GLOBAL CULTURE

Nationalism, globalization and modernity

A Theory, Culture & Society special issue

edited by

MIKE FEATHERSTONE

SAGE Publications

London · Newbury Park · New Delhi

GLOBAL CULTURE

CONTENTS

Global Culture: An Introduction

Mike Featherstone

Is there a global culture? If by a global culture we mean something akin to the culture of the nation-state writ large, then the answer is patently a negative one. On this comparison the concept of a global culture fails, not least because the image of the culture of a nation-state is one which generally emphasizes cultural homogeneity and integration. According to this line of reasoning, it would be impossible to identify an integrated global culture without the formation of a world state — a highly unlikely prospect. Yet if we move away from the static polarity suggested by our original question and try to employ a broader definition of culture and think more in terms of processes, it might be possible to refer to the globalization of culture. Here we can point to cultural integration and cultural disintegration processes which take place not only on an inter-state level but processes which transcend the state-society unit and can therefore be held to occur on a trans-national or trans-societal level. It therefore may be possible to point to trans-societal cultural processes which take a variety of forms, some of which have preceded the inter-state relations into which nation-states can be regarded as being embedded, and processes which sustain the exchange and flow of goods, people, information, knowledge and images which give rise to communication processes which gain some autonomy on a global level. Hence there may be emerging sets of 'third cultures', which themselves are conduits for all sorts of diverse cultural flows which cannot be merely understood as the product of bilateral exchanges between nation-states. It is therefore misleading to conceive a global culture as necessarily entailing a weakening of the sovereignty of nation-states which, under the impetus of some form of teleological evolutionism or other master logic, will necessarily become absorbed into larger units and eventually a world state which produces cultural homogeneity and integration. It is also misleading to regard the emergence of third

Theory, Culture & Society (SAGE, London, Newbury Park and New Delhi), Vol. 7 (1990), 1–14

cultures as the embodiment of a logic which points to homogenization. The binary logic which seeks to comprehend culture via the
mutually exclusive terms of homogeneity/heterogeneity, integra-
tion/disintegration, unity/diversity, must be discarded. At best,
these conceptual pairs work on one face only of the complex prism
which is culture. Rather we need to inquire into the grounds, the
various generative processes, involving the formation of cultural
images and traditions as well as the inter-group struggles and interdependencies, which led to these conceptual oppositions becoming
frames of reference for comprehending culture within the state-
society which then become projected onto the globe.

Postmodernism is both a symptom and a powerful cultural image
of the swing away from the conceptualization of global culture less
in terms of alleged homogenizing processes (e.g. theories which
present cultural imperialism, Americanization and mass consumer
culture as a proto-universal culture riding on the back of Western
economic and political domination) and more in terms of the
diversity, variety and richness of popular and local discourses, codes
and practices which resist and play-back systemicity and order.
Modes of understanding which operated within a strict symbolic
hierarchy and a bound context are now asked to accept that all
symbolic hierarchies are to be spatialized out and that the context is
boundless. The focus on the globe is to suggest that a new level of
conceptualization is necessary. Yet the conception of culture as
having escaped the bounded nation-state society also points to a
limit, the image of the globe as a single place, the generative frame
of unity within which diversity can take place. At the same time, the
temptation of the postmodern mood is to eschew such theoretical
complications and to regard the changes which point to a global
culture as opening up another space onto which can be inscribed
speculative theorizations, thin histories and the detritus of the exotic
and spectacular. The challenge for sociology, still attempting to
come to terms with the upsurge of interest in culture in the 1980s
which has seen a lowering of the boundaries between it and the other
social sciences and the humanities, is to both theorize and work out
modes of systematic investigation which can clarify these globalizing processes and distinctive forms of social life which render problematic what has long been regarded as the basic subject matter for
sociology: society, conceived almost exclusively as the bounded
nation-state.[1]

The argument that the rise and development of sociology has been too dominated by the special case of the rise of the modern nation-state, in which the particular characteristics of a national integration process have been generalized into a model of social integration, in which society becomes the key frame of reference for sociology, is gaining wider acceptance (see in this collection the pieces by Robertson, Arnason, Mennell and Turner). Wallerstein (1987), for example, has argued that this identification of sociology with the study of society should be rejected on two counts. Firstly, it developed in the nineteenth century as part of an antithetical tandem, the other half of which was the state, in which society was seen as a substratum of manners and customs which held people together. Secondly, this 'artificial' division between the political and social — and we should add the economic — which gave rise to the separate disciplines of politics, sociology and economics in the nineteenth century, should be rejected in favour of a more integrated social science approach combined with history: a historical social science.[2] Yet it is a mistake to regard sociology as being solely preoccupied with the nation-state society: an interest in global and universal processes can be traced back at least as far as the Enlightenment. Furthermore there exist important sub-traditions within sociology which have endeavoured to follow the broader approach which Wallerstein endorsed. We find various blends of the social sciences, history and philosophy not only content to universalize Western models of modernization, rationalization, industrialization, revolution and citizenship to the rest of the world, a world conceived as bound together by a universal history; but also the universalization of an egalitarian concern with doing justice to particularities and differences, with *humanity*. From the point of view of those at the forefront of the upsurge of interest in culture and perspectives such as postmodernism, the assumptions of the rationalization, modernization and industrialization models are to be treated with suspicion. In effect, the assumption is that we have moved beyond the logic of the universal 'iron cage' rationalization process (Haferkamp, 1987). As Margaret Archer argues, in her contribution, the various brands of industrialization, convergence and post-industrialization theory which were popular in the 1960s and 1970s subordinated culture to structural development and shelved the question of the relationship between culture and agency. Likewise, in his article in this collection, Alain Touraine argues that the idea of revolution which has been at the heart of the Western representation of modernization entailed a belief in the logic of the system, a society without actors.

From the vantage point of the late twentieth century it seems that the era of revolution is now finally over. It is these issues plus an increasing sensitivity to the particularities and 'exhaustion' of Western modernity, in a global circumstance in which other cultural and civilizational traditions are becoming impossible to ignore, that has led some to argue that sociology's basic undergraduate teaching programme should shift from revolving around local societies to focus on internationalization and global issues (Tiryakian, 1986).

Within the French tradition the emphasis on the idea of humanity, the new universal secular religious ideal which can be traced back to Saint-Simon and Comte, came to full development in the later writings of Durkheim. For Durkheim, as societies expanded and increased in complexity, the degree of social and cultural differentiation developed to the point at which, even for members of the same society, the only thing they retained in common was their humanity. This 'idea of the human person', which developed out of individualist morality, was for Durkheim the natural successor to Christianity (Lukes, 1973: 338ff.). For Durkheim the sacredness of the person could become one of the few cultural ideals capable of providing a crucial point of unification for an increasingly differentiated, yet interdependent, world. In his contribution, Tenbruck discusses a related cultural ideal, the dream of a secular ecumene, which also can be traced back to the grounds of Christendom. The idea of a secular ecumene which gained its historical dynamic from the French Revolution has undergone transformations into the powerful cultural imagery of socialism, with its dream of a global culture and, in the post-war era, the equally potent ideal of 'development' — both of which set off a whole series of global cultural struggles.

The debates about the place of culture in world-systems theory brings to the fore many of the issues we have just raised. It is Wallerstein's reiteration of one of his central tenets, in his piece on culture and the world system, that the world-system is 'based on a particular logic, that of the ceaseless accumulation of capital' which raises questions about his conceptualization of culture. Boyne's argument that Wallerstein still employs a view of culture as merely derivative and reactive to the 'brute and disinterested objectivism of world-systems theory', meets an equally forceful defence in his exchange with Wallerstein. A similar criticism is made by Worsley who wishes to contest Wallerstein's conflation of the 'three worlds' into his central concepts of core and periphery. For Worsley, Wallerstein's model is another variant of political economy which does not sufficiently take culture into account; he remarks that 'without the cultural dimension it is impossible to make sense of a modern world in which nationalism, religion and inter-ethnic hostility has been far more important than internationalism and secularism'.

This argument is developed further by Bergesen in his contribution 'Turning World Systems Theory on its Head'. Bergesen argues that there is a common neo-utilitarian basis to both world-systems analysis and international relations theory which neglects the power relations and cultural relations which preceded the inter-state system. (Bergesen's argument here is analogous to the culturally embedded economy arguments of Durkheim about the non-contractual basis of contract and Simmel's quest to 'build a storey beneath historical materialism', variants of which can also be detected in the work of Weber and Marx.) For Bergesen, Wallerstein commits the individualist error of working from parts to wholes in which the sub-units, the individual states, are assumed to acquire their definitive properties prior to participation in the world-system. Rather, he argues 'for the vast majority of the world's states, the international system preceded their existence and moreover made that existence possible in the first place'. A system which was forcefully created through conquest and colonization, through power not exchange. Likewise international relations theory focuses on inter-state relations and neglects the international state system in the form of culture (independent diplomatic languages — Latin then French — and systems of representation linked to the Church and dynastic families in the Middle Ages) which arose alongside state action and made it possible.

Bergesen's argument can also be related to the theory of globalization developed by Robertson in which nation-states are not seen to simply interact but to constitute a world, a global context in which the world becomes a singular place with its own processes and forms of integration (see also Moore, 1966). Robertson, whose piece in this collection extends the argument he has developed over a number of years, emphasizes the autonomy of the globalization process, which should be seen not as the outcome of inter-state processes, but to operate in *relative* independence of conventionally designated societal and socio-cultural processes. For these reasons Robertson maintains that the term globalization is preferable to internationalization (literally inter nation-state exchanges) as it draws attention to *the form* within which the world becomes 'united'. It points to the process of global compression which has led to the current high degree of global complexity and intensified cultural conflicts over 'the definition of the global situation'. A globalization process which could, in theory, have rendered the world into a singular place through a variety of trajectories: through the imperial hegemony of a single nation or power bloc, or the triumph of a trading company, the universal proletariat, a form of religion, or the world-federalist movement. All these are historical possibilities which could have produced various blends and forms of cultural integration and differentiation. All of them, as well as the current phase of the globalization process, could be said to entail the production of global cultures. For Robertson the phase of accelerated globalization has taken place since the 1880s. The shift towards the idea of the homogeneous unitary nation-state was itself one aspect of this process and should not be misunderstood as an impediment, for it was itself an idea which became rapidly globalized. Also significant have been: the increase in the numbers of international agencies and institutions, the increasing global forms of communication, the acceptance of unified global time, the development of global competitions and prizes, the development of standard notions of citizenship, rights and conception of humankind.

This globalization process which points to the extension of global cultural interrelatedness can also be understood as leading to a global ecumene, defined as a 'region of persistent culture interaction and exchange' (Kopytoff, 1987: 10; Hannerz, 1989). A process whereby a series of cultural flows produce both: *firstly*, cultural homogeneity and cultural disorder, in linking together previously isolated pockets of relatively homogeneous culture which in turn produces more complex images of the other as well as generating identity-reinforcing reactions; and also *secondly*, transnational cultures, which can be understood as genuine 'third cultures' which are orientated beyond national boundaries. As Appadurai remarks in his piece, the complexity of the global cultural flows now taking place cast doubt on the continuing usefulness of centre-periphery models. Appadurai suggests we can conceive of five dimensions of global cultural flows which move in non-isomorphic paths. Firstly, there are *ethnoscapes* produced by flows of people: tourists, immigrants, refugees, exiles and guestworkers. Secondly, there are *technoscapes*, the machinery and plant flows produced by multi-national and national corporations and government agencies. Thirdly, there are *finanscapes*, produced by the rapid flows of money in the currency markets and stock exchanges. Fourthly, there are *mediascapes*, the repertoires of images and information, the flows which are produced and distributed by newspapers, magazines, television and film. Fifthly, there are *ideoscapes*, linked to flows of images which are associated with state or counter-state movement ideologies which are comprised of elements of the Western Enlightenment world-view — images of democracy, freedom, welfare, rights etc. While Appadurai has emphasized the disjunction between these cultural flows, it should be added that states, multinationals — as well as other agencies, institutions and interest groups — will attempt to manipulate, channel (close or open up) the cultural boundaries of others to these flows with varying degrees of success in relation to their relative power resources. We will now look in more detail at some of the trans-national cultural flows, and then turn to the hermeneutic problems entailed.

The changes in the world economy which have taken place in the 1970s and 1980s, which some have referred to as a new phase of capitalism 'disorganized capitalism' or 'post-Fordism' (Lash and Urry, 1987; Offe, 1985; Lipietz, 1987), are generally represented as entailing the de-monopolization of economic structures with the deregulation and globalization of markets, trade and labour. The globalization of capital flows with 24-hour stockmarket trading, which gained pace after the 'Big Bang' of October 1986, not only deregulated local markets and made local capital vulnerable to the strategies of corporate raiders, it necessitated new norms for the market too. The globalization of capital, Dezalay remarks in his contribution to this collection, also entailed the globalization of the market in services to finance, commerce and industry. A new category of professionals: international lawyers, corporate tax accountants, financial advisers and management consultants were required as the various business and financial interests sought to chart and formalize the newly globalized economic space. This reintroduction of competition and market imperatives in the world of law led to a process of homogenization and interconnection between national legal systems. The breaking down of barriers favoured the strongest performer: the North American law firms which had already experienced the emergence of 'mega-law firms' and the creation of 'law factories'. In this sense the globalization of the market for legal services was in many ways an Americanization. It also made space for a new generation of lawyers — less tied to the quasi-aristocratic ideals and disdain for marketing characteristic of the gentleman lawyers. Now the emphasis was upon technical competence, aggressive tactics and a meritocratic ethos which made the new lawyers perfect auxiliaries to the new breed of corporate raiders. A similar process of deregulation and globalization occurred within related professional activities such as architecture and advertising. To these we could add a range of specialists in the film, video, television, music, image and consumer industries which King refers to as 'design professionals'. This coterie of new specialists and professionals not only work outside the traditional professional and organizational cultures of the nation-state, they experience the problems of inter-cultural communication at first hand. This, plus the necessity of moving backwards or forwards between different cultures, various imperfect proto-'third cultures' necessitate new types of flexible personal controls, dispositions and means of orientation, in effect a new type of habitus. They not only operate in a compressed global space made possible by new means of communication, but frequently work in and inhabit a specific type of urban space: the redeveloped inner city areas. King (1990) refers to these as global or 'world cities', cities in which the global financial and banking services and culture industries are concentrated. Yet in practice, as Hannerz (1989) points out, global cultural centres whether of the traditional type (e.g. focal points of high culture and fashion such as Paris) or new forms of popular culture industries (e.g. film and television in Los Angeles, Bombay and Hong Kong) do not necessarily correspond to economic (e.g. Tokyo) and political (e.g. Washington) centres. Although there are of course instances in which all three functions are concentrated together (e.g. New York, London).

One consequence of these changes is that more and more people are now involved with more than one culture, thus increasing the practical problems of interculture communication. As Gessner and Schade point out, intercultural communication has developed as a new research area since the end of the late 1960s to investigate the practical problems and misunderstandings encountered by private persons, agencies and organizations which are brought into contact for a variety of reasons such as, for example, cross-border legal disputes. While such people, and the cultural specialists and professionals we have mentioned, may as a consequence develop 'third cultures' for transnational communication, it is by no means clear that this necessarily entails the generation of a cosmopolitan outlook.[3]

Indeed, as Hannerz suggests in his article in this collection, we can envisage a range of responses between the polarities of localism (territorially anchored or 'bounded' cultures involving face-to-face relations among people who do not move around a great deal) and cosmopolitanism (transnational cultural networks extended in space in which there is a good deal of overlapping and mingling which encourages an orientation to engage with the other). Some of the people who travel widely, such as businessmen and expatriates, are often locals at heart who do not really want to leave home. For these there is an expanding literature of do-it-yourself travel guides on how to find home comforts abroad and how to avoid the embarrassment of unintended cultural insults and *faux pas* towards foreign hosts. The majority of present-day tourism is of the 'home plus' (sun, sea, sand, wildlife, etc.) variety, in which new and potentially disturbing experiences are strictly controlled. As Zygmunt Bauman argues, most tourism seeks to reduce hermeneutic problems by directing tourists to special enclaves in which functional mediators play the boundary maintaining role. In contrast we can posit varieties of cosmopolitanism, such as in diplomacy, in which the other culture is largely mastered and there is the capacity to communicate the fruits of this competence to others via third languages, such as diplomatic languages. A further example of cosmopolitanism is the transnational intellectuals who keep in touch via global cultural flows and who are not only at home in other cultures, but seek out and adopt a reflexive, metacultural or aesthetic stance to divergent cultural experiences.

One complication to the local–cosmopolitan dichotomy, is the stranger. For Bauman the stranger — someone who comes today and stays tomorrow — cannot be integrated into the cosmopolitan/local, friend/enemy forms of sociation; indeed the stranger introduces a disturbing indeterminacy into attempts at classificatory clarity. Within the urban environments of modernity, the alien or stranger appears inside the lifeworld and refuses to participate in the state's construction of an 'imagined community', its efforts to eliminate strangers and redefine them as friends through nationalistic assimilation policies. Yet for Bauman these attempts to attain cultural uniformity and homogeneity ultimately fail. Modernity with its project of imposing order on the world and social engineering projects reaches its limits and state-led cultural crusades are abandoned. The shift towards a contemporary postmodern culture, Bauman holds, offers a greater chance of tolerance as we move into an era in which national and cultural boundaries are constantly re-drawn and crossed more easily.

The resilience of the *ethnie*, the ethnic cores of nations, the pre-modern traditions, memories, myths, values and symbols woven together and sustained in popular consciousness, is emphasized by Anthony Smith in his contribution. Yet, for Smith like Robertson, this does not necessarily lead to tolerance for the globalization process and the intensification of contacts and sense that the world is one place also brings nations closer together in cultural prestige competitions. A world of competing national cultures seeking to improve the ranking of their states, offers the prospect of global 'cultural wars' with little basis for global projects of cultural integration, *lingua francas*, and ecumenical or cosmopolitan 'unity through diversity' notions, despite the existence of the necessary technical communications infrastructures. The latter, especially the global mass media, have been characterized by some theorists as offering the spectre of cultural homogenization often in the form of 'cultural imperialism' or 'Americanization'. Schiller (1985), for example, regards transnational corporations as breaking down national broadcasting and telecommunications entities so that they can saturate the defenceless cultural space of the nation (see Schlesinger, 1987). While particular television programmes, sport spectacles, music concerts, advertisements may rapidly transit the globe, this is not to say that the response of those viewing and listening within a variety of cultural contexts and practices will be anything like uniform (Featherstone, 1987; forthcoming; Wernick, forthcoming). Friedman, in his article, discusses some interest-ing examples of the ways in which groups in various national contexts in different parts of the world handle consumer commod-ities and tourism through a variety of strategies to re-constitute identity.

The varieties of response to the globalization process clearly suggest that there is little prospect of a unified global culture, rather there are global cultures in the plural. Yet, as several contributors have pointed out, the intensity and rapidity of today's global cul-tural flows have contributed to the sense that the world is a singular place which entails the proliferation of new cultural forms for encounters. While this increasingly dense web of cosmopolitan – local encounters and interdependencies can give rise to third cultures and increasing tolerance, it can also result in negative reactions and intolerance. John O'Neill, for example, discusses the global panic generated by AIDS, as leading to both an intensification of the sense that the world is one place which must pull together to fight off threats to world order, and at the same time, a de-globalizing reaction arising from the difficulty of sealing off the nation-state from global viral flows. In a similar vein, Beyer points to the ways in which the globalization of religion produces a situation in which there are no outsiders who can serve as a repository of evil. With globalization, the person who was unequivocally outside now becomes a neighbour, with the result that the inside/outside distinction fails. This can lead to responses of ecumenicism, tolerance and universalism in which everyone is included, or resistance to globalization in the form of counter movements, such as the various non-Western fundamentalisms which react against 'Westoxication' or, in the West, seek to embark on a neoconservative programme of de-differentiation to restore Western Christendom. In this context the analogies between a national culture and global culture again break down. While we can refer to the process of formation of national identities and the role of intellectuals in mobilizing the *ethnie* in attempting to develop a unified national culture, we are made painfully aware of the alternative traditions and histories, the layers of local cultures which were suppressed as a result of this project. It becomes impossible to talk about a common culture in the fuller sense without talking about who is defining it, within which set of interdependencies and power balances, for what purposes, and with reference to which outside culture(s) have to be discarded, rejected or demonified in order to generate the sense of cultural identity.[4] To contemplate this on a global level means imaginatively to construct an 'outside' to the globe, the sphere of global threat captured only in the pages and footage of science fiction accounts of space invaders, inter-planetary and inter-galactic wars. In addition the transnational cosmopolitan intellectuals (serving which masters we might ask?) would have a long way to go to re-discover, formulate and agree upon global equivalents to the *ethnie*.

It is also all too evident that discussion of a global culture is generated from within a particular time and place and practice. This one within a Western European academic setting in English, as we move towards the end of the twentieth century. It is hard for us to imagine from the centrality of our English academic discourse, as Walter Benjamin (1968: 80) remarks, having to think of the problems of translating our language into that of non-Western languages and how this might effect their sense of place within the world (Polier and Roseberry, 1989). Yet it is all too clear that the Indian scientist or intellectual in New Delhi who wishes to develop contacts to exchange information with his Japanese opposite numbers, must do so in English. We are slowly becoming aware that the West is both a particular in itself and also constitutes the universal point of reference in relation to which others recognise themselves as particularities (Sakai, 1988). The debates about how to characterize Japan on the Western continuum of pre-modernity, modernity and post-modernity bring this problem into prominence. While economically Japan has become a major global presence, global culture flows into and, especially out of, Japan have been well regulated. The extent to which the talk of a new 'age of culture' in Japan in the 1980s (see Harootunian, 1989) will materialize into a self-confident global cultural project, remains to be seen. Nevertheless, we are becoming aware that the 'orientalization of the world' (Maffesoli, 1988) is a distinct global process — although the task of unpacking the range of cultural associations summoned up by this concept, and their place in the continuing struggles to define the global cultural order, has yet to begin.

Notes

This issue would not have been possible without the pioneering work on globalization by Roland Robertson who brought this particular set of problems into the journal *Theory, Culture & Society* in the early 1980s. The conceptualization of the issue and final blend of papers has benefited greatly from our discussion over the years and from his advice and suggestions. Roy Boyne also made a number of important comments and suggestions. I would also like to thank Janet Abu Lughod, Josef Bleicher, Mike Hepworth, Hans Mommaas, Daniel Poor, Bryan S. Turner and Schuichi Wada for the various ways in which they have helped in putting together this issue.

1. Zygmunt Bauman (1989: 152) makes this linkage explicit when he writes 'the models of postmodernity, unlike the models of modernity, cannot be grounded in the realities of the nation state'.

2. It is interesting to note that in this argument for an integrated historical social science Wallerstein has no place for psychology. For an approach which also seeks to go beyond the nation-state-society frame of reference but argues for integrated social science which includes psychology, see Moscovici (1988 and forthcoming). Elias (1978, 1982, 1985) has also developed historical and processual approaches which

synthesize many of the accustomed 'levels' and 'territorial domains' of social science, including the psychological and sociological, which are normally kept apart (see also, Elias, 1969).

3. Third cultures may lead to a process of routinization and formalization of contacts in order to reduce ambiguity given the high demands such encounters place upon individuals' personal accomplishments. Yet it is also possible that processes of informalization and the 'formalization of informalization' may occur once the contacts have become less emotionally threatening (see Wouters, 1986; forthcoming).

4. For an account of the problems of participating in the writing of a world history — the project of writing a revised version of the officially described *History of the Scientific and Cultural Development of Mankind* sponsored by UNESCO which pulled together historians from all parts of the world — see Burke (1989).

References

Bauman, Z. (1989) 'Sociological Responses to Postmodernity', in C. Mongardini and M.L. Maniscalco (eds), *Modernismo e Postmodernismo*. Roma: Bulzoni Editore.

Benjamin, W. (1968) *Illuminations*. New York: Harcourt, Brace and World.

Burke, P. (1989) 'New Reflections on World History', *Culture and History* 5.

Elias, N. (1969) 'Sociology and Psychiatry', in S.H. Foulkes and G.S. Prince (eds), *Psychiatry in a Changing Society*. London: Tavistock.

Elias, N. (1978) *The Civilizing Process, Volume I*. Oxford: Blackwell.

Elias, N. (1982) *The Civilizing Process, Volume II*. Oxford: Blackwell.

Elias, N. (1985) 'On the Sociogenesis of Sociology', *Sociologisch Tijdschrift* 11(1).

Featherstone, M. (1987) 'Consumer Culture, Symbolic Power and Universalism', in G. Stauth and S. Zubaida (eds), *Mass Culture, Popular Culture and Social Life in the Middle East*. Boulder: Westport Press.

Featherstone, M. (forthcoming) 'Postmodernism, Consumer Culture and Global Disorder' in *Postmodernism and Consumer Culture*. London: Sage.

Haferkamp, H. (1987) 'Beyond the "Iron Cage" of Modernity?', *Theory, Culture & Society* 4(1).

Hannerz, U. (1989) 'Notes on the Global Ecumene', *Public Culture* 1(2).

Harootunian, H. (1989) 'Visible Discourses Invisible Ideologies' in M. Miyoshi and H. Harootunian (eds), *Postmodernism and Japan*. Durham, NC: Duke University Press.

King, A (1990) *Global Cities*. London: Routledge.

Kopytoff, I. (1987) 'The International African Frontier: The Making of African Political Culture', in *The African Frontier*. Bloomington: Indiana University Press.

Lash, S. and Urry, J. (1987) *The End of Organized Capitalism*. Oxford: Polity Press.

Lipietz, A. (1987) *Miracles and Mirages: the Crisis of Global Fordism*. London: Verso.

Lukes, S. (1973) *Emile Durkheim: His Life and Work*. Harmondsworth: Allen Lane.

Maffesoli, M. (1988) *Le Temps des Tribus*. Paris: Klincksieck.

Moore, W.E. (1966) 'Global Sociology: the World as a Singular System', *American Journal of Sociology* 71(5).

Moscovici, S. (1988) *La machine a faire des dieux*. Paris: Fayard.

Moscovici, S. (forthcoming) 'Questions for the Twenty-First Century', *Theory, Culture & Society*.

Offe, K. (1985) *Disorganized Capitalism*. Oxford: Polity Press.

Polier, N. and Roseberry, W. (1989) 'Triste Tropes: Postmodern Anthropologists Encounter the Other and Discover Themselves', *Economy and Society* 18(2).

Sakai, N. (1988) 'Modernity and its Critique. The Problem of Universalism and Particularism', *South Atlantic Quarterly* 87(3).

Schiller, H.I. (1985) 'Electronic Information Flows: New Basis for Global Domination?', in P. Drummond and R. Patterson (eds), *Television in Transition*. London: British Film Institute.

Schlesinger, P. (1987) 'On National Identity: Some Conceptions and Misconceptions Criticised', *Social Science Information* 26(2).

Tiryakian, E.A. (1986) 'Sociology's Great Leap Forward: the Challenge of Internationalization', *International Sociology* 1(2).

Wallerstein, I. (1987) 'World-Systems Analysis', in A. Giddens and J. Turner (eds), *Social Theory Today*. Oxford: Polity Press.

Wernick, A. (forthcoming) 'Promo Culture: the Cultural Triumph of Exchange', *Theory, Culture & Society* 7(4).

Wouters, C. (1986) 'Formalization and Informalization: Changing Tension Balances in Civilizing Processes', *Theory, Culture & Society* 3(2).

Wouters, C. (forthcoming) 'Social Stratification and Informalization in Global Perspective', *Theory, Culture & Society* 7(4).

Mike Featherstone teaches Sociology at Teesside Polytechnic. He is author of *Postmodernism and Consumer Culture* and co-editor of *Body, Culture and Society*, both of which will be published by Sage in late 1990.

Mapping the Global Condition: Globalization as the Central Concept

Roland Robertson

Nothing will be done anymore, without the whole world meddling in it.
Paul Valéry (quoted in Lesourne, 1986: 103)

We are on the road from the evening-glow of European philosophy to the dawn of world philosophy.
Karl Jaspers (1957: 83–4)

Insofar as [present realities] have brought us a global present without a common past [they] threaten to render all traditions and all particular past histories irrelevant.
Hannah Arendt (1957: 541)

The transformation of the medieval into the modern can be depicted in at least two different ways. In one sense it represents the trend towards the consolidation and strengthening of the territorial state . . . In another sense it represents a reordering in the priority of international and domestic realms. In the medieval period the world, or transnational, environment was primary, the domestic secondary.
Richard Rosencrance (1986: 77)

My primary interest in this discussion is with the analytical and empirical aspects of *globalization*. On the other hand, I want to raise some general questions about social theory. As far as the main issue is concerned, I set out the grounds for systematic analysis and interpretation of globalization since the mid-eighteenth century — indicating the major phases of globalization in recent world history and exploring some of the more salient aspects of the contemporary global circumstance from an analytical point of view. On the general-theoretical front I suggest that much of social theory is both a product of and an implicit reaction to — as opposed to a direct engagement with — the globalization process.

Thus I emphasize the need to redirect theory and research toward explicit recognition of globalization. While there *is* rapidly growing interest in that topic, much of it is expressed very diffusely and there

Theory, Culture & Society (SAGE, London, Newbury Park and New Delhi), Vol. 7 (1990), 15–30

is considerable danger that 'globalization' will become an intellectual 'play zone' — a site for the expression of residual social-
theoretical interests, interpretive indulgence, or the display of
world-ideological preferences. In any case I think that we must take
very seriously Immanuel Wallerstein's (1987: 309) contention that
'world-systems' analysis is not a theory about the world. It is a
protest against the ways in which social scientific enquiry was structured for all of us at its inception in the middle of the nineteenth
century.' Even though I do not subscribe to world-system theory in
the conventional sense of the term, primarily because of its economism (Robertson and Lechner, 1985) and am not pessimistic about the
possibility of our being able to accomplish significant theoretical
work vis-à-vis the world-as-a-whole, I consider it to be of the utmost
importance for us to realize fully that much of the conventional
sociology which has developed since the first quarter of the
twentieth century has been held in thrall by the virtually global
institutionalization of the idea of the culturally cohesive and sequestered national society during the main phase of 'classical' sociology
(Robertson, 1990a). Ironically, the global aspect of that phenomenon has received relatively little attention (Meyer, 1980).

Globalization and the Structuration of the World
The present discussion is a continuation of my previous efforts to
theorize the topic of globalization, a task made all the more difficult
by the recent and continuing events in China, the USSR and Europe
which have disrupted virtually all of the conventional views
concerning world order. At the same time those events and the
circumstances which they have created make the analytical effort all
the more urgent. We have entered a phase of what appears to us in
1990 as great global uncertainty — so much so that the very idea of
uncertainty promises to become globally institutionalized. Or, to
put it in a very different way, there is an eerie relationship between
the ideas of postmodernism and postmodernity and the day-by-day
geopolitical 'earthquakes' which we (the virtually *global* we) have
recently experienced.

We need to enlarge our conception of 'world politics' in such a
way as to facilitate systematic discussion of the relationship between
politics in the relatively narrow sense and the broad questions of
'meaning' which can only be grasped by wide-ranging, empirically
sensitive interpretations of the global-human condition as a whole.

Specifically, I argue that what is often called world politics has in the twentieth century hinged considerably upon the issue of the response to modernity, aspects of which were politically and internationally thematized as the standard of 'civilization' (Gong, 1984) during the late-nineteenth and early-twentieth centuries in particular reference to the inclusion of non-European (mainly Asian) societies in Eurocentric 'international society' (Bull and Watson, 1984).

Communism and 'democratic capitalism' have constituted alternative forms of acceptance of modernity (Parsons, 1964) — although some would now argue that the recent and dramatic ebbing of Communism can in part be attributed to its 'attempt to preserve the integrity of the premodern system' (Parsons, 1967: 484–5) by invoking 'socialism' as the central of a series of largely 'covert gestures of reconciliation . . . toward both the past and the future' (Parsons, 1967: 484).[1] On the other hand, fascism and neo-fascism have, in spite of their original claims as to the establishment of *new* societal and international 'orders' (as was explicitly the case with the primary Axis powers of the Second World War, Germany and Japan), been directly interested in *transcending or resolving* the problems of modernity. The world politics of the global debate about modernity have rarely been considered of relevance to the latter and yet it is clear that, for example, the 'the sense of the past of the major belligerents in World War I reveals a striking contrast between the temporalities of the nations of each alliance system and underlying causes of resentment and misunderstanding' (Kern, 1983: 277), with the nations whose leaders considered them to be relatively deprived — most notably Germany and Japan — being particularly concerned to confront the problem of modernity in political and military terms.[2] It may well be that the Cold War which developed after the defeat of big-power fascism constituted an interruption and a partial freezing of the world-cultural politics of modernity and that now with the possible ending of the Cold War those politics will be resumed in a situation of much greater global complexity — in the interrelated contexts of more intense globalization, the discourse of postmodernity and 'the ethnic revival' (Smith, 1981), which itself may well be considered as *an aspect of* the contemporary phase of globalization (Lechner, 1984).

Any attempt to theorize the general field of globalization must lay the grounds for relatively patterned discussion of the politics of the global-human condition, by attempting to indicate the structure of any viable discourse about the shape and 'meaning' of the world-as-a-whole. I regard this as an urgent matter partly because much of the contemporary discussion about the global scene is being conducted by interpreters operating under the umbrella of 'cultural studies' with exceedingly little attention to the issue of global complexity and structural contingency, except for frequently invoked cliches about 'late capitalism' and/or the salience of 'the multinational corporation'. This is not at all to say that the economic factor is unimportant, nor certainly that the textual (or 'power-knowledge') aspect of the 'world system' is of minor significance. Rather, I am insisting that both the economics and the culture of the global scene should be analytically connected to the general structual and actional features of the global system.

I maintain that what has come to be called globalization is, in spite of differing conceptions of that theme, best understood as indicating the problem of *the form* in terms of which the world becomes 'united', but by no means integrated in naive functionalist mode (Robertson and Chirico, 1985). Globalization as a topic is, in other words, a conceptual entry to the problem of world order in the most general sense — but, nevertheless, an entry which has no cognitive purchase without considerable discussion of historical and comparative matters. It is, moreover, a phenomenon which clearly requires what is conventionally called interdisciplinary treatment. Traditionally the general field of the study of the world as a whole has been approached via the discipline of international relations (or, more diffusely, international studies). That discipline (sometimes regarded as a subdiscipline of political science) was consolidated during particular phases of the overall globalization process and is now being reconstituted in reference to developments in other disciplinary areas, including the humanities (Der Derian and Shapiro, 1989). Indeed, the first concentrated thrust into the study of the world as a whole on the part of sociologists, during the 1960s (discussed in Nettl and Robertson, 1968), was undertaken mainly in terms of the idea of *the sociology of international relations*. And there can be little doubt that to this day the majority of social scientists think of 'extra-societal' matters in terms of 'international relations' (including variants thereof, such as transnational relations, non-governmental relations, supranational relations, world politics and so on). Nonetheless that tendency is breaking down in conjunction with considerable questioning of what Michael Mann (1986) calls the unitary conception of society. While there have been attempts to carve-out a new discipline for the study of the world as a whole, including the long-historical making of the contemporary 'world system' (e.g. Bergesen, 1980), my own position is that it is not so much that we need a new discipline in order to study the world as a whole but rather that social theory in the broadest sense — namely as a perspective which stretches across the social sciences and humanities (Giddens and Turner, 1987: 1) and even the natural sciences — should be refocused and expanded so as to make concern with 'the world' a central hermeneutic, and in such a way as to constrain empirical and comparative-historical research in the same direction.

Undoubtedly there *have* been various attempts in the history of social theory to move along such lines but the very structure of the globalization process has inhibited such efforts from taking-off into a full-fledged research program (Robertson, 1990a) — most notably during the crucial take-off period of globalization itself, namely 1880–1925. In so far as that has indeed been the case then we are led to the position that exerting ourselves to develop *global* social theory is not 'merely' an exercise demanded by the transparency of the processes rendering the contemporary world as a whole as a single place (Robertson, 1987a, 1989) but also that our labors in that regard are crucial to the empirical understanding of the bases upon which the matrix of contemporary disciplinarity and interdisciplinarity rests. There has been an enormous amount of talk in recent years about self-reflexiveness, the critical-theoretic posture, and the like; but ironically much of that talk has been about as far removed from discussion of the real world — in the *two*-fold sense of quotidian contemporary realities *and* the concrete global circumstance — as it could be. In other words much of fashionable social theory has favored the abstract and, from a simplistic global perspective, 'the local' to the great neglect of the global and civilizational contours and bases of western social theory itself. (As will be seen, the distinction between the global and the local is becoming very complex and problematic — to such an extent that we should now speak in such terms as the global institutionalization of the lifeworld and the localization of globality.)

During the second half of the 1980s 'globalization' (and its problematic variant, 'internationalization') became a commonly used term in intellectual, business, media and other circles — in the process acquiring a number of meanings, with varying degrees of precision. This has been a source of frustration — but not necessarily a cause for surprise or alarm — to those of us who had sought earlier in the decade to establish a relatively strict definition of globalization as part of an attempt to come to terms systematically with major aspects of contemporary 'meaning and change' (Robertson, 1978). Nevertheless a stream of analysis and research *has* been developed around the general idea, if not always the actual concept, of globalization. And it is my intention here to take stock of some of the most pressing issues in this area — not so much by surveying and evaluating different approaches to the making of the contemporary world-system, world society, global ecumene, or whatever one chooses to call the late-twentieth century world-as-a-whole; but rather by considering some relatively neglected analytical and historical themes.

I deal with globalization as a relatively recent phenomenon. In fact I argue that it is intimately related to modernity and modernization, as well as to postmodernity and 'postmodernization' (in so far as the latter pair of motifs have any analytical purchase). Let it be emphatically clear, however, that in attempting to justify that proposal I am by no means suggesting that work within the frame of the globalization paradigm should be limited to the relatively recent past. All that I am maintaining is that the concept of globalization per se should be applied to a particular series of developments concerning *the concrete structuration of the world as a whole*. The term 'structuration' has been calculatedly chosen. Although I will shortly consider some aspects of Anthony Giddens's venture into 'the global scene', I cannot address in this paper the general problems which arise from the concept of structuration (Cohen, 1989). I will say only that if the notion of structuration is to be of assistance to us analytically in the decades ahead it has to be moved-out of its quasi-philosophical context, its confinement within the canonical discourses about subjectivity-and-objectivity, individual-and-society, voluntarism and determinism and so on (Archer, 1988). It has to be made directly relevant to *the world* in which we live. It has to contribute to the understanding of how the global system has been and continues to be *made*. It has to be focused upon the production and reproduction of 'the world' as the most salient plausibility structure of our time (Wuthnow, 1978: 65). The same applies to the cultural-agency problematic which Margaret Archer (1988) has recently theorized.

Human history has been replete with ideas concerning the physical structure, the geography, the cosmic location, and the spiritual and/or the secular significance of the world (Wagar, 1971);

movements and organizations concerned with the patterning and/or the unification of the world-as-a-whole have intermittently appeared for at least the last two thousand years; ideas about the relationship between the universal and the particular have been central to all of the major civilizations; and so on. Even something like what has recently been called 'the global-local nexus' (or the 'local-global nexus') was thematized as long ago as the second century BC when Polybius, in his *Universal History*, wrote in reference to the rise of the Roman empire: 'Formerly the things which happened in the world had no connection among themselves . . . But since then all events are united in a common bundle' (Kohn, 1971: 121).[3] However, the crucial considerations are that it has not been until relatively recent times that it has been realistically thought that 'humanity is rapidly becoming, physically speaking, a single society' (Hobhouse, 1906: 331), nor is it until quite recently that considerable numbers of people living on various parts of the planet have spoken and acted in direct reference to the problem of the 'organization' of the entire, heliocentric world. It is upon this heavily contested problem of the concrete patterning of the world — including resistance to globality — that I seek to center the concept and the discourse of globalization.

The world-as-a-whole could, in theory, have become the reality which it now is in ways and along trajectories other than those which have actually obtained (Lechner, 1989). The world could, in principle, have been rendered as a 'singular system' (Moore, 1966) via the imperial hegemony of a single nation or a 'grand alliance' between two or more dynasties or nations; the victory of 'the universal proletariat'; the global triumph of a particular form of organized religion; the crystallization of 'the world spirit'; the yielding of nationalism to the ideal of 'free trade'; the success of the world-federalist movement; the world-wide triumph of a trading company; or in yet other ways. Some of these have held sway at certain moments in world history. Indeed, in coming to terms analytically with the contemporary circumstance we have to acknowledge that some such possibilities are as old as world history in any meaningful sense of that phrase and have, in fact, greatly contributed to the existence of the globalized world of the late twentieth century. Moreover, much of world history can be fruitfully considered as sequences of 'miniglobalization', in the sense that, for example, historic empire formation involved the unification of previously sequestered territories and social entities. There have also been shifts in the opposite direction, as was the case with the deunification of medieval Europe — although the rise of the territorial state also promoted imperialism and thus conceptions of the world-as-a-whole.

Nonetheless, when all is said and done no single possibility has — or so I claim — been more continuously prevalent than another. There may have been periods in world history when one such possibility was more of a 'globalizing force' than others — and that must certainly be a crucial aspect of the discussion of globalization in the long-historical mode — but we have not as a world-people moved into the present global-human circumstance along one or even a small cluster of these particular trajectories. And yet in the present climate of 'globality' there is a strong temptation for some to insist that the single world of our day can be accounted for in terms of one particular process or factor — such as 'westernization', 'imperialism' or, in the dynamic sense, 'civilization'. Indeed, as I argue elsewhere (Robertson, 1990b) the problem of globality is very likely to become a basis of major ideological and analytical cleavages of the twenty-first century.[4]

While I certainly do not subscribe to the view that social theorists should at all costs attempt to be neutral about these and other matters, I am certainly committed to the argument that one's moral stance should be *realistic* — that one should have no vested interest in the attempt to map this or any other area of the human condition. More precisely, I argue that systematic comprehension of the macrostructuration of world order is essential to the viability of any form of contemporary theory and that such comprehension must involve analytical separation of the factors which have facilitated the shift towards a single world — e.g. the spread of capitalism, western imperialism and the development of a global media system — from the *general and global* agency-structure (and/or culture) theme. While the empirical relationship between the two sets of issues is of great importance (and, of course, complex) conflation of them leads us into all sorts of difficulties and inhibits our ability to come to terms with *the basic and shifting terms* of the contemporary world order.

Thus we must return to the question of *the actual* form of recent and contemporary moves in the direction of global interdependence and global consciousness. In posing the basic question in this way we immediately confront the critical issue as to the period during which the move towards the world as a singular system became more or less inexorable. If we think of the history of the world as consisting for a very long time in *the objectiveness* of a variety of different civilizations existing in varying degrees of separation from each other, our main task now is to consider the ways in which the world 'moved' from being merely 'in-itself' to the problem or the possibility of its being 'for itself'. However, before coming directly to that vital issue I must attend briefly to some basic analytical matters. This I do via the recent statement of Giddens (1987: 255–93) on 'Nation-states in the Global State System'.

Giddens makes much of the point that 'the development of the sovereignty of the modern state from its beginnings depends upon a reflexively monitored set of relations between states' (Giddens, 1987: 263). More specifically, he argues that the period of treaty making following the First World War 'was effectively the first point at which a reflexively monitored system of nation-states came to exist globally' (Giddens, 1987: 256). I fully concur with both the emphasis upon the importance of the post-First World War period and Giddens's claim that 'if a new and formidably threatening pattern of war was established at this time, so was a new pattern of peace' (Giddens, 1987: 256). More generally, Giddens's argument that the development of the modern state has been guided by increasingly global norms concerning its sovereignty is, if not original, of great importance. However, he tends to conflate the issue of the homogenization of the state (in Hegel's sense) — what Giddens calls 'the universal scope of the nation-state' (Giddens, 1987: 264) — and the issue of relationships between states.

My argument is that it is important to make a distinction between, on the one hand, the diffusion of expectations concerning the external legitimacy and mode of operation of the state and, on the other, the development of regulative norms concerning the relationships between states; while readily acknowledging that the issue of the powers and limits of the state has indeed been *empirically* linked to the structuring of the relationships between states and, moreover, that it constitutes a crucial axis of globalization. James Der Derian (1989) has recently drawn attention to an important aspect of that theme by indicating the proximity of the formal Declaration of the Rights of Man that sovereignty resides in the nation to Jeremy Bentham's declaration in the same year of 1789 that there was a need for a new word — namely, 'international' — which would 'express, in a more significant way, the branch of law which goes commonly under the name of the *law of nations*' (Bentham, 1948:326).

Thus while undoubtedly the two issues upon which I have been dwelling via Giddens's analysis have been and remain closely inter-dependent, it is crucial to keep them analytically apart in order that we may fully appreciate variations in the nature of the empirical connections between them. In sum, the problem of contingency arising from state sovereignty and the development of relational rules between sovereign units is not the same as the issue of the crystallization and diffusion of conceptions of national statehood (Smith, 1979). Nor is it the same as the development and spread of conceptions of the shape and meaning of 'international society' (Gong, 1984). The second set of matters is on a different 'level' than that addressed by Giddens.

My primary reason for emphasizing this matter is that it provides an immediate entry to what I consider to be the most pressing general problem in the contemporary discussion of globalization. Giddens's analysis is a good example of an attempt to move toward the global circumstance via the conventional concerns of socio-logical theory. While readily conceding that it is his specific concern to talk about the modern nation-state and the internal and external violence with which its development has been bound-up, the fact remains that in spite of all of his talk about global matters at the end of his analysis, Giddens is restricted precisely by his having to center 'the current world system' within a discussion of 'the global *state* system' (Giddens, 1987: 276-7; emphasis added). Even though he eventually separates, in analytical terms, the nation-state system (with the ambiguity which I have indicated) as the political aspect of the world system from the 'global information system' (as relating to 'symbolic orders/modes of discourse'); the 'world-capitalist economy' (as the economic dimension of the world system); and the 'world military order' (as concerning 'law/modes of sanc-tion') — along lines reminiscent of approaches of the 1960s (Nettl and Robertson, 1968) and, ironically, of a general Parsonian, func-tional-imperative approach — Giddens ends-up with a 'map' of what he reluctantly calls the world system, which is centered upon his conflated characterization of the rise of the modern state system.

'Mapping' the world social-scientifically is, of course, a common procedure, it having crystallized during the 1960s with the diffusion of perceptions concerning the existence of the Third World, on the one hand, and polarized First (liberal-capitalist) and Second (industrializing-communist) Worlds, on the other. Ever since that period — the beginning of the current phase of contemporary, late twentieth-century globalization — there has proliferated a large number of different and, indeed, conflicting ideological and/or 'scientific' maps of the world system of national societies — so much so that it is reasonable to say that the discourse of mapping is a vital ingredient of global-political culture, one which fuses geography (as in the use of North–South and East–West terminology) with political, economic, cultural and other forms of placement of nations on the global-international map. Much of this overall effort has resulted in significant work — as, for example, in Johan Galtung's *The True Worlds* (1980) and Peter Worsley's (1984) lengthy discussion of the cultures of 'the three worlds'. Indeed, the kind of work which has strongly reminded us of the major cleavages and discontinuities in the world-as-a-whole is a significant antidote to those who now speak blithely in 'global village' terms of a single world. Nonetheless there can be no denying that the world is much more singular than it was as recently as, say, the 1950s. Thus the crucial question remains as to the basic form or structure in terms of which that shift has occurred. That that form has been *imposed* upon certain areas of the world is, of course, a crucial issue — but until the matter of form (more elaborately, structuration) is adequately thematized our ability to comprehend the dynamics of the world-as-a-whole will be severely limited.

A Minimal Phase Model of Globalization

What I am offering here is what I call and advocate as a necessarily minimal model of globalization. This model does not make grand assertions about primary factors, major mechanisms, and so on. Rather, it indicates the major constraining tendencies which have been operating in relatively recent history as far as world order and the compression of the world in our time are concerned.

As I have indicated, one of the most pressing tasks in that regard is to confront the issue of the undoubted salience of the unitary nation state — more diffusely, the national society — since about the mid-eighteenth century and at the same time to acknowledge its historical uniqueness, indeed its abnormality (McNeil, 1986). The homogenous nation state — homogenous here in the sense of a culturally-homogenized, administered citizenry (Anderson, 1983) — is thus a construction of a particular form of life. That we are ourselves have been increasingly subject to its constraints does not mean that for analytical purposes it has to be accepted as *the* departure point for analyzing and understanding the world. Thus I have argued not merely that national societies should be regarded as constituting *but one* general reference point for the analysis of the global-human circumstance, but that we have to recognize even more than we do now that the prevalence of the national society in the twentieth century is *an aspect of globalization* (Robertson, 1989) — that the diffusion of *the idea of* the national society as a form of institutionalized societalism (Lechner, 1989) was central to the accelerated globalization which began to occur just over one-hundred years ago. I have also argued more specifically (Robertson, 1987a, 1989, 1990b) that the two other major components of globalization have been, in addition to national societies and the system of international relations, conceptions of *individuals* and of *humankind*. It is in terms of the shifting relationships between and the 'upgrading' of these reference points that globalization has occurred in recent centuries.

With such considerations in mind I now propose — in unavoidably skeletal terms — that the temporal-historical path to the present circumstance of a very high degree of *global density and complexity* can be delineated as follows:

Phase I — *the germinal phase*, lasting in Europe from the early fifteenth until the mid-eighteenth century. Incipient growth of national communities and downplaying of the medieval 'transnational' system. Accentuation of concepts of the individual and of ideas about humanity. Heliocentric theory of the world and beginning of modern geography; spread of Gregorian calendar.

Phase II — *the incipient phase*, lasting — mainly in Europe — from the mid-eighteenth century until the 1870s. Sharp shift towards the idea of the homogenous, unitary state; crystallization of conceptions of formalized international relations, of standardized citizenly individuals and a more concrete conception of humankind. Sharp increases in conventions and agencies concerned with international and transnational regulation and communication. Beginning of problem of 'admission' of non-European societies to 'international society'. Thematization of nationalism–internationalism issue.

Phase III — *the take-off phase*, lasting from the 1870s until the mid-1920s. Increasingly global conceptions as to the 'correct outline' of an 'acceptable' national society; thematization of ideas concerning national and personal identities; inclusion of some non-European societies in 'international society'; international formalization and attempted implementation of ideas about humanity. Very sharp increase in number and speed of global forms of communication. Rise of ecumenical movement. Development of global competitions — e.g. Olympics, Nobel Prizes. Implementation of World Time and near-global adoption of Gregorian calendar. First *World* war. League of Nations.

Phase IV — *the struggle-for-hegemony phase*, lasting from the early 1920s until the mid-1960s. Disputes and wars about the fragile terms of the globalization process established by the end of the take-off period. Globewide international conflicts concerning forms of life. Nature of and prospects for humanity sharply focused by Holocaust and atomic bomb. United Nations.

Phase V — *the uncertainty phase*, beginning in the 1960s and displaying crisis tendencies in the early 1990s. Inclusion of Third World and heightening of global consciousness in late 1960s. Moon landing. Accentuation of 'post-materialist' values. End of Cold War and spread of nuclear weapons. Number of global institutions and movements greatly increases. Societies increasingly face problems of multiculturality and polyethnicity. Conceptions of individuals rendered more complex by gender, ethnic and racial considerations. Civil rights. International system more fluid — end of bipolarity. Concern with humankind as a species-community greatly enhanced. Interest in world civil society and world citizenship. Consolidation of global media system.

As I have said, this is a necessarily skeletal sketch, with much detailed and more rigorous discussion of the shifting relationships between and the relative autonomization of each of the four major components to be added. Clearly, one of the most important empirical questions has to do with the extent to which the form of globalization which was set firmly in motion during the period 1880–1925 will 'hold' in the coming decades. In more theoretical vein, much more needs to be done so as to demonstrate the ways in which the selective responses of relevant collective actors — most particularly societies — to globalization play a crucial part in the making of the world-as-a-whole (Robertson, 1987b).[5] Different forms and degrees of societal participation in the globalization process make a crucial difference to its precise form. In any case, my main point is that there is a general autonomy and 'logic' to the globalization process — which operates in *relative* independence of strictly societal and other more conventionally studied sociocultural processes.[6] The global system is not an outcome of processes of basically intra-societal origin (contra Luhmann, 1982) or even of the development of the inter-state system. Its making has been much more complex and culturally rich than that.

Notes

1. It is of more than passing interest to note that in speaking of communism as a radical branch of one of the 'the great "reform" movements of postmedieval Western history' — namely, socialism — Talcott Parsons said in 1964 that 'it seems a safe prediction that communism will, from its own internal dynamics, evolve in the direction of the restoration — or where it has yet not existed, the institution — of political democracy' (Parsons, 1964: 396–7). On the other hand, Parsons insisted that the *internationalism* of communism had made a crucial contribution to world order.

2. Ronald Inglehart (1990: 33) observes in the course of his empirical analysis of culture in advanced industrial societies 'that the publics of the three major Axis powers, Germany, Japan, and Italy, all tend to be underachievers in life satisfaction. The traumatic discrediting of their social and political systems that accompanied their defeat in World War II may have left a legacy of cynicism that their subsequent social change and economic success has still not entirely erased.'

3. I owe the precise phrases 'local-global nexus' and 'global-local nexus' to Chadwick Alger.

4. I argue specifically in this connection that images of world order are central to global culture as responses to globality (Robertson, 1990b).

5. I discuss the growing significance of globe-oriented movements in Robertson (1989, 1990b).

6. I argue also (Robertson, forthcoming) that at a higher level of generality globalization can be analyzed in terms of the global institutionalization of the relationship between the universal and the particular (see also Robertson, 1987a, 1989). In a manner which differs from the position of Albert Bergesen (see his piece in this volume of *TCS*), I try to turn world-systems theory 'on its head' by emphasizing *culture* and the *agency* aspect of the making of the global system.

References

Anderson, B. (1983) *Imagined Communities*. London: Verso.

Archer, M. (1988) *Culture and Agency: The Place of Culture in Social Theory*. Cambridge: Cambridge University Press.

Arendt, H. (1957) 'Karl Jaspers: Citizen of the World', pp. 539–50 in P.A. Schlipp (ed.), *The Philosophy of Karl Jaspers*. La Salle: Open Court.

Bentham, J. (1948) *The Principles of Morals and Legislation*. New York: Lafner.

Bergesen, A. (1980) 'From Utilitarianism to Globology: the Shift from the Individual to the World as a Whole as the Primordial Unit of Analysis', pp. 1–12 in A. Bergesen (ed.), *Studies of the Modern World-System*. New York: Academic Press.

Bull H., and Watson, A. (eds) (1984) *The Expansion of International Society*. Oxford: Clarendon Press.

Cohen, I.J. (1989) *Structuration Theory: Anthony Giddens and the Constitution of Social Life*. New York: St. Martin's Press.

Der Derian, J. (1989) 'The Boundaries of Knowledge and Power in International Relations', pp. 3–10 in J. Der Derian and M.J. Shapiro (eds), *International/Intertextual Relations: Postmodern Readings of World Politics*. Lexington, MA: Lexington Books.

Der Derian, J. and Shapiro, M.J. (eds) (1989) *International/Intertextual Relations: Postmodern Readings of World Politics*. Lexington, MA: Lexington Books.

Galtung, J. (1980) *The True Worlds: A Transnational Perspective*. New York: Free Press.

Galtung, J. (1985) 'Global Conflict Formations: Present Developments and Future Directions', pp. 23–74 in P. Wallersteen, Johan Galtung and Carlos Portales (eds), *Global Militarization*. Boulder: Westview Press.

Giddens, A. (1987) *The Nation-State and Violence*. Berkeley: University of California Press.

Giddens, A. and Turner J. (1987) 'Introduction', pp. 1–10 in A. Giddens and J. Turner (eds), *Social Theory Today*. Stanford: Stanford University Press.

Gong, G.W. (1984) *The Standard of 'Civilization' in International Society*. Oxford: Clarendon Press.

Hobhouse, L.T. (1906) *Morals in Evolution. A Study in Comparative Ethics, Vol. I.* New York: Henry Holt.

Inglehart, R. (1990) *Culture Shift in Advanced Industrial Society*. Princeton: Princeton University Press.

Jaspers, K. (1957) 'Philosophical Autobiography', pp. 3–94 in P.A. Schlipp (ed.), *The Philosophy of Karl Jaspers*. La Salle: Open Court.

Kern, S. (1983) *The Culture of Time and Space, 1880–1918*. Cambridge, MA: Harvard University Press.

Kohn, H. (1971) 'Nationalism and Internationalism', pp. 119–34 in W.W. Wagar (ed.), *History and the Idea of Mankind*. Albuquerque: University of New Mexico Press.

Lechner, F.J. (1984) 'Ethnicity and Revitalization in the Modern World System', *Sociological Focus* 17:243–56.

Lechner, F.J. (1989) 'Cultural Aspects of the Modern World-System', pp. 11–28 in W.H. Swatos (ed.), *Religious Politics in Global Perspective*. New York: Greenwood Press.

Lesourne, J.F. (1986) *World Perspectives: A European Assessment*. New York: Gordon and Breach.

Luhmann, N. (1982) 'The World Society as a Social System', *International Journal of General Systems* 8:131–8.

McNeil, W.H. (1986) *Polyethnicity and National Unity in World History*. Toronto: University of Toronto Press.

Mann, M. (1986) *The Sources of Social Power: Volume I, A History of Power from the Beginning to A.D. 1760*. Cambridge: Cambridge University Press.

Meyer, J.W. (1980) 'The World Polity and the Authority of the Nation-State', in A. Bergesen (ed.), *Studies of the Modern World-System*. New York: Academic Press.

Moore, W.E. (1966) 'Global Sociology: the World as a Singular System', *American Journal of Sociology* 71:475–82.

Nettl, J.P. and Robertston, R. (1968) *International Systems and the Modernization of Societies: The Formation of National Goals and Attitudes.* London: Faber.

Parsons, T. (1964) 'Communism and the West: The Sociology of Conflict', pp. 390–9 in A. and E. Etzioni (eds), *Social Change: Sources, Patterns and Consequences.* New York: Basic Books.

Parsons, T. (1967) *Sociological Theory and Modern Society.* New York: Free Press.

Robertson, R. (1978) *Meaning and Change.* Oxford: Blackwell.

Robertson, R. (1987a) 'Globalization Theory and Civilization Analysis', *Comparative Civilizations Review* 17 (Fall): 20–30.

Robertson, R. (1987b) 'Globalization and Societal Modernization: A Note on Japan and Japanese Religion', *Sociological Analysis* 47(S): 35–42.

Robertson, R. (1989) 'Globalization, Politics and Religion', pp. 10–23 in J.A. Beckford and T. Luckmann (eds), *The Changing Face of Religion.* London: Sage.

Robertson, R. (1990a) 'After Nostalgia? Wilful Nostalgia and the Phases of Globalization', in B.S. Turner (ed.), *Theories of Modernity and Postmodernity.* London: Sage.

Robertson, R. (1990b) 'Globality, Global Culture and Images of World Order', in H. Haferkamp and N. Smelser (eds), *Social Change and Modernity.* Berkeley: University of California Press.

Robertson, R. (forthcoming) 'Social Theory, Cultural Relativity and the Problem of Globality', in A.D. King (ed.), *Culture, Globalization and the World System.*

Robertson, R. and Chirico, J. (1985) 'Humanity, Globalization and Worldwide Religious Resurgence: A Theoretical Exploration', *Sociological Analysis* 46: 219–42.

Robertson, R. and Lechner, F. (1985) 'Modernization, Globalization and the Problem of Culture in World-Systems Theory', *Theory, Culture & Society* 2 (3): 103–18.

Rosencrance, R. (1986) *The Rise of the Trading State: Commerce and Conquest in the Modern World.* New York: Basic Books.

Smith, A.D. (1979) *Nationalism in the Twentieth Century.* New York: New York University Press.

Smith, A.D. (1981) *The Ethnic Revival.* New York: Cambridge University Press.

Wagar, W.W. (ed.) (1971) *History and the Idea of Mankind.* Albuquerque: University of New Mexico Press.

Wallerstein, I. (1987) 'World-Systems Analysis', pp. 309–24 in A. Giddens and J. Turner (eds), *Social Theory Today.* Stanford: Stanford University Press.

Worsley, P. (1984) *The Three Worlds: Culture and Development.* London: Weidenfeld and Nicolson.

Wuthnow, R. (1978) 'Religious Movements and the Transition in World Order', pp. 63–79 in J. Needleman and G. Baker (eds), *Understanding the New Religions.* New York: Seabury Press.

Roland Robertson is Professor of Sociology at the University of Pittsburgh and the author of numerous papers and books on various aspects of the global situation, including his forthcoming *Globalization* (Sage).

Culture as the Ideological Battleground of the Modern World-System

Immanuel Wallerstein

> It is not our human nature that is universal, but our capacity to create cultural realities, and then to act in terms of them. (Mintz, 1988: 14)

I

Culture is probably the broadest concept of all those used in the historical social sciences. It embraces a very large range of connotations, and thereby it is the cause perhaps of the most difficulty. There is, however, one fundamental confusion in our usage which I shall address.

On the one hand, one of the basic building stones of social science's view of the world, most explicitly emphasized by the anthropologists, is the conviction that, while all persons share some traits with all others, all persons also share other traits with only some others, and all persons have still other traits which they share with no one else. That is to say, the basic model is that each person may be described in three ways: the universal characteristics of the species, the sets of characteristics that define that person as a member of a series of groups, that person's idiosyncratic characteristics. When we talk of traits which are neither universal nor idiosyncratic we often use the term 'culture' to describe the collection of such traits, or of such behaviors, or of such values, or of such beliefs. In short, in this usage, each 'group' has its specific 'culture'. To be sure, each individual is a member of many groups, and indeed of groups of very different kinds — groups classified by gender, by race, by language, by class, by nationality, etc. Therefore, each person participates in many 'cultures'.

In this usage, culture is a way of summarizing the ways in which

Theory, Culture & Society (SAGE, London, Newbury Park and New Delhi), Vol. 7 (1990), 31–55

groups distinguish themselves from other groups. It represents what is shared within the group, and presumably simultaneously not shared (or not entirely shared) outside it. This is a quite clear and quite useful concept.

On the other hand, culture is also used to signify not the totality of the specificity of one group against another but instead certain characteristics *within* the group, as opposed to other characteristics within the same group. We use culture to refer to the 'higher' arts as opposed to popular or everyday practice. We use culture to signify that which is 'superstructural' as opposed to that which is the 'base'. We use culture to signify that which is 'symbolic' as opposed to that which is 'material'. These various binary distinctions are not identical, although they all seem to go in the direction of the ancient philosophical distinctions between the 'ideal' and the 'real', or between the 'mind' and the 'body'.

Whatever the merits of these binary distinctions, they all go in a quite different structural direction from the other use of culture. They point to a division within the group rather than to the unity of the group (which of course is the basis of division between groups). Now, this 'confusion' of the two tonalities of the concept, 'culture', is so long-standing that it cannot be a mere oversight, especially given the fact that the discussion of culture in general and of its definition in particular has been so voluminous throughout the nineteenth and twentieth centuries.

It is safest to presume that long-standing intellectual confusions are deliberate and the fact of the confusion should itself be the starting-point of the analysis. Since this voluminous discussion has in fact taken place largely within the confines of a single historical system, the capitalist world-economy, it may be that not only the discussion but the conceptual confusion are both the consequence of the historical development of this system and reflect its guiding logic.

The philosophical distinctions between the 'ideal' and the 'real' and between the 'mind' and the 'body' are very ancient, and have given rise, broadly speaking, to two perspectives, at least within the context of so-called Western philosophy. Those who have promoted the primacy of the 'ideal' or of the 'mind' have tended to argue that the distinction points to an ontological reality, and that the 'ideal' or the 'mind' is more important or nobler or in some way superior to the 'real' or the 'body'. Those who have promoted the primacy of the 'real' or the 'body' did not however take the inverse position.

Instead, they tended to argue that the 'ideal' or the 'mind' are not distinct essences but rather social inventions, and that only the 'real' or the 'body' truly exist. In short they have tended to argue that the very concept of the 'ideal' or the 'mind' are ideological weapons of control, intended to mask the true existential situation.

Let us thus designate as culture (usage I) the set of characteristics which distinguish one group from another, and as culture (usage II) some set of phenomena which are different from (and 'higher' than) some other set of phenomena within any one group. There is one great problem about culture (usage I). Who or what has such a culture? It seems that 'groups' have. But if 'culture' is the term in our scientific vocabulary which has the broadest and most confusing usage, 'group' is the term that has the vaguest usage. A 'group' as a taxonomic term is anything anyone wishes to define as a group. There exists no doubt, to follow the *ultima ratio* of such a term, a 'group' of all those who are of a given height, or who have a certain color hair. But can such 'groups' be said to have 'cultures'? There would be few who would claim so. Obviously, it is only certain 'groups' then that have 'cultures'.

We could try this exercise starting from the other direction. To what kinds of groups are 'cultures' (usage I) normally attributed? Nations are often said to have a national culture. 'Tribes' and/or 'ethnic groups' are often said to have a culture. It is not unusual to read about the 'culture' of 'urban intellectuals', or of the 'urban poor'. More rarely, but frequently, we might read of the 'culture' of 'Communists' or of 'religious fundamentalists'. Now what those 'groups' presumed to have 'cultures' (always usage I) share in common is that they seem to have some kind of self-awareness (and therefore a sense of boundaries), some shared pattern of socialization combined with a system of 'reinforcement' of their values or of prescribed behavior, and some kind of organization. The organization may be quite formalized, as in the case of a nation-state, or it can be quite indirect, as for example the shared newspapers, magazines, and possibly the voluntary associations which act as communication networks between 'urban intellectuals'.

However, as soon as I raise the question of who or what has a culture, it becomes immediately obvious how slippery is the terrain. What is the evidence that any given group has a 'culture'? The answer is surely not that all presumed 'members' of any of these groups act similarly to each other and differently from all others. At most, we could argue for a statistically significant relationship between group 'membership' and certain behavior, or value-preferences, or whatever.

Furthermore, if we press the matter a little further, it is quite clear that our statistical findings would vary constantly (and probably significantly) over time. That is to say, behavior or value-preferences or however one defines culture is of course an evolving phenomenon, even if it is a slowly-evolving one, at least for certain characteristics (say, food habits).

Yet, on the other hand, it is surely true that people in different parts of the world, or in different epochs, or in different religious or linguistic communities do indeed behave differently from each other, and in certain ways that can be specified and fairly easily observed. For example, anyone who travels from Norway to Spain will note that the hour at which restaurants are most crowded for the 'evening meal' is quite different in the two countries. And anyone who travels from France to the US will observe that the frequency with which foreign strangers are invited to homes is quite different. The length of women's skirts in Brazil and Iran is surely strikingly different. And so on. And I have only cited here elements of so-called everyday behavior. Were I to raise more metaphysical issues, it would be easy, as everyone knows, to elucidate group differences.

So, on the one hand, differences are obvious — which is what the concept of culture (usage I) is about. And yet the degree to which groups are in fact uniform in their behavior is distressingly difficult to maintain. When Mintz says that we have a 'capacity to create cultural realities and then to act in terms of them', I cannot but agree. But I then wonder how we can know who the 'we' are who have this capacity. At that point, I become skeptical that we can operationalize the concept of culture (usage I) in any way that enables us to use it for statements that are more than trivial. The anthropologists, or at least some of them, have argued convincingly that the concept of 'human nature' cannot be used to draw meaning-ful implications about real social situations. But is this not equally true of their proposed substitute, culture?

This then is where I begin. Culture (usage I) seems not to get us very far in our historical analyses. Culture (usage II) is suspect as an ideological cover to justify the interests of some persons (obviously the upper strata) within any given 'group' or 'social system' against the interests of other persons within this same group. And if, indeed, the very distinction of 'ideal' and 'real', 'mind' and 'body' were acknowledged to be an ideological weapon of control, then the confusion of the two usages of culture would be a very logical consequence, since it would no doubt add to the process of masking the true existential situation. I would like therefore to trace the actual development of the 'culture' (in either or both usages) over time within the historical system which has given birth to this extensive and confusing use of the concept of culture, the modern world-system which is a capitalist world economy.

II

Let us begin by reviewing some of the realities of the evolution of this historical system, as they have affected the way its participants 'theorized' it. That is, I am concerned with the degree to which this historical system became conscious of itself and began to develop intellectual and/or ideological frameworks which both justified it, and impelled its forward movement, and thereby sustained its reproduction. I shall mention six such realities which have implications for the theoretical formulations that have come to permeate the system.

1. The capitalist world-economy is constructed by integrating a geographically vast set of production processes. We call this the establishment of a single 'division of labor'. Of course, all historical systems are based on a division of labor, but none before was as complex, as extensive, as detailed, and as cohesive as that of the capitalist world-economy. The political framework within which this division of labor has grown up has not however been that of a world empire, but instead that of an interstate system, itself a product of the historical development of this system. This interstate system has been composed of, and given birth and legitimacy to, a series of so-called sovereign states, whose defining characteristic is their territorial distinctiveness and congruence combined with their membership in and constraint by this interstate system. It is not the inter-state system, however, but the separate states that control the means of violence. Furthermore, their control is in theory exclusive within their respective jurisdictions. Although such total control is a myth, state pre-emption of violence is at least massive, if never exclusive.

This organization of social life where the predominant 'economic' pressures are 'inter-national' (a bad term, but the one in common use), and the predominant 'political' pressures are 'national' points to a first contradiction in the way participants can explicate and justify their actions. How can one explain and justify them nationally and internationally simultaneously?

2. The capitalist world-economy functions, as do most (perhaps all) historical systems by means of a pattern of cyclical rhythms. The most obvious, and probably the most important, of these rhythms is a seemingly regular process of expansion and contraction of the world-economy as a whole. On present evidence, this cycle tends to be from fifty to sixty years in length, covering its two phases.

The functioning of this cycle (sometimes called 'long waves', sometimes Kondratieff cycles) is complex and I will not review it here (see, for example, Wallerstein, 1982). One part, however, of the process is that, periodically, the capitalist world-economy has seen the need to expand the geographic boundaries of the system as a whole, creating thereby new loci of production to participate in its axial division of labor. Over 400 years, these successive expansions have transformed the capitalist world-economy from a system located primarily in Europe to one that covers the entire globe.

The successive expansions that have occurred have been a conscious process, utilizing military, political, and economic pressures of multiple kinds, and of course involving the overcoming of political resistances in the zones into which the geographic expansion was taking place. We call this process 'incorporation', and it too is a complex one (see Hopkins and Wallerstein, 1987). This process points to a second contradiction which the populations of each successively incorporated zone faced. Should the transformations that were occurring in their zone be conceived of as changes from a local and traditional 'culture' to a world-wide modern 'culture', or were these populations rather simply under pressure to give up their 'culture' and adopt that of the Western imperialist power or powers? Was it, that is, a case of modernization or of Westernization?

3. Capitalism is a system based on the endless accumulation of capital. It is therefore a system which requires the maximum appropriation of surplus value. There are two ways to increase the appropriation of surplus value. One is that workers work harder and more efficiently, thereby creating greater output with the same amount of inputs (other than human labor-time). The second way is to return less of the value that is produced to the direct producers. In short, capitalism by definition involves a pressure on all direct producers to work more and to be paid less.

This requirement however runs afoul of the logic of the individual's pursuit of his/her own interest. The most obvious incentive for hard work is higher recompense. One can substitute coercion for higher recompense, but of course coercion also has a cost and thereby its use also reduces surplus value. It follows that, unless one can substitute (at least partially) some other motivation for work other than recompense or fear, it is very difficult to obtain simultaneously the twin goals of harder work and lower pay. How can one think about this system in such a way as to achieve this objective?

4. Capitalism as a system requires movement and change, at least formal change. The maximal accumulation of capital requires not only goods and capital to circulate but manpower as well. It requires in addition a constant evolution in the organization of production in terms both of the nature of the leading sectors and of the sites of production. We usually analyze these phenomena under two labels — that of economic innovation and that of the rise and fall of nations.

One principal consequence of this reality is the enormous emphasis placed within the modern world-system on the virtues of 'newness'. No previous historical system has ever been based on a theory of progress, indeed a theory of inevitable progress. But the emphasis on newness, and its constant implementation (at least at the level of form) raises precisely the question of legitimacy — legitimacy of the historical system in general; legitimacy of its key political institution, the various sovereign states, in particular. From Bodin to Weber to Mao Zedong the question of legitimacy has been constantly debated and seen as an extremely knotty issue to resolve. It is particularly difficult because the very advocacy of the virtues of newness undermines the legitimacy of any authority, however laboriously the legitimacy was achieved.

5. The capitalist system is a polarizing system, both in its reward pattern and in the degree to which persons are increasingly forced to play socially polarized roles. It is, however, also an expanding system and therefore one in which all the absolute parameters have taken the form of a linear upward projection over time. Since its outset, the capitalist world-economy has had ever more productive activity, ever more 'value' produced, ever more population, ever more inventions. Thus, it has had ever more outward signs of wealth.

And yet, if it has been a polarizing system, it must at the least be true that this increase of wealth has been going to only a small proportion of the world's population. It might even be the case that real consumption per world capita has not been keeping pace. For example, it is surely the case that there is less physical space per capita and fewer trees per capita now than 400 years ago. What does this mean in terms of that elusive but very real phenomenon, the 'quality of life'?

The contradiction therefore that needs to be handled is that between 'progress' and deterioration, between visibly increasing wealth and very real impoverishment. The only way to defuse the resulting angers may well be denial, but how is it possible to deny phenomena that are so public, and whose public character is indeed one of the exigencies of the system? That is, the endless accumulation of capital requires as one of its mechanisms a collective orientation towards consumption.

6. Finally, the capitalist world-economy is an historical system. And being historical, it has a life cycle and, as any other such system, must at some point cease to function as the consequence of the aggregated results of its eventually paralyzing contradictions. But it is also a system which is based on a particular logic, that of the ceaseless accumulation of capital. Such a system therefore must preach the possibility of limitless expansion.

Limitless expansion can seem euphoric, as in the image of wafting upward into heaven, or disastrous, as in the image of hurtling downward into space. In a sense, both images constrain action since there seems to be little an individual can do to affect the pattern. The mundane reality however is more complex, more unsettling, but also more subject to human will.

As systems move towards their natural demise they find themselves in 'transition' to uncertain futures. And the very uncertainty, which at one level is liberating, is also disconcerting. Thus we are faced with the dilemma of how to think about such transformation, whether to deny the process of systemic 'death' or instead to welcome the process of systemic 'birth'.

III

The 'culture', that is the idea-system, of this capitalist world-economy is the outcome of our collective historical attempts to come to terms with the contradictions, the ambiguities, the complexities of the socio-political realities of this particular system. We have done it in part by creating the concept of 'culture' (usage I) as the assertion of unchanging realities amidst a world that is in fact ceaselessly changing. And we have done it in part by creating the concept of 'culture' (usage II) as the justification of the inequities of the system, as the attempt to keep them unchanging in a world which is ceaselessly threatened by change.

The question is how is this done? Since it is obvious that interests fundamentally diverge, it follows that such constructions of 'culture' are scarcely neutral. Therefore, the very construction of culture becomes a battleground, the key ideological battleground in fact of the opposing interests within this historical system.

The heart of the debate, it seems to me, revolves around the ways in which the presumed antinomies of unity and diversity, universalism and particularlism, humanity and race, world and nation, person and man/woman have been manipulated. I have previously argued that the two principal ideological doctrines that have emerged in the history of the capitalist world-economy — that is, universalism on the one hand and racism and sexism on the other — are not opposites but a symbiotic pair. I have argued that their 'right dosage' has made possible the functioning of the system, one which takes the form of a continuing ideological zigzag (Wallerstein, 1988).

It is this zigzag which is at the base of the deliberate confusions inherent in the two usages of the concept of 'culture'. I should like to illustrate the issues by analyzing some comments made by a political intellectual in Jamaica, Rex Nettleford, in a speech he gave in 1983 to a political party meeting, a party that calls itself the People's National Party. The speech itself, when reprinted, bore the title 'Building a Nation, Shaping a Society'. Nettleford wished to emphasize the importance of a 'sense of history' in building a nation against those who 'teach our young that they have no history worth studying, only a future which . . . they are expected to conquer'. Here is what Nettleford said:

> 'Black' does not merely mean skin in the history of the Americas. It means culture — a culture woven out of the encounters between the millions of West Africans brought as slaves and the millions of Europeans who came as masters, settlers or indentured labourers. In Jamaica and the Caribbean the substance of a truly indigenous life, for all its texture, has been forged in the crucible of the black majority's early efforts to come to terms with the new environment and to survive. That was a struggle of a fundamental and elemental kind, and it is that struggle which is being denied its proper place in the economic, social and cultural

ethos of this society. I sense a *deblackening* of the ethos, a persistent contempt in official and cocktail circles for the fruits of our people's labours, and a hypocritical refuge is being taken in our national motto by those who prefer to emphasize the word 'many' since to them the 'one' may mean the majority. 'Out of many one people' becomes 'out of many one'. So we keep the country pluralist and divided with the marginalized majority remaining marginal, and a privileged few (with many 'roast breadfruits' among them) holding on to the economic, social and cultural power in the land.

The real truth is that our people are better than we like to think: we are not that unsophisticated to be racist, but we are not that foolish not to be race conscious. And on that delicate balancing of sensibilities rests the unusual sophistication of the mass of this population. It is that sophistication which misleads not only our own leaders, but those from outside who say they want to help us. Our people who have gone through centuries of struggle know that 'what is pertinent today is not simply freedom from foreign oppression (which in our own primitive way we can deal with), but the creation within this country of socio-economic and political frameworks which accord high values to the human personality'. We are very uptight about our personae, about our personal recognition and status, and we hold suspect any class of people inside or outside our nation, who would agree with a once influential Jamaican private sector leader, who in criticising the policies of a certain regime in the recent past said that during the seventies 'our rich national culture had been reduced, shrunken to fit into the narrow concept of a vigorous black culture'. She was saying this in a country where the vast majority are hopelessly of that 'culture.' Anything that expresses the image of the majority is a 'reduction' and a 'shrinking'! We are not likely to shape a society or build a nation with such beliefs in place, and especially if they are to be found among those in the power structure; and so I implore this forum to think seriously on these things. (Nettleford, 1986: 9–10)

Notice in this analysis that the definition of a culture is central. Nettleford wants to build and shape an entity he calls a nation or a society. This is of course standard language and seems to refer to culture (usage I), a usage which presumably emphasizes the ways in which Jamaicans are alike. But he proceeds to observe that others, 'found among those in the power structure' of this same Jamaica, also claim they wish to do the same.

The two groups seem to be using the national motto 'out of many one people' to mean opposite things. Those who Nettleford calls the 'privileged few' emphasize 'pluralism' within and unity without ('freedom from foreign oppression'). Nettleford says this neglects entirely the 'black majority' who are 'marginalized' and who are seeking 'the creation within [Jamaica] of socio-economic and political frameworks which accord high values to the human personality' (which presumably means an increase in economic and social equality).

How are the privileged few doing this? By 'a *deblackening* of the ethos', by hypocritically emphasizing the 'many' in the national motto, by failing to teach a fact (one that is a fact however not of the history of Jamaica, but of the history of the Americas, and therefore of the world-system). This fact is that 'millions of West Africans [were] brought as slaves' while 'millions of Europeans . . . came as masters, settlers or indentured labourers'. The historic encounters of these two groups 'in Jamaica and the Caribbean' forged the 'texture' of a 'truly indigenous life'. 'Black' is the term of the resultant 'culture', which is 'vigorous' and not a 'reduction' or a 'shrinking'.

So, in the end, what is being said is that the assertion of 'blackness' as constitutive of the national 'culture' of Jamaica (culture here in usage I) is the mode by which the 'marginalized majority' can hope to protect themselves against the claims of the 'privileged few' to represent a higher 'culture' (usage II). Thus what seems particularist at the level of the world-system ('blackness') serves as an assertion of a universalist theme ('high values to the human personality'). This, says Nettleford, is being 'race conscious' but not 'racist', which he admits requires a 'delicate balancing of sensibilities'. In this complicated reasoning, which seems to me correct, the more 'blackness' that Jamaica would exhibit, the more color-blindness (or humanist values) it would exhibit.

Yes, you may respond, perhaps so, but where does this argument end? At what point do we cross the line from 'race consciousness' to 'racism'? For there are clearly many, many cases across the world where the assertion of the particularist 'culture' of the (national) 'majority' to the exclusion of the minority or minorities could be seen as oppressive? Have Bretons no 'cultural' claims in France, Swedes in Finland, Ainu in Japan, Tamils in Sri Lanka, Kurds in Turkey, Hungarians in Romania?

Nettleford might agree — I do not know — that all these latter groups have legitimate claims to their 'cultural' assertion, and still argue that the situation is historically different in Jamaica. Why? Essentially because in Jamaica it is the majority that has been historically 'marginalized', and not the various 'minorities'. And, as long as that remains true, then negritude or any similar particularism may serve as the negation of the negation, as Sartre (1949) argued in 'Black Orpheus.'[1]

What the Nettleford quote does is to demonstrate how tangled is the skein of cultural debate in the capitalist world-economy, but also how covered with nettles, and therefore how careful we need to be if we wish to understand and evaluate this ideological battleground.

IV

I would like to take each of the six contradictions of the capitalist world-economy and show how the ideologies of universalism and of racism-sexism help contain each of the contradictions, and why therefore the two ideologies are a symbiotic pair.

1. Since the capitalist world-economy is a world-system, and for some time now one that has expanded to cover the entire globe, it is easy to see how universalism reflects this phenomenon, and indeed this has been one of the most explicit explanations of the ideologists. Today we have a network of United Nations structures, based in theory on the Universal Declaration of Human Rights, asserting the existence of both international law and values of all humanity. We have universal time and space measurements. We have a scientific community who assert universal laws. Nor is this a phenomenon merely of the twentieth century. Universal science was already being proclaimed in the sixteenth century, and indeed far earlier. Grotius was writing about a universal 'law of the seas' in the first half of the seventeenth century. And so on.

At the same time, of course, we have been erecting a network of 'sovereign states' with clear territorial boundaries and with national laws, assemblies, languages, passports, flags, money, and above all citizens. The entire land area of the globe is today exhaustively divided into such units, which now number over 150.

There are two ways we can consider these 150 or so sovereign states. We can see them as very strong institutions whose raison d'être is to limit the validity of universal rules. Sovereignty means in theory the right to do within the frontiers of the country whatever the internal (and constitutionally appropriate) authorities decide to do. But of course, at the same time, these 150 or so units are an immense reduction from the number of political authorities (to use a vague term) which existed in the world as of say 1450. Almost every one of the 150 or so units comprises an area that in 1450 included more than one political authority. Thus most of these sovereign states face the issue of how they are to treat this 'coming together' historically of what were previously separate entities. All of them, without any exception, do it on the principle of citizenship, a principle which today usually asserts that all persons born in that state are citizens (plus certain others) and that all such citizens enjoy equal rights. (The most notorious exception, South Africa, which as a state refuses to acknowledge the legitimacy of this theory of citizenship, is considered for that very reason a world scandal.) Thus, each state is proclaiming the universality of the equality of citizens, and virtually all states are accepting this principle as a sort of universal moral law.

We can assert, if we wish, that the principle of universalism both on a world-wide scale and within each of the sovereign states that constitute the interstate system is hypocritical. But it is precisely because there is in reality a hierarchy of states within the interstate system and a hierarchy of citizens within each sovereign state that the ideology of universalism matters. It serves on the one hand as a palliative and a deception and on the other as a political counter-weight which the weak can use and do use against the strong.

But racism-sexism as an ideology equally serves to contain the contradiction involved in creating sovereign states within an inter-state system that contains a single division of labor. For racism-sexism is precisely what legitimates the real inequalities, the always existing (if continually shifting) hierarchies both within the world-system as a whole and within each sovereign state. We know that the peoples of color were subjected to formal colonization as well as to slave labor during the history of this world-system. We know that there exist many formal discriminations concerning the movements of peoples. And we know that these phenomena have been justified by racist theories, sometimes based on pseudo-science (thereby deferring to the ideology of universalism) and sometimes based on unmitigated prejudice, as in the talk of a Yellow Peril which was so widespread in the White areas of the world in the beginning of the twentieth century.

At the state level, the phenomenon of justification by racism of an internal political, economic, and social hierarchy is so familiar that it is scarcely worth recounting. I would only point out two things. Where internal hierarchies cannot be based on skin color, they can always be based on other particularist criteria, as say in Northern Ireland. Secondly, everywhere — in all the states individually, and in the interstate system as a whole — the racist idelogy takes the same form. It is argued that one group is genetically or 'culturally' (note here, culture in usage II) inferior to another group in such a way that the group said to be inferior cannot be expected to perform tasks as well as the presumably superior group. This is said to hold true either eternally or for a very long period into the future (pending, in another deference to universalist doctrine, some very long-term educational process).

So racism is used, as we all know, to justify these hierarchies. But sexism? Yes, sexism too, and in two ways. First, if one examines racist terminology, one will find that it is regularly clothed in sexist language. The superior 'race' is considered to be more masculine, the inferior one to be more feminine. It is as though sexism was even more deeply rooted than racism. Whereas a purely racist ideology might occasionally fail to persuade, the ideologues can find their clinching argument by adding the sexist overtones. So we hear arguments that the dominant group is more rational, more disciplined, more hard-working, more self-controlled, more independent, while the dominated group is more emotional, more self-indulgent, more lazy, more artistic, more dependent. And this is of course the same set of characteristics that sexist ideology claims distinguish men from women.

There is a second way in which sexism doubles with racism. The dominated racial group, because it is said to be more self-indulgent, is thereby thought more aggressive sexually (and more pan-sexual as well). The males of the dominated group therefore represent a threat to the females of the dominant group who, although women and not men, are somehow more 'self-controlled' than the males of the dominated group. But since they are nonetheless physically weaker, because they are women, they therefore require the active physical protection of the males of the dominant group.

Furthermore, we can turn this sexist argument around and still justify world hierarchies. Now that, as a result of recent political developments, women have gained more rights of various kinds in Western countries, the fact that they have not yet done as well politically in some Third World countries, say those countries in which Islam is strong, becomes itself a further justification of racist ideology. The Moslems, it is argued, are not culturally capable of recognizing the same universal principles of man–woman relations that are said to be accepted in the Western (or Judeo–Christian world) and from this it is said to follow that they are also capable of many other things.

2. We have noted that the historic expansion of a capitalist world-economy originally located primarily in Europe to incorporate other zones of the globe created the contradiction of moder-

nization versus Westernization. The simple way to resolve this dilemma has been to assert that they are identical. In so far as Asia or Africa 'Westernizes,' it 'modernizes'. That is to say, the simplest solution was to argue that Western culture is in fact universal culture. For a long time the ideology remained at this simple level, whether it took the form of Christian proselytization or of the famous '*mission civilisatrice*' of France's colonial empire.

Of course, this sometimes took the slightly more sophisticated form of arguing that only Western civilization, of all world civilizations, was somehow capable of evolving from a pre-modern form to modernity. In a sense, this is what Orientalism as a discipline clearly implied. Clothed in the legitimation of particularism — Islam or India or China represented complex, high cultures which a Westerner could only appreciate after long, difficult, and sympathetic study — the Orientalists also suggested that these high Oriental cultures were historically frozen and could not evolve, but could only be 'destroyed' from without. Various versions of anthropological theory — the search for the pristine pre-contact culture, but also the universalist distinction of structuralist anthropology between cold and hot cultures — led to the same conclusions. The West had emerged into modernity; the others had not. Inevitably, therefore, if one wanted to be 'modern' one had in some way to be 'Western' culturally. If not Western religions, one had to adopt Western languages. And if not Western languages, one had at the very minimum to accept Western technology, which was said to be based on the universal principles of science.

But at the very same time that the universalist ideologues were preaching the merits of Westernization or 'assimilation', they were also (or others were also) preaching the eternal existence and virtue of difference. Thus a universalist message of cultural multiplicity could serve as a justification of educating various groups in their separate 'cultures' and hence preparing them for different tasks in the single economy. The extreme version of this, and an explicitly theorized one, is *apartheid*. But lesser versions, perhaps less coherently articulated, have been widespread within the system.

Furthermore, racism and sexism can be justified by a rejection of Westernization which can take the form of legitimating indigenous ideological positions (a so-called revival of tradition) that include blatantly racist and sexist themes. At which point, we have a renewed justification of the world-wide hierarchy. It becomes legitimate to treat Iran as a pariah nation, not only because Iran uses 'terrorist' tactics in the international arena, but because Iranian women are required to wear the *chador*.

3. The problem of getting workers to work harder at lower pay is inherently a difficult one. It runs against the grain of self-interest. The question is therefore whether there can exist an ideological motivation which might help achieve this contradictory objective of world capital. Let us see in what ways universalism and racism-sexism can serve this end.

Universalism can become a motivation for harder work in so far as the work ethic is preached as a defining centerpiece of modernity. Those who are efficient, who devote themselves to their work, exemplify a value which is of universal merit and is said to be socially beneficial to all. This is true not only at the individual level but at the collective level. Thus states that are low in the hierarchy of the world-system, groups that are low in the hierarchy of states, are adjured to overcome the handicap of lower status by joining in the universal ethos. By becoming 'competitive' in the market, individuals and groups may obtain what others already have, and thus one day shall achieve equality. Until then, inequality remains inevitable.

Thus, the universal work ethic justifies all existing inequalities, since the explanation of their origin is in the historically unequal adoption by different groups of this motivation. States that are better off than other states, groups that are better off than other groups, have achieved this advantage by an earlier, stronger, and more enduring commitment to the universal work ethic. Conversely, those who are worse off, therefore those who are paid less, are in this position because they merit it. The existence of unequal incomes thus becomes not an instance of racism-sexism but rather of the universal standard of rewarding efficiency. Those who have less have less because they have earned less.

But racism and sexism complement this universalizing theorem very well. Racism and sexism, when institutionalized, create a high correlation between low group status and low income. Thus, those at the lower end of the scale are easily identifiable by what may then be termed cultural criteria (culture, that is, in usage II). Culture (usage II) now becomes the explanation of the cause. Blacks and women are paid less because they work less hard, merit less. And they work less hard because there is something, if not in their biology, at least in their 'culture', which teaches them values which conflict with the universal work ethos.

Furthermore, we can enlist the dominated groups in their own oppression. In so far as they cultivate their separateness as 'cultural' groups, which is a mode of political mobilization against unequal status, they socialize their members into cultural expressions which distinguish them from the dominated groups, and thus into some at least of the values attributed to them by racist and sexist theories. And they do this, in a seeming paradox, on the grounds of the universal principle of the equal validity of all cultural expressions.

4. Modernity as a central universalizing theme gives priority to newness, change, progress. Through the ages, the legitimacy of political systems had been derived from precisely the opposite principle, that of oldness, continuity, tradition. There was a straightforwardness to pre-modern modes of legitimation which does not exist anymore. Political legitimacy is a much more obscure objective within the realities of the capitalist world-economy, yet states of course seek constantly to achieve it. Some degree of legitimacy is a crucial element in the stability of all regimes.

Here is where culture (usage I) can be very helpful. For in the absence of the personalized legitimacy of monarchical-aristocratic systems, where real power normally defines the limits of legitimacy, a fictionalized collectivity with a collective soul, a hypothetical 'nation' whose roots are located in days of yore, is a marvelous substitute. Few governments in the history of the capitalist world-economy have failed to discover the power of patriotism to achieve cohesion. And patriotism has quite often been reinforced by or transformed into racism (jingoist chauvinism, opposition of the citizen to the stranger or immigrant) and sexism (the presumed martial nature of males).

But in the real world of the capitalist world-economy with its regular rise and decline of nations, a multifarious set of patriotisms offers little in the way of explanation, especially for the losers in the cyclical shifts. Here then legitimacy can be restored by appealing to the universalizing principles of appropriate political and social change which, by a change in state structure (a 'revolution') will make possible (for the first time or once again) national development. Thus, by appealing to culture (usage II), the advanced elements of the nation can place the state in the line of universal progress.

Of course, such 'revolutions' work to restore (or create) legitimacy by seeking to transform in some significant way the position of the state in the hierarchy of the world-system. Failing that, the revolution can create its own tradition about itself and link this self-appraisal to a perhaps revised but still fictive history of the state. Thus, if culture (usage II) is inefficacious or becomes so, one can fall back on culture (usage I).

5. The capitalist world-economy does not merely have unequal distribution of reward. It is the locus of an increasing polarization of reward over historical time. Here however there is an asymmetry between the situation at the level of the world-economy as a whole and that at the level of the separate sovereign states which compose the interstate system. Whereas at the level of the world-system, it seems clear that gap of income between states at the top and the bottom of the hierarchy has grown, and has grown considerably over time, it does not necessarily follow that this is true within each state structure. Nonetheless, it is also the case that one of the moral justifications of the capitalist world-economy, one that is used to justify hard work at low pay (the issue just discussed in the previous section), is that inequalities of reward have been diminishing over time, that such inequalities as exist are transitory and transitional phenomena on the road to a more prosperous, more egalitarian future.

Here, once again, we have a blatant discord between official ideology and empirical reality. How has this been contained? The first line of defense has always been denial. The rising standard of living has been a central myth of this world-system. It has been sustained both by arithmetic sleight of hand and by invoking the paired ideologies of universalism and racism-sexism.

The arithmetic sleight of hand is very straightforward. At the world level, it consists first of all of talking about the numerator and not the denominator, and ignoring the dispersion of the curve. We talk about the numerator when we recite the expanded world volume of production, or total value produced, while failing to divide it by world population. Or we analyze quality of life by observing some linear trends but failing to count others. Thus we measure age of mortality or speed of travel but not average number of hours of work per year or per lifetime, or environmental conditions.

But the real sleight of hand is to engage in national rather than global measures, which involves a double deception. First of all, in an unequal and polarizing world-system, there is geographical dispersion. Hence, it is perfectly possible for real income, as measured by GNP per capita say, to rise in some countries while going down in others and in the system as a whole. But since the countries in which the rise occurs are also those most extensively studied, observed, and measured, it is easy to understand how facile but false generalizations take root. In addition, despite the better statistical systems of such core countries, it is undoubtedly the case that they do not measure adequately the non-citizen component of the population (often illegally in residence). And since this is the poorest component, the bias is evident.

Still, misperception of reality is only a first line of defense, and one that is increasingly difficult to sustain. Hence, in the last fifty years, a world-wide schema of 'developmentalism' has been erected and propagated which legitimates the polarization. By this point you will realize how repetitive is the pattern of ideological justification. First of all, there is the universalist theme. All states can develop; all states shall develop. Then come the racist themes. If some states have developed earlier and faster than others, it is because they have done something, behaved in some way that is different. They have been more individualist, or more entrepreneurial, or more rational, or in some way more 'modern'. If other states have developed more slowly, it is because there is something in their culture (usage I at the state level, usage II at the world level) which prevents them or has thus far prevented them from becoming as 'modern' as other states.

The seesaw of ideological explanation then continues into the hypothetical future. Since all states can develop, how can the underdeveloped develop? In some way, by copying those who already have, that is, by adopting the universal culture of the modern world, with the assistance of those who are more advanced (higher present culture, usage II). If, despite this assistance, they are making no or little progress, it is because they are being 'racist' in rejecting universal 'modern' values which then justifies that the 'advanced' states are scornful of them or condescending to them. Any attempt in an 'advanced' state to comprehend 'backwardness' in terms other than wilful refusal to be 'modern' is labeled Third-Worldism, or reverse racism or irrationalism. This is a tight system of justification, since it 'blames the victim', and thereby denies the reality.

6. Finally, let us turn to the contradiction of limitlessness and organic death. Any theory of limitless expansion is a gambler's paradise. In the real world, it is not possible. Furthermore, to the limited extent that the theory has seemed to accord with the existential reality of the capitalist world-economy as a world-system, it has not seemed to accord with the realities of the separate states. Even the strongest and the wealthiest of states, *especially* the strongest

and wealthiest, have risen and declined. We are currently living the beginnings of the long-term relative decline of the United States, only recently still the hegemonic power of the world-system.

Thus the world-system as a whole must deal with the problem of its eventual demise and, within the ongoing system, the strong states must deal with the problem of their relative decline. The two problems are quite different, but regularly fused and confused. There are basically two ways to deal with demise or decline: to deny them or to welcome the change.

Once again, both universalism and racism-sexism are useful conservative ideologies. First of all, racism-sexism serves to sustain denial. Demise or decline is at most a temporary illusion, caused by momentarily weak leadership, because by definition it is said it cannot occur, given the strength or the superiority of the dominant culture (usage II). Or, if it is really occurring, it is because culture (usage II) has ceded place to a deceptive world humanism in the vain hope of creating a world culture (usage I). Thus, it is argued, the demise or decline, which it is now admitted may really be occurring, is due to insufficient emphasis on culture (usage II) and hence to admitting 'lower' racial groups or 'women' to political rights. In this version of ideology, demise or decline is reversible, but only by a reversion to a more overt racism-sexism. Generally speaking, this has been a theme throughout the twentieth century of what we today call the extreme, or neo-fascist, right.

But there is a universalizing version to this exercise in denial. The demise or decline has perhaps not been caused, or not primarily caused, by an increased political egalitarianism, but much more by an increased intellectual egalitarianism. The denial of the superiority of the scientific elite, and their consequent right to dictate public policy, is the result of an anti-rationalist, antinomian denial of universal culture (usage I) and its world-wide culture-bearers (usage II). Demands for popular control of technocratic elites is a call for 'the night of the long knives', a return to pre-modern 'primitivism'. This is the heart of what is today called neo-conservatism.

But if the overtly 'conservative' versions of the ideologies are inadequate to the task, one can put forward 'progressive' versions. It is not too difficult to 'welcome' the 'transition' in ways that in fact sustain the system. There is the universalizing mode, in which progressive transition is seen as inevitable. This can lead on the one hand to postponing the transition until the equally inevitable 'preconditions' of transition are realized. It can lead on the other hand to interim measures whose reality is the worsening of conditions on the grounds that this 'speeds up' the realization of the preconditions. We have known many such movements.

Finally, the 'welcoming' of the transition can have the same conservative effect in a racist form. One can insist that it is only the presently 'advanced' groups that can be the leaders of the next presumed 'advance'. Hence, it is only on the basis of presently-realized culture (usage II) that the transition to a new world will be realized. The more 'backward' regions must in some way wait on the more 'advanced' ones in the process of 'transition.'

V

The paired ideologies of universalism and racism-sexism then have been very powerful means by which the contradictory tensions of the world-system have been contained. But of course, they have also served as ideologies of change and transformation in their slightly different clothing of the theory of progress and the conscientization of oppressed groups. This has resulted in extraordinarily ambivalent uses of these ideologies by the presumed opponents of the existing system, the antisystemic movements. It is to this last aspect of culture as an ideological battleground that I should like now to turn.

An antisystemic movement is a movement to transform the system. An antisystemic movement is at the same time a product of the system. What culture does such a movement incarnate? In terms of culture (usage I), it is hard to see how the antisystemic movements could conceivably have incarnated any culture other than that of the capitalist world-economy. It is hard to see how they could not have been impregnated by and expressed the paired ideologies of universalism and racism-sexism.

However in terms of culture (usage II) they have claimed to have created a new culture, a culture destined to be a culture (usage I) of the future world. They have tried to elaborate this new culture theoretically. They have created institutions presumably designed to socialize members and sympathizers into this new culture. But of course it is not so easy to know what shall be the culture, a culture, of the future. We design our utopias in terms of what we know now. We exaggerate the novelty of what we advocate. We act in the end, and at best, as prisoners of our present reality who permit ourselves to daydream.

This is not at all pointless. But it is surely less than a sure guide to appropriate behavior. What the antisystemic movements have done, if one considers their global activities over 150-odd years, has been essentially to turn themselves into the fulfillers of the liberal dream while claiming to be its most fulsome critics. This has not been a comfortable position. The liberal dream — the product of the principal self-conscious ideological *Weltanschauung* within the capitalist world-economy — has been that universalism will triumph over racism and sexism. This has been translated into two strategic operational imperatives — the spread of 'science' in the economy, and the spread of 'assimilation' in the political arena.

The fetishism of science by the antisystemic movements — for example, Marx's designation of his ideas as 'scientific socialism' — was a natural expression of the post-1789 triumph of Enlightenment ideas in the world-system. Science was future-oriented; it sought total truth via the perfectibility of human capacities; it was deeply optimistic. The limitlessness of its ambitions might have served as a warning-signal of the deep affinity of this kind of science to its world-system. But the antisystemic thinkers interpreted this affinity to be a transitory misstep, a surviving irrationality, doomed to extinction.

The problem, as the antisystemic movements saw it, was not that there was too much science, but too little. Sufficient social invest-ment in science was still lacking. Science had not yet penetrated into enough corners of economic life. There were still zones of the world from which it was kept. Its results were insufficiently applied. The revolution — be it social or national or both — would at last release the scientists to find and to apply their universal truths.

In the political arena, the fundamental problem was interpreted to be exclusion. The states were the handmaidens of minorities; they must be made the instrument of the whole of society, the whole of humanity. The unpropertied were excluded. Include them! The minorities were excluded. Include them! The women were excluded. Include them! Equals all. The dominant strata had more than others. Even things out! But if we are evening out dominant and dominated, then why not minorities and majorities, women and men? Evening out meant in practice assimilating the weaker to the model of the strong. This model looked suspiciously like Everyman — the man with simple but sufficient means, hard-working, morally upright and devoted to family (friends, larger community).

This search for science and assimilation, what I have called the fulfillment of the liberal dream, was located deep in the consciousness and in the practical action of the world's antisystemic movements, from their emergence in the mid-nineteenth century until at least the Second World War. Since then, and particularly since the world cultural revolution of 1968, these movements, or at least some of them, have begun to evince doubts as to the utility, the reasonableness of 'science' and 'assimilation' as social objectives. These doubts have been expressed in multiple forms. The green movements, the countercultural movements have raised questions about the productivism inherent in the nineteenth-century adulation of science. The many new social movements (of women, of minorities) have poured scorn upon the demand for assimilation. I do not need to spell out here the diverse ways in which this has been manifested.

But, and this is the crucial point, perhaps the real triumph of culture (usage I), the antisystemic movements have hesitated to go all the way. For one thing, the priorities of one kind of antisystemic movement have often been at odds with that of another kind (e.g. ecologists v. Third World liberation movements). For another thing, each kind of movement itself has been internally divided. The debates within the women's movements or Black movements over such questions as political alliances or the desirability of 'protective' legislation for the 'weaker' groups are instances of the tactical ambivalences of these movements.

As long as the antisystemic movements remain at the level of tactical ambivalence about the guiding ideological values of our world-system, as long as they are unsure how to respond to the liberal dream of more science and more assimilation, we can say that they are in no position to fight a war of position with the forces that defend the inequalities of the world. For they cede, by this ambivalence, the cultural high-ground to their opponents. The advocates of the system can continue to claim that scientism and assimilation represent the true values of world culture (usage I) and that their practitioners are the men of culture (usage II), the high priests of this culture (usage I). And, as long as this remains true, we are all enveloped in the paired ideologies (and the false antinomy) of universalism and racism-sexism.

The cultural trap in which we are caught is a strong one, overlain by much protective shrubbery which hides its outline and its ferocity from us. Can we somehow disentangle ourselves? I believe it is possible, though at most I can only indicate some of the directions in which, if we moved along them, I believe we might find ways to disentangle.

Beyond scientism, I suspect there lies a more broadly defined science, one which will be able to reconcile itself dramatically with the humanities, such that we can overcome what C.P. Snow (1959) called the division of the two cultures (note the term again, here in usage II). I suspect we may have to reverse the history of science and return from efficient causes to final causes. I think, if we do, that we may be able to scrape away all that is contingent (that is, all that is Western) to uncover new possibilities.

This will make possible a new rendezvous of world civilizations. Will some 'universals' emerge out of this rendezvous? Who knows? Who even knows what a 'universal' is? At a moment of world history when the physical scientists are at last (or is it once again?) beginning to talk of the 'arrow of time', who is able to say that there are any immutable laws of nature?

If we go back to metaphysical beginnings, and reopen the question of the nature of science, I believe that it is probable, or at least possible, that we can reconcile our understanding of the origins and legitimacies of group particularisms with our sense of the social, psychological, and biological meanings of humanity and humaneness. I think that perhaps we can come up with a concept of culture that sublates the two usages.

I wish that I saw more clearly how this could be done, or where it is leading. But I have the sense that in cultural terms our world-system is in need of some 'surgery'. Unless we 'open up' some of our most cherished cultural premises, we shall never be able to diagnose clearly the extent of the cancerous growths and shall therefore be unable to come up with appropriate remedies. It is perhaps unwise to end on such a medical analogy. Medicine, as a mode of knowledge, has only too clearly demonstrated its limitations. On the other hand, the art of medicine represents the eternal human response to suffering, death, and transition, and therefore incarnates hope, however much it must be tempered by an awareness of human limitations.

Notes

This article has also been published in the Japanese journal *Hitotsubashi Journal of Social Studies*, Vol. XXI, August 1989.

1. Jean-Paul Sartre (1949: 237) calls negritude 'antiracist racism'.

References

Hopkins, Terence, K. and Wallerstein, Immanuel (1987) 'Capitalism and the Incorporation of New Zones into the World-Economy', *Review* 10(5/6): 763–79.

Mintz, Sidney W. (1988) *The Power of Sweetness and the Sweetness of Power*. 8th Duijker Lecture. Deventer: Van Loghum Slaterus.

Nettleford, Rex (1986) 'Building a Nation, Shaping a Society', pp. 9–10 in J. Wedderburn (ed.), *A Caribbean Reader on Development*. Kingston.

Sartre, Jean-Paul (1949) 'Orphée noir', pp. 229–88 in *Situations*, III. Paris: Gallimard.

Snow, C.P. (1959) *The Two Cultures and the Scientific Revolution*. New York: Cambridge University Press.

Wallerstein, Immanuel (1982) 'Crisis as Transition', pp. 11–54, esp. 12–22 in S. Amin et al. (eds), *Dynamics of Global Crisis*. New York: Monthly Review Press.

Wallerstein, Immanuel (1988) 'The Ideological Tensions of Capitalism: Universalism versus Racism and Sexism', pp. 3–9 in J. Smith et al. (ed), *Racism, Sexism, and the World-System*. Westport, CT: Greenwood Press.

Immanuel Wallerstein is the Director of the Fernand Braudel Center (SONY-Binghamton), and the author of *The Modern World-System*.

Culture and the World-System

Roy Boyne

Immanuel Wallerstein's essay begins by quoting Sidney Mintz to the effect that what is universal is 'our capacity to create cultural realities'. That view, however, does not truly animate Wallerstein's reflection on culture. A more accurate theme for his essay would refer to our capacity to utilize cultural *strategies* in the deception of ourselves and others.

He begins by articulating a typically structuralist and monotonal view of culture, which, for him, is a concept pointing *either* to characteristics shared within a group which distinguish that group from other groups *or* to hierarchical distinctions within groups which value one set of characteristics rather than another. An example of the former use of the concept would be its deployment as an indexical expression in a comparison between, say, the shared values and life-patterns of a particular tribe of American Indians and the shared values of the first and subsequent generations of white settlers into North America. An example of the latter use of the concept would be its utilization in a comparison of the culture of the Victorian bourgeois family, with their values of work, letters, art, and obedience, and the lack of standards thought to be typical within the Victorian underclass. For Wallerstein, these are *the* two tonalities of the concept of culture; the former representing harmony within a group, the latter representing division. What is really crucial, however, is that he thinks that such cultural judgements typically imply an attribution of rank and desert, with all the functions of rationalization or righteous opposition thereby made available.

Wallerstein holds that there has been long-standing intellectual confusion between the two usages of the idea of culture, and he further holds that this may be the consequence of the historical development of the world system and a reflection of its logic.

This is an extremely broad thesis, but it is not one that is easy to

Theory, Culture & Society (SAGE, London, Newbury Park and New Delhi), Vol. 7 (1990), 57–62

sustain. A glance through the Bible, or Plato's *Republic*, or Shakespeare, or Confucius, is enough to confirm that questions of the internal coherence or division within a group, and issues of distinctions between different groups have *always* been central both to the ways in which individuals and groups have understood themselves and to the varieties of rhetorical manoeuvres available to those who seek to persuade others of the importance to the group of one course of action rather than another. If the concept of culture has only these two tonalities, one suspects that to account for them in terms of the logic of the modern world system is somewhat specious, for the internal and external status of the group has always been of major moment for all social processes. If there is a *one single* longstanding intellectual confusion as far as the concept of culture is concerned, it is much more likely to be attributable to factors of social ontology rather than to comparatively recent historical development.

Does, however, the concept of culture only have these two tonalities? If the concept of culture were only about issues of internal and external harmony and difference, then perhaps the answer to that might be affirmative. But is not culture also about the definition and pursuit of interests which are deemed to be (within a specific sociohistoric cultural complex) vital, autonomous, and specific to the agents pursuing them? At another level, do not the ethologists claim that human culture may be studied as a part of animal behaviour? At still another level, is it not necessary to include the physical environment in any general understanding of culture — and we need not go back to the archaic anthropology of Rousseau's *Essay on the Origin of Languages* here, for, as David Harvey (1985) reminds us, increasing urbanization makes the urban the immediate level of social action and consciousness formation. In short, a brief and by no means exhaustive reflection on the concept of culture must show that group harmony vis-a-vis other groups and group disharmony vis-a-vis its own constitution do not alone provide the major tonalities of the concept of culture. In fact, if there is a case to be made for finding one or more major tonalities, it probably rests upon the idea — implicit within the whole anthropological tradition, and even into Lévi-Strauss's version of it — of rich description: culture is that which needs to be described, that which cannot be anticipated on the basis of some theoretical premise.

Furthermore, if we turn to writers who are concerned with culture under the sign of group harmony vis-a-vis other groups and group disharmony vis-a-vis its own constitution we have to question Wallerstein's assertion that there has been a long-standing intellectual confusion over the idea. Wilhelm Dilthey, for example, writing in 1883, was very clear that these were alternative modes of thought:

> In sciences of systems of culture, one thinks of psychological elements in various individuals, chiefly, only with respect to their role in a system of purposes. There is a way of looking at things different from this, one which considers external organization of society, that is, relations of community, of external association, of domination, and of subordination of wills in society. The same tendency of abstraction is operative whenever one distinguishes political history from cultural history. (Dilthey, 1988:115)

In actual fact, however, these points would not be of great interest to Wallerstein, for he somewhat disingenuously suggests that the concept of culture is not worth the effort. What evidence, he asks, can be adduced to show that a particular group has a culture? Can we operationalize the concept of culture, he wonders, in such a way that we can use it to make statements that are more than trivial? His negative responses to these positivistic questions bespeak a certain narrowness of approach such that differences between groups do not assist the quest for historical understanding, and cultural differences within groups tend to function as ideological cover for the advancement of interests. Has Wallerstein not read Max Weber or thought about the mechanisms of prejudice or listened to advice about where it is not safe to walk alone? The point is, of course, that skilled social actors are skilled precisely by virtue of their operationalization of concepts of cultural difference; and even if such mundane sociological matters are outside of Wallerstein's frame of reference, does he really hold that differences between, say, Protestant and Catholic are of no use in understanding the history of European society?

The underlying reason for Wallerstein's critique of the concept of culture is not, in fact, that it has been a site of intellectual confusion, nor that it possesses only a specious analytical utility. It is rather that it opens onto a form of analysis and social understanding which is opposed to the brute and disinterested objectivism of world system theory. On the one side we have the cunning plasticity of culture, on the other side the certain realities of the virtually tangible structures of the capitalist world economy. As Wallerstein reviews them in his essay, some of the *realities* (his term) and their cultural consequences of the evolution of the capitalist world economy are

1. an unprecedentedly complex, detailed and cohesive *international* division of labour which co-exists contradictorily with the multitude of differentially privileged *national* polities which cultural attributes like racial characteristics are held to justify;

2. a complex rhythmic cycle, repeated every fifty or sixty years, of expansion and contraction, with each pulse of the cycle concluding with the 'modernization' of another part of the system;

3. a bifurcated logic of capital accumulation on the part of the firm and individual reward as the principal motivation, buttressed by making the work ethic the very centre of modernity, ensuring participation in the system;

4. relentless technical, organizational and product development, mirrored by too-often unsatisfied demands for national progress, whose energy can fuel various forms of political movement;

5. a constant dual process of wealth accumulation and impoverishment, in which the wealth accrues out of talent, energy and application, and the impoverishment will supposedly end once inappropriate cultural traits are left behind; and

6. finally, the system is a historical one and, as such, it must eventually face the demise that, in preaching the gospel of limitless development, it denies, doing so by blaming weak leadership for temporary setbacks, or by self-castigation for inappropriate cultural standards which now must be overturned by, for example, equal opportunities legislation, or by blaming the scientists and the technocrats.

Wallerstein believes therefore that the notion of culture is a part of that set of ideas which have been developed in response to the ambiguities, contradictions and complexity of this real historical system in which we find ourselves. The notion of culture has, for him, two principle functions. In its emphasis on the differences between groups, on unique and still relevant cultural traditions, it highlights a certain solidity, something to hold on to even though we are all adrift in a world that is ceaselessly changing. On the other hand, in so far as culture refers to differences within groups, it points to those mechanisms that divert attention from the economic divisions which are at the heart of the capitalist system even while underpinning them. It is this double function of culture: (falsely?) to persuade us that we do not live solely in accordance with the logic of economic production, and duplicitously to divert us from dwelling too much on what the other groups have — *for they are different* from us — which explains the title of Wallerstein's essay, 'Culture as the Ideological Battleground of the Modern World-system'.

Just what he means by 'battleground' is explained using a quotation from a speech made by the Jamaican politician, Rex Nettleford, in 1983. Wallerstein uses the speech to show that the two functions of culture can be locked into conflict with each other. Crudely, arguments for national standing vis-a-vis other nations can arrest discontent over internal inequalities, and can even celebrate them as part of a rich cultural heritage (certain speeches of Winston Churchill spring to mind); while, conversely, the radical reformer can blame the outside for perverting the real and homogeneous cultural identity of the inside, and can go on to promise recovery of that identity.

We can see pretty clearly that the distinction between universalism and particularism is central to Wallerstein's understanding of the notion of culture. He thinks that both universalistic principles and particularist prejudices have served ideological functions, that they have been weapons deployed upon the battleground of the modern world-system. The universalist idea of citizenship, for example, works to conceal differences; but it can also operate to protect less privileged groups. On the other hand, racism and sexism, often justified by reference to the universalist aspirations of pseudo-scientific statements regarding genetic inheritance or psychological disposition, are particularist notions that have served to justify inequalities. It is not hard to see where this is leading: for Wallerstein, surveying the world from the objective edifice of world-system theory, all culture is derivative. Even if one agrees with Nelson and Grossberg (1988: 3) that 'reflection theories, however qualified and problematized, play a necessary and constitutive role, not only for all later and sophisticated Marxisms, but also in all historically or politically grounded interpretation', it is remarkable that a theorist of Wallerstein's stature presents the rich variety of human thought, achievement, consciousness, pain, stupidity and evil as but a mechanical reflex of world-systemic economic structures.

What Wallerstein does is to provide a framework of understanding. But a framework is all that it is. World-system theory is like a house without glass in the windows, fuel in the fireplace, food in the cupboards, or beds upon which to sleep. Even if we grant the status of uncontestable reality to the main supports of the structure, and we should not do so lightly since we would be saying thereby that the human sciences have arrived at a shared epistemology in regard to which we can expect no radical shifts, it does not follow that the understanding of culture will be exhausted by providing an account of the way that it keeps the structure from breaking apart. Few would contest that some aspects of culture can be analysed in that way, but that is far from all there is to it.

It is probably in the case of the treatment of racism and sexism in Wallerstein's essay that we see just how poverty-stricken an analysis of racism and sexism would be if it were presented from the standpoint of world-system theory alone. Why is this? It is because the explanation offered by Wallerstein treats racism and sexism as epiphenomenal, as incidental to the level of the real. There is no mention of lynchings, of child molestation, of back street abortions, of the burning of witches, of the Ku Klux Klan. The fact is that racisms and sexisms come in an infinite variety of guises and draw upon a veritable *Malleus Maleficarum* of reproductive transmogrifying strategies. This *Malleus Maleficarum* is just one facet of a cultural reality which is just as momentous as the reality which Wallerstein describes in terms which are themselves cultural through and through. To misquote Tennyson, Wallerstein's culture is for a very small crowd.

References

Dilthey, Wilhelm (1988) *Introduction to the Human Sciences*, translated from the German (1883) by Ramon J. Betanzos. London: Harvester-Wheatsheaf.

Harvey, David (1985) *Consciousness and the Urban Experience*. Oxford: Blackwell.

Nelson, Cary and Grossberg, Lawrence (eds) (1988) *Marxism and the Interpretation of Culture*. London: Macmillan.

Roy Boyne teaches Sociology at Newcastle Polytechnic.

Culture is the World-System:
A Reply to Boyne

Immanuel Wallerstein

It's a great pity the world is not as we would like it to be. But does it do any good to kill the messenger? Roy Boyne starts his piece by asserting that I claim to be talking about the 'capacity to create cultural realities', whereas in fact I am talking about the 'capacity to utilize cultural strategies'. I gather the former is commendable, but the latter is dubious, or manipulative. The pure create realities; the impure utilize strategies. Roy Boyne clearly has a finer sense of discernment than I have; he knows when someone or some group is creating a reality rather than merely utilizing a strategy. I admit that I have found no practical way to draw the line, and I gave the effort up long ago. The historical social sciences should no doubt be informed by and based on moral options. But I don't believe social scientists serve any purpose by moralizing. Utilizing strategies is not in any case immoral, and the use of strategies is very much a cultural reality.

What shall I say to Roy Boyne's loud denunciations, that I really have stopped beating my wife: that I admit that culture involves 'rich description' (who could ever think otherwise, but do not 'politics' or 'economics' also involve 'rich description'?); that I do not think that one can only make 'trivial' statements about culture (why else would I bother writing this article, and others, with 'culture' in the title?); that I do not believe culture is merely 'derivative' (how could I think that when I deny the presumed ontological autonomy of three spheres of economics, politics and culture?); that I don't think racism and sexism are 'epiphenomenal' (when in fact I have said time and again that they are fundamental, defining realities of the modern world-system)?

Boyne apparently thinks that I think that economic structures have 'mechanical reflexes,' that they are 'tangible' (have you or

Theory, Culture & Society (SAGE, London, Newbury Park and New Delhi), Vol. 7 (1990), 63–65

anyone, Mr. Boyne, ever touched a 'rising rate of interest' or a 'falling rate of profit'?). Enough of slogans.

We get only one definition of culture in Boyne's article: 'culture is that which needs to be described, that which cannot be anticipated on the basis of some theoretical premise'. I wrote a whole book, called *Historical Capitalism*, in which I explained the use of my somewhat unusual locution in the title as reflecting my feeling that most analyses of capitalism were derived from theoretical premises and that I believed its analysis must begin with a description of what historically actually occurred. This attitude I thought I was continuing in my article on 'Culture as the Ideological Battleground of the Modern World-system'. I was seeking to spell out how 'culture' as a concept has been historically used in the last two centuries or so, and what I thought was lying behind its use, including what I think have been the systematic confusions in its usage. (No doubt Dilthey also saw a double usage; so what?) I treated the concept of culture exactly as I would treat any other concept (e.g., rent, bourgeoisie, the people, democracy, sovereignty, surplus-value, and so forth *ad infinitum*) as historically formed, created and recreated, not merely a tool of analysis but an object of analysis. I make no apology for this effort. Of course, culture is ultimately 'derivative'. Every concept, by being a concept, implies a derivation. There is nothing special in this about culture.

Why then is Roy Boyne, and many others, so agitated about, so defensive about, the *chasse gardée* of culture? I suspect that he sees in 'culture' the expression of human freedom and free will against the evil mechanical oppressive demons that govern us (the 'political economy'?). If so, he is truly barking up a wrong tree. If anything, culture is a word that describes what constrains us (in the most effective way possible, by shaping our 'will' that seeks to assert its 'freedom'), and is not a word that describes our ability to escape these constraints. Herbert Marcuse, in *Eros and Civilization*, inveighs against those who wish to redefine Freudian concepts by giving a greater role to socio-cultural factors in the formation of our personalities. He notes that this is the road to our being remolded by 'society'. He argues that the Freudian id, in so far as it is based precisely on biology and *not* on culture, is the only safeguard of our freedom, the only way in which we can ever hope to escape the shackles of 'brute and disinterested objectivism'.

There are two matters ultimately at issue in this debate. One is the issue of agency: can those who suffer (from say racism) do anything about it, anything that matters? The second is whether there is something called 'culture' which deserves a place, even a privileged place, in our epistemology?

On agency, I permit myself to repeat what I previously said in a discussion of Walter Rodney's views on agency, with which I was much in sympathy:

> The issue of agency is not a simple one. It plagues the social sciences. As those who denigrate generalizations in the name of idiographic uniqueness never tire of saying, any structural analysis implies that an individual, a group is caught in some web not of their making and out of their control. And so it does, except that this web is in turn formed by the sum of wills that are in turn formed by the structural conditions (constraints) — a perfect circle. If one adds to this conundrum the fact that in virtually any social situation, the actors may be ranked in a hierarchy of power — some stronger, some weaker — it follows logically that the stronger 'get their way' more frequently than the weaker. Else, in what sense are they stronger? This social reality is transformed into a problem of the analyst when we discuss agency. Should the analyst describe history from the top down or the bottom up? The obvious answer is the analyst should do neither, since the two are inextricably linked. The two are analytically one. (Wallerstein, 1986)

On the second issue, the importance of studying 'culture', I feel about it the same way as I feel about studying 'economics' or 'politics'. It is a non-subject, invented for us by nineteenth-century social science. The sooner we unthink this unholy trinity, the sooner we shall begin to construct a new historical social science that gets us out of the many cul-de-sacs in which we find ourselves. Emphasizing 'culture' in order to counterbalance the emphases others have put on the 'economy' or the 'polity' does not at all solve the problem; it in fact just makes it worse. We must surmount the terminology altogether.

I confess I have no easy solution to offer. I am as much a victim of my education as my colleagues. So I too fall back on using the existing misleading conceptual languages in order to communicate. But I assert that I am in search of better, and that world-systems analysis, if it has any value whatsoever, is part of this search, one incarnation of our collective quest for a radically-revised concepticon.

Reference

Wallerstein, Immanuel (1986) 'Walter Rodney: The Historian as Spokesman for Historical Forces', *American Ethnologist* 12(2): 330–36.

Turning World-System Theory on its Head

Albert Bergesen

In sociology and political science the prevailing theoretical approach to explaining international order is quite similar. In international relations theory the realist and neo-realist position argues that the international state system is a product of struggles for power between sovereign states in a condition of international anarchy. It is an assumption which can be traced back to Thucydides (1951) and was classically articulated by Hobbes (1964) for the actions of the modern state system. Given the obvious absence of a world state, this seems quite reasonable. Within sociology the world-system perspective associated with Immanuel Wallerstein (1983; 1989) makes a somewhat similar set of assumptions. Here the world is seen as developed and underdeveloped states, or zones, the interaction of which, through unequal exchange processes, produces a global core-periphery division of labor. Here trade and exchange constitute the principal social mechanism for integrating this global system.

These two perspectives are similar as they both make the common theoretical assumption that the component zones, or states, precede, and make possible, the subsequent structures and processes of the larger world, or international, system. In effect, both positions begin with sub-parts of the world-system, from which they derive, albeit with different logics, the larger global totality. The neo-Hobbesian rational choice bias of realist international relations theory has been heatedly discussed (Ashley, 1984), and the Smithian bias of Wallerstein's world division of labor has been criticized by Brenner (1971), who emphasizes the primacy of class relations within nations over exchange relations between them, as the most fundamental source of capitalism on a world scale. Although they are antithetical political positions, there is a common neo-utilitarian basis to the sociologists of the world-system perspective (a Smithian division of labor) and the political scientists of the neo-realist international relations perspective (a Hobbesian struggle for power).

Theory, Culture & Society (SAGE, London, Newbury Park and New Delhi), Vol. 7 (1990), 67–81

The Neo-utilitarian Consensus

I can be more specific about the similar conceptual foundations of international relations and world-system theory. Both represent the general utilitarian paradigm, which can be summarily represented in three assumptions they make in the construction of their specific theories of world order.

First, and most fundamentally, is the assumption that the sub-units of the larger world-system acquire their defining properties prior to their participation in the international system. Both theoretical paradigms begin with the individualist assumption that we begin with an aggregate of states and then move toward international order, rather than the collectivist assumption that we begin with an international order and only then derive the presence of states and national economies. In classic utilitarian thinking this took the form of assuming individuals had innate needs, desires, or wants to truck and barter, and that realizing these wants resulted in arrangements such as the Smithian division of labor and the Hobbesian social contract. These structures became the two institutional hallmarks of the utilitarian theory of the modern political and economic order. In theorizing about world order, this same logic reappears in the form of underived assumptions about nations' social structure and level of economic development, which are now assumed to exist *prior* to their coming together to form a larger network of international relations or a world-system of trade and unequal exchange.

For the neo-realist international relations theorist, this takes the form of assuming that state power capabilities are pre-international in origin. Again, the analog with the classical and neo-classical economic models which assume people exist in a pre-social state of nature where their internal dispositions, needs, wants, and goals are, by and large, anterior to social relations with others, making such relations the product of the pursuit of those wants/needs in an aggregated context. At the global level the components of this model are no longer biological individuals, but now national states, and the equivalent internal disposition of need and want are now national security concerns, power aspirations, and level of economic development.

Interestingly, from this point of view Lenin's theory of imperialism makes similar assumptions. In arguing that imperialism is the highest stage of capitalism, he posits that intra-societal transformations (advanced capitalist development) result in states reaching out to other regions of the globe, creating a web of inter-societal political/economic structures (colonialism or imperialism). But the key assumption is that change *within* national economies set off, or determine, relations *between* societies. From a global perspective, this is clearly an individualist bias (again, where the individuals here are capitalist states). This, though, is rarely noted because the actors at the world level are now whole countries and when they act it seems more social, but what is social, and what is individual, is relative. From the national, state, or societal perspective, persons or sub-groups are individual parts and the social formation the whole. But globally, societal wholes are but smaller global parts. Societies, states, and national economies are the individual components of the now larger global totality.

Second, having assumed already existing internal differences, the political scientists and sociologists then assume states interact to maximize these given power and economic interests. International political economy theorists have a neo-classical economic bias seemingly opposed to the neo-Marxism of imperialism/dependency/world-system theorists. Yet both are quite similar. Their reasoning is from parts to wholes, where the parts are states or national economies, and the whole the international or world-system. Both models assume that interaction between states or economic zones *follows from*, or is determined by, political or economic strength within states or zones.

Third, there is the resultant assumption that because of these international interactions (whether economic, political, or cultural), the by-product is some kind of international order, which takes the two most prominent utilitarian forms: contract and division of labor. The social contract on a global scale is the political scientist's emphasis upon regime formation, treaties, and international coalition formation. Here contractual relations between states constitute the very substance of international order itself. To put it more bluntly, the presence of social structure at a global level for international relations regime theorists is nothing but the contractual agreements and understandings of so many discrete state actors. For the world-system theorists, global order takes the form of a division of labor — now global and now unequal — but nonetheless a division of labor. World order, from the Wallersteinian perspective, is nothing more than patterns of trade and unequal exchange.

What then is wrong with these theories? Most simply, their logic is backward. Their most important, and taken-for-granted assumption, that state power precedes the emergence of international economic and political relations, is simply wrong. In point of fact, for the vast majority of the world's states, the international system *preceded* their existence and moreover made that existence possible in the first place. It also continues to reaffirm/reproduce their global position and resultant level of national development.

World-system Theory Turned on Its Head

To see this parts-to-whole logic in operation, we can turn to Wallerstein's conception of the world-economy, which he views as a chain of production points linked throughout the world. Wallerstein's 'commodity' chains run from periphery to core, third to first world, and form a world division of labor: 'To talk of commodity chains means to talk of an extended social division of labor' (Wallerstein, 1983: 30). The classic neo-utilitarian assumption. For Wallerstein this global division of labor among different production processes developed over time and became more hierarchical, that is, 'led to an ever greater polarization between the core and peripheral zones of the world-economy', where polarization means 'real income levels', 'quality of life' and the 'accumulation of capital' (Wallerstein, 1983: 30).

Now, this brings us to the key problem: the origin of inequality and exploitation on a global scale. The contested point is Wallerstein's understanding of how this division of the world into rich and poor (core and periphery) was produced and continues to be reproduced. He says, 'Initially, [speaking here of the 'hierarchization' of the commodity chains] the spatial differentials were rather small, and the degree of spatial specialization limited. Within the capitalist system, however, whatever differentials existed (whether for ecological or historical reasons) were exaggerated, reinforced, and encrusted' (Wallerstein, 1983: 30). And just what did the exaggerating: centuries of unequal exchange.

> How did this unequal exchange work? Starting with any real differential in the market occuring because of either the (temporary) scarcity of a complex production process, or artificial scarcitites created *manu militari*,[1] commodities moved between zones in such a way that the area with the less 'scarce' item 'sold' its item to the other area at a price that incarnated more real input (cost) than an equally-priced item moving in the opposite direction. What really happened is that there was a transfer of part of the total profit (or surplus) being produced from one zone to another. (Wallerstein, 1983: 31)

But this is an inversion of the historical process as it actually occurred. First, there are not any 'real differential(s) in the market' which begin the process, for the differences between core and periphery are not part of nature but are forcefully created through conquest and colonization; through power, not exchange. 'Initially' there are not real differences which are through time magnified by unequal exchanges between different 'areas,' because initially there is the exercise of force, power, and the conquest of European colonial expansion which not only subjugates areas of the world to core political domination, but through such force, such non-economic or extra-economic coercion, transforms these areas into plantations, large-scale ranches, mines, and all the economic infrastructures we call underdevelopment. Second, European/non-European power relations form a structure of world power which continues to reaffirm the subordinate position of colonial areas. It is only then, *after* the conquest, *after*, the establishment of a set of global relations of subordination, that we get anything like 'unequal exchange'.

This element of force and power, the political and economic dominance of the European core over the rest of the world, is not only missing in Wallerstein's exposition, but mystified by his analysis. When he suggested a 'struggle' over 'price' between 'buyer' and 'seller,' where the core is the buyer and the periphery the seller, it implies the relative independence to buy and sell on the world market.

But when did the Aztecs or Incas ever decide to 'sell' on the world market? When did they, as Wallerstein's 'producers' located somewhere along one of his 'commodity chains', ever struggle over price with the Europeans? Never, obviously! And why? Because Aztecs and Incas did not start out with any real 'differential' in the world market, nor did Cortez or Pizarro ever engage them in a 'struggle over price', for there never was any 'unequal exchange' between Europe and the Aztecs or Incas. What differentials existed were *created* through political struggle between Europe and the rest of the world.

Therefore, given conquest, not unequal exchange; given political power and social control, not commodity chains of buying and selling; given the establishment of global social relations between the European core and the conquered world, then, and only then, do differences come into being. These 'differentials' are politically created, not starting points in nature, for conquest sets in place a global structure of domination — colonialism — making the production of raw materials a *necessity*, and not a *decision* by buyers and sellers in a mythical supply and demand determined world market.

Wallerstein's theoretical misconception arises for three reasons. First, he mistakenly generalizes from the Baltic trade between politically independent Eastern and Western Europe to the world as a whole. While the Baltic trade peripheralized Poland as a producer of primary commodities, the relations between Western Europe and the rest of the world did not involve sovereign states, but areas that had been conquered. The Aztecs are not the Poles, and while trade and unequal exchange may have underdeveloped Poland, it was conquest which established the political framework of colonialism within which trade with the Americas took place. It was conquest and colonial relations which structured peripheral production and thereby created underdevelopment, and, since the colonial relation characterized most of the world (by 1914 some 84 percent of the world was, or had been, under colonial rule), this made the colonial relation, not the Baltic-like unequal exchange relation, the key core-periphery relation for the world economy as a whole.

Second, the suggestion that 'the transnationality of commodity chains is as descriptively true of the sixteenth century capitalist world as of the twentieth-century' (Wallerstein , 1983: 31) is misleading, because the colonial periphery was not composed of sovereign states. Colonies are not states, and to describe colonial plunder and surplus transfers as 'transnational' trade is misleading. As colonies became independent they became states, but for the world-system as a whole, with the first colony being established in Ceuta in 1415, we don't have a politically sovereign ex-colony until 1776, and even with the decolonization of the rest of the Americas in the first half of the nineteenth century, we don't have the decolonization of Africa, Asia, and India until after 1945.

Third, Wallerstein focuses upon state boundaries as the political relation in the world, which then makes it seem that 'almost all commodity chains of any importance have traversed these state frontiers' (Wallerstein, 1983: 31) such that it seems that the world economy, as such chains, is an economic system outside the political structure of the world-system. As such the world economy appears external to political power and domination structures that might constrain or shape the direction of surplus extraction and accumulation. But this is true only when core-periphery relations are seen as economic exchange, and not political power relations. Actually, this is quite a general problem, as orthodox Marxists also feel that only societal relations of production frame and determine the extraction of surplus from direct producers, and although they have been quite critical of Wallerstein, they too end up arguing that the totality of production relations exist only regionally, as in nineteenth-century slave modes of production in the American South and capitalist modes in Britain.

The important theoretical point here is not that there are no such social relations of production, but that there are also relations of production on a world scale, *global relations of production*, in the form of the ownership and control of colonial social formations by core states, that constrain and determine the societal modes which are but the infrastructures of the larger global mode of production.

From this point of view, individual core states collectively constitute *a class of states* that have a common political/economic relation to the rest of the world, establishing the basis for a theoretical discussion of truly world class relations. These relations define a world mode of production which frames and structures, that is, sets limits and determines, Wallerstein's core-periphery economic exchanges (including unequal exchange). Wallerstein's commodity chains therefore are not outside the exercise of global political constraints, because the important political/production relations of the world-system are not state-society or state-economy relations, but are core-periphery political relations. Viewing the world as a whole, states and colonies have common political relations of domination and subordination, which constitute a set of *global property relations* or *global class relations*, that are larger than the power and authority of any single state or the social production relations of any single societal mode of production.

While unequal exchange and commodity chains may have been transnational since the sixteenth century, they are not transcolonial, and that is the important point. Wallerstein's commodity chains are external to individual state structures but *internal* to core-periphery political structures of global power. And that is the important point. By focusing upon the externality of global surplus flows to any single state, he masks the control core states exercise *collectively*, as a class, vis-a-vis the surplus flows from the underdeveloped world. His commodity chains parcelize the unity of the global production process, and thereby mystify and mask the underlying global relations of production.

By so missing this core-periphery production relation, Wallerstein makes the classic utilitarian error of deriving the structural location of core and periphery from their exchanges, rather than seeing that it is the core-periphery political/production relation that brings forth their unequal economic exchange relation.

In short, trade, unequal exchange, or long commodity chains do not construct the core-periphery structure of power and domination, but the core-periphery domination relation makes possible the surplus extraction and the directionality of its flow — that is, makes unequal exchange possible and reproduces it over the centuries.

For Wallerstein, unequal exchange results in 'a transfer of part of the total profit (or surplus) being produced from one zone to another . . . [such that] we can call the losing zone a "periphery" and the gaining zone a "core"' (Wallerstein, 1983: 32). Note: in this analysis, core and periphery are consequences — not causes — of surplus transfer. The process, though, works just the other way around. He speaks of the vertical integration of production processes shifting more of the total surplus toward the core, which provides more funds for 'further mechanization, which allows producers in core zones to gain additional competitive advantages in existing products and . . . to create ever new rare products with which to renew the process' (Wallerstein, 1983: 32). But again, it is not that Spain produced more competitive products than the Aztec or Incas.

There simply was no a priori world market into which Spaniard and Aztec stepped. Nor did unequal exchange between these 'areas' result in a transfer of the surplus profit the Aztecs had created at their point on the commodity chain, nor did this 'exchange' link American 'producers' with European 'producers'.

That kind of reasoning makes no sense at all, for something is missing. The conquest! Not just as a fact of political domination but as the mechanism whereby Aztec or Inca economies were destroyed and reconstituted as mines, plantations, and ranches, which did generate surplus that only then moved to Europe. But not because of unequal exchange. When Spain, Portugal, England, or France shipped manufactured goods to their colonies and from them was taken cattle, wheat, indigo, or cotton, this was not exchange or trade. Not even unequal exchange. Colonies — precisely because they are colonies, because that is a *global property relation* — have no choice but to ship surplus. Peripheral production is not determined by struggles over price, nor the vagaries of the market, nor monopolistic practices of core producers. Peripheral production is determined by the fact that colonies are owned by the core and that ownership relation, that global property relation, is masked and mystified by calling it an unequal exchange relation. Colonies — by definition — are not sovereign actors and don't freely trade nor get caught in unequal exchanges because there is no exchange in the first place.

No commodity chains, and no production process in the core and again in the periphery. Once the world economy and global mode of production come into existence, there is only one social property relation on a world scale, and only one production process, and only one class relation, and that is the core ownership and control of peripheral production. This also means there is only one mode of production — a global mode of production.

Turning International Relations Theory on Its Head

If power relations precede trade relations in world-system theory, it is also true that cultural relations precede political relations in international relations theory. The key point here is the same as the sociological critique of utilitarianism, except now it is a sort of globological critique of neo-realist international relations theory. Let's start with the sociological critique, which was manifested in the writings of Marx, Weber and Durkheim. Their general point was that individual action implies the presence of some kind of social order, not the other way around. In Durkheim (1933) this took the form of noting the pre-contractual foundations of contract. Individuals do not come together in a state of rude nature to form the contractual bonds of society, for to interact at all presupposes institutions like language which implies a set of mutually agreed upon symbols and trans-individual meanings, that is, implies the presence of some form of social order. It is because of such precontractual contracts that interaction can occur in the first place. For Weber (1958) it was the cultural presuppositions of the Protestant Ethic that undergrid the seemingly rational acts of the utilitarian capitalist. It was not just economic avarice that made capitalism the rationalistic system it was; rationality was culturally rooted. For Marx the argument was directly against the assumptions of economists such as Adam Smith who assumed the propensity to truck and barter was natural and not social in origin. To paraphrase Marx's famous statement, it is not buying and selling which makes a person a capitalist, but capitalism which makes a person buy and sell. It is the external class relations of capitalism that make men sell their labor. It was never a free choice.

Starting from that point, I will argue that it is not the nation-state in trade, diplomacy, or war that makes an international system, but an international system that makes a state trade, act diplomatically, and go to war. This inversion of the utilitarian logic is at the heart of the globological (sociology on a world scale) critique of international relations theory. Just as earlier sociologists overcame the fiction that no man exists outside or prior to, society, so must we today overcome the fiction of an international state of nature, of international anarchy, populated by self-seeking realist states. Since the inception of the modern state system in the fifteenth century, it is safe to say there has been no state that has existed outside of, or prior to, this international order.

Just as an individual cannot interact without the pre-existence of culture, so too does state action imply a commonality that *precedes* state interaction. This is the global analog to Durkheim's precontractual understandings.

Take the example of the necessity of language for interpersonal interaction. There is an analog with states. A state acts and communicates through a diplomatic language independent of the local vernacular, at first Latin and later French, and diplomatic representatives (ambassadors, emissaries, couriers, etc.) and in earlier centuries through linked dynastic families. The point here is that the presence of these linkages precedes state interaction, and further, makes it possible in the first place.

From this point of view the international system, in the form of its culture (diplomatic language and systems of representation) does not follow the interaction of states, but makes that possible. The modern state does not start out in some rude state of 'international nature' without a common culture or social relations to go forth and contractually form diplomatic language, international regimes, and all the other culture collectively known as the international system. The point to remember is that the vast majority of the 150 or so states in existence today were created out of an already existent international system. Those states did not create this system. They came into existence *after* the culture and structure of the international system was already in place, whether we are talking about international law and alliances or global structures of domination (colonialism) that undergrid the more surface core-periphery division of labor.

Now the question can be raised about the inception of the modern interstate system. Did not that involve states' interacting for the first time to produce a larger network of interstate relations? At stake here is the larger question of the validity of the collectivist sociological perspective. That is, if one argues that the social precedes and makes possible the individual, from whence comes such collective order? This is Thompson's (1978) critique of Althusser's (1971) sociology and the reaffirmation of the conscious acting subject not only in history, but making history. When it is put like this: do people make history or does history make people, it seems an impossible question and some sort of compromise seems necessary. There is external structure, yes, but there is also willed conscious action, agency. Agency and structure, the duality of human existence. As Marx tried to put the same question: men do make history but not under conditions of their choosing. At the level of the concrete analysis of actual historical situations, this middle road between the conscious rational actor and the omnipresent sociological structure seems reasonable. Certainly no one would argue that all is determined, nor that all is a matter of moment to moment choice. But this is not the issue here. The question is one of theoretical paradigms, and the problem with the halfway solution is that it is no answer at all to the question of whether the international system is composed a priori of self-interested states or whether that very interest is a function of positional location within the larger system. The position I will adopt here is that the modern state does not precede the international system. Both arise at once, along with the advent of modern colonialism, making the sociologists' world-system a reality at the same time as the political scientists' international state system. Actor (state) and system (world) are temporally inseparable, and if anything the cultural and structural relations of pre-modern Europe laid the foundation, and thereby preceded, the emergence of the modern state. If there is an edge in this chicken–egg question, it lies with the world-system, not the state.

Cultural Pre-suppositions of the Modern State System

We can address the question of the origins of the state system by remembering how it in fact arose from the larger system of Latin Christendom, a point classically made in the international relations literature by Wight (1977). He argues that the international framework of the state system preceded the emergence of states, and was provided by the organizational structure of the Latin Church and the cultural universalism of Christendom. This was represented, in part, by the commonality of Christian princes whose dynasties were linked to each other and to the medieval past. The various international congresses that characterized the developing state system arose from earlier councils of the Church, so that, again, some order preceded the establishment of the modern international order. It was simply not a Hobbesian self-orginating system. 'The Church was the international organization of the "Respublica Christana" and its conciliar machinery provided the model for the states-system' (Wight, 1977: 144). The point here is that as councils were declining, the secular congresses were growing. For instance, the Council of Constance (1414–18), whose purpose was to end the Great Schism, was also involved in current conflicts between England, France, Poland and the Teutonic Knights. It was followed by the Council of Basle (1431–45) and its successor of Ferrara-Florence (1438–45). During this time the more secular congresses were commencing, like the Congress of Arras of 1435 involving England, France, and Burgundy. These early secular congresses often had the papacy as mediator, reflecting the diminishing role of the Church in the politics of the state system (Wight, 1977: 144).

The point is not the concrete historical origin of modern diplomatic machinery, but the implication of this historical record for our more general theoretical model of how the state system arose. From the early state conferences being part of the later Church councils, to the presence of an extra-state language for diplomacy, to the hereditary linkage of princes, there was an international order which arose at the same time as states, such that one cannot separate out the state as coming first and the international system as second. In fact, this international culture often preceded state action, and certainly made it possible, such that what Durkheim (1933) noted about the utilitarians, that contractual order was not the source of society but society the source of contracts, must now be applied to international relations and world-system theory. Again, most of the world's states appeared after this system was set in place, much like people are born into an ongoing, already existing society. This means that the emphasis upon international anarchy only acts to mask the presence of international structure the same way that the individual bias of utilitarianism masks societal structure.

Bringing the Collective into International Theory

Power provides the social element missing in the atomistic picture of a world division of labor the same way culture provides the social element for the Hobbesian picture of the international relations theorists. In both cases, the collective must be reintroduced into these accounts. The heart of the world-system, then, is not trade and exchange, just like the heart of the international state system is not contractual regimes between self-seeking state actors in a universe of international anarchy. In both cases, we have the neo-utilitarian world view devoid of culture/power and populated with actors who have somehow acquired their attributes prior to and independent of their participation in the global system. But as noted before, most states of the world came out of the actions of the world-system itself. Colonialism established their boundaries, and their national identities were forged in anti-colonial struggle. It is not accidental that the weakness of Spain is tied to the independence movement in Latin America or the exhaustion of Europe after 1945 to the decolonization of Africa and Asia, nor that these independence movements were encouraged and supported by the newly emerging hegemonic power at the time. England encouraged and quickly recognized the independence movements in Latin America and the United States in Asia/Africa. Therefore, there is no way that the very creation of most of the world's states can be seen as anything other than, if not the product of, at least the interaction with, the larger international/world-system. Wallerstein's world division of labor certainly exists. Different parts of the world produce and exchange different kinds of products. Of that there is no doubt. But, that is only the surface. Below and behind lies the structure of global power which has made such trade relations possible and continues to enforce them today.

Trade and exchange — and to include the political scientists — war and diplomacy — do not make the world or international system, but the international/world-system makes states trade, exchange, and go to war! Until this is fully realized, both the international relations tradition in political science and the world-system tradition in sociology will perpetuate a false and misleading picture of the nature of international life and, most importantly, continue to mask the deeper sets of culture/power relations that undergrid and make possible the more secondary and surface interactions that presently represent the heart of these two theoretical traditions.

Geographical Progressivity, Theoretical Regressivity
I would like to close with an irony. The initial impulse of the world-system perspective was to deal with questions of underdevelopment from a more theoretically progressive point of view. National models, whether neo-classical or Marxist, had the same difficulty. They saw development, whether by evolution or revolution, as an essentially intra-societal process. But capitalism was a world-wide phenomena and its most dynamic processes were thought to be at this global level. It was a progressive move in shifting the level of analysis to the globe and in discussing capitalism as a global phenomena. That geographical shift, though, also involved a theoretical move backward, in that this global economic entity was conceptualized in the atomistic terms of a division of labor. The place of the collective, of cultural and power relations, was now missing. A progressivity in levels of analysis was lost in a regression to the pre-sociological models of the Smithian/Hobbesian variety. What is required now is the final intellectual reconstruction of social theory, the same transformation of individualistic thought that the sociologists did for theory in the nineteenth century. Simply specifying processes at the world level is no longer sufficient, particularly when they are flawed with the presocial assumptions of atomism that mask global culture and power. There is one more step for the fledgling world-system perspective to take, and that is to place culture and power at the heart of the analysis and replace the individualism implied in the idea of a division of labor, unequal or not.

Notes
I would like to thank Elisabeth Clemens and Andre Gunder Frank for helpful comments. This research was supported by the University of Arizona.

1. Although power is mentioned here, it is almost entirely the case in Wallerstein's writings that unequal exchange relations are the predominate source of defining and reproducing the core-periphery structure.

References
Althusser, L. (1971) *Lenin and Philosophy*. New York: Monthly Review.
Ashley, R. (1984) 'The Poverty of Neo-Realism', *International Organization* 5(2): 225–86.
Brenner, R. (1971) 'The Origins of Capitalist Development: A Critique of Neo-Smithian Marxism', *New Left Review* 104: 25–92.

Durkheim, E. (1933) *The Division of Labor in Society*. New York: Free Press.

Hobbes, T. (1964) *Leviathan*. New York: Washington Square Press.

Thompson, E.P. (1978) *The Poverty of Theory and Other Essays*. New York: Monthly Review.

Thucydides (1951) *The Peloponnesian War*. New York: Modern Library.

Wallerstein, I. (1983) *Historical Capitalism*. London: Verso.

Wallerstein, I. (1989) *The Modern World-System III: The Second Era of Great Expansion of the Capitalist World-Economy, 1730–1840s*. New York: Cambridge.

Weber, M. (1958) *The Protestant Ethic and the Spirit of Capitalism*. New York: Scribner's.

Wight, M. (1977) *System of States*, Hedley Bull (ed.). Leicester: Leicester University Press.

Albert Bergesen teaches Sociology at the University of Arizona, Tucson.

Models of the Modern World-System

Peter Worsley

I have often been credited with inventing the Third World. In fact, the honour goes to the French demographer, Alfred Sauvy, who first used the term in an article in the newspaper, *L'Observateur*, on 14 August 1952, entitled 'Trois Mondes, Une Planète'. That it arose in France, and not in the Third World itself, may seem paradoxical. It was a product of the Cold War, the epoch in which two super-powers tried to dominate the entire globe. The claims, by each of them, that they alone represented the interests of humanity as a whole, was, however, widely rejected by people who resisted being sucked into either 'camp'; in France by the Gaullists on the Right, with their insistence on finding a 'third', national 'way'; and on the Left, by the democratic but radical socialists fighting both against US hegemony over the Atlantic Alliance and, internally, the large Stalinist French Communist Party.

By the end of the Second World War, only a few ex-colonial countries, notably India, had achieved their independence. But two years later China, the most populous country on earth, achieved its liberation from imperialist domination through force of arms. Through the 1950s and 1960s, the number of new Afro-Asian states steadily increased. They now began to come together with increasing frequency to work out a new position in world affairs quite distinct from either of the blocs headed by the superpowers. Some had fought for independence through armed struggle. In Vietnam, a nation of peasants defeated the French Army; in Algeria, another bitter armed struggle was going on. Although that revolution was contained militarily, and the 'Mau Mau' Rising in Kenya was also defeated by the British, the two major colonial Powers now realized that they could not go on holding down world-wide revolution by force for ever.

So the 'winds of change' blew powerfully in Africa: seventeen new states in the single year of 1961.

Theory, Culture & Society (SAGE, London, Newbury Park and New Delhi), Vol. 7 (1990), 83-95

The first commitment of these new states was to 'nation-building' internally and to the liberation of the remaining colonies. Having freed themselves from capitalist European domination, they had no desire to fall under another European hegemony, that of the communist bloc. So when they came together at Bandung in 1955, they eventually constituted themselves as a force independent of either 'camp', not as yet another *bloc*, but as a loose Afro-Asian *grouping* (Singham and Hune, 1986).

They therefore saw themselves, and were seen by others, as a new, *Third* World. At the beginning, this was primarily a political grouping, in which radical governments such as those of Nkrumah and Nasser had played a major part, and where liberation movements, including that of Cuba and even the communist government of China were invited. Over the years, most of the more radical governments were either destabilized or in other ways displaced by military or other forms of monocentric, usually one-party regimes. By this time, most of the elites in power in the new African states who jointly constituted the Organization of African Unity had become more concerned with consolidating boundaries drawn in colonial times than in putting the Pan-African ideal into practice. Nationalism and ethnic prejudice were freely exploited by the more chauvinist elites.

By the 1970s, wars between ex-colonial states had become common, even wars between communist countries, notably China and Vietnam — a phenomenon unthinkable to nineteenth-century European pioneers of socialism. Movements for secession, such as that in Biafra, had been crushed. The image of the 'Third World' as 'a vital new force in international affairs', to use the sub-title the publisher added to my 1964 book, *The Third World*, had become tarnished.

These developments were not simply attributable to imperialist machinations nor to the converse, to some ineradicable quality of the spirit of nationalism. Sinister interventions and manipulations there certainly were, sometimes bloody, as in post-Independence Zaïre, sometimes clandestine, using proxies. But governments of all political complexions, which had come to power on a wave of popular anti-colonialist but also nationalist enthusiasm, increasingly found themselves unpopular, because they had built for themselves a fearsome machine of power centralized in the hands of a new state elite. In the neo-colonial equation of power, therefore, there were two terms; the external power of strong foreign governments and of the world market, and the internal power of the new single-party states.

The deliberately balkanised micro-states such as those of Africa and the Caribbean, especially, were quite unable to exert any influence over a world market controlled by the developed industrial countries. More and more, too, the power exercised over them was being exercised not by the states which had formerly been their colonialist oppressors (from whose control they thought they had definitively escaped), but by a new kind of non-governmental agency, the multinational corporation.

These were developments which many of the new leaderships had not foreseen. In the euphoria of independence, Tanzania, for instance, had talked about dispensing with an army altogether. Within a couple of decades, Tanzania was obliged to invade neighbouring Uganda, and further to impoverish herself in the process, in order to end the butchery of the Idi Amin regime which had spread across the border. In the economic field, Nyerere ruefully admitted, years later, they had believed that political independence would give them control over their own economic development. This had proved to be far from the case.

It was therefore at this stage that the Non-Aligned Movement shifted from primarily political preoccupations, such as the liberation of the remaining colonies, towards a focus upon economic underdevelopment as the root cause of their political impotence.

The first major breakthrough came with the formation of UNCTAD in 1964, when, against the opposition of the West, the UN was forced to put Third World underdevelopment seriously on its agenda for the first time. By 1974, the OPEC oil cartel struck a blow at Western domination which plunged the developed world into crisis. A new weapon, it seemed, had been forged which could bring the West to heel; the organization of similar cartels by producers of primary goods.

This proved not to be the case, firstly because the developed economies are capable either of living without most Third World primary goods, such as bananas, or can develop substitutes for them, or can find complaisant trading partners within the Third World who break the solidarity needed for any cartel to be effective.

The capacity of world capitalism to retain its stranglehold over formally independent countries by non-political means, which came as a surprise to the new Third World states, was, however, a quite familiar phenomenon to theorists, technocrats and governing elites in the countries of Latin America. Because they had been politically independent for more than a century, they had not shown much interest in the political preoccupations of the new states. At the time of Bandung, therefore, the Third World had been an Afro-Asian world. But the experience of Latin America became increasingly relevant to the new states. True, US political and, in Central America, direct military intervention had been commonplace. But that power was usually mediated through agrarian oligarchs and local 'colonels', the man on a white horse, in the nineteenth century, and later by a fiercely anti-communist military trained in US staff colleges.

Military intervention usually took the form of palace coups d'état, for no serious challenge to a social order based on the domination of the landowning class and of the Church took place until the turn of the century; notably, the Mexican Revolution of 1910. The superpower of the continent in the nineteenth century, Britain and the twentieth-century hegemon, the US, normally relied on the exercise of economic power.

It was natural, then, that dependency theory should emerge first in Latin America. In its most popular version, and the one which made most impact upon the world outside that continent, that of A.G. Frank, it was a model of the world-system which saw the entire world as polarized between 'core' countries and those on the 'periphery'. A similar Manichaean alternative existed in the field of policy; only two choices were available — in the sub-title of one of Frank's (1969) books: underdevelopment or revolution.

During the 1960s and 1970s however, it became obvious that a number of formerly agrarian ex-colonies were, in fact, well advanced along the road to industrialization — the so-called 'newly-industrializing countries' — notably Mexico and Brazil and the 'four little tigers' of East Asia, Taiwan, South Korea, Hong Kong and Singapore, to name no others. Stepping out of the plane into the smog-laden industrial pollution of Mexico City or São Paulo was enough to put the Frankian assumption of the inevitability of underdevelopment under capitalism in doubt.

The second of his two alternatives, revolution, was by now by no means as realistic a possibility as it had seemed when a handful of guerrillas landed from the *Granma* and went on to win a stunning victory with an army that only numbered 2000 a year before Havana fell. The death of Ché Guevara in Bolivia marked the turn of the tide for revolution in that continent.

Where the tide of revolution did still flow powerfully, notably in southern Africa, post-independence governments in Mozambique and Angola, and in Nicaragua, were viciously destabilized from outside. Vietnam found herself engaged in further war against her communist neighbours, China and Kampuchea. But revolutionary regimes, even apart from these disasters, also showed themselves unable to organize the development of the economy with the machinery they had developed to fight revolutionary wars.

Newer kinds of development theory therefore began to reflect these changes. Elsewhere, I have criticized Wallerstein's (1974, 1979) version, for all its impressive scholarly foundations, because of its insistence that there is only one single world-system (Worsley, 1980). There can be no doubt that the expansion of capitalism outside Europe began not because people in the West were moved by a spirit of abstract geographical enquiry: it was a search for gold and spices. Nor can there be any doubt about the persisting dynamism of contemporary capitalism: about its capacity to innovate and to expand into new zones. To take the two dimensions of labour and prices, world capitalism has uprooted from their homes and distributed around the globe far more millions than were displaced during and after the Second World War. Changes in world prices on the commodity exchanges of New York, London or Chicago affect every primary producer, even those within the COMECON bloc, and are particularly disastrous for micro-countries dependent on one or two exports. Parallel with this economic power is the cultural hegemony of the mass media, particularly radio and television, which has implanted capitalist values in the minds of millions in the Second and Third Worlds. Night after night, on the TV screens of any country south of New Orleans, the images of the good life are images of life among the wealthy in the USA, and the dream is to get, not to New York or Chicago, but to Miami.

Yet the model finds capitalism everywhere: even the communist countries are simply parts of the world economic system, while capitalism is also projected backwards into history as the dominant world-system, even as early as the sixteenth century. Yet capitalism in its mercantilist phase of expansion outside Europe — to the New World and to the East — which Weber labelled 'booty capitalism', was a quite different and much more limited phenomenon compared to the later capitalism which transformed agriculture along capitalist lines, and implanted mines, plantations and eventually industry. The unimportance of Europe is reflected in the way the Grand Vizier of Turkey addressed the French Ambassador, in 1666, not simply as 'a Giaour (unbeliever)' but also as 'a hogge, a dogge, a turde eater'.

Turning to more recent times, the distinctive characteristics of both the Second World and the Third World are also made to disappear in the Wallerstein model; as 'worlds', they are simply decomposed, and their component states simply allocated to one category or the other of the model, as either 'core', 'peripheral' or 'semiperipheral' countries — and nothing else.

In my view, *per contra*, there are profound political, economic and cultural differences between the First World and communist countries in each of these domains and not simply in terms of the economy alone. In the political sphere, until 1989, state power lay with the Communist Party; the economy, too, has been controlled by the state and planned from the centre; and forms of cultural life were based upon the values of a distinctive ideology. For the entire postwar period up to this year, therefore, it was inadequate simply to bypass these differences by simply classifying Hungary, say, or Spain, let alone India or North Korea, as either 'peripheral' or 'semi-peripheral' units. The possibility that most of Eastern Europe, at least, of the older communist states, might become economically attached to the capitalist world market is a new possibility, not one of long-standing, as the Wallerstein model has insisted.

But despite these and other theoretical shortcomings, Wallerstein did perceive the need to introduce a category, in between the simple binary opposition between 'core' and 'periphery' — that of 'semi-periphery' — the significance of which I underestimated at the time. Moreover, the model did have a place for the individual state, whatever the restrictions upon its autonomy because of its subordinate position in the world-system.

These modifications of the Frankian schema reflect developments in the real world which earlier generations of theorists on the Left had deemed to be impossible — the industrialization of Third World economies under capitalism.

Such development was still usually denigrated, however, as '*dependent* development' — merely a new way in which global capital in the heartlands was now penetrating every corner of the globe, no longer in search simply for raw materials, cheap labour, or markets for manufactured goods, but as branch plant subsidiaries in what was now a worldwide division of *productive* labour, manipulated, masterminded and initiated from the centre, in the interests of the centre. Pioneers of the theory of the New International Division of Labour (Froebel et al., 1980) for instance insisted that what industrial development was taking place was only in sectors of obsolete technology which the West was happy to discard, textiles especially, using cheap, unskilled and un-unionized and mainly young, female labour.

The implantation of a massive automobile industry in the ABC triangle of Brazil, near São Paulo, was certainly the work of Volvo, Mercedes-Benz, Ford, and VW, like most other industrial development in Brazil, while even in Mexico, where a substantial sector has been developed by national capital, two-thirds of manufacturing industry was US-owned in 1980.

And in Hong Kong, as Siu-Lun Wong (1988) has shown, the first stage of that city-state's industrialization took place under Chinese, not Western auspices. Shanghainese entrepreneurs fleeing the Communist advance in China in 1949 used the capital they brought to Hong Kong to develop a textile industry which was one of the most advanced in the world. They sent their sons, not to Harvard or Oxford, but to the best centres in the world for textile technology: to Bolton College of Technology in the UK and to Lowell Institute of Technology in Massachusetts.

The second stage of growth — the introduction of modern semiconductor industries — was indeed the doing of foreign, mainly US and Japanese multinationals, though even here domestic capital is developing its share of the market. But, as Jeffrey Henderson (1989) has shown, development of new kinds is taking place; Hong Kong is no longer simply a centre for assembly; final testing of transistors assembled elsewhere and design operations are turning the city into a regional centre.

Multinational investors, indeed, went there in the first place because industrialization had already started. They were attracted by the availability of masses of unskilled labour, though unskilled labour was abundant in other parts of East Asia and elsewhere. But the State — in this case, a British colonial government — also actively set out to attract investment via tax and other incentives and the provision of an adequate infrastructure. The state also embarked upon an ambitious programme to turn out the technicians, scientists and engineers modern microchip and other industry needed.

And as far as the unskilled workforce is concerned, they are no longer among the most wretched of the earth. Their political docility and absence of militant trade unionism was attractive to multinational investors: in part because of the discouragement of unionization by the colonial authorities, in part because of political divisions within the Chinese labour movement and the damping-down of any tendencies to militancy by representatives of Peking. But of crucial importance also are the welfare policies of the British colonial government — the provision of a system of welfare in a country which, fifteen years ago, was notorious for the absence of social services: low-cost housing (80 percent of the working class housed in the world's largest public housing programme); universal secondary education and a large tertiary sector; a system of public health services, and the provision of cheap food (as well as investment in job-producing industry) by China: a subsidy to household income of the order of 50 percent. This strategy of development, then — what one might call authoritarian Welfareism — is quite different from the more brutal pattern in societies like South Korea and Taiwan which Jon Halliday described, in their formative period of industrialization as 'semi-militarized societies', though in these countries, too, democracy is slowly making significant headway as a result of popular struggles.

Such differences, however, are passed over in world-system theories in which the system seems to proceed according to an immanent logic, without reference to powerful actors, decision-makers or institutions. Writers such as Nigel Harris, however, using Trotsky's notion of 'state capitalism', and impressed by the evident activity of the interventionist state we described above, have singled out the state as the central agency of development, while the very institution which does operate globally — the multinational corporation — is dismissed:

> Economic growth in the newly industrializing countries appears to be everywhere associated with the expansion of the public sector and the role of the state. It has not been 'free enterprise' nor multinational capital which has led the process (Harris, 1987:143)

Using data from Brazil and Mexico, and the East Asian 'four little tigers', Harris argues that these countries represent the future for the entire Third World. To sustain that argument, he has to ignore most of the Third World, in particular the uncomfortable fact that 'the average rich-world cat consumes around $500 worth of food a year — more than the GNP per capita of the seven poorest nations on earth; Chad, Bangladesh, Ethiopia, Nepal, Mali, Burma or Zaïre' (Ichiyo, 1984).

One novel feature of some recent writing by left-wing unilinealists has been the abandonment of the traditional denunciation of capitalism as a system of hyper-exploitation, which they justify by referring to Marx's writings on British rule in India. Few have gone as far, however, as Bill Warren (1980), who celebrates capitalism as the force which will bring welfareism to every corner of the globe, an instance of optimistic unilineal evolutionism which would have been thoroughly acceptable to nineteenth-century believers in the inevitability of progress.

While these left-wing exponents of world-system theory have been abolishing the Third World, analysts in international organizations have been multiplying worlds. Their methodological starting-point is the World Bank's strategy of ranking each country from number 1 to number 128 in terms of GNP per capita, life expectancy at birth, etc. The Bank then separates out high-income oil exporters, industrial market economies (i.e. the First World), and East European non-market economies, before dividing the Third World into low-income economies, lower and upper middle-income economies and high-income economies.

Other analysts, using a wider range of criteria of development such as miles of paved road, number of telephones per capita have classified Third World countries into more elaborate sets. Thus Goldthorpe (1977) distinguished rich countries, 'anomalies', intermediate countries, the USSR and Eastern Europe, the better-off poor, the middling poor, the poorer, the poorest (separating out China, North Korea, then North Vietnam, plus Cuba, presumably on political grounds), and other 'small countries'.

More recently, Wolf-Phillips (1987) has argued that we should distinguish a Fourth World of the least developed countries. The term has more often been used, usefully, to describe tribal and other 'nations without states' (McCall, 1980). But the problem with introducing the concept of a Fourth World in purely economic terms is that there is no reason why one should not go on to distinguish Fifth, Sixth, or Seventh 'worlds'. Methodologically speaking, the dividing-line between Senegal, which had $380 per capita per annum and Mauretania, $450 is a quite arbitrary one (*World Development Report 1986*). Yet one is put into the 'low-income' category and the other into 'lower middle-income'. For these are simply observers' constructs. One could draw the line anywhere one liked to create larger or smaller 'worlds' and, too, any number of them. If one were to introduce political and cultural distinctions, the number of possible 'worlds' becomes too large to be useful.

Let us turn now to the actors' perspective, for there is a real-life Third World out there in practical life with its own institutions, notably the Non-Aligned Movement, which now embraces virtually the entire underdeveloped world. To these people, underdevelopment remains a reality from which they are unlikely to escape in the visible future, and they still see that they share a common life-fate with other poor countries. Given the number of countries, the grouping is inevitably very heterogeneous, which has led some observers of a more *Realpolitik* turn of mind, to conclude, with General Haig, that the Third World as a concept is a 'myth' or, with Jeanne Kirkpatrick, that the Non-Aligned Movement is an ineffective and irrelevant organization whose members ought to face up to choosing between the 'free' and the 'totalitarian' worlds — precisely what the Third World rejected in its beginnings and continues to challenge.

On the Left, Régis Debray has scornfully dismissed the Third World as merely an 'annexe' of the First; Manuel Castells argues that 'modern technology has laid to rest the very notion of a "Third" World' (though he goes on to use the term freely). Debray is right when he argues that whatever unity the Third World does possess is a function of its common relationship to imperialism. The weaker countries of the world are still disadvantaged on the world market which even the richest of them, such as the OPEC states, cannot control; and because world-wide confrontation between the Superpowers and their dependents and their attempt to bend the world to their interests still persists.

None of the models so far discussed take culture into account. All of them are variants of one kind or another of political economy, though without the cultural dimension it is impossible to make sense of a modern world in which nationalism, religion and inter-ethnic hostility have been far more important than internationalism and secularism. Models based on political economy alone, therefore, are quite incapable of explaining such phenomena as the rise of a modern version of Islam which is wrongly labelled 'fundamentalism', or the contradiction between the claims of that religion to universal community and the reality of the harnessing of Islam to the interests of the nation-state, notably during the Iran-Iraq War.

The relative impotence of the majority of the world's population to control its own life-fate is symbolized in the limits upon the effectiveness of the Non-Aligned Movement, for all its power to win votes at the UN in Manhattan.

But the self-consciousness and self-activity of the peoples of the Third World are not confined to the activities of elites at international meetings. All across the globe, non-governmental popular organizations such as the Consumers' Association of Penang, or the Kerala Popular Science Movement (KSSP), or SEWA, the organization set up by illiterate Outcaste women workers in Ahmedabad, denied membership of male-dominated trade unions, who went on to establish their own bank, are constantly, day in and day out, fighting to change the world, and to improve their life-circumstances. Like their contemporaries in Eastern Europe, too, they have been far more concerned with the struggle to establish democracy: with the right to self-expression and self-determination: than with differences of economic system.

Unfortunately, one unintended by-product of well-motivated Western charity organizations has been that they have to stir consciences in the West by depicting the Third World as a disaster-zone. The result is that the stereotype of the Third World most people have today is of a starving African child with his hands held out for food. This image entirely omits the vast transformation of the newly-industrializing countries and of the shift from a world dominated by reliance on agriculture to a world in which the majority of humanity live in cities. It also omits the self-activity of the people themselves, who are not waiting for Western technology, or Western know-how, and are using both the indigenous experience of millennia as well as modern technologies.

In the West, the superiority of our science and technology is no longer taken for granted. The majority have little awareness of the knowledges and skills accumulated and transmitted from generation to generation by other cultures. But they do know that we are all threatened by nuclear extinction and by the steady destruction of the environment, and that these things have been part and parcel of the development of Western science and industry.

The initiative of the Soviet Union in taking the crucial steps towards the wind-down of the arms-race, and the subsequent transformation of Eastern Europe once the Soviet stranglehold was loosened, have however, opened up a new world of possibilities. Not all of these are positive: the recrudescence of xenophobic nationalism inside the USSR itself is one obvious danger. But we are entering a new epoch and moving out of the appalling Ice Age of the Cold War and of Superpower hegemony.

All the models we have discussed, even world-system theory, paradoxically, take the nation-state as their unit of analysis. Yet all of us belong to communities which are both smaller and wider than the nation-state. Hence, as one anthropologist has put it, as long as there are 'ten thousand societies inhabiting 160 nation-states' which refuse to recognize their cultural and political rights, minority peoples will continue to struggle to run their own affairs, by force of arms if need be.

Conversely, the modern world has been shaped by cultural communities, from the Catholic Church and Islam to secular ideologies and movements like communism which transcend the boundaries of even the largest and most centralized state.

It is now possible that by redirecting expenditure on war we could start on solving the problem which has always been technically possible but has so far proved beyond human capability; the elimination of world poverty. Young people are aware of these possibilities where their elders are often fearful of change or inured by experience to cynicism and resignation. The young are also more concerned with the world as a whole. Thus the biggest event in the history of human communications — the Band Aid television rock concert organized by Bob Geldof — was a project to raise money for the Third World. Eventually, the politicians in the West will become more responsive to these shifts in political imagination just as even the most conservative of them now takes pains at least to talk Green.

Note

An earlier version of this paper was presented at a Conference organized by the Institut für Vergleichende Sozialforshung, Berlin, June 1989.

References

Frank, A.G. (1969) *Latin America: Underdevelopment or Revolution?* New York: Monthly Review Press.

Froebel, F., Heinrichs, J. and Kreye, O. (1980) *The New International Division of Labour.* Cambridge: Cambridge University Press.

Goldthorpe, J.E. (1977) *The Sociology of the Third World.* Cambridge: Cambridge University Press.

Harris, Nigel (1987) *The End of the Third World: Newly Industrializing Countries and the Decline of an Ideology*. Harmondsworth: Penguin.

Henderson, Jeffrey (1989) *The Globalization of High Technology Production: Society, Space and Semiconductors in the Restructuring of the Modern World*. London: Routledge.

Ichiyo: Muto (1984) *Development in Crisis*. Penang: Consumers' Association of Penang.

McCall, Grant (1980) 'Four Worlds of Experience and Action', *Third World Quarterly* 2(3): 36–45.

Singham, A.W. and Hune, Shirley (1986) *Non-Alignment in an Age of Alignments*. London: Zed Books.

Wallerstein, Immanuel (1974) *The Modern World-System: Capitalist Agriculture and the Origins of the World-Capitialist Economy in the Sixteenth Century* (2 vols). New York: Academic Press.

Wallerstein, Immanuel (1979) *The Capitalist World-Economy*. Cambridge: Cambridge University Press.

Warren, Bill (1980) *Imperialism: Pioneer of Capitalism*. London: Verso.

Wolf-Phillips, Leslie (1987) 'Why "Third World"?', *Third World Quarterly* 9(4): 1311–27.

Wong, Siu-Lun (1988) *Emigrant Entrepreneurs: Shanghai Industrialists in Hong Kong*. Hong Kong: Oxford University Press.

World Development Report 1986 (1987) Oxford: Oxford University Press.

Worsley, Peter (1980) 'One World or Three? A Critique of the World-system Theory of Immanuel Wallerstein', pp. 298–338 in R. Milliband and J. Saville (eds), *Socialist Register 1980*. London: Merlin Press.

Peter Worsley is Emeritus Professor of Sociology at the University of Manchester.

Theory, Culture and Post-Industrial Society

Margaret S. Archer

The human being and the social agent are not identical. One sign of
an adequate social theory is that it performs the introduction
between them punctiliously: defective theories settle for reduction
of the one to the other. Basically, introducing them is necessary
since to be human is simultaneously to be social. Equally fundamentally, reducing them is mistaken, because a human being is
much more than a social agent. None of this is nullified by our
awareness that society contains a larger register of cultural meanings
and a bigger repository of structural resources than can ever be
drawn upon by one person, nor its corollary, that all people necessarily do draw upon them. It should be acknowledged with the same
alacrity that without reference to people's biology and psychology,
their nature and spirituality, their Weberian 'non-social' relations to
both the phenomenal and noumenal worlds, we are left with 'plastic
man' (Hollis, 1977) whose selective permutations on meanings and
resources can only be explained by an infinite regress to prior social
determination.

Yet it is precisely this selective, reflective, mediatory and inno-
vatory capacity of individuals and groups which is needed to explain
the constitution and reformulation of the register and the reposi-
tary. In contrast, *Homo Sociologicus* is a dull fellow: seemingly his
salvation from humanoid status lies with his ineluctable production
of unintended consequences, but since these are handled in robotic
direction-finding and error-correcting fashion, there is no re-birth
of 'autonomous man'. The relevance of this to theories of industrial
society is embedded in their treatment of culture itself — its subordination to structural developments or its denigration effectively
leave us with a parade of humanoids — 'Industrial Man', 'Modernistic Man', his offspring 'Post-Modern Man' and the infant
'Information Man'. Robertson's (1988) concept of metaculture is

Theory, Culture & Society (SAGE, London, Newbury Park and New Delhi), Vol. 7
(1990), 97–119

pertinent here for the cluster of industrial society theorists have come to share a peculiarly impoverished one. Metacultures

> constrain conceptions of culture, mainly in terms of deep-rooted, implicit assumptions concerning relationships between parts and wholes, individuals and societies, societies and the world-as-a-whole. . . . They also shape the different ways in which — and, indeed, the degree to which — substantive culture will be invoked and applied to 'practical action'. (Robertson, 1988: 14)

Impoverishment consists principally in the progressive subordination of culture until it becomes an epiphenomenon of structure. It can be further denuded by its trivialization: for Daniel Bell the movement from 'the end of ideology' (Bell, 1962) to 'the shambles of modern culture' (Bell, 1979: 169) was downhill all the way.

This subordination of culture has gathered momentum within industrial society theory, especially over the last decade. Earlier qualms or hopes about ideas acting as independent, critical or contradictory factors appear to have been stifled amongst both the advocates and the opponents of Information Society. The consequence is that this subordination of culture robs mankind of any independent moral vantage point for the evaluation of post-industrial trends or for articulating 'techno-choices' (Badham, 1986), that is, principles guiding the uses to which information technology should be put. Correspondingly, in the broader context of social theory, the major problem of linking structure and agency is shelved once again by yet another metaculture of the marionette.

Phase 1 — The Industrial Convergence Thesis

The treatment of culture from within industrial society theory will be illustrated by looking at three phases in its development; only in the middle one were the problems presented by cultural epiphenom-enalism and cultural monism seriously addressed. The latest phase witnesses the 'third wave' innundating the cultural realm and sweeping all before it, in a belated fulfilment of the Comtean Law of Three Stages. In examining these theories, the focus will be upon their inadequate treatment of culture. Their structural deficiencies have readily attracted criticism, an imbalance which itself says a great deal about the pervasiveness of their metaculture.

Perhaps the key book to retrieve and recycle nineteenth-century theories of positivism for twentieth-century circumstances and consumption was Clark Kerr et al.'s *Industrialism and Industrial Man* (1962). Its central assumptions, crude as they were, gradually became axiomatic for later theorizing. The core notion was simply an extended celebration of the impact of industrialization on society in general. Industrialism was represented as a prime mover, a new axial principle of social life, which standardized social structures by 'the pure logic of the industrialization process' (Kerr et al., 1962: 33). This logic was deterministic and universalistic, irresistibly exerting 'the tug of industrialism whatever . . . initial differences' (Kerr et al., 1962: 52) of socio-cultural organization it encountered. Consequently, it furthered world-wide convergence towards a single stereotype — modern society.

What is crucial about this stereotype is that it bundled together structural changes and cultural changes as part of the parcel that was 'modern society'. With simultaneity and complementarity, changes in the structural domain (the tug towards urbanization, pluralism and bureaucratization) were directly paralleled by congruent changes in the cultural realm (the pull towards instrumental education, the nuclear family, rationalization and secularization, including 'Industrial Man' himself, the plastic product of a homogeneous process). Questions of cultural incompatibility, contradiction or resistance did not arise: the 'pure logic' was so purely irresistible that even the notion of 'cultural lag' could be abandoned after the initial stage. Everyone would rapidly converge with the United States. Cultural differences would be ironed out to the extent that 'Industrial man is seldom faced with real, ideological alternatives within his society' (Kerr et al. 1962: 283).

The industrial convergence thesis was subject to telling criticism by Goldthorpe (1964, 1971), Archer and Giner (1971), Westergaard (1972), Mann (1970) and Bottomore (1973) among many others. What is interesting is that despite their own substantial differences all the opponents of the thesis homed in on its *structural* deficiencies when quite rightly attacking its inbuilt technological determinism, evolutionism, functionalism and universalism. Significantly, it was not subjected to sustained *cultural* critique. Certainly, Goldthorpe properly condemned 'the exaggeration of the degree of determinism which is exercised upon social structures by "material" exigencies' (1964: 117) and most of the above would concur. Nevertheless, what was remarkable for its absence was an extended discussion of culture as an independent variable in the modernization process or the relative autonomy of culture to direct industrial societies in different ways — not just at the beginning but in perpetuity.

It is tempting and reassuring to suppose that the critics of the original industrial convergence thesis regarded their structural objections as so devastating as to make picking over the cultural ruins a pointless exercise. In retrospect this is not convincing: on the contrary, in challenging the structural premises of the thesis, most were aiming at what they saw as its *weaker* flank. Not only is there evidence of a growing and generalized endorsement of the prime postulates of the metaculture, rationalization and secularization, but this is also the time when Peter Berger wrote that 'the secularizing potency of capitalistic-industrial rationalization is not only self-perpetuating but self-aggrandizing' (1969: 126). Even more significantly, those critics stressing egalitarian ideals in opposition to meritocratic ones did not transcend the industrial society perspective. Instead they focused only upon those limited forms of egalitarianism associated with it — extending educational opportunity, growing occupational mobility and increasing political pluralism. Effectively then, they endorsed the cultural credo of the industrial convergence thesis by limiting their critique to the confines of its parameters.

Phase 2 — Post-industrialism

If the 1960s version of industrial society theory had allowed for some initial cultural diversity which was ironed out as modernity gathered momentum, the story could end with structure and culture bundled together and bound by the functional dictates of industrialism itself. At the very most, tenacious cultural differences were what made Japanese industrialism just a little different. The 1970s versions of the post-industrial thesis, of which there were plenty, all worked the other way around. In common they began with bold and uncompromising statements about the *conflation* of structure and culture. The two were no longer a rough bundle but reciprocally constitutive of post-industrial society.

The following statement of Ernest Gellner's in *Thought and Change* is the starting point for the post-industrial conflationists: 'Modern science is inconceivable outside an industrial society: but modern industry is equally inconceivable without modern science. Roughly, *science is the mode of cognition of industrial society, and industry is the ecology of science*' (1972: 179, my italics). Such conflation became the new metaculture of opponents and advocates of post-industrialism alike and both pursued it relentlessly. What halted them was the realization that they were heading straight into cultural monism. Both were equally aware that if this were endorsed for the entire population they would deprive themselves of any independent vantage point for evaluating post-industrialism (whether positively or negatively) and would render moral debate on the Good Life inert within modern society. As conflationism began to look like handing a moral blank cheque to post-industrialism, the question became: was it too late to disentangle themselves from the powerful metaculture they had helped to spin? Much more importantly, could Modernist Man be morally emancipated? (In any cultural *sauve qui peut* the intellectuals always make it to the exit — how else could generations of theorists have endorsed relativism with impunity and self-immunity?)

Theorists of post-industrialism are numerous and diffuse. In order to get to the heart of the above issues I will concentrate on two of the most mutually antagonistic to see how they both entered and then tried to extricate themselves from the same (formal) metacultural impasse. On the one hand there is the neo-Durkheimian Daniel Bell, whose books in the 1970s were an attempt to re-write the last chapter of *The Division of Labour* with a happy ending (Bell 1976, 1979). On the other hand there is Jürgen Habermas, continuing the Frankfurt school's revisionism, who rewrote Marx's economics as if Galbraith were at his shoulder but wanted to retain Marx's emancipatory vision. As I have mentioned, structural considerations are not the interest of this paper and as far as these two theorists are concerned, they are not very interesting for they merely parade the orthodoxy of the early 1970s — economic growth, the application of science to production, increased welfare, decreased conflict, diminished politicization, etc. Vastly more intriguing are their similarities and differences in the treatment of culture.

Let us begin with Bell who in the beginning advanced much the same cultural message as Aron, Lipset, Shils and too many others. The message was simplicity itself — *The End of Ideology* (Bell, 1962): the mechanism was conflation. With the rise of the service class, this unprecedented amount of collective mobility incorporated the majority into industrial society, endowed them with vested material interests, particularly in increased consumption, and correspondingly reduced their ideological divisions or utopian designs. For, as Lipset argued, now the 'fundamental problems of the industrial revolution have been solved' (1969: 406). Yet conflation involved much more than the assumption that advances in industrialization constituted progress, namely that people in general now thought that was what progress was. Thus the post-political and post-ideological age also heralded the arrival of a new techno-rationality in culture which relegated the remaining socio-political problems to the status of technical questions for which technical solutions would be forthcoming. Thus in Aron's words

> Beyond a certain stage in its development industrial society itself seems to me to widen the range of problems referable to scientific examination and calling for the skill of the social engineer. Even forms of ownership and methods of regulation, which were the subject of doctrinal or ideological controversies during the past century seem to . . . belong to the realm of technology. (1967: 164-5)

Yet from then on both Bell (1976) and Aron (1972) draw back from the monism that such a metaculture would imply, stressing the durability of individualism and egalitarianism as cultural values antipathetic to advanced industrial societies. And the further Bell explored (1979) the substance of this individualism, the more he came to see that one hundred years of industrialism had fathered a cultural monstrosity. The structural combination of fast communications media, high living standards and a mass consumption market had generated a hedonistic cultural ethos which 'is prodigal, promiscuous, dominated by an anti-rational, anti-intellectual temper in which the self is taken as the touchstone of cultural judgements, and the effect on the self is the measure of the aesthetic worth of experience' (1979: 37). This trivial self-expressionism was engulfing: already it had brought about 'Death of the Bourgeois World View' with its rationalism, sobriety and deferred gratification, for which postmodernism now substituted enslavement to instinctual gratification as 'impulse and pleasure alone are real and life-affirming: all else is neurosis and death' (1979: 51).

Why, however, does this represent a subordination of culture? Basically because of its nature it has no capacity to direct society ideationally: since it cannot articulate principles of structural change it remains parasitic upon existing structures. Junk culture is the spoilt brat of affluence, but in its ceaseless acts of profanation and unprincipled celebrations of novelty, it also denies the possibility of any debate on the Good Society predicated as that must be on enduring, if contested, principles and on rational discourse for their contestation. The culture of modernism is subordinate because of its impotence — it can neither sustain, nor criticize, nor redirect post-industrial society.

As the con-celebrants of spontaneity grow, the restless quest for novelty means no *avant garde* can run fast enough to stay out in front and excesses of profanity become the main outlet. But ceaseless desecration is no *modus vivendi*: on the contrary it leads via nihilism to entropy. Consequently, Bell too has to address the question of cultural emancipation — of Modernistic Man, to restore his motivation, and of Post-Industrial Society, to ensure its moral regulation. Bell has come back full-circle to Durkheim's problem at the end of *The Division of Labour* — where is the new socio-cultural cement to be found?

Durkheim's answer, of course, was to invent it: a new form of secular civic morals, necessary in his view since the demise of religion was also the loss of any social binding power. Bell's reply is precisely the opposite, a return to religion, construed *contra* Durkheim as residing in a psychological not a sociological need, though servicing the latter.

> Despite the shambles of modern culture, some religious answer will surely be forthcoming, for religion is not (or no longer) a 'property' of society in the Durkheimian sense. It is a constitutive part of man's consciousness: the cognitive search for the pattern of the 'general order' of existence; the affective need to establish rituals and to make such conceptions sacred; the primordial need for relatedness to some others, or a set of meanings which will establish a transcendent response to the self; and the existential need to confront the finalities of suffering and death. (Bell, 1979: 169)

The difficulties of this emancipatory-cum-regulatory response seem both theological and sociological. On the one hand Bell simply re-endorses the Durkheimian definition of religion, i.e. that which maintains a distinction between the sacred and the profane and he wants 'it' reinstated. . . .

> If there is no separation of realms, if the sacred is destroyed, then we are left with the shambles of appetite and self-interest and the destruction of the moral circle which engirds mankind. Can we — must we not — re-establish that which is sacred and that which is profane? (Bell, 1979: 171)

The difficulty is that whilst the Christian has no difficulty with linking emancipation and regulation ('in Thy service is perfect freedom'), Bell (1979: 170) is looking for some 'new rite of incorporation': no existing version will do since they beg the question of 'who is God and who is the Devil' (Bell, 1979: 169). But the trouble with 'new rites' is that they have to be written, by someone, they do not just surface from some generic religious consciousness; and once written, embodying that 'author's' designation of the sacred, then imposed, for if social consensus existed it would not have needed writing; and because imposed, the *secular* relationship between regulation and emancipation resurfaces as an antinomy. Bell thus seems to want the benefits of religion for the individual without the burden of Revelation and its blessings on society without the Church to pronounce the benediction: in other words he wants something very similar to what Durkheim wanted and appears just as unlikely to get it.

Habermas, on the contrary, seeks a thoroughly secular solution to what he views as a thoroughgoing secular problem. The similarity is that he too begins with a conflation of the structural and the cultural in which the latter is the subordinate partner and he too ends with an attempt at the cultural emancipation of the human race. Basically, economic revisionism is the source of cultural conflation. 'Scientific–technical progress has become an independent source of surplus value' (1968: 104), its effects are the end of scarcity and class struggle now that 'the Biblical curse of necessary labour is broken technologically' (1972: 58), but also a new form of legitimation since this can no longer come from classical economic notions of just exchange in a free market. Market economics are finished even as ideas, and, since the institutionalization of science and technology involves rationalization which is death to tradition, where is the legitimation of advanced industrial society to come from? The answer is 'by having technology and science *also* take on the role of an ideology' (1968: 104). But this entails no mystificatory imposition of one class's values upon another, but rather the universal spreading of a 'technocratic consciousness' deriving from the domination of the empirical-analytical sciences whose application to production was the source of self-propelling economic growth.

Technocratic consciousness results in depoliticization and thus represents another version of The End of Ideology thesis and another form of cultural conflation. The difference is that science too is ideological, not in the old sense of resting upon misrepresentation and manipulation, but because it discloses knowledge subject to an interest in securing and extending control over the object world, whilst other interests are simultaneously repressed. Thus as 'the reified models of the sciences migrate into the socio-cultural life-world' (1968: 110) they become repressive of the human race's 'emancipatory interest', because people and human relations are also treated as objectified processes over which technical control is to be gained.

The essence of modern scientific ideology lies in misapplication rather than mendacity. As it embraces the social sciences then the knowing subject — man who can reflect upon and change his actions — is lost to sociology and himself. Thus in the social sciences, observed regularities (like the connection between measured intelligence and school achievement or the persistence of gender roles) are taken as invariant, with no reflection about whether they merely express forms of social domination. Equally, in personal life, self-understanding shadows scientific progress (we think of ourselves as 'extroverts', 'late developers', or 'hyperactive'): we view ourselves as determined and objectified entities without self-mastery at the mercy of 'maternal deprivation', 'depression' or 'hormonal imbalance' and to solve our problems we swallow pills. Human communication is distorted because people think and talk about themselves in terms of scientific objectivity and make decisions about what are seen as purely technical problems, thus again rendering moral debate inert (Archer, 1988: 62f.).

In order to avoid positivistic monism and to overcome cultural subordination Habermas had to locate an alternative source of emancipatory values and a means of achieving them. After brief but disappointed hopes in the student movement of the late 1960s, his efforts in the 1970s were devoted to elaborating upon the 'ideal speech situation' where communication free from restraint could foster critical reflection promotive of emancipation. The difficulties of this solution have been well rehearsed: what is significant is that it was *structural* obstacles which were singled out. First came the charge of circularity — how could undistorted communication produce emancipation since it depended upon equality of opportunity to participate in the dialogue which presumed that emancipated speakers already existed. This Habermas took on board, agreeing that

> only in an emancipated society, whose members' autonomy and responsibility have been realized, would communication have developed into the non-authoritarian and universally practised dialogue. . . . To this extent the truth of statements is based on anticipating the good life. (1972: 314)

To that extent, however, critical reflection remained an

(intellectual) speciality outside public consciousness while ever the positivist heritage held sway. Then followed the obvious objection of potential collapse into intellectual authoritarianism. The riposte that this form of academic discourse constituted a model towards which the universities might lead society as a whole met the counter-charge that it was not transferable to other structural settings — particularly the most inegalitarian such as workers and management, where there would be reciprocal resistance to open dialogue. The psycho-analytical analogue upon which the 'ideal speech situation' had drawn heavily, assumed a common therapeutic purpose of the parties involved which was utterly lacking in a stratified society.

All of this is pretty straightforward, the interesting twists and turns are associated with the Frankfurt School's cultural attempts to re-establish metaphysics and reflection in the realm of rational discourse which positivistic philosophers had restricted to the phenomenal world of 'fact', observation and experience. Critical reflection was intended to produce human emancipation: exercised in the ideal speech situation it would generate the consensual truths which set men free. The latter requires some independent criterion of truth and the former a model of emancipated man. Critics have argued that both were lacking.

On the one hand, consensuality or collective certitude are certainly inadequate criteria for validating truth claims. Yet if nothing but this arbitrates on critical discourse, what protects against the pretence that 'deep seated prejudices were heaven-sent intuitions' (Kolakowski, 1978: 789). And, with a final turn of the screw, if the participants themselves are the final arbiters (as in psycho-analysis) what prevents descent into that very self-expressive syndrome which Bell detested for undermining epistemological and ethical foundations? On the other hand (again as in psycho-analysis) it is valid and necessary to ask how we would *recognize* an emancipated person; the question is *not* how do they *feel*. Yet here it appeared that no non-empirical model of man was forthcoming, which meant that 'emancipation' received a negative definition. It was always a state of being freed *from* social constraints *x*, *y*, and *z*, but without some conception of the final goal how could one know that the state had been achieved and the list of distorting factors exhausted?

One can have the greatest respect for the task Habermas set himself — the defence of metaphysics and the rehabilitation of a discourse based on 'good reason' rather than scientific 'proof'. One can agree that positivism is

> the source of illusion, and the treatment of this reality as the source, object or test of knowledge that is the true origin of irrationality. The true reality, and the object of negative reason or critical theory, is identified with a more fundamental realm of existence representing both the source of the phenomenal world and an ideal state beyond the limitations imposed by this world. To take existing empirical facts or appearances as reality, to dwell only in this world, and to identify an awareness of its laws with knowledge, results in the failure to recognize its subordinate and limited nature, and hinder the potential development towards a more ideal state. (Badham, 1984: 80)

One can do all this and still find the metaphysics of the Frankfurt school empty and their model of critical discourse not up to the job specification.

Phase 3 — The Third Wave — Information Society

By the start of the eighties this critical concern with shoring up a cultural platform from which people could evaluate, criticize and seek to re-direct structural change, was submerged by the Third Wave. The arrival of Information Society, offspring of the union between computing and telecommunications, was formally christened the Third Wave by Alvin Toffler (1981). Like previous technological breakers it washed up new structures and washed away cultural redoubts: but this was the biggest, the Great Tidal Bore (the twentieth-century mega-equivalent of Gellner's Great Divide in the nineteenth century) and you either rode it or went under. For 'what is occurring now is, in all likelihood bigger, deeper and more important than the industrial revolution . . . the present moment represents nothing less than the second great divide in human history' (Toffler, 1975: 21). On the other side of the new divide was full-blown cultural monism: where science and technology were utterly synonymous with knowledge and knowledge was completely conflated with the structure of the new Information Society. By 1980 Daniel Bell had pocketed both his pessimism about disintegrative cultural modernism and his optimism about religious revival and joined in the celebration of the new axial principle — computer-assisted 'theoretical knowledge' universalized by telecommunications.

A new social framework was presented as the autonomous effect of information technology with its deterministic consequences for everything social — from domestic life to international relations, through leisure activities to industrial relations, no sphere was left untouched by informatics (Lyon, 1988). This one-dimensional theory of social change presumed the emergence of a monistic set of values which operated as objective and neutral guides for action. Again, it is this on which I want to concentrate rather than upon the structural deficiencies of the thesis, though the two have an important interrelationship. Structural objections have wreaked havoc with the simplistic notion of a 'march through the sectors', a great trek which had supposedly ended with 'information workers' in the majority throughout the OECD countries. Thus Gershuny and Miles (1983; 1986) demonstrated the misleading characterization of economic history as a steady and systematic movement from societies being mainly agricultural, then mainly industrial and finally mainly service-oriented. Like the 'service class' of post-industrial theory, the 'information sector' is a heterogeneous category, a statistical artifact produced by lumping together as it were the telecommunications expert and the TV repair man. However, precisely because empirical data on the structural constitution of an 'information sector' do not hold up, so the thesis about the dawn of Information Society ultimately depends on the argument about its new cultural axial principle being upheld.

This principle is really nothing more than Comte's Third Stage flowering late; what could be called positivism with peripherals. Positive science rules, in public and private life with the boundary between the two dissolving as information technology invades the home and, it is claimed, rules supreme. It rules through its self-evidently beneficial effects: user-friendly technology has thus become like health, obviously a good thing. Hi-tech hopefuls never look to 'the reversal of priorities Marx saw in the factory whereby the dead (machines) dominate the living (workers) is extended by the computer into the realm of knowledge' (Poster, 1984: 166). Instead, the image is of man and machines together becoming able to 'subdue many, perhaps in time most, of the world's afflictions' (Michie and Johnson, 1985: 244). To see such universal beneficence needs strenuous tunnel vision, which sights the welfare benefits of computer-assisted medical diagnosis and averts the eyes from the warfare potential of computer-guided missile systems.

It rules to the exclusion of other modes of thought and thus without opposition. Metaphysics are dead: moral philosophy has been put out of business. What remains is not even the philosophy of science (which sometimes used to demarcate a metaphysical domain whose talk was not meaningless), but philosophy *for* science, a servile subject which cleans up the ideational environment. It clarifies the nature of scientific knowledge, demonstrates its progressive and advantageous character, and above all reveals the absurdity of alternative philosophies which are not able to stand up to what Popper once called the 'strain of civilization'. It thus rules out any stance capable of inverting the question and asking whether civilization can stand the strain of rampant technology.

Finally, it rules by changing our model of Man through reversing the way in which Man is modelled. The notion of the computer as the extension of human (computational, cross-referencing, retrieval) capacities has been turned around to yield the concept of superior 'artificial intelligence'. Whether this is presented as a straightforward process in which men remake themselves in the image of technology (Bolter, 1984) or as a more subtle form of technological definition of identity, i.e. we know exactly what we are once we have modelled it, and what we do not yet know about ourselves in that way is an exact specification of the future modelling programme for AI (Mefford, 1987) — the result is the same, computer dominated self-knowledge. Moreover, it will be an increasingly denigratory one which tells us how we fall short; and not just that we are no match in computing the biggest known prime number. Yet the notion of the *superior* capacity of computers has a lot more to do with reconceptualizing what it is to be human than with machines having captured the essence of the human mind. For what has been downgraded if not excluded from the latter concept are human abilities for exercising wisdom, judgement, empathy, sympathy, discernment, responsibility, accountability and self-sacrifice. David Bolter (1984) would not want me to add 'imagination' to that list, for Turing's Man is indeed one whose imagination has been captured and captivated by the machine.

In other words, if the whole cultural realm becomes subordinate to information technology, then there is no other basis than the instrumental rationality which it fosters on which to criticize it, evaluate it, decide how to deploy it or when to restrict it. We are left with what Weizenbaum called the 'imperialism of instrumental reason' (1976). Depressingly, the critics of Information Society indeed appear to have been culturally colonized. Critical emphasis is exclusively *structural* and is placed on how we can obtain a better

technological mix or fix — Schumacher's 'intermediate technology' (1978), Roszak's 'selective industrialization' (1973), Illich's
'convivial production' (1975) or Dickson's 'alternative
technology' (1974).

A cultural technique is glaringly absent even amongst those who
think they are totally hostile. Temperate hostility settles for quantitative reduction (small is beautiful; but it is only a smaller version of
the same thing, so beauty is like slimming). Immoderate hostility
means a 'Luddite response'; kicking at the bars of what David
Lyon calls 'the new electronic cage' (1988: 140). Yet if self-con-
fessed Luddites such as Michael Shallis (1984) confront a 'self-
augmenting' process (in Jaques Ellul's terms [1980]) or have come
to think that they do, then their actions are impotent protests like
smashing the first looms.

If culture is indeed subordinate, then reactions to information
technology become matters of taste: one goes in to technophilia or
technophobia. The technophiliac, with instrumental reason on his
side, can at least give grounds for his optimism — every technical
problem can have a technical solution. The technophobic, without a
cultural critique to call upon, just emanates pure hate. In either case
the process rolls on with the people reduced to spectators who make
their approving or disapproving noises without being able to affect
their predicament. Yet this passivity only arises if culture genuinely
is subordinate. If it is not, then neither are we confined to technophilia or technophobia but are confronted with 'techno-choices'.
We the people, working through our contemporary decision-
making structures, have to choose between, for example, directing
science and technology to maximize production or decrease working
hours, for participatory politics or the surveillance state, for
military expansion or welfare extension, to protect the environment
or to increase commodities (Badham, 1986). Such choices depend
upon ideals and value conflict and ethical debate. However,
industrial society theorists belong to that part of the sociological
tradition which has severed its links with moral philosophy and
which, therefore, ends up 'sociologizing' morals, in their case
subordinating them to the categorical imperative of technology.
This kind of sociology

insofar as it has been able to produce general interpretations of the contemporary
world, has done so with a lack of moral conviction. The conceptions that have
predominated since the 1950s till today bear witness to that. They are particularly
empty of a moral vision: the 'mass society', the 'industrial society', the 'post-

industrial society' and, the newest candidate in this succession, the 'information society' all fit this assertion. *The fact that there are either optimistic or pessimistic versions of each one of these conceptions does not mean that they are in any way grounded in moral philosophy.* (Giner, 1987: 79, my italics)

In order to activate 'techno-choices' this grounding needs to be re-established, but to do that means challenging the central theoretical and empirical premises of industrial society theory: we have to go for both its jugular and its great aorta to release culture from subordination, to restore its relative autonomy and retrieve its moral potency.

Post-Industrialism and Moral Philosophy

I will begin by charging industrial society theorists (with the exceptions noted under Phase 2) guilty of the Fallacy of Amoral Objectivity, as Giner (1987) termed it. The charge is conspiracy to make ethics superfluous, to reduce morality to a mere by-product of social forces, in this case the powerful constraints of technological change, and therefore to promote moral agnosticism within the social science community. The charge sheet could read more briefly — they are held guilty of culpable scientism.

In their case the Fallacy of Amoral Objectivity arises from the view that it is possible to side-step any truck with moral philosophy when assessing the 'progressiveness' of social arrangements. Basically, post-industrial theorists do this by arguing that technology provides the means which enable mankind to achieve its desires, thus the changes taking place in response to desire are progressive for those involved and only require amoral objective monitoring on the part of the investigator. The formula is really: desire + instrumental rationality + technology = progress, and it is one which supposedly leaves the theorists preening themselves on their 'ethical neutrality' towards these goings-on. However, there are major problems with each term and connection in the formula and because of this proper 'ethical neutrality' degenerates into amoral objectivism.

To begin with, 'desires' are postulated without any general theory of humanity (which has the job *inter alia* of distinguishing between propensities and conduct in such terms as good/evil, virtue/vice, grace/sin, rational/irrational, free/determined, etc.) Since our theorists turn their backs on this job yet want to make other people's desires carry the moral burden, then the simple act of wanting something has to be seen as rationally desirable on this view, otherwise the blank ethical cheque cannot be issued. In other words, good reason is presumed to be forthcoming from anyone who desires anything: the only way of making ethical check-outs redundant. Then such actors harness their wants to *Zweckrationalität*, they survey the technological means available, and the end result is dubbed 'progressive' for mankind as a whole. Yet instrumental rationality is simply expedient to those who have the greatest resources to achieve their desires. As Weber noted, subjective wants generally get arranged on a scale of urgency by power. To judge the outcome, i.e. the ensuing technological changes, as a unilinear process of *general* human advancement is to affirm that might is right, whatever the specific costs particular technologies impose on definite sections of the population. In other words, whatever results is 'progress' in the absence too of any notion of the Good Society. Because of its absence, what results can never be viewed as the unintended and undesirable consequence of social interaction. On this account post-industrial societies can never take a form which is seriously inimical to parts of the population, nor can its theorists entertain the real possibility that the structure of an industrial society (like any other) can indeed be what *nobody* wants.

In short, the attempt to avoid moral philosophical concerns by making technology the means to achieve mankind's desires cannot deem any and all outcomes to be progress and thus cannot dispense with a consideration of the Good Society. As Horkheimer and Adorno once put it, instrumental reason alone gives us 'rationality with reference to means and irrationality with references to human existence' (1972; 31-2). Consequently, it must be a central concern to theorists, as to different sections of the population, to define and justify which forms of technological development are socially 'progressive' and 'advantageous' — and for this the *Wertrational* has to come into play for the *Zweckrational* cannot do that job.

Of course, this condemnation of the industrial society theorists' formula can only appeal to defenders of Autonomous Man against *Homo Sociologicus Industrialis*, of the human being against the humanoid, of actors against agents. For we have to follow something like the scenario sketched out by Hollis (1977).

> What starts as a search for an active model of man leads first to a demand for actions which are self-explanatory because fully rational, thence to an account of rationality in terms of real interests, thence into ethics and finally to that ancient problem about the nature of the Good Society. *Yet it should come as no surprise that questions in ethics and politics should attend an analysis of human nature.*

We cannot know what is rational without deciding what is best. (Hollis, 1977: 137, my italics)

Those who do the opposite can, of course, endow their humanoid with appropriately pre-programmed desires — moral determinism by society was the main way in which sociology could part company with moral philosophy in the first place and continue to do so. For example,

> Structural-functionalism, during its mature and hegemonic Parsonian dispensation, left no room for a philosophical theory of morality. Man's moral choices became 'dilemmas of action' whose resolution rested on personality structures which were in turn underpinned by cultural determinants and socialization processes. (Giner, 1987: 73)

This is precisely the source of the Amoral Objectivity Fallacy — the Infallibility of Society.

Obviously, it begs the question of how it can be avoided: of the proper relationship between the study of advanced industrial (or any other kind of) society and moral philosophy. I will confine myself to three points, the first of which concerns the necessity of a relationship. Social theory must pay its real respects to the morality of actors as a generic part of its model of man. This means more than a simple acknowledgement that people think and (to some extent) act in terms of what is good, right and proper, for so does the morally determined humanoid. It entails both a respect for moral differences *and* the human capacity to endorse different morals. They are not socially pre-programmed (there is no moral determinism though there may be ethical conditioning) and by nature they can change their minds in moral matters, defining the good, the right or the proper otherwise. Social theory thus has to tangle with the moral realm but simultaneously must concede it some autonomy. Although there may well be contributory social factors in accounts of individual or collective morality, they are not sufficient to account for the conversion of a Saul into a Paul. Hence, we must shun the nineteenth-century parting of the ways between social theory and moral philosophy which was based on the programme of 'sociologizing' man's morals. The degenerative phase of this programme was the attempt to 'psychologize' that which could not be successfully 'sociologized' — dismally substituting the 'unstable personality' for the exercise of moral autonomy. If we grant relative moral autonomy, then when we proceed to construct our models of man it would be foolish to forgo an interchange between the sociological imagination and the philosophical and theological imaginations. An interchange about what should be for humanity in relation to what could be for society.

A second point stems from Weber's just conviction that ethical systems make claims to substantive rationality which sociology cannot adjudicate between. Since it cannot be our job to arbitrate on metaphysical matters, can we do more than understand their meanings for those holding them (with as much hermeneutic ingenuity as possible) plus explicating their relationship to action and exploring the social consequences of their being held? I want to argue that we can and that there is a particular area of collaborative endeavour.

Any ethical system, including those advanced by *engagé* social theorists, faces a shared problem. Namely, there is a gap between the ethical conspectus itself and its embodiment in a concept of the Good Society. This gap is inescapable since the concrete contours of the Good Society, which is good because it expresses the realization of the moral precepts in question, is never directly derivable from them. This is most obvious when an old ethical system confronts changed social circumstances and when a new ethical system faces up for the first time to what social changes would constitute its actualization. Formally, the problem is identical for religious beliefs and secular ethics and formally social theory can make the same contribution.

Metaphorically, when trying to conceptualize the kingdom of heaven on earth, moral advocates tend to be pretty bad sociologists and this is equally true of our *engagé* colleagues who have a go. This comment needs tempering with charity, for what they are attempting is an exercise in mental prediction without the protection of the *ceteris paribus* clause, since other things never are equal in the real world. The predictions consist in judging what practical social arrangements will encapsulate their precepts: such judgements may be inappropriate (or contested) and they are always at the mercy of the unforeseen and the unintended. This is equally the case for the Catholic Church with its systematic social doctrine, starting with *Rerum Novarum*, for the English Utilitarians seeking the institutional arrangements compatible with the pleasure principle, for modern feminists searching for a social framework fostering gender equality and for Daniel Bell whose socialism in economics, liberalism in politics and conservatism in culture are triune positions which have to be accommodated in a reconceptualization of social structure. These instances are cited purely for their diversity. For despite this diversity, sociology can perform several services, all of which help the group in question to make better 'techno-choices' and none of which entail illicit metaphysical incursion. (Of course, who we choose to help is a matter of personal 'value relevance', though even a hefty critical kick may not be unhelpful, and how we go about it could involve more restricted questions of 'professional ethics'.) To begin with we can explore *whether* the lineaments of the proposed Good Society actually are consonant with the respective precepts (was state intervention in education consistent with Utilitarian *laissez-faire* principles?). Often this would feed-back to preceptive clarification or elaboration — for example, are egalitarians seeking equality of opportunity or satisfied with nothing short of equality of outcome in whatever domain? Next, *would* the Society proposed produce the expected Good — would Bell's 'Public Household' work, would positive institutional discrimination have no undesirable consequences for the status of women, would the very pursuit of a social policy lead to its perversion — as Leo XII (1891) noted in *Rerum Novarum*:

> It is not easy to define the relative rights and the mutual duties of the wealthy and of the poor, of capital and of labour. And the danger lies in this, that crafty agitators constantly make use of these disputes to pervert men's judgements and to stir up the people to sedition.

To 'crafty agitators' have to be added other perverse effects, intervening variables and new unforeseeable factors: all of which may mean back to the drawing board. Finally, were it achieved, *what* further repercussions are entailed and are those which could be anticipated fully consistent with the originating precepts?

In short, sociology could act as a permanent Devil's Advocate for any notion of the Good Society which enters the lists: for individual theorists this will usually mean assuming the proper title, Promoter of the Faith, but for all it would entail a self-imposed moral asceticism — passionate endorsement of any precepts must go hand in hand with the most suspicious scrutiny of their social expression. The same asceticism entails that detestation of some ethical system does not dispense us from the most scrupulous assessment of the consistency, workability and consequences of its model society. The main thing then that the sociologist as moral ascetic has to say to the sociologist as Amoral Objectivist, is that the latter make life easy for themselves and unliveable for many others by transforming ethical concerns into (im)purely social ones.

The third and last point is one of contrast with and criticism of industrial society theorists and their treatment of culture. I have been dwelling upon the necessity of dialogue between sociology and moral philosophy in a joint enterprise of clarifying which 'techno-choices' should be made to attain the forms of social development that different ethical communities would deem 'progressive'. In so doing, I have assumed that the *Wertrationalität* is not in short supply and I believe the assumption correct. However, a leitmotif of industrial society theory is cultural monism: the problem of the Phase 2 theorists was how if possible to avert it *given* the End of Ideology proper. Part then of their subordination of the cultural domain was its depopulation. In this they are again true heirs of Comte; they have taken on board his zero-sum formula for religious — metaphysical — positivistic ideas and gone overboard about the hegemony of the latter in post-industrial society. Lying behind this is, I believe, another major fallacy whose deficiencies complement the Fallacy of Amoral Objectivism to disastrous effect. This is the Myth of Cultural Integration (Archer, 1985; 1988). This Myth embodies 'one of the most deep seated fallacies in social science . . . the . . . assumption of a high degree of consistency in the interpretations produced by societal units' (Etzioni, 1968: 146). Yet it projected an image of culture so powerful that it scored the retina, leaving a perpetual after-image, which distorted subsequent perception.

Its more distant origins lie in Comte and German historicism (*Historismus*), its more proximate ones are the heritage of anthropology. Despite definitional wranglings over the term 'culture', there was substantial accord amongst anthropologists about its main property — strong and coherent patterning. This central notion of culture as a monistic integrated whole echoes down the decades. Malinowski's concept of 'an individual culture as a coherent whole' (1944), Ruth Benedict's 'cultural patterns' (1961), Kroeber's 'ethos of total culture' (1963) resurface in Mary Douglas's notion of 'one single, symbolically consistent universe' (1966), to be enshrined in the Parsonian central value-system and to gain monumental reinforcement by its adoption into Western Marxism as 'hegemonic culture' and its offspring 'the dominant ideology'. What we see in industrial society theorists is simply the latest generation held in thrall by it.

Two features of this heritage deserve underlining. On the one hand its strong aesthetic rather than analytical orientation, which led to an endorsement of 'artistic' hermeneutics as the method for grasping the inner sense of cultural wholes' (Merquior, 1979: 48). On the other hand, this approach, based on the intuitive understanding of cultural configurations, entailed a crucial pre-judgement, namely an insistence that coherence was there to be found, that is a mental closure against the discovery of cultural inconsistencies, clashes between different beliefs, and consequently attaching any importance to them. Both are hallmarks of post-industrial society theorists. Read Habermas and such is his artistic persuasiveness that technocratic positivism seems to invade every cranny of the *Lebenswelt*: read Bell on the same advanced industrial societies and self-expressive modernism is everywhere to be found. The former is struggling for an emancipation which the latter finds rampant and dangerous, whilst the latter in turn longs for a return to religion which he believes dead. Empirical work on cultural cartography is thin on the ground but should supply an antidote to cultural monism.

But more is required than an empirical demonstration that the *Wertrationalität* is alive and well in modern societies. There is also the vastly important theoretical job which is passed-up by all who endorse the Myth of Cultural Integration of tracing how cultural contradictions within and between belief systems make just as important a contribution to social change as anything going on in the structural domain (Archer, 1988). (Even our Phase 2 theorists could only think of a legitimation crisis as a relationship between culture and structure.) The subordination of culture in theories of industrial society rules out a priori any significance of cultural contradictions. Viewing culture as subordinate is really what makes for an industrial society theorist — they have a limited 'industrial imagination' which conflates structure with culture, instrumental rationality with morality and technical advance with social progress. In this context postmodernism now shows all the excesses typical of a counter-revolution.

References

Archer, Margaret S. (1985) 'The Myth of Cultural Integration', *British Journal of Sociology* 36(3).

Archer, Margaret S. (1988) *Culture and Agency: The Place of Culture in Social Theory*. Cambridge: Cambridge University Press.

Archer, Margaret S. and Giner, Salvador (eds) (1971) *Contemporary Europe: Class, Status and Power*. London: Weidenfeld and Nicolson.

Aron, Raymond (1967) *The Industrial Society*. London: Weidenfeld and Nicolson.

Aron, Raymond (1972) *Progress and Disillusion: The Dialectics of Modern Society*. Harmondsworth: Penguin.

Badham, Richard (1984) 'The Sociology of Industrial and Post-Industrial Societies', *Current Sociology* 32(1).

Badham, Richard (1986) *Theories of Industrial Society*. Beckenham: Croom Helm.

Bell, Daniel (1962) *The End of Ideology*. New York: Collier.

Bell, Daniel (1976) *The Coming of Post-Industrial Society*. New York: Collier.

Bell, Daniel (1979) *The Cultural Contradictions of Capitalism*. Harmondsworth: Penguin.

Bell, Daniel (1980) 'The Social Framework of the Information Society', in M. Dertouzos and J. Moses (eds) *The Computer Age: a Twenty Year View*. Cambridge, MA: M.I.T. Press.

Benedict, Ruth (1961) *Patterns of Culture*. London: Routledge and Kegan Paul.

Berger, Peter (1969) *The Social Reality of Religion*. London: Faber and Faber.

Bolter, David (1984) *Turing's Man: Western Culture in the Computer Age*. London: Duckworth.

Bottomore, T.B. (1973) *Sociology: A Guide to the Problems and Literature*. London: Allen and Unwin.

Dickson, David (1974) *Alternative Technology: The Politics of Technical Change*. Glasgow: Fontana/Collins.

Douglas, Mary (1966) *Purity and Danger*. London: Routledge and Kegan Paul.

Ellul, Jacques (1980) *The Technological System*. New York: Continuum.

Etzioni, Amitai (1968) *The Active Society*. London: Free Press

Gellner, Ernest (1972) *Thought and Change*. London: Weidenfeld and Nicolson.

Gershuny, Jonathan and Miles, Ian (1983) *The New Service Economy*. London: Frances Pinter.

Giner, Salvador (1987) 'Sociology and Moral Philosophy', *International Review of Sociology*, new series, no. 3.

Goldthorpe, John (1964) 'Social Stratification in Industrial Society', in P. Halmos (ed.), *The Development of Industrial Societies*. Sociological Review Monograph, No 8, Keele University.

Goldthorpe, John (1971) 'Theories of Industrial Society', *European Journal of Sociology* 12(2).

Habermas, Jürgen (1968) *Toward a Rational Society*. London: Heinemann.

Habermas, Jürgen (1972) *Knowledge and Human Interests*. London: Heinemann.

Hollis, Martin (1977) *Models of Man; Philosophical Thoughts on Social Action*. Cambridge: Cambridge University Press.

Horkheimer, Max and Adorno, Theodor (1972) *The Dialectic of Enlightenment*. New York: Herder and Herder.

Illich, Ivan D. (1975) *Tools for Conviviality*. Glasgow: Fontana,

Kerr, Clark et al. (1962) *Industrialism and Industrial Man*. London: Heinemann.

Kolakowski, Leszek (1978) *Main Currents of Marxism*, Vol. 2. Oxford: Clarendon Press.

Kroeber, A.L. (1963) *Anthropology; Culture, Patterns, and Processes*. New York: Harcourt Brace.

Lipset, S.M. (1969) *Political Man*. London: Heinemann.

Lyon, David (1988) *The Information Society: Issues and Illusions*. Cambridge: Polity Press.

Malinowski, B. (1944) *A Scientific Theory of Culture*. Chapel Hill: University of North Carolina Press.

Mann, Michael (1970) 'The Social Cohesion of Liberal Democracy', *American Sociological Review* 38(3).

Mefford, Dwain (1987) 'Analogical Reasoning and the Definition of the Situation: Back to Snyder for Concepts and Forward to Artificial Intelligence for Method', in C.F. Herman, C.W. Kegely and J.N. Rosenau (eds) *New Directions in the Study of Foreign Policy*. Boston: Allen and Unwin.

Merquior, J.G. (1979) *The Veil and the Mask*. London: Routledge and Kegan Paul.

Michie, Donald and Johnson, Rory (1985) *The Knowledge Machine: Artificial Intelligence and the Future of Man*. New York: Morrow.

Miles, Ian and Gershuny, Jonathan (1986) 'The Social Economics of Information Technology', in Marjorie Ferguson (ed.) *New Communication Technologies and the Public Interest*. London and Beverly Hills: Sage.

Poster, Mark (1984) *Foucault, Marxism and History*. Cambridge: Polity Press.

Rerum Novarum (1891) *The Condition of Labour*. Vatican: Polyglot Press.

Robertson, Roland (1988) 'The Sociological Significance of Culture: Some General Considerations', *Theory, Culture & Society* 5(1).

Roszak, Theodor (1973) *Where the Wasteland Ends: Politics and Transcendence in the Post-Industrial Society*. London: Faber and Faber.

Schumacher, E. (1978) *Small is Beautiful: A Study of Economics as if People Really Mattered*. London: Abacus.

Shallis, Michael (1984) *The Silicon Idol*. Oxford: Oxford University Press.

Toffler, Alvin (1975) *Future Shock*. London: Pan.

Toffler, Alvin (1981) *The Third Wave*. London: Pan.

Weizenbaum, Joseph (1976) *Computer Power and Human Reason*. New York: W.H. Freeman and Co.

Westergaard, John H. (1972) 'The Myth of Classlessness', in Robin Blackburn (ed.) *Ideology in Social Science*. London: Fontana/Collins.

Margaret S. Archer is Professor of Sociology at the University of Warwick. Her most recent book is *Culture and Agency* (Polity Press).

The Idea of Revolution

Alain Touraine

1. *Tabula Rasa*

The idea of revolution is at the heart of the Western representation of modernization. European experience, which dominated the world stage for so long, drew its force, its violence, and its formidable capacity for expansion, from the central affirmation that modernity had to be produced solely by the force of reason, and that nothing should resist that universal inspiration which would destroy all social and cultural tradition, all beliefs, privileges and communities.

The West, first European and then American, has maintained for centuries that modernization is nothing other than modernity at work, that its purpose has not been the effective mobilization of resources but the replacement of custom by reason. Modernization must be therefore endogenous, and the role of the state or of intellectuals should be limited to the removal of obstacles to the exercise of reason. This identification of modernity with the process of modernization, this absolute confidence in the 'progress of the human spirit', to quote the title of one of Condorcet's works, and in the necessity of destroying the old world, was so total, so obvious to the majority of Westerners, that still today, at the end of a century defined by a great diversity of modes of modernization and resource development — from Soviet type revolutions to religious fundamentalism by way of 'Third World' nationalisms and the neo-Bismarckian industrialization of the Far East — the Western countries resist every analysis of their own specific mode of modernization, so convinced are they of their own incarnation of universal modernity itself. There may have been doubts and criticisms raised against this idea, but today it has been powerfully reinforced by the generalized failures of communist and nationalist modernization, and by the belief that the rationalist mode — which we might also call capitalist — of development is the only one which

Theory, Culture & Society (SAGE, London, Newbury Park and New Delhi), Vol. 7 (1990), 121–141

has universal value and which leads, despite the difficulties, to the certain enrichment of democracy.

This belief in endogenous development, this *Enlightenment* philosophy, elaborated in England and France during the eighteenth century, which dominated the principal centres of industrial development in Great Britain and then in the United States, through the nineteenth and twentieth centuries, produced a model of social and political action which can best be defined as revolutionary. At the beginning of the seventeenth century, Descartes sought to construct rational thought from the standpoint of a *tabula rasa*, freed from all received ideas and all customary habits of thought. More than two centuries later, the song which would become the most universal symbol of the workers' revolutionary movement, *The Internationale*, proclaims, '*du passé faisons table rase*'. The absolute opposition between reason and tradition, between science and religion, entails that between the future and the past, and it founds the general call to destroy the past which would later be found, for example, in Schumpeter's definition of capitalism as creative destruction.

When we speak of industrial revolution, or of political revolution, or of sexual revolution, economic, social and cultural changes are always seen as mutations and as the triumph of reason, most often understood as a kind of natural force, over the artificial constructions erected to protect parochial interests and traditional beliefs. The conflicts and the struggles, which this revolutionary conception of modernity regards as necessary, are not internal conflicts within the truly social realm, but the confrontation of modern, open, rational society with its enemies, all the absolutisms, and all the forms of irrationality and stagnation. The social actor engaged in these struggles is not to be identified with and cannot be assigned to a particular category like a class, but is taken to be as one with the natural world of reason and of needs opposed to particular interests. The principal agent of progress has in fact to be the nation seen as a creation out of popular sovereignty and construed as the defender of universal principles like liberty and equality. At the very least, in anticipation of the new world order promised by Hegel and Marx, the nation-state has to root out particularism and overthrow despotic forms of state power.

The idea of revolution is thus that of a struggle against an *ancien régime*, prosecuted in the name of natural laws of progress by a nation which has emancipated itself from the traditional forms of power. Natural progress, the nation, and, on the negative side, the old order, are the three components whose association makes up the idea of revolution which triumphed in the West during the eighteenth and nineteenth centuries, and which went on to spill over across the rest of the world with the Soviet and then Chinese revolutions. Let us now illustrate this definition in the context of some of its more important expressions, beginning with the French Revolution and Marxist thought.

2. The French Revolution

The truly revolutionary aspect of the destruction of the structure and power of the *ancien régime* in France between 1789 and 1799 is the affirmation of national sovereignty. For the date of their national holiday, the French people should have chosen, not 14 July which was the day of one of the bloodiest riots of the period, but 17 June, the day on which the representatives of the Third Estate transformed themselves into a National Assembly, an act confirmed three days later by the 'oath of the Jeu de Paume', and which was followed by a gradual process over the next few days which saw deputies from the clergy and the nobility rallying to the Assembly. This affirmation of the nation was already present in the English *Bill of Rights* of 1689 — although, in this text, reference back to traditions still impeded the affirmation of a universal principle — and above all in the founding texts of American independence like those declarations of rights, on a par with the Declaration of Independence itself, drawn up by various states, particularly Virginia, Massachusetts, and Pennsylvania, texts which were inspired by the philosophy of the Enlightenment and by theories of natural law.

Interpretations of the French revolution in terms of social conflict, or, more precisely, in terms of class struggle, miss the essential point: the nation, identified with the progress of reason, overcomes the obstacles set up during the march of despotism, the privileges and power of the priests. This is completely different from the struggle of the bourgeoisie or the peasants against the aristocracy. The logic of the French revolution is not social but political. The war abroad and the civil war at home reinforce this predominance of truly political action which culminates with the brief leftist episode of the 'cult of reason', but above all with the permanent denunciation of the enemies of the revolution as traitors against the nation and enemy agents. Proclamations of the class struggle were hardly made at all, unless they came from marginal radical groupings such as the *enragés* or, later, the followers of François Babeuf. Still less was it a question of creating a democracy which would represent opposing interests and frame the negotiations between them within the limits of the law. It was a question of creating and defending the unity of the nation, identified with the universal principles of reason, liberty and equality, against all its internal and external enemies. The radicalization of the revolutionary process did not result from an aggravation of social conflict, but, on the contrary, from the stronger and stronger hold of a logic internal to the denunciation and expurgation of increasingly weak and distant populist mobilizations. This is Jacobinism, the action of the Jacobin club, and it is at the heart of the revolution: its non-elected power, which was to be Robespierre's after September 1792, replacing that of the Convention, and itself increasingly displaced by the Committee of Public Safety and the Committee of General Security — the double politburo of the revolution.

3. Marxist Thought

The idea of revolution is inseparable from the domination of political action, and even of a properly political agent, over social action. This affirmation may seem paradoxical and we can immediately set Marx's thought against it, above all his incessant denunciations of the political illusion, beginning with his *Critique of Hegel's Philosophy of Right* and *The Economic and Philosophical Manuscripts* of 1844 and on to his historical analyses of the 1848 Revolution and his writings on the Paris Commune, and even to his (1875) *Critique of the Gotha Programme*. Is it not Marx who appeals to civil society and to the proletarian revolution against the dangerous and grotesque illusions of the Montagnards of 1849, against the majority of the Commune in 1871, and against Lasalle in 1875? However, beyond this essential critique of political illusion and revolutionary rhetoric, Marx remains entirely faithful to the revolutionary spirit; that is to say, to the critique of particular interests in the name of a totality, to that which the young Hegel called *schöne Totalität*. The very meaning of historical materialism is the elimination of every analysis couched in terms of social actors. What made it a major historical force is that it proclaims the revolutionary capacity of negativity, of the alienated proletariat. Nothing is more foreign to Marx and Marxism than the idea of the workers' movement. In that sense, it was Althusser who was right against the defenders, often Christians, of a Marxist humanism. Marx is not the defender of the rights and liberties of the workers, nor of social justice. He affirms, on the contrary, that absolute proletarianisation creates the agent (and not the actor) who makes manifest the contradictions of the system. If there are class struggles, struggles between historical actors, this can only be between governing classes or between fractions of governing classes, as Marx explained in particular with reference to the revolution in France in February 1848 where he saw the replacement of the finance bourgeoisie by the bourgoisie as a whole who were subsequently powerful enough to determine the form of the Republic. Revolutions lead neither to the domination of the proletariat nor to the creation of a workers' state, but to the dissolution of all classes, and thus of the state, in a reconciliation of society and nature, of objective and subjective, in a humanization of nature and a naturalization of human beings which allows simultaneously the complete blossoming of the individual and the triumph of reason.

History has shown that this conception of the actor, reduced to being the negation of the negation, leads to new forms of Jacobinism, to the absolute power of the revolutionary intellectuals who alone are capable of interpreting not the demands of actors but the natural movement of history, and who will guide it toward its inevitable entry into a world delivered from its contradictions. It is true that the Soviet revolution did not appeal to the nation but to the workers and peasants; it was not a patriotic revolution, but a proletarian one; however, the logic of communist regimes is the same as that of the Robespierrist regime: in both cases one can hear the same call to totality, to reason and to nature, against its enemies both without and within, leading to the same politics of exclusion, purges, and purifying executions.

Looking to other historical examples takes us no further. They all lead us to the same conclusion, and it is one which becomes all the more clearer the more rapid and radical is the revolutionary process concerned. A wealth of documents, emanating particularly from the participants, have shown for example at what point the Cultural Revolution of the Red Guards became merely an instrument at the service of the political faction in power. The same conclusion applies to the Ethiopian revolution.

Social revolution is a contradiction in terms, for the essence of revolution is that it imposes total power so that no part of society can be defined outside of its relations of sociality, domination, specialization or negotiation. The greatest political force of the twentieth century has been Marxism–Leninism, which is to say the fusion of the proletarian revolution with an anti-imperialist and anti-colonial national liberation. This constitutes a double rupture which dramatically reinforces the absolute power of the leaders of the revolution who refuse any autonomy to particular social actors. The closer one gets to the burning core of revolution, the more we find social actors consumed in its flames, and the more the logic of party and revolutionary state prevails over that of social actors with their interrelations and their conflicts.

4. The Capitalist Revolution

It is not as easy, although necessary, to show that the liberal conception of social change is close to the revolutionary model of modernization. Was not Karl Polanyi right to affirm that the key thing about the great transformation of the West was that it radically separated the world dominated by instrumental rationality from the rest of the social organization, with its political compromises, cultural traditions, national character, religious practices, all of which constituted so many forces of fragmentation, equilibrium, and resistance faced with the truly revolutionary power of reason transformed into technology, administrative organizations, calculations, interests and markets?

Liberals have in common with the other revolutionaries that they eliminate social actors and their relations and subsume the whole of social life under a central universal principle which, in this case as well, is defined as rational and natural. Can Marx's thought be understood if we do not see it first of all as a 'critique of political economy', which is to say a reinterpretation of the thought of the great English economists, of that vision therefore which reduced human beings to pieces of merchandise, for they sell not their labour but their labour power for the price of their biological reproduction.

The brutality of European industrialization relies upon the negation of all social actors. Political actors can wield influence only if they are quite precise with regard to the interests that they serve, and only if they are well aware of the economic logic which must fashion their actions, or, on the contrary, if they intervene in defence of the forces of resistance to modernization. Capitalism merits the adjective *revolutionary* which Marx gave it. What Weber analysed is not the formation of the modern rationalized economy and society, but more precisely the birth of the capitalist spirit in its truest sense, in other words the splitting apart of economic agents from their community and their roots, which would create an availability and absolute uncertainty leading to independence and the secularization of economic action which characterizes capitalism. This does not place one class in opposition to another; it imposes the absolute power of reason over those who would resist: over women driven by their nature and their passions, over children determined by their instincts, over idle workers hiding behind the walls of their corporatism, over ignorant and vicious colonials whom the administrators must drag and force into the modern way of life. The spirit of capitalism is not opposed to the revolutionary spirit; they belong to the same ensemble. What each is opposed to, as clearly in the one case as in the other, are those reformist modes of modernization — forms of political integrationism or religious fundamentalism — which may arise within nationalist and populist regimes. If the United States and other countries with a similar history of European colonization have not seemed susceptible to the revolutionary ethos, it is because the juridical consciousness of the New England colonists, the frontier spirit of new lands to conquer. and the incorporation of immigrants have all added to the originally European capitalist spirit. What has been added here is an opening-up and a will to look after their own affairs that the European countries have not sought. The colonial conquest, led by Europe, had opposite effects to the conquest of an open frontier: it did not transform the societies of origin.

5. The Swabian Peasantry in 1525

Weber's work is so clear in its explanation of the relations between economic modernity and the protestant ethic that we are able to supplement those revolutionary movements nourished by the Enlightenment with movements of religious revolution which while apparently dissimilar are actually closely related. The example of the Peasant War of 1525, which played such a central and lasting role in the history of the German nation and culture, readily shows this *rapprochement*. The great movement of secularization destroyed the complex equilibrium between spiritual and temporal power, pulling them apart. With Jules II, the papacy became a temporal power of the modern form, at the same time as Machiavelli theorized the state and politics apart from any religious reference, and, in parallel, as Christian eschatology became secular with Luther's idea that every man is a priest. This is the central theme of the dozen articles produced by the Swabian peasants in 1525, perhaps partly under the influence of Thomas Muntzer, but which nevertheless are in the same line as Luther who, some weeks later, in a display of dreadful viciousness, called upon the German princes to butcher these peasant revolutionaries. A peasant or an urban collectivity is like a church; it has to respond to the demands of its priests; it has a divine right. The peasant insurrection is by divine right just as much as is the power of the princes. Is not this theme of the people of God found across the centuries with the simultaneously revolutionary and fundamentalist spirit of those Latin American communities animated by liberation theology? Again therefore we see a revolutionary movement formed in conscience of the order of the world and the meaning of history. The demands of the peasants, which were not new and which over the course of a century gave rise to an uprising every three years, became revolutionary through this appeal to the divine law, to a principle as absolute as that of reason. Revolution always responds to the imperative of a law, punishing its adversaries with the same force as the sword of justice.

6. A Society without Actors

For actors to become revolutionary, they must abandon themselves to a law of nature which may also be a law of God. Hence the revolution demands sacrifices in the name of that biblical imperative to replenish the earth. It also follows that revolution is egalitarian. Revolutions are often associated with general crises of society, and particularly with military disasters. Is it not the case that Germany in 1918, and Russia in 1905 and 1918 demonstrate the force of the links between war, defeat and revolution? Reciprocally, war stimulates revolutionary energies, as the French and Soviet cases have shown. But in making these points, one defines only the negative conditions of revolution: crises of social controls and social institutions, and, more profoundly, the decomposition of social actors. Revolution, however, does not occur if the dissolution of actors is not accompanied by the formation of a commanding elite who can appeal to the truths of nature and history for a revolution even in the face of those actors and the crises that have broken them apart.

No society has been more favourable to the formation of revolutionary actions than capitalist society because it is not only positivistic and scientific, it has also destroyed occupations and guilds. Marx refused to recognize that skilled workers have a particular role despite the fact that in his time they formed the first unions. He saw skilled work as a combination of simple tasks, something which was essential to his intention to reduce the working class to that proletarian condition which, representing an absolute alienation, would trigger off the total liberation of humanity.

The nineteenth-century European, at once capitalist and revolutionary, had a dynamic conception of society. Lévi-Strauss was right to see the steam-engine as the symbol of a social mechanism functioning between poles of heat and cold, between the capitalist entrepreneurs and proletarianized workers.

The central feature of this society is its elimination of every reference to social actors. We speak of capitalists and workers, but the nineteenth century referred overwhelmingly to industry, capital, work, and the social question. As to the world of the worker, no one saw this world as providing a major social subject. Marx, like Smith and Ricardo, thought in systemic terms about the contradictions between the capitalist system and nature. He did not think that it would be the action of the workers which would reverse capitalism, but rather that it would be the developing contradiction between the forces and relations of production; and he saw communist society certainly not as a workers' society, but as a society of natural needs, as a return to use-value as against the reign of the commodity and interest. Society here is conceived like a machine or like an organism functioning in accordance with a basic logic of universal scope. For a long time, the representation of society left only a marginal, residual place to politics, and the Marxists, like the liberals, dreamed of the withering away of the state. Politics is here identified with the functioning of the capitalist system. It is not about the management of change or the elaboration of reforms; it is a principle of order. This is why political action functions in terms of all or nothing. If the notion of class has been so important in this type of society, it is because it defines the social or political actor by its place within a system of production, within the social machine or organism. *Stände*, and even more, castes are defined by a principle, whether religious or military, which is neither functional nor really social, only the third estate being defined, although very widely, in economic terms. Classes, on the contrary, have a definition which is purely functional and which does not refer to any other trait of behaviour, neither to such principles as honour or belief, nor to such aims as liberty, justice or the good life. It is not by chance that the notion of class is so vaguely defined in Marx, and that the text devoted to its definition is not merely incomplete but virtually empty. The thing is that Marx's analysis is not couched in terms of class, but in terms of relations between classes, or better still, in terms of the capitalist system. What is not reduced in Marx to the logic of capitalism is referred to the level of the universal, to human nature, to species-being and not to the project of a collective worker–actor.

Revolution and social movement are mutually incompatible notions. This statement may shock or even scandalize, such is the extent to which the European tradition has habitually identified the one with the other, or at least has seen them as closely associated. If we conceive a social movement to be, as the European tradition has defined it, the organized expression of a social conflict central to whose objectives are the social utilization of resources and cultural models, at the level of investment, knowledge and ethics, noting just what is most important, we introduce the image of two or more actors confronting each other in the name of their opposing interests, but sharing the same cultural model, such that each actor is defined negatively by their will to fight an adversary *and* positively by their will to be the agent of realization of cultural models. It is as if the industrialists and the workers' movement were fighting their adversary and affirming their mission as agents of progress at the same time, identifying themselves with work, production, energy, with, in other words, the cultural foundations of a society of production and technology. This vision has corresponded with real historical situations, as well as French and Irish syndicalist movements on the brink of the First World War, there was also the foundation by Samuel Gompers of the American Federation of Labour, which, reformist though it might have been, rested entirely on the idea of direct confrontation of employers and wage-earners. Now, in these cases, whether the actions are moderate or radical, these social movements are outside of the conception of revolution properly understood, both because they give priority to the taking of power over the transformation of the conditions of work, and above all because the revolutionary idea is about system and totality, while all social movements construe the world in terms of actors and conflicts. The principal author of the *Charter of Amiens*, V. Griffuelhes, provides a clear account of the underlying nature of direct action syndicalism: because France has long since achieved democratic institutions, he said in 1906, its syndicalism can devote itself to direct class struggle, without having to concern itself with the transformation of the state that has been already realized. Syndicalism was therefore, for him, not revolutionary, but post-revolutionary. It is always wrong to define a social movement as either reformist or revolutionary, for these words refer to a conception of social change, while a social movement is an actor in the interior of an economic and social system. This much is clearly shown by Marx, and even more by Lenin who mistrusted the syndicates because they were located within the, admittedly besieged, capitalist sector of Russian society, whereas the Party had to transform the general crisis of the regime into a revolution and a total transformation of the society. So one should hardly be astonished that the leaders of the workers' opposition are to be found among the first victims of the Leninist dictatorship.

This opposition between revolution and social movements appears within historical studies themselves. Marxist historians have produced numerous economic analyses, and one part of modern historiography, in particular the French Annales school, has eliminated political history in favour of a history of the *longue durée* which is more than anything a history of economic systems and international commerce. The passage from this economic history to social history has almost never been successful, as is shown by the failure of the French school of E. Labrousse. In a totally different spirit, there has been the development of a social history of the workers' movement, inspired above all by E.P. Thompson and by a number of young researchers, mostly English and American, whose inspiration is close to the sociology of social movements. On the one hand, we find a belief in the logic of the system, its formation, its functioning, and its downfall; on the other hand, we find a belief in a mixture of the traditional and the modern, of the economic and the communitary, of politics and religion, in the formation of political action.

7. Diachrony against Synchrony

These observations lead us to the most central definition of the revolutionary idea. A society will see itself in revolutionary — or counter-revolutionary — terms to the extent that its problems of historical mutation prevail over its problems of social functioning, more concretely today, to the extent that its difficulties of industrialization take precedence over the internal conflicts arising out of being an industrial society. Revolution is a notion which depends upon a diachronic analysis, whereas the social movement is a concept which is linked to synchronic analysis. However, a property of European society has been the belief that modernity was about pure movement: progress of the human spirit, development of production or of consumption. While it is true that this way of seeing things is not shared by everyone, nevertheless it does correspond both to revolutionary thought and to liberal ideology, whereas the social-democratic conception is based on the idea of the social movement, of conflict and of transforming that conflict into a means of economic growth through the enlargement of the internal market and the destruction of perquisites and privileges.

The liberal image of society, the idea of a constant flux, always diversified and never to be mastered, whether by internal or, above all, by external changes, belongs to the same ensemble as the idea of revolution. Whereas, the social-democratic politics of collective negotiation depends on another ensemble that might be referred to, following the English tradition from the Fabians to T.H. Marshall, as the construction of industrial democracy and a new citizenship. This social-democratic conception is strong exactly where the spirit of the Enlightenment has been relatively weak, where an enlightened bourgeoisie has not been strong enough to impose its conception of modernity as work, as destruction of the past, and as rationalization, and where it has only been possible to see modernity as the result of a voluntaristic effort of modernization. It is absolutely not paradoxical to say that the revolutionary spirit has always been associated with the presence of an executive group, be they intellectuals or pacesetters of the bourgeoisie, who identify themselves with science and the Enlightenment. Revolution is the other side of Enlightenment progressivism, just as populism is the other side of social-democracy. In the first ensemble, everything appears in terms of becoming and of historical laws; in the second, it is a question of concrete actors who are always more or less a people or a nation even at the same time that they are a class. Liberals and revolutionaries have in common that they do not think in terms of actors but in terms of the rationality of a system, whether it is a question of the laws of the market or of scientific socialism. Whereas social-democrats and populists, while opposed to each other just as much as liberals and revolutionaries are, have in common that they think in terms of the mobilization of actors, socially, culturally and nationally defined.

The revolutionary idea has obviously been most central in France, but also — and this may come as a surprise — this is true of Great Britain, Italy, Spain, and of the Latin-American countries, dominated by a secular, anti-clerical and freemasonic middle class, as it is of Germany, Japan and Turkey, whose modernization was directed by nationalist forces, or the Scandinavian countries, transformed in the 1930s by a voluntaristic social-democracy which created the most advanced industrial democracies. The Soviet Union was created by revolutionary intellectuals, heirs to the materialism stemming from the eighteenth century and from Marx, and they proceeded simultaneously to smash the revolutionary populism of the Socialist Revolutionary Party (SRP) and the social-democratic spirit of the Menshevik syndicates.

In a word, if social movements are actors within civil society, revolutions are located within the order of the state. If classes or other similar categories are some of the functioning elements of one type of society, they cannot be agents of historical mutation: how can capitalists create capitalism? It is therefore always the state which is the central agent of these mutations, and revolutionary action consists in seizing control of the state in order to direct the change, which is both a matter of historical necessity and of resisting pressures and invasions from the outside.

Today, at a time when post-revolutionary regimes are relaxing and renouncing their ambition to make a new society and a new social being, we can see to what little extent social and cultural behaviour has been changed, and with what force religious beliefs and national sentiment, cultural taste and patterns of work have for decades been resistant to a power which was only essentially that of the state apparatus. This explains the surprising ease with which a culturally free social life, laden with tradition, has been revived in those countries where a revolutionary fairy once anaesthetized both Beauty and the forest in which she lay.

The virtues that the leaders of the revolution call upon are the loyalty to the collectivity, the courage of the people, vigilance against traitors and enemies, and it is uncommon for a revolutionary mobilization not to provide itself quickly with a nationalist significance. When, however, national sentiment is strongly hostile to revolutionary power, as in Poland and some other countries, this power cannot reach down to sink into the roots of the society.

Revolution is the inverted image of a society, and the opposition between the logic of the social and the logic of revolution is inevitably developed to the point where revolutionary power loses all contact with the society. A *coup d'Etat* may then reverse the situation, as was the case with Thermidor; but, if this power establishes its hold over a long period, it may itself come to recognize, as the post-revolutionary Soviet regime is doing today, its inability to manage the economy, to appreciate the needs of the people, and to resist the abuses of bureaucracy. Revolutions are in their nature caught up in a spiral of radicalization and struggle against successive minorities, a spiral which transforms the power which speaks in the name of the majority into that of a minority, then a clan, and finally into personal power.

8. In Reply to a Limited Thesis

The analyses above are so far from the most current interpretation of revolution that we must ask why this conception has not been used up to this point. What exactly is it? It is that social demands are not in themselves revolutionary, but that they become so if the political institutions are incapable of responding to them, of adapting to them, and of integrating them into the systems of norms and forms of organization in force. In a word, it is not a matter of analysing revolution, but of questioning the institutional responses in the face of certain social demands. The force of this interpretation is that it shows how the same social demands, for example salary claims, may or may not become revolutionary depending upon the negotiating ability of the various enterprises and the state. If the door remains closed when one knocks, isn't it tempting to kick it open? The simplicity of this account is seductive, but it is extremely deficient. It can be understood that institutional obstruction can provoke violence or resignation, but why a revolution? It must be admitted that the nature of demands is such that the political system or its social adversaries absolutely cannot respond to them all positively. This would take us to an analysis of the demands and not merely to an analysis of the political response. While it is tempting to say that the more that protesters are violent in their methods and global in their aspirations, the more they will totally reject the established order or dominant value system, and the more engaged action will become revolutionary, this explication risks being tautological. How can we be sure that a contestation is total if not by its revolutionary outcome? But what in this thesis, above all, is contradicted by our observations above, and by many others is that revolutionary situations are most certainly not those where actors — classes or other social groups — confront each other directly. Such situations lead maybe to war, maybe to negotiation. Revolutionary situations are, on the contrary, those where actors are the most absent, where a commanding elite, in power or in opposition, calls not on active social forces but on natural or historical laws, on necessity rather than on will, for the property of revolutionary action is that it is undertaken in the name of actors who are absent or silent, whether they are considered to be exploited, alienated or colonized. As soon as we are within a schema of social demands and political responses, we are no longer in a revolutionary situation: grievances, occupations, and picketing, on the one side, redundancies and lock-outs, on the other, are not elements of a revolutionary scenario, but are merely violent forms of that tension which is inseparable from negotiation with employers or the exertion of pressure on the state. The violence which arises out of the absence of adequate institutional response still belongs to the reformist and transactional mode of social change, for the frontiers of what is acceptable are here placed continually in question, and no democracy can function solely by consensus or even by compromise; every situation has its violent aspect. Revolution belongs to another condition, one where not only do the partners not negotiate but where there are no partners, no contests, no institutional rules, where everything takes place between good and evil, between the national and the foreign, between life and death.

Revolution does not come from kicking down the door; it destroys the very building which is seen as an obstruction on a road which leads somewhere else. The domain of revolution, which is beyond that of violence, is entered when the social movement is replaced by its opposite, by what I have called a social anti-movement, in which actors are no longer defined by their conflictual relations with other actors, but by their rupture from each and by the negation of their existence as actors, so that every adversary becomes an enemy or a traitor, and where the objective is not the creation of a plurality, but of homogeneity and even purity. The revolutionary world is a world of essence, not of change, a world of war, not of politics.

To affirm that it is the degree to which institutions are open or closed which makes social demands revolutionary or not is naïvely to believe in the total power of institutions, as if a society were only a market, as if democracy had unlimited powers of intervention. Revolution begins with the negation of the other; it ends with the dissolution or destruction of those who proclaimed that negation, and it can only be followed by chaos or by an absolute power.

9. In Reply to an Opposed Thesis

The reply which I have just made can lead to a totally contrasting conception, but one which is opposed to everything in the analyses I have presented here. Are not the most recent revolutionary situations very different from the ones that I have described? Wouldn't we, here at the end of the twentieth century, spontaneously identify revolution as a movement of national liberation mobilized against the economic and political penetration of the West? Are not revolutions more anti-imperialist than anti-capitalist, and is it not this mutation which distinguishes Marxism–Leninism, or rather Leninism–Maoism, from the European Marxism prior to the Russian revolution? In brief, am I not the captive of an image of revolution which is both archaic, having its proper place in the nineteenth century, and Eurocentric?

Obviously, one can decide to use a word to designate one type or other of social phenomena without being made prisoner of the oldest traditions, but it ought at least to be recognized that many of the political upheavals which have been called revolutions have nothing in common with the European experience of revolution, and are even the very opposite of it. It is for this reason that I refer to them as *anti-revolutions*, which is not to deny certain revolutionary aspects that may be found in them.

The first of them, historically speaking, at least from among the most important political transformations, was the Mexican Revolution 1910–20. While the French revolution combined the destruction of an *ancien régime* with belief in progress and the formation of a nation founded upon universal principles, the Mexican revolution rejected a capitalist development which had been led by the secular and positivistic *Científicos*, advisers to President Porfirio Diaz, and which had been conducted largely to the profit of foreign capital, and exalted the idea of the *raza*, Mexico's own union of Mexican and Spanish. In its final phase, and during the 1920s, the revolution was influenced by the Russian revolution, with fluttering red flags a common sight, at the same time as an anti-religious and anti-clerical action was developing which ended by triggering off a veritable *Vendée*. But this revolution, despite its European aspects, was more particularist than universal, more populist and nationalist than rationalist, and its most active social component was the small peasantry of Morelos, mobilized by Zapata against the spreading exploitation of the capitalist sugar industry.

At the other end of the century, is not the Iranian revolution, here also, directed against the white revolution of Pahlevi and against the penetration of foreign capital? It depends upon the uprooted urban masses at the same time as upon the anti-Westernism of the intellectuals moulded by Chariati and other Islamic thinkers. In both cases, the appeal to a *Volk*, along German lines, is the opposite of the French or Soviet appeal to the nation and to the proletariat, and the resistance to imperialism is the opposite of the progressivism of the Jacobins or the Marxists. The construction or re-birth of a national identity, as a defence against foreign penetration and imperialism rather than as an expression of confidence in the development of the forces of production, the role of the state as an agent of integration rather than of modernization, these are so many characteristics which distinguish these anti-revolutions from revolutions properly so called, or, if one objects to this vocabulary, which underline the difference in nature between revolutions of the French or Soviet type and those of the Mexican or Iranian type.

In the immense space which separates revolutions from anti-revolutions, the overthrowing of ancient regimes in the name of progress from the reconstruction of stolen identities, we find those mixed, complex and confused cases which mingle Marxism and populism, belief in the future with the cult of the past. Nasser's revolution, in Egypt, was marked across its whole range by the combination and conflict of Arab nationalism and Marxist universalism. The Latin-American revolutionaries have been less constant in associating populism and anti-imperialism, vacillating continually between guerilla movements, which are far from revolutionary since there is no question of mass mobilization, and great populist alliances such as the one that the Brazilian Communist Party accepted in 1945 which accorded priority to the campaign for the return of Getulio Vargas over the class struggle. But can we understand these revolutions which, like Janus, look out in two opposite directions, without first referring them to the insurmountable opposition between those revolutions which submit to the laws of history and those which bend history to their need for identity?

10. After the Revolutions

We have left behind the era of revolutions as analogously defined by the Marxist, Eric Hobsbawm, and the liberal, Francois Furet. But the multiplicity of exit routes should make us better understand the revolutionary phenomenon in its historical reality. For there are at least three great types of socio-political regime which have been bequeathed to us by the revolutionary period.

The first is the triumph of the capitalist system, which is to say the strengthening of a social and economic system, based on the rational defence of interests and their negotiated combination, which dissolves its virtual actors — classes or interest groups — in the changing life of the economic or political marketplace. A century after the death of Marx, the capitalist economy has prospered, the bourgeoisie has been superseded by shifting levels of capital and of decision-making, and class-based parties grow weak throughout Europe, even in Italy where the Communist Party is drawn to Euro-leftism.

A second post-revolutionary outcome is the formation of social movements and the organization of collective agreements, reinforced by social laws, and which lead to the creation of a redistributive Welfare State. The theme of social justice and of the redistribution of income through taxation and systems of social security is inseparable from that of social struggle, and it is the unions who have been, in Great Britain as in France, the principal agents behind the creation of the first systems of social security. In the course of the twentieth century, the workers' movement, after having reached its height, in the 1920s in Great Britain, in the 1930s in the United States, Sweden and France, in the 1960s in Italy, has little by little been absorbed by the political system, in which the unions have become important actors. But new social movements are formed in response to the rapidly growing power of the culture-industries. These movements, however, increasingly get rid of the revolutionary references which had once been upheld in the workers' movement. Those attempts, important during the 1970s, to relocate these new social movements in the line of thought and revolutionary action inherited from the nineteenth century, led throughout to complete failure.

In a word, revolutions have been reversed, as we have seen, into anti-revolutions, as they travel the whole of that line which separates English and French evolutionism from the German historicism of the end of the eighteenth century.

The revolutionary era was the common trunk of the modern world, necessary for entry into that world. Wherever the breath of revolution has not been felt and the hope is maintained of linking the future and the past without discontinuity, by a movement of progressive torsion, leading finally to a society set apart from its traditions without losing them, the effect of this has not really been the introduction of modernity, but its peripheralization as something which has always seemed foreign.

The history of the twentieth century has been dominated by attempts to avoid revolution and by the violent refusal of the Western model of the *tabula rasa*. By mid-century, these attempts seemed to have succeeded; ideas of modernization and development had shattered into a thousand pieces with nationalisms liberating themselves from the colonial system, each searching for their proper vision of a modernity which is everywhere different. But the century comes to an end on the ruins of these efforts. At the moment when all socialisms are renouncing their hopes and when the nationalisms are choking on their refusals, exhausted in the face of the power of the central economies, it seems that only one model of modernization has conquered the world, the Western model. Are we witnessing, then, the triumph of the capitalist revolution? Such an impression would be mistaken, for the revolutionary, rationalist model is as exhausted as the nationalist and culturalist models of development. We have to renounce, throughout all parts of the world, the idea that one unique principle is enough to move a society, whether that principle is rationalist or nationalist, materialist or voluntarist. For development is always a combination of the universalism of reason and the particularism of a historical mode of mobilization of economic and social resources. The West believed in the total power of reason, and the revolutionaries shared that belief and illusion with the liberals. Elsewhere, populists and nationalists held that the collective will and the mobilization of a culture would provide entry for their country into modernity. Their error was the reverse of that of the West, but was still deep for all that. For Western rationalism impeded the formation of social actors, of cultural resistance, and of the political process to a lesser extent than communist or Third World voluntarism set itself against the requirements of rationality. The presence of the fact of revolution in the heart of the Western rationalist model is more visible and more effective than the presence of pockets of technical rationality — often managed by foreigners — in the core of voluntarist regimes.

The combination of instrumental reason and national and cultural mobilization is everywhere indispensable and everywhere difficult. It is at the point that the West ceased to mobilize culturally, at the moment when Enlightenment rationalism had won its long battle with religion, that the revolutions burst. Has not the struggle against religion always been at the centre of every revolution? It is at this point that we encounter the triumph of the idea of rational society, to which the left opposition, in the aftermath of the Soviet revolution, gave the form of a great central planning machine. It is against this revolutionary rationalism that the demand economy which led to mass consumption, social movements as well as rejecting the identification of social life with the power of a commanding elite who equate themselves with rationality, have struggled. The whole evolution of Western societies has consisted in covering over that blank sheet, supposedly the surface upon which would be inscribed the great calculus of reason, with a multiplicity of memories and projects, conflicts and compromises. Those countries which have not been through revolution, and which have often been led by a political or even military elite, whether communist parties installed by the Red Army or post-colonial military dictatorships, must abandon some of their cherished memories and projects, to allow them to seize the future from the past in a way that is both rationalist and revolutionary, and, just as importantly, so that they can distinguish both the general problem to be resolved — the installation of modernity — and the solution appropriate to their historical situation, which is to say the mix of rationalism and culture, of universalism and particularism which enables the creation of a modern society at once similar to and yet always different from the others.

The era of revolutions is over, as is that of their converse, cultural nationalism. Every country must find a particular combination of modern rationalism and the specificity of a mode of mobilization of historically determined resources. If this is not found, they will be led towards violence in all its forms and into the corruption of development, whether their society becomes enclosed in an 'iron cage' of technology without any socio-cultural rationale, or whether it will be delivered up into the arbitrary power of princes and priests who are contemptuous of rationality. Avoidance of these two parallel forms of decomposition, of Dr Strangelove on the one hand and the Ayatollahs on the other, means that societies have to understand themselves not as having to chose between economic and political revolution and one form or other of populism, but in terms of finding the most certain middle way possible between submission to reason and the creation of an open society which recognizes both social conflicts and the links that unite the past to the future.

Today it is not possible just to be revolutionary, or liberal, or even nationalist. We must learn to reduce the distance between these apparently contradictory but actually complementary elements of development.

Note

This paper was first presented at the Amalfi Prize for European Sociology and Social Science Conference, Amalfi, May 1989, at which Serge Moscovici was awarded the prize. It has been translated by Roy Boyne.

Alain Touraine is Director of the Centre d'Analyse et d'Intervention Sociologiques, Paris.

Modernity and Ambivalence

Zygmunt Bauman

There are friends and enemies. And there are *strangers*.

Friends and enemies stand in an opposition to each other. The first are what the second are not, and vice versa. Which does not, however, testify to their equal status. Like most other oppositions which order simultaneously the world in which we live and our life in the world, this one is a variation of the master-opposition between the inside and the outside. The outside is negativity to the inside's positivity. The outside is what the inside is not. The enemies are the negativity to the friends' positivity. The enemies are what the friends are not. The enemies are flawed friends; they are the wilderness which violates friends' homeliness, the absence which is a denial of friends' presence. The repugnant and frightening 'out there' of the enemies is, as Derrida would say, a supplement: both the addition to, and displacement of the cosy and comforting 'in here' of the friends. Only by crystallizing and solidifying what they are not, or what they do not wish to be, or what they would not say they are into the counter-image of the enemies, may the friends assert what they are, what they want to be and what they want to be thought as being.

Apparently, there is a symmetry: there would be no enemies were there no friends, and there would be no friends unless for the yawning abyss of enmity outside. Symmetry, however, is an illusion. It is the friends who define the enemies. It is the friends who control the classification and the assignment. The opposition is an achievement and self-assertion of the friends. It is the product and the condition of friends' narrative domination, of the friends narrative as the domination.

The rift between friends and enemies makes *vita contemplativa* and *vita activa* into mirror reflections of each other. More importantly, it guarantees their co-ordination. Subjected to the same principle of structuration, knowledge and action chime in unison,

Theory, Culture & Society (SAGE, London, Newbury Park and New Delhi), Vol. 7 (1990), 143–169

so that knowledge may inform the action and the action may confirm the truth of knowledge.

The friends/enemies opposition sets apart truth from falsity, good from evil, beauty from ugliness. It also sets apart proper and improper, right and wrong, tasteful and unbecoming. It makes the world readable and thereby instructive. It dispels doubt. It enables one to go on. It assures that one goes where one should. It makes the choice look like nature-made necessity — so that man-made necessity may be immune to the vagaries of choice.

Friends are reproduced by the pragmatics of co-operation, enemies by the pragmatics of struggle. Friends are called into being by responsibility and moral duty. The friends are those for whose well-being I am responsible before they reciprocate and regardless of their reciprocation; only on this condition the co-operation, ostensibly a contractual, two-directional bond, can come into effect. Responsibility must be a gift if it is ever to become an exchange. Enemies, on the other hand, are called into being by renunciation of responsibility and moral duty. The enemies are those who refuse responsibility for my well-being before I relinquish my responsibility for theirs, and regardless of my renunciation; only on this condition the struggle, ostensibly a two-sided enmity and reciprocated hostile action, may come into effect. Though anticipation of friendliness is not necessary for the construction of friends, anticipation of enmity is indispensable in the construction of enemies. Thus the opposition between friends and enemies is one between doing and suffering, between being a subject and being an object of action. It is an opposition between reaching out and recoiling, between initiative and vigilance, ruling and being ruled, acting and responding.

With all the opposition between them, or — rather — *because* of that opposition, both sides of the opposition stand for relationships. Following Simmel, we may say that friendship and enmity, and only they, are forms of sociation; indeed, the archetypal forms of all sociation, the two-pronged matrix of sociation. Between themselves, let us add, they make the frame within which sociation is possible, they make for the possibility of 'being with others'. Being a friend, and being an enemy, are the two forms in which the other may be recognized as another subject, construed as a 'subject like the self', admitted into the self's life-world, be counted, become and stay relevant. If not for the opposition between friend and enemy, none of this would be possible. Without the possibility of breaking the bond of responsibility, no responsibility would impress itself as a duty. If not for the enemies, there would be no friends. Without the possibility of difference, says Derrida (1974:143), 'the desire of presence as such would not find its breathing space. That means by the same token that the desire carries in itself the destiny of its non-satisfaction. Difference produces what it forbids, making possible the very thing that it makes impossible.'

Against this cosy antagonism, this conflict-torn collusion of friends and enemies, the stranger rebels. The threat he carries is more awesome than that which one can fear from the enemy. The stranger threatens the sociation itself — the very possibility of sociation. He calls the bluff of the opposition between friends and enemies as the compleate mappa mundi, as the difference which consumes all differences and hence leaves nothing outside itself. As that opposition is the foundation on which all social life and all differences which patch and hold it together rest, the stranger saps social life itself. And all this because the stranger is neither friend nor enemy; and because he may be both. And because we do not know, and have no way of knowing, which is the case.

The stranger is one (perhaps the main one, the archetypal one) member of the family of undecidables — those baffling yet ubiquitous unities that, in Derrida's (1981a: 71) words again, 'can no longer be included within philosophical (binary) opposition, resisting and disorganizing it, without ever constituting a third term, without ever leaving room for a solution in the form of speculative dialectics'. Here are a few examples of 'undecidables' discussed by Derrida:

The *pharmakon*: the Greek generic term which includes both remedies and poisons, used in Plato's *Phaedrus* as a simile for writing, and for this reason indirectly responsible — through the translations which aimed at eschewing its inherent ambiguity — for the direction taken by the post-Platonian Western metaphysics. *Pharmakon*, as it were, is 'the regular, ordered polysemy that has, through skewing, indetermination, or overdetermination, but without mistranslation, permitted the rendering of the same word by "remedy", "recipe", "poison", "drug", "filter" etc.' (Derrida, 1981a: 99). Because of this capacity, *pharmakon* is, first and foremost, powerful because ambivalent and ambivalent because powerful: 'It partakes of both good and ill, of the agreeable and disagreeable (Derrida, 1981b: 99). *Pharmakon*, after all, 'is neither remedy nor poison, neither good or evil, neither the inside nor the outside'.

The *hymen*: a Greek word again, standing for both membrane

and marriage, which for this reason signifies at the same time the virginally uncompromising difference between the 'inside' and the 'outside', and its violation by the fusion of self and other. In the result, *hymen* is 'neither confusion nor distinction, neither identity nor difference, neither consummation nor virginity, neither the veil nor the unveiling, neither the inside nor the outside, etc.'.

The *supplement*: in French, this word stands for both an addition, and a replacement. It is, therefore, the other that 'joins in', the outside that enters the inside, the difference that turns into identity. In the result, the *supplement* 'is neither a plus nor a minus, neither an outside nor the complement of an inside, neither accident nor essence, etc.' (Derrida, 1981b: 42–3).

Undecidables are all *neither/nor*, that is, simultaneously, *either/or*. Their underdetermination is their potency: because they are nothing, they may be all. They put paid to the ordering power of the opposition. Oppositions enable knowledge and action; undecidables paralyze. They brutally expose the fragility of a most secure of separations. They bring the outside into the inside, and poison the comfort of order with suspicion of chaos.

This is exactly what the strangers do.

The Horror of Indetermination

Cognitive (classificatory) clarity is a reflection, an intellectual equivalent of behavioural certainty. They arrive and depart together. How closely they are tied, we learn in a flash when landing in a foreign country, listening to a foreign language, gazing at foreign conduct. The hermeneutic problems which we then confront offer a first glimpse of the awesome behavioural paralysis which follows the failure of classificatory ability. To understand, as Wittgenstein suggested, is to know how to go on. This is why hermeneutical problems (which arise when the meaning is not unreflectively evident) are experienced as annoying. Unresolved hermeneutical problems mean uncertainty as to how the situation ought to be read and what response is likely to bring the desired results. At best, uncertainty is felt as discomforting. At worst, it carries a sense of danger.

Much of the social organization can be interpreted as sedimentation of a systematic effort to reduce the frequency with which hermeneutical problems are encountered and to mitigate the vexation such problems cause once faced. Probably the most common is the method of territorial and functional separation. Were this method applied in full and with maximum effect, hermeneutical problems would diminish as the physical distance shrinks and the scope and frequency of interaction grow. The chance of misunderstanding would not materialize, or would cause but a marginal disturbance when it occurs, if the principle of separation, the consistent 'restriction of interaction to sectors of assumed common understanding and mutual interest' (Barth, 1969: 15), were meticulously observed.

The method of territorial and functional separation is deployed both outwardly and inwardly. Persons who need to cross into a territory where they are bound to cause and to encounter hermeneutic problems actively seek enclaves marked for the use of visitors and the services of functional mediators. The tourist countries, which expect a constant influx of large quantities of 'culturally undertrained' visitors, set aside such enclaves and train such mediators in anticipation.

Territorial and functional separation is both a reflection of existing hermeneutical problems and a most powerful factor in their perpetuation and reproduction. With segregation continuous and closely guarded, there is little chance that the probability of misunderstanding (or at least the anticipation of such misunderstanding) will ever diminish. Persistence and constant possibility of hermeneutic problems can be seen therefore as simultaneously the motive and the product of boundary-drawing efforts. As such, they have an in-built tendency to self-perpetuation. As boundary-drawing is never foolproof and some boundary-crossing is difficult to avoid — hermeneutic problems are likely to persist as a permanent 'grey area' surrounding the familiar world of daily life. That grey area is inhabited by unfamiliars; the not-yet classified, or rather classified by criteria similar to ours, but as yet unknown to us.

The 'unfamiliars' come in a number of kinds, of unequal consequence. One pole of the range is occupied by those who reside in *practically* remote (that is, rarely visited) lands, and are thereby limited in their role to setting the limits of familiar territory (the *ubi leones*, written down as danger warnings on the outer boundaries of the Roman maps). Exchange with such unfamiliars is set aside from the daily routine and normal web of interaction as a function of special category of people (say, commercial travellers, diplomats or ethnographers), or a special occasion for the rest. Both (territorial and functional) means of institutional separation easily protect — indeed, reinforce — the unfamiliarity of the unfamiliars, together with their daily irrelevance. They also guard, though obliquely, the secure homeliness of own territory. Contrary to widespread opinion, the advent of television, this huge and easily accessible peephole through which the unfamiliar ways may be routinely glimpsed, has neither eliminated the institutional separation nor diminished its effectivity. McLuhan's 'global village' has failed to materialize. The frame of a cinema or TV screen staves off the danger of spillage more effectively still than tourist hotels and fenced off camping sites; the one-sidedness of communication further entrenches the unfamiliars on the screen as, essentially, incommunicado. The most recent invention of 'thematic' shopping malls, with Carribean villages, Indian reserves and Polynesian shrines closely packed together under one roof, has brought the old technique of institutional separation to the level of perfection reached in the past only by the zoo.

The phenomenon of strangehood cannot be, however, reduced to the generation of — however vexing — hermeneutic problems. Insolvency of the learned classification is upsetting enough, yet perceived as something less than a disaster as long as it can be referred to a missing knowledge: if only I learned that language; if only I studied those strange customs. . . . By themselves, hermeneutic problems do not undermine the trust in knowledge and attainability of behavioural certainty. If anything, they reinforce both. The way in which they define the remedy as learning another method of classification, another set of oppositions and meanings of another set of symptoms, only corroborates the faith in essential orderliness of the world and particularly in the ordering capacity of knowledge. A dose of puzzlement is pleasurable, as it resolves in the comfort of reassurance. This, as any tourist knows, is a major part of the attraction held by foreign trips, the more exotic the better. The difference is something one can live with. The different is not really different. 'There' is like 'here' — just another orderly world inhabited by either friends or enemies with no hybrids to distort the picture and perplex the action.

The strangers are not, however, the 'as-yet-undecided'; they are, in principle, undecidables. They are that 'third element' which should not be. The true hybrids, the monsters: not just unclassified, but unclassifiable. They therefore do not question this one opposition here and now: they question oppositions as such, the very principle of the opposition, the plausibility of dichotomy it suggests. They unmask the brittle artificiality of division — they destroy the world. They stretch the temporary inconvenience of 'not knowing how to go on' into a terminal paralysis. They must be tabooed, disarmed, suppressed, exiled physically or mentally — or the world may perish.

Territorial and functional separation cease to suffice once the mere unfamiliar turns to be the stranger, aptly described by Simmel (1971: 143) as 'the man who comes today and stays tomorrow'. The stranger is, indeed, someone who refuses to stay in the 'far away' land or go away and hence a priori defies the easy expedient of spatial or temporal segregation. The stranger comes into the life-world and settles here, and so — unlike in the case of mere 'unfamiliars', it becomes relevant whether he is a friend or a foe. He made his way into the life-world uninvited, thereby casting me on the receiving side of his initiative, making me into the object of action of which he is the subject — all this being a notorious mark of the enemy. Yet, unlike other, 'straightforward' enemies, he is not kept at a secure distance, not on the other side of the battle line. Worse still, he claims a right to be an object of responsibility — the well known attribute of the friend. If we press upon him the friend/enemy opposition, he'd come out simultaneously under and over-determined. And thus, by proxy, he'd expose the failing of the opposition itself. He is a constant threat to the world order.

Not for this reason only, though. There are more. For instance, the unforgettable and hence unforgivable original sin of the late entry: the fact that he had entered the realm of the life-world at a point of time which can be exactly determined. He did not belong 'initially', 'originally', 'from the very start', 'since time immemorial'. The memory of the event of his coming makes of his very presence an event in history, rather than a fact of nature. His passage from the first to the second would infringe on an important boundary in the map of existence and is all the more impossible for being resolutely resisted; such a passage would amount, after all, to the admission that nature is itself an event in history and that, therefore, the appeals to natural order or natural rights deserve no preferential treatment. Being an event in history, having a beginning, the presence of the stranger always carries the potential of an end. The stranger has a freedom to go. He may be also forced to go — or at least forcing him to go may be contemplated without violating the order of things. However protracted, the stay of the stranger is temporary — another infringement on the division which ought to be kept intact and preserved in the name of secure, orderly existence.

Even here, however, the treacherous incongruity of the stranger does not end. The stranger undermines the spatial ordering of the world: the fought-after co-ordination between moral and topographical closeness, the staying-together of friends and the remoteness of enemies. The stranger disturbs the resonance between physical and psychical distance — he is physically near while remaining spiritually remote. He brings into the inner circle of proximity the kind of difference and otherness that are anticipated and tolerated only at a distance — where they can be either dismissed as irrelevant or repelled as inimical. The stranger represents an incongruous and hence resented 'synthesis of nearness and remoteness' (Simmel, 1971: (45)). His presence is a challenge to the reliability of orthodox orientation points and the universal tools of order-making. His proximity (as all proximity, according to Levinas [1982: 95–101]) suggests a moral relationship, while his remoteness (as all remoteness, according to Erasmus, [1974: 74, 87]) permits solely a contractual one: another important opposition compromised.

As always, the practical incongruity follows the conceptual one. The stranger who refuses to go gradually transforms his temporary abode into a home territory — all the more so as his other, 'original' home recedes in the past and perhaps vanishes altogether. On the other hand, however, he retains (if only in theory) his freedom to go and so is able to view local conditions with an equanimity the native residents can hardly afford. Hence another incongruous synthesis — this time between involvement and indifference, partisanship and neutrality, detachment and participation. The commitment the stranger declares cannot be trusted, as it comes complete with a safety valve of easy escape which most natives often envy yet seldom possess.

The stranger's unredeemable sin is, therefore, the incompatibility between his presence and other presences, fundamental to the world order; his simultaneous assault on several crucial oppositions instrumental in the incessant effort of ordering. It is this sin which rebounds in the constitution of the stranger as the bearer and embodiment of incongruity; indeed, the stranger is a person afflicted with incurable sickness of multiple incongruity. He may well serve as the archetypal example of Sartre's *le visquex* or Mary Douglas's the slimy — an entity sitting astride an embattled barricade (or, rather, a substance spilled over the top of it and making it slippery both ways), blurring a boundary line vital to the construction of a particular social order or a particular life-world. No binary classification deployed in the construction of order can fully overlap with essentially non-discrete, continuous experience of reality. The opposition, born of the horror of ambiguity, becomes the main source of ambivalence. The enforcement of any classification means inevitably production of anomalies (this is, phenomena which are perceived as 'anomalous' only as far as they span the categories whose staying apart is the meaning of the order). Thus 'any given culture must confront events which seem to defy its assumptions. It cannot ignore the anomalies which its scheme produces, except at risk of forfeiting confidence' (Douglas, 1966: 39). There is hardly an anomaly more anomalous then the stranger. He stands between friend and enemy, order and chaos, the inside and the outside. He stands for the treacherousness of friends, for the cunning of enemies, for fallibility of order, penetrability of the inside.

Fighting Indeterminacy

Of the pre-modern, small-scale communities which for most of its members were the universe in which the whole of the life-world was inscribed, it is often said that they had been marked by dense sociability. This shared verdict is however variously interpreted. Most commonly, 'dense sociability' is misinterpreted as a Toennies-style intimacy, spiritual resonance and disinterested cooperation; in other words, as friendship with no, or with suppressed, enmity. Friendship, however, is not the only form of sociation; enmity performs the function as well. Indeed, friendship and enmity constitute together that framework inside which the sociation becomes possible and comes about. The 'dense sociability' of the past strikes us, in retrospect, as distinct from our own condition not because it contained more friendship than we tend to experience in our own world, but because its world was tightly and almost completely filled with friends and enemies — and friends and enemies only. Little room, and if any then a marginal room only, was left in the life-world for the poorly defined strangers. Thus the semantic and behavioural problems the friends/enemies opposition cannot but generate arose but seldom and were dealt with quickly and efficiently in the duality of ways the opposition legitimized. Community effectively defended its dense sociability by promptly reclassifying the few strangers coming occasionally into its orbit as either friends or enemies. Ostensibly a temporary station, strangehood did not present a serious challenge to the neat and solid duality of the world.

All supra-individual groupings are first and foremost processes of collectivization of friends and enemies. The lines dividing friends from enemies are co-ordinated, so that many individuals share their friends and their enemies. More exactly, individuals sharing a common group or category of enemies treat each other as friends. For communities characterized by 'dense sociability', this was the whole story, or almost a whole story. And this could remain the whole story as long as reclassifying strangers into one of the two opposite categories of either friends or enemies was easy and within the community power.

The last condition is not, however, met in modern urban environment. The latter is marked by the divorce between physical density and dense sociability. Aliens appear inside the confines of the life-world and refuse to go away (though one can hope that they will in the end). This new situation does not stem necessarily from the increased restlessness and mobility. As a matter of fact, it is the mobility itself which arises from the state-enforced 'uniformization' of vast spaces — much too large for being assimilated and domesticated by old methods of mapping and ordering deployed by individuals. The new aliens are not visitors, those stains of obscurity on the transparent surface of daily reality, which one can bear with as long as one hopes that they will be washed off tomorrow (though one can still be tempted to do this right way). They do not wear swords; nor do they seem to hide daggers in their cloaks (though one cannot be sure). They are not like the enemies one knows of. Or at least that is what they pretend. However, they are not like the friends either.

One meets friends at the other side of one's responsibility. One meets enemies (if at all) at the point of the sword. There is no clear rule about meeting the strangers. Intercourse with the strangers is always an incongruity. It stands for the incompatibility of the rules the confused status of the stranger invokes. It is best not to meet strangers at all. Now, when one cannot really avoid the space they occupy or share, the next best solution is the meeting which is not quite meeting, a meeting pretending not be one, a (to borrow Buber's term) mismeeting (*Vergegnung*, as distinct from meeting, *Begegnung*). The art of mismeeting is first and foremost a set of techniques of de-ethicalizing the relationship with the other. Its overall effect is a denial of the stranger as a moral object and a moral subject. Or, rather, exclusion of such situations as can accord the stranger moral significance. This, however, is a poor substitute for the ideal perhaps lost, but at any rate now unattainable: when the opposition between friends and enemies is not challenged at all, and thus the integrity of the life-world can be sustained with the simple semantic and behavioural dichotomies operated matter-of-factly by community members.

Like all the other self-perpetuating social groupings, both territorial and non-territorial, the national states collectivize friends and enemies. In addition to this universal function, however, they also eliminate the strangers; or at least they attempt to do so. Nationalist ideology — says John Breuilly (1982: 343) — 'is neither an expression of national identity (at least, there is no rational way of showing that to be the case) nor the arbitrary invention of nationalists for political purposes. It arises out of the need to make sense of complex social and political arrangements.' What has to be made sense of in the first place, and thus become 'livable with', is a situation in which the traditional, tested dichotomy of friends and enemies cannot be applied matter-of-factly and has been therefore compromised — as a poor guide to the art of living. *The national state is designed primarily to deal with the problem of strangers, not enemies.* It is precisely this feature that sets it apart from other supra-individual social arrangements.

Unlike tribes, the nation-state extends its rule over a territory before it claims the obedience of people. If the tribes can assure the needed collectivization of friends and enemies through the twin processes of attraction and repulsion, self-selection and self-segregation, territorial national states must enforce the friendship where it does not come about by itself. National states must artificially rectify the failures of nature (to create by design what nature failed to achieve by default). In the case of the national state, collectivization of friendship requires conscious effort and force. Among the latter, the mobilization of solidarity with an imagined community (the apt term proposed by Benedict Anderson [1983]), and the universalization of cognitive/behavioural patterns associated with friendship inside of the boundaries of the realm, occupy the pride of place. The national state re-defines friends as natives; it commands to extend the rights ascribed 'to the friends only' to all — the familiar as much as the unfamiliar — residents of the ruled territory. And vice versa, it grants the residential rights only if such an extension of friendship rights is desirable (though desirability is often disguised as 'feasibility'). This is why nationalism seeks the state. This is why the state spawns nationalism. This is why for the duration of the modern era, now two centuries old, nationalism without the state has been as flawed and ultimately impotent as state without nationalism — to the point of one being inconceivable without the other.

It has been stressed repeatedly in all analyses of modern states that they 'attempted to reduce or eliminate all loyalties and divisions within the country which might stand in the way of national unity' (Schafer, 1955: 119). National states promote 'nativism' and construe their subjects as 'natives'. They laud and enforce the ethnic, religious, linguistic, cultural homogeneity. They are engaged in incessant propaganda of shared attitudes. They construct joint historical memories and do their best to discredit or suppress such stubborn memories as cannot be squeezed into shared tradition. They preach the sense of common mission, common fate, common destiny. They breed, or at least legitimize and give tacit support to animosity towards everyone standing outside the holy union (Alter, 1989: 7ff.). In other words, national states promote uniformity. Nationalism is a religion of friendship; national state is the church which forces the prospective flock into submission. The state-enforced homogeneity is the practice of nationalist ideology.

In Boyd C. Shafer (1955: 121) witty comment, 'patriots had to be made. Nature was credited with much by the eighteenth century, but it could not be trusted to develop men unassisted.' Nationalism was a programme of social engineering, and the national state was to be its factory. National state was cast from the start in the role of a collective gardener, set about the task of cultivating sentiments and skills otherwise unlikely to grow. In his addresses of 1806 Fichte wrote

> The new education must consist essentially in this, that it completely destroys freedom of will in the soil which it undertakes to cultivate, and produces, on the contrary, strict necessity in the decision of will, the opposite being impossible. . . . If you want to influence him at all, you must do more than merely talk to him; you must fashion him, and fashion him, and fashion him in such a way that he simply cannot will otherwise than you wish him to will. (quoted in Kedouri, 1960: 83)

And Rousseau advised the Polish king on the way to manufacture Poles (at a distance, the 'man as such' was better seen in his true quality of the national patriot):

It is education that must give souls a national formation, and direct their opinions and tastes in such a way that they will be patriotic by inclination, by passion, by necessity. When first he opens his eyes, an infant ought to see the fatherland, and up to the day of his death he ought never to see anything else. . . . At twenty, a Pole ought not to be a man of any other sort; he ought to be a Pole. . . . The law ought to regulate the content, the order and the form of their studies. They ought to have only Poles for teachers. (1953: 176–7)

Were the national state able to reach its objective, there would be no strangers left in the life-world of the residents-turned-natives-turned-patriots. There would be but natives, who are friends, and the foreigners, who are current or potential enemies. The point is, however, that no attempt to assimilate, transform, acculturate, or absorb the ethnic, religious, linguistic, cultural and other heterogeneity and dissolve it in the homogeneous body of the nation has been thus far unconditionally successful. Melting pots were either myths or failed projects. The strangers refused to split neatly into 'us' and 'them', friends and foes. Stubbornly, they remained hauntingly indeterminate. Their number and nuisance power seem to grow with the intensity of dichotomizing efforts. As if the strangers were an 'industrial waste' growing in bulk with every increase in the production of friends and foes; a phenomenon brought into being by the very assimilatory pressure meant to destroy it. The point-blank assault on the strangers had to be from the start aided, reinforced and supplemented by a vast array of techniques meant to make a long-term, perhaps permanent, cohabitation with strangers possible. And it was.

Assimilation, or the War against Ambivalence

Literally, assimilation means making alike. Some time in the seventeenth century the reference field of the term had been stretched, to embrace its at present most familiar and common social uses. Since then, the concept began to be applied freely and widely. Like other terms born of the novel experience of rising modernity and naming heretofore unnamed practices, it sharpened contemporary eyes to previously unnoticed aspects of distant times and places. The processes the new term tried to capture were now, retrospectively, postulated, sought, found and documented in past societies whose consciousness contained neither the concept nor the visions it awoke. A conscious, historically framed action has been, so to speak, 'dehistoricized', and envisaged as a universal process, characteristic of all social life. It suddenly seemed that everywhere and at all times differences between the ways human beings behave tend to disappear or at least blur; that whenever and wherever human beings of distinct habits lived close to each other, they would tend, with the passage of time, to become more like each other; some habits would gradually give way to others, so that more uniformity will result. This understanding stood in a stark contradiction to the quite recent and previously unquestioned, but now rapidly suppressed and forcibly forgotten, pre-modern practice which accepted the permanence of differentiation, considered 'sticking to one's kin' a virtue, penalized emulation and boundary-crossing — and on the whole viewed the differences with equanimity as a fact of life calling for no more remedial action than spring storms or winter snows.

If the metaphorical origin of the term 'culture' has been amply documented, the same is not true of the concept of assimilation. This is regrettable, as the beginnings of modern uses of 'assimilation' provide a unique key to the sociological hermeneutics of the term, i.e. to the disclosure of such strategies of social action as originally sought expression in the borrowed trope, only to hide later behind its new 'naturalized' interpretations; and of such aspects of those strategies as made the borrowed term 'fit' in the first place. We learn from the OED that the earliest recorded use of the term 'assimilation', which preceded the later metaphorical applications by a century, was biological. In the biological narrative of the sixteenth century (OED records 1578 as the date of the first documented use) the term 'assimilation' referred to the acts of absorption and incorporation performed by living organisms. Unambiguously, 'assimilation' stood for conversion, not a self-administered change; an action performed by living organism on its passive environment. It meant 'to convert into a substance of its own nature'; 'the conversion by an animal or plant of extraneous material into fluids and tissues identical with its own'. First inchoate metaphorical uses of the term date from 1626, but it was not before the middle of the eighteenth century that the meaning was generalized into an unspecific 'making alike'. The contemporary use, in which the onus is shifted towards the 'absorbed material' and away from the converting organism ('to be, or become like to . . .'), came last, and became common currency only about 1837.

It seems that what made the established term attractive to those who sought a name for new social practices was precisely the asymmetry it implied; the unambiguous uni-directionality of the process. As a part of biological narrative 'assimilation' stood for the activity of the foraging organism, that subordinated parts of the environment to its own needs and did it by transforming them so that they become identical with its own 'fluids and tissues' (the organism as, simultanously, *causa finalis*, *causa formalis* and *causa efficiens* of the process and its outcome). The imagery that the concept evoked was one of a living, active body, bestowing or impressing its own form and quality upon something different from itself, and doing it on its own initiative and for its own purpose; of a process, in the course of which the form and quality of the other entity went through a radical change, while the identity of 'assimilating' body was maintained and, indeed, kept constant in the only way it could. It was this imagery that made the biological concept eminently suitable for its new, social, semantic function.

The metaphorical function of the concept captured the novel drive to uniformity, expressed in the comprehensive cultural crusade on which the new, modern nation-state had embarked. The drive reflected and augured the coming intolerance to difference.

Modern state power meant disempowerment of communal self-management and local or corporative mechanisms of self-perpetuation; it meant, therefore, sapping the social foundations of communal and corporative traditions and forms of life. This, in turn, broke the unthinking automaticism and the 'matter-of-factness' with which the patterns of human behaviour used to be reproduced and maintained. Human conduct lost its appearance of naturalness; lost as well was the expectation that nature would take its course even if (or particularly if) unattended and left to its own devices. With the backbone of communal self-reproduction disintegrating or crushed, the modern state power was bound to engage in deliberate management of social processes on an unheard of scale. Indeed, it needed to generate by design what in the past could be relied upon to appear on its own. It did not 'take over' the function and the authority of local communities and corporations; it did not 'concentrate' the previously dispersed powers. It presided over the formation of an entirely new type of power, of unprecendented scope, depth of penetration, and ambition (see Bauman, 1987: Chapters 3 and 4).

The ambition was to create artificially what nature could not be expected to provide; or, rather, what it should not be allowed to provide. The modern state was a designing power, and designing meant to define the difference between order and chaos, to sift the proper from the improper, to legitimize one pattern at the expense of all the others. The modern state propagated some patterns and set to eliminate all others. All in all, it promoted similarity and uniformity. The principle of a uniform law for everybody residing on a given territory, of the identity of the citizen status, proclaimed that members of society, as objects of attention and vigilance of the state, were indistinguishable from each other, or at least were to be treated as such. By the same token, whatever group-distinctive qualities they might have possessed were illegitimate. They also arose anxiety: they testified to the non-completion of the task of order-building.

In its essence, therefore, assimilation was a declaration of war on foreign substances and qualities. More importantly still, it was a bid on the part of one section of the society to exercise a monopolistic right to define certain other sections and their qualities as foreign, out of tune and out of place, and thereby in need of radical reform. It was one of the many paragraphs in the overall plan of replacement of the natural state of things by an artificially designed order; and hence it was a bid on the part of the designers to exercise a mono- polistic right to sort out the 'fitting' from the 'unfitting', the 'worthy' from the 'unworthy' categories, and to spell out the condi- tions under which passage from the second to the first may take place.

Above all, the vision of assimilation was a roundabout confirma- tion of social hierarchy, of the extant division of power. It assumed the superiority of one form of life and inferiority of another; it made their inequality into an axiom, took it as a starting point of all argu- ment, and hence made it secure against scrutiny and challenge. It effectively reinforced this inequality through ascribing the discrimi- nation of the 'inferior' sectors of the power structure to their own flaws, imperfections and their very 'otherness'. The acceptance of the assimilation as a vision and as a framework for life strategy was tantamount to the recognition of the hierarchy, its legitimacy, and above all its immutability.

The vision and the programme of assimilation was also an important weapon in the effort of the modern state to further sap the coherence and the power of resistance of those competitive institutions of social control which potentially limited its ambition of absolute sovereignty. Inferiority of the 'foreign' was defined, upheld and enforced as a feature of the category as a whole; of a collectively maintained, communal way of life. The offer of escaping the stigmatizing classification through acceptance of a non-stigmatized form of life was, on the other hand, extended to the individuals. Assimilation was an invitation, extended to individual members of the stigmatized groups, to challenge the right of those groups to set proper standards of behaviour. It was an offer extended over the heads of, and as a direct challenge to, communal and corporative powers. Assimilation was, therefore, an exercise in discrediting and disempowering the potentially competitive, communal or corporative, sources of social authority. It aimed at loosening the grip in which such competitive groups held their members. It aimed, in other words, at the elimination of such groups as forces of effective and viable competition.

Once this effect had been achieved — communal authorities robbed of their prestige and their legislative powers rendered ineffective — the threat of a serious challenge to the extant structure of domination was practically eliminated. The potential competitors were shorn of their power to resist and engage in a dialogue with even a remote chance of success. Collectively, they were powerless. It was left to the individual members to seek to wash off the collective stigma of foreignness by meeting the conditions set by the gate-keepers of the dominant group. The individuals were left at the mercy of the gate-keepers. They were objects of examination and assessment by the dominant group, who held complete control over the meaning of their conduct. Whatever they did, and whatever meaning they intended to invest in their actions, a priori reaffirmed the controlling capacity of the dominant group. Their clamouring for admission automatically reinforced the latter's claim to dominance. The standing invitation to apply for entry, and the positive response to it, confirmed the dominant group in its status of the holder, the guardian and the plenipotentiary of superior values, by the same token giving material substance to the concept of value superiority. The very fact of issuing the invitation established the dominant group in the position of the arbitrating power, a force entitled to set the exams and mark the performance. Individual members of the categories declared as sub-standard were now measured and valued by the extent of their conformity with dominant values. They were 'progressive' if they strove to imitate the dominant patterns and to erase all traces of the original ones. They were labelled 'backward' as long as they retained loyalty to the traditional patterns, or were not apt or fast enough in ridding themselves of their residual traces.

The standing invitation was represented as a sign of tolerance. In fact, however, the assimilatory offer derived its sense from the stiffness of discriminatory norms, from the finality of the verdict of inferiority passed or nonconformist values. The tolerance, understood as the encouragement of 'progressive attitudes' expressed in the search of individual 'self-improvement', was meaningful only as long as the measures of progress were not negotiable. Within the policy of assimilation, tolerance aimed at individuals was inextricably linked with intolerance aimed at the collectivities, their values and above all their value-legitimating powers. Indeed, the first was a major instrument in the successful promotion of the second.

The effective disfranchisement of alternative value-generating and value-legitimating authorities was represented as the universality of values supported by the extant hierarchy. In fact, however, the alleged universality of the authoritatively hailed and promoted values had no other material substratum but the expediently protected sovereignty of the value-adjudicating powers. The more effective was the suppression of possible sources of challenge, the less chance there was that the bluff of universality would be called, and that the pretence of the absolute validity of value-claims would be unmasked as a function of power monopoly. The degree to which the locally dominant values could credibly claim a supra-local validity was a function of their local supremacy.

Chasing Elusive Targets

From the standpoint of the grandiose yet unimplementable project of assimilation, some insufficiently emphasized, often overlooked facets of modern society and its uneasy, hate–love relationship with modern culture can be better seen.

Assimilation, as distinct from cross-cultural exchange or cultural diffusion in general, is a typically modern phenomenon. It derived its character and significance from the modern 'nationalization' of the state, i.e. from the bid of the modern state to linguistic, cultural and ideological unification of the population which inhabits the territory under its jurisdiction. Such a state tended to legitimize its authority through reference to shared history, common spirit, and a unique and exclusive way of life — rather than to extraneous factors (like, for instance, dynastic rights or military superiority), which, on the whole, are indifferent to the diversified forms of life of subjected population.

The gap between uniformity inherent in the idea of the nation and the practical heterogeneity of cultural forms inside the realm under unified state administration constituted therefore a challenge and a problem, to which national states responded with cultural crusades, aimed at the destruction of autonomous, communal mechanisms of reproduction of cultural unity. The era in which national states were formed was characterized by cultural intolerance; more generally, by nonendurance of, and impatience with all difference. Practices that departed from, or not fully conformed to, the power-assisted cultural pattern, were construed as alien and potentially subversive for, simultaneously, the national and political integrity.

The nationalization of the state (or, rather, etatization of the nation) blended the issue of political loyalty and trustworthiness (seen as conditions for granting citizenship rights) with that of cultural conformity. On one hand, the postulated national model served as the ideal objective of cultural crusade, but on the other it was deployed as the standard by which membership of the body politic was tested, and the exclusive practices were explained and legitimized which had been applied to those disqualified as having failed the test. In the result, citizenship and cultural conformity seemed to merge; the second was perceived as the condition, but also as a means to attain the first.

In this context, obliteration of cultural distinctiveness and acquisition of a different, power-assisted culture was construed and perceived as the prime vehicle of political emancipation. The consequence was the drive of politically ambitious, advanced sectors of 'alien' populations to seek excellence in practising the dominant cultural patterns and to disavow the cultural practices of their communities of origin. The prospect of full political citizenship was the main source of the seductive power of the acculturation programme.

The drive to acculturation put the ostensible identity of politics and culture to the test, and exposed the contradictions with which the fusion was inescapably burdened and which in the long run proved responsible for the ultimate failure of the assimilatory programme.

(a) Cultural assimilation was an intrinsically individual task and activity, while both political discrimination and political emancipation applied to the 'alien' (or otherwise excluded) community as a whole. As the acculturation was bound to proceed unevenly and involve various sections of the community to a varying extent and at varying speed, the advanced sectors seemed to be held back by the relatively retarded ones. Cutting the ties with the community offered no way out from the impasse, as the collective maturity for acceptance, like the capacity of a bridge, would be measured by the quality of the weakest section. On the other hand, acting as a cultural broker or missionary on behalf of the dominant culture in order to accelerate the cultural transformation of native community as a whole only reinforced the commonality of fate between the acculturated and the 'culturally alien' sections of the community and further tightened the already stiff conditions of political acceptance.

(b) The evidently acquired character of cultural traits gained in the process of acculturation jarred with the inherited and ascribed nature of national membership hiding behind the formula of common culture. The fact that their cultural similarity had been achieved, made the acculturated aliens different from the rest, 'not really like us', suspect of duplicity and probably also ill intentions. In this sense, cultural assimilation in the framework of a national state was self-defeating. As it were, national community, though a cultural product, could sustain its modality as a nation only through emphatic denial of a 'merely cultural', i.e. artificial, foundation. Instead, it derived its identity from the myth of common origin and naturalness. The individual was or was not its member; one could not choose to be one.

(c) Though it effectively alienated its agents from their community of origin, assimilation did not lead therefore to a full and unconditional acceptance by the dominant nation. Much to their dismay, the assimilants found that they had in effect assimilated solely to the process of assimilation. Other assimilants were the only people around who shared their problems, anxieties and preoccupations. Having left behind their original community and lost their former social and spiritual affinities, the assimilants landed in another community, the 'community of assimilants' — no less estranged and marginalized than the one from which they escaped. Moreover, the new alienation displayed a marked tendency to self-exacerbation. The *Weltanschauung* of the assimilants was now forged out of the shared experience of their new community, and given shape by a discourse conducted mostly inside its framework. In the event, it showed a marked tendency to underline the 'universalistic' character of cultural values and militate against all and any 'parochiality'. This circumstance set their perceptions, their philosophy and their ideals apart from the 'native' ones and effectively prevented the gap from being bridged.

The modern project of cultural unity produces the conditions of its own unfulfilment. By the same token, it creates the unpredecented, exuberant dynamism which characterises modern culture.

Order and chaos are both modern ideas. They emerged together — out of the disruption and collapse of the divinely ordained world, which knew of neither necessity nor accident, the world which just was. This world which preceded the bifurcation into order and chaos we find difficult to describe in its own terms. We try to grasp it mostly with the help of negations: we tell ourselves what that world was not, what it did not contain, what it was unaware of. That world would hardly have recognized itself in our descriptions. It would not understand what we are talking about. It would not survive such understanding. The moment of understanding would be (and it was) the sign of its approaching death. And of the birth of modernity.

We can think of modernity as of a time when order — of the world, of human habitat, of human self, and of the connection between all three — is a matter of thought, of concern, of a practice aware of itself. For the sake of convenience (the exact dating of birth is bound to remain contentious: the insistence on dating is itself a phenomenon of modernity, alien to the process of its conception and gestation) we can agree with Stephen L. Collins, who in his recent study (1989: 4,6,7,28, 29, 32) took Hobbes's vision for the birth-mark of the consciousness of order, that is of modern consciousness, that is of modernity ('Consciousness', says Collins, 'appears as the quality of perceiving order in things'):

> Hobbes understood that a world in flux was natural and that order must be created to restrain what was natural. . . . Society is no longer a transcendentally articulated reflection of something predefined, external, and beyond itself which orders existence hierarchically. It is now a nominal entity ordered by the sovereign state which is its own articulated representative . . . [40 years after Elizabeth's death] order was coming to be understood not as natural, but as artificial, created by man. And manifestly political and social. . . . Order must be designed to restrain what appeared ubiquitous [that is, flux]. . . . Order became a matter of power, and power a matter of will, force and calculation. . . . Fundamental to the entire reconceptualization of the idea of society was the belief that the commonwealth, as was order, was a human creation.

Collins is a scrupulous historian wary of the dangers of projectionism and presentism, but he can hardly avoid imputing to the pre-Hobbsian world many a feature akin to the post-Hobbsian world of ours — if only through indicating their absence; indeed, without such strategy of description the pre-Hobbsian world would stay numb and meaningless for us. To make that world speak to us, we must lay bare its silences: to spell out what that world was unaware of. We must force that world to take stance on issues to which it remained oblivious: that oblivion was what made it that world, a world so different and so incommunicado with our own.

And thus if it is true that we know that the order of things is not natural, this does not mean that that other, pre-Hobbsian, world thought of the order as the work of nature: it did not think of order at all, not in the sense we think of it now. The discovery that order was not natural was discovery of order as such. The concept of order appears in consciousness only simultaneously with the problem of order, of order as a matter of design and action. Declaration of the 'non-naturalness of order' stood for an order already coming out of hiding, out of non-existence, out of silence: nature was, after all, the silence of man. If it is true that we think of order as a matter of design, this does not mean that that other world was complacent about designing and expected the order to come and stay on its own and unassisted. That other world lived without such alternative; it would not be the other world, were it giving its thought to it. If it is true that our world is shaped by the suspicion of brittleness and fragility of the artificial man-made islands of order among the sea of chaos, it does not follow that the other world believed that the order stretches over the sea and the human archipelago alike; it was, rather, unaware of the distinction between land and water.[1]

We can say that the existence is modern inasmuch as it forks into order and chaos. The existence is modern inasfar as it contains the alternative of order and chaos.

Indeed: order and chaos. Order is not aimed against an alternative order; the struggle for order is not a fight of one definition against another, of one way of articulating reality against a competitive proposal. It is a fight of determination against ambiguity, of semantic precision against ambivalence, of transparency against obscurity, clarity against fuzziness. Order is continuously engaged in the war of survival. What is not itself, is not another order: any order is always the order as such, with chaos as its only alternative.

'The other' of order is the miasma of the indeterminate and unpredictable: uncertainty, the source and archetype of all fear. The tropes of 'the Other of Order' are: undefinability, incoherence, incongruence, incompatibility, illogicality. Chaos, 'the Other of Order', is pure negativity. It is a denial of all that the order strives to be. It is against that negativity that the positivity of Order constitutes itself. But the negativity of chaos is a product of order's self-constitution; its side-effect, its waste, and yet the condition sine qua non of its possibility. Without the negativity of chaos, there is no positivity of order; without chaos, no order.

We can say that the existence is modern inasmuch as it is saturated by the 'without us, a deluge' feeling. The existence is modern inasmuch as it is guided by the urge of designing what otherwise would not be there: designing of itself.

The raw existence, the existence free of intervention, the unordered existence, becomes now nature: something singularly unfit for human habitat — something not to be trusted and not to be left to its own devices, something to be mastered, subordinated, remade so as to be readjusted to human needs. Something to be held in check, restrained and contained, transferred from the state of shapelessness into form — by effort and by application of force. Even if the form has been preordained by nature itself, it won't come about unassisted and won't survive undefended. Living according to nature needs a lot of designing, organized effort, and vigilant monitoring. Nothing is more artificial than naturalness; nothing less natural than abiding by the laws of nature. Power, repression, purposeful action stand between nature and that socially effected order in which artificiality is natural.

We can say that existence is modern inasmuch as it is effected and sustained by social engineering. The existence is modern inasmuch as it is managed and administered by powerful, resorceful, sovereign agencies. Agencies are sovereign inasmuch as they claim and defend the right to manage and administer existence: the right to define order and, by implication set aside chaos, as the leftover that escapes the definition.

It was the intention to engage in social engineering which made the state modern. The typically modern practice of the state, the substance of modern politics, was the effort to exterminate ambivalence: to define precisely — and to suppress or eliminate everything that could not or would not be precisely defined. 'The Other' of the modern state is the no-man's or contested land: the under or over-definition, ambiguity. As the sovereignty of the modern state is the power to define and to make the definitions stick, everything that self-defines or eludes the state-legislated definition is subversive. 'The Other' of sovereignty is obfuscation, opacity, and confusion. Resistance to definition sets the limit to sovereignty, to power, to the power of sovereign state, to order. That resistance is the stubborn and grim reminder of the flux which order wished to contain but in vain; of the limits to order; of the necessity of ordering. State ordering creates chaos. But the state needs chaos to go on creating order.

We can say that consciousness is modern inasmuch as it is suffused with the awareness of inconclusiveness of order; moved by the inadequacy, nay non-feasibility, of the social engineering project. Consciousness is modern inasmuch as it reveals ever new layers of chaos underneath the lid of power-assisted order. Modern consciousness criticizes, warns, and alerts. It spurs into action by unmasking its ineffectiveness. It perpetuates the ordering bustle by disqualifying its achievements and laying bare its defeats.

Thus there is a hate–love relation between modern existence and modern culture (in the most advanced form of self-awareness), a symbiosis fraught with civil wars. In the modern era, culture is that obstreperous and vigilant Her Majesty's Opposition which makes the government feasible. There is no love lost, harmony, nor similarity between the two: there is only mutual need and dependence, the complementarity which comes out of the opposition; which is opposition. It would be futile to decide whether modern culture undermines or serves modern existence. It does both things. It can do each one only together with the other. Opposition is it positivity. Dysfunctionality of modern culture is its functionality. The modern powers' struggle for artificial order needs culture that explores the limits and the limitations of the power of artifice. The struggle for order informs that exploration and is in turn informed by its findings. In the process, the struggle sheds its initial hubris: the pugnacity born of naivety and ignorance. It learns, instead, to live with its own permanence, inconclusiveness — and prospectless-ness. Hopefully, it'll learn in the end the difficult skills of modesty and tolerance.

The history of modernity is one of the tensions between social existence and its culture. Modern existence forces its culture into opposition to itself. This disharmony is precisely the harmony modernity needs. The history of modernity draws its uncanny and unprecedented dynamism from it. For the same reason, it can be seen as a history of progress: as the natural history of humanity.

Postscript
Three aspects of contemporary change usually subsumed under the concept of postmodernity, may — just may — put a time limit to the validity of preceding analysis.

1. A pronounced, though by no means conclusive tendency toward 'denationalization of the state'. 'privatization of nationality', or, more correctly, toward separation between the state and the nation (similar, in a way, to the last century separation between the state and the church). This process has been sometimes described as 'resurgence of ethnicity'. The latter term puts in the forefront the unanticipated flourishing of ethnic loyalties inside national minorities. By the same token, it casts a shadow on what seems to be the deep cause of the phenomenon: the growing separation between the membership of body politic and ethnic membership (or more generally, cultural conformity) which removes much of its original attraction from the programme of cultural assimilation. This separation, in turn, is more than incidentally related to the establishment of alternative, mostly non-cultural and non-ideological, foundations of the state's power. For all practical intents and purposes, the era of state-led cultural crusades grinds to a halt.

2. Culture itself, having lost its instrumental role in servicing the systemic reproduction and underwriting the social integration, has been freed from obtrusive and constraining interest of the state and tends to become a part of the private domain. Ethnicity has become one of the many categories of tokens, or 'tribal poles', around which flexible and sanction-free communities are formed and in reference to which individual identities are construed and asserted. There are now, therefore, much fewer centrifugal forces which once weakened ethnic integrity. There is, instead a powerful demand for pronounced, though symbolic rather than institutionalized, ethnic distinctiveness.

3. Under these conditions, ethnic differences may — just may — generate less antagonism and conflict than in the past. It is true that various aspects of heterophobia associated with the boundary-drawing preoccupations are still in operation; but the continuous re-drawing of boundaries typical of contemporary (post-modern)

culture and the easiness with which they are crossed in the absence of state-hired border-guards renders the antagonisms somewhat more shallow, short-lived and less venomous or radical. With the state declaring (and practising) its indifference to cultural and ethnic pluralism, tolerance stands a better chance than ever before.

Between themselves, these three tendencies may well render the drama of the anti-ambivalence war of assimilation a matter of mostly historical interest well before it has reached the conclusion for which it vainly strove.

Note

1. An example: 'The individual experienced neither isolation nor alienation' (Collins, 1989: 21). In fact, the individual of the pre-modern world did not experience the absence of the experience of isolation or alienation. He did not experience belonging, membership, at-home-being, togetherness. Belonging entails the awareness of being together or a part of; thus belonging, inevitably, contains the awareness of its own uncertainty, of the possibility of isolation, of the need to stave off or overcome alienation. Experiencing oneself as 'unisolated' or 'unalienated' is as much modern as the experience of isolation and alienation.

References

Alter, Peter (1989) *Nationalism* (translated by Stuart McKinnon-Evans). London: Edward Arnold.

Anderson, Benedict (1983) *Imaginary Communities*. London: Verso.

Barth, Frederick (1969) *Ethnic Groups and Boundaries. The Social Organization of Cultural Differences*. Bergen: Universitet Ferlaget.

Bauman, Zygmunt (1987) *Legislators and Interpreters*. Oxford: Polity Press.

Breuilly, John (1982) *Nationalism and the State*. Manchester: Manchester University Press.

Collins, Stephen L. (1989) *From Divine Cosmos to Sovereign State: An Intellectual History of Consciousness and the Idea of Order in Renaissance England*. Oxford: Oxford University Press.

Derrida, Jacques (1974) *Of Grammatology* (translated by Gayatri Chakravosty Spivak). Baltimore: Johns Hopkins University Press.

Derrida Jacques (1981a) *Disseminations* (translated by Barbara Johnson). London: Athlone Press.

Derrida, Jacques (1981b) *Positions* (translated by Alan Bass). Chicago: Chicago University Press.

Douglas, Mary (1966) *Purity and Danger*. London: Routledge.

Erasmus, Charles J. (1974) *In Search of the Common Good*. New York: Free Press.

Kedouri, Elie (1960) *Nationalism*. London: Hutchinson.

Levinas, Emmanuel (1982) *Ethics and Infinity, Conversations with Phillippe Nemo*, (translated by Richard A. Cohen). Pittsburgh: Duquene University Press.

Rousseau, Jean Jacques (1953) *Considerations on the Present of Poland*. London: Nelson.

Schafer, Boyd C. (1955) *Nationalism, Myth and Reality*. London: Gollancz.
Simmel, Georg (1971) 'The Stranger', in *On Individuality and Social Forms*. (original edition, 1908). Chicago: Chicago University Press.

Zygmunt Bauman is Professor of Sociology at the University of Leeds. His latest book is *Modernity and the Holocaust* (Polity Press, 1989).

Towards a Global Culture?

Anthony D. Smith

The initial problem with the concept of a 'global culture' is one of the meaning of terms. Can we speak of 'culture' in the singular? If by 'culture' is meant a collective mode of life, or a repertoire of beliefs, styles, values and symbols, then we can only speak of cultur*es*, never just culture; for a collective mode of life, or a repertoire of beliefs, etc., presupposes different modes and repertoires in a universe of modes and repertoires. Hence, the idea of a 'global culture' is a practical impossibility, except in interplanetary terms. Even if the concept is predicated of *homo sapiens*, as opposed to other species, the differences between segments of humanity in terms of lifestyle and belief-repertoire are too great, and the common elements too generalized, to permit us to even conceive of a globalized culture.

Or are they? Can we not at last discern the lineaments of exactly that world culture which liberals and socialists alike had dreamed of and hoped for since the last century? In the evolutionary perspective, the hallmark of history was growth: growth in size, population, knowledge and the like. Small-scale units everywhere were giving way to densely-populated societies on a continental scale, so that even the largest of nation-states was but a staging post in the ascent of humanity. For liberals, from Mill and Spencer to Parsons and Smelser, the adaptive capacity of humanity was increasing by definite stages, as modernization eroded localism and created huge, mobile and participant societies, whose flexibility and inclusiveness presaged the dissolution of all boundaries and categories of a common humanity.[1]

A similar hope was entertained by socialists of all varieties. Despite the many ambiguities revealed in the scattered writings of Marx and Engels on the subject of superseding humanity's divisions, they both looked forward to the withering away of the nation-state and the internationalization of literary cultures. If they and

Theory, Culture & Society (SAGE, London, Newbury Park and New Delhi), Vol. 7 (1990), 171–191

their communist successors accepted the present realities of national boundaries and cultures, and even conceded the need to conduct the class struggle within those boundaries, they nevertheless looked forward to the day when the socialist revolution would infuse proletarian values into ethnic and national cultures, and when humanity's divisions would be transcended without being formally abolished.[2]

The Rise of Transnational Cultures

It is these hopes that have re-emerged after 1945 out of the ruins of a divided Europe and world. Before 1945, it was still possible to believe that the medium-sized nation-state was the norm of human organization in the modern era and that national culture was humanity's final goal and attribute. A world of nations, each sovereign, homogenous and free, cooperating in the League of Nations, was humanity's highest aspiration, and the guarantee of political justice through diversity and pluralism.

The Second World War destroyed that vision and aspiration. It revealed the bankruptcy of the world of nations posited by nationalists and accepted in good faith by so many. It demonstrated the hold of 'supranational' ideologies over large segments of humanity: of racism, capitalism and communism. It also brought the hegemony of 'superpowers', continental states which won the War, relegating the former 'great powers' to the middle or lower ranks of world status.

In the postwar world, a world of power blocs and ideological camps, humanity was re-divided, but in such a way as to give rise to the hope of transcending the greatest obstacle to a truly global politics and culture: the nation-state. In the postwar world, the nation-state was clearly obsolete, along with nationalism and all its rituals. In its place arose the new cultural imperialisms of Soviet communism, American capitalism, and struggling to find a place between them, a new Europeanism. Here lay the hope of eroding the state and transcending the nation.

Fundamental to the new cultural imperialisms has been the need to create a positive alternative to 'national culture.' If the nation was to be 'superseded', it could not simply be through a process of depoliticization, a 'withering away' of nationalism. To separate and destroy national*ism*, but keep the organizational culture of nations intact, was to risk the renewal of that very nationalism which was to be abolished. This was in fact the Soviet approach since the

1920s (Goldhagen, 1968; G.E. Smith, 1985). But the communist authorities also realized the dangers of their policies towards nationalities, and therefore proposed the creation of a new 'Soviet' man, a citizen of the Soviet Union, whose loyalty would be an ideological one to the new 'political community', even where he or she retained a sense of emotional solidarity with their ethnic community. In the end, these ethnic communities and republics would, after a period of growing cooperation, fuse together to produce a truly 'Soviet culture' (Fedoseyev et al., 1977).

In America, too, the hope for a continental culture of assimilative modernization based on the 'American Creed' of liberty and capitalism, was counterposed to the 'narrow nationalisms' of Europe and the Third World, as well as to the communist rival. America, the land of immigrants and minorities, was held up in the 1950s as the exemplar of 'melting pot' assimilation and, when that vision proved to be a mirage, of integration through diversity. In this version, 'symbolic' attachments to particular ethnic communities are valued, and their needs and rights are politically recognized, so long as they are ultimately subordinated to the overarching political community and its complex of myths, memories and symbols. Ethnicity has become one of the basic, if informal, organizing principles of American society, but not in such a way as to impair the overriding allegiance of each citizen to America, its values, heroes, flag, Revolutionary myths and the Constitution. To this 'official nationalism', we can add a more diffuse attachment to the culture and landscapes of America, its prairies, deserts and mountain ranges, its early settlements and folk arts (Glazer and Moynihan, 1975; Kilson, 1975; Gans, 1979).

If the Soviet and American experiences demonstrated the possibilities of the new cultural imperialisms in transcending nationalism, the project of a truly 'European Community' presaged the manner in which a global culture might be created. Since the inception of the European movement in 1948, there has been much debate on the future shape of such a 'supranational' community. On the one hand, there was the Gaullist formulation of a *Europe des Patries*, shared by some British governments; on the other hand, a vision of a truly united states of Europe, politically as well as economically, of the kind that earned the name of 'super-nation' from its detractors (see Galtung, 1973). In between were various shades of federalism or confederalism, linked by a common Rhine-based culture harking back beyond the epoch of the nation-state to earlier and looser identities — the Holy Roman Empire, the Carolingians, Christendom, even Rome itself — from which a new European cultural unity might be forged with the instruments of telecommunications and economic interdependence. In the age of television and computer, it is perfectly feasible to construct a new European culture which would match its American and Soviet rivals, and demonstrate once again the vitality of the new cultural imperialisms in a post-industrial era.

Like the American model, this new formulation of European community depends on the fashionable notion of 'unity in diversity', which suggests the possibility of cultural imperialism coexisting with vital cultural identities. Just as there is a balance between common economic regulation from Brussels and the specific social and economic policies of the member states of the Community; just as there is a sharing of political sovereignty between the member states and the political centres in Strasbourg and Brussels, a condominium of overlapping jurisdictions; so, in the sphere of culture, a common European heritage which will spawn the new 'European citizen' is balanced by the still lively, if cross-fertilized, cultures of Europe's many nations, but in such a way as to subordinate them to the 'cultural imperatives' of the continent in a post-industrial era (see Schlesinger, 1987).

A 'Post-industrial' Global Culture?

It is not difficult to see what lies behind such formulations of the new cultural imperialism. Broadly speaking, it is argued that the era of the nation-state is over. We are entering a new world of economic giants and superpowers, of multinationals and military blocs, of vast communications networks and international division of labour. In such a world, there is no room for medium or small-scale states, let alone submerged ethnic communities and their competing and divisive nationalisms. On the one hand, capitalist competition has given birth to immensely powerful transnational corporations with huge budgets, reserves of skilled labour, advanced technologies and sophisticated information networks. Essential to their success is the ability to deliver suitably packaged imagery and symbolism which will convey their definitions of the services they provide. While they have to rely on a transnational lingua franca, it is the new systems of telecommunications and computerized information networks which enable them to by-pass differences in language and culture to secure the labour and markets they require. In other words, the resources, range and specialized flexibility of transnational corporations' activities enable them to present imagery and information on an almost global scale, threatening to swamp the cultural networks of more local units, including nations and ethnic communities (see Said and Simmons, 1976).

On the other hand, an alternative perspective claims that we have entered, not just a post-national, but also a post-industrial, some would say 'postmodern', era. Nations and nationalism may have been functional for a world of competing industrial states, but they are obsolete in the 'service society' of an interdependent world based upon technical knowledge. It is not capitalism and its transnational corporations which have eroded the power of nation-states, but the possibilities of constructing much larger institutional units on the basis of vast telecommunications systems and computerized networks of information. In this situation, any attempt to limit such networks to national boundaries is doomed to failure; today, 'culture' can only be continental or global. But, by the same token, these same communications networks make possible a denser, more intense interaction between members of communities who share common cultural characteristics, notably language; and this fact enables us to understand why in recent years we have been witnessing the re-emergence of submerged ethnic communities and their nationalisms (Richmond, 1984).

This last point echoes Marx and Engels' concession to 'national culture' in a socialist world. Nations, Marx admitted, would be likely to persist as cultural forms, and a truly cosmopolitan culture did not rule out residual folk cultures, to which Engels referred disdainfully as so many 'ethnographic monuments' with their dying customs, creeds and languages (see Fisera and Minnerup, 1978; Cummins, 1980; Connor, 1984). Similarly, today, movements of ethnic autonomy in Western Europe have sometimes linked their fate with the growth of a European Community that would supersede the bureaucratic straitjacket of the existing system of nation-states, which have signally failed to give peripheral ethnic minorities their due in the post-War world. Only in a broader, looser European Community would such neglected minorities find recognition and equal opportunities (see Esman, 1977; A.D. Smith, 1981).

Yet, the main thrust of 'late-capitalism' and/or 'post-industrialism' analyses is away from the small-scale community and towards a world of cultural imperialism, based on economic, state and communications technology and institutions. Whether the imperial-isms are ideological or political or economic, their cultural base is always technical and elitist. They are, as with every imperialism, cultures of state or states, promoted 'from above', with little or no popular base and with little or no reference to the cultural traditions of the peoples incorporated in their domain.

But there is an important difference from earlier cultural imperialisms. Earlier imperialisms were usually extensions of ethnic or national sentiments and ideologies, French, British, Russian, etc. Today's imperialisms are ostensibly non-national; 'capitalism' and 'socialism', and in a different sense 'Europeanism', are by defini-tion and intention 'supranational', if not universal. They are supported by a technological infrastructure which is truly 'cosmopolitan', in the sense that the same telecommunications base will eventually erode cultural differences and create a genuinely 'global culture' based on the properties of the media themselves, to which the 'message' will become increasingly incidental. For the rest, tourism and museology alone will preserve the memory of an earlier era of 'national cultures', of the kind that Donald Horne has given us such a vivid record (Horne, 1984).

What is the content of such a post-industrial 'global culture'? How shall we picture its operations? Answers to such questions usually take the form of extrapolation from recent western cultural experiences of 'postmodernism'. Beneath a modernist veneer, we find in practice a pastiche of cultural motifs and styles, underpinned by a universal scientific and technical discourse. A global culture, so the argument runs, will be eclectic like its western or European progenitor, but will wear a uniformly streamlined packaging. Standardized, commercialized mass commodities will nevertheless draw for their contents upon revivals of traditional, folk or national motifs and styles in fashions, furnishings, music and the arts, lifted out of their original contexts and anaesthetized. So that a global culture would operate at several levels simultaneously: as a cornucopia of standardized commodities, as a patchwork of dena-tionalized ethnic or folk motifs, as a series of generalized 'human values and interests', as a uniform 'scientific' discourse of meaning, and finally as the interdependent system of communications which forms the material base for all the other components and levels.[3]

It might be argued that there is nothing especially new about a 'global culture', that earlier cultural imperialisms were every whit as eclectic and simultaneously standardized. After all, the hellenization that Alexander's armies carried throughout the ancient Near East, drew on a variety of local motifs as well as giving them expression in the Greco-Macedonian forms of theatre, assembly, marketplace and gymnasium. And the same was true of the pax Romana throughout the Mediterranean world (see Tcherikover, 1970; Balsdon, 1979).

Yet, those pre-modern cultural imperialisms were neither global nor universal. They were ultimately tied to their places of origin, and carried with them their special myths and symbols for all to recognize and emulate. Today's emerging global culture is tied to no place or period. It is context-less, a true melange of disparate components drawn from everywhere and nowhere, borne upon the modern chariots of global telecommunications systems.

There is something equally timeless about the concept of a global culture. Widely diffused in space, a global culture is cut off from any past. As the perennial pursuit of an elusive present or imagined future, it has no history. A global culture is here and now and everywhere, and for its purposes the past only serves to offer some decontextualized example or element for its cosmopolitan patchwork.

This sense of timelessness is powerfully underlined by the pre-eminently technical nature of its discourse. A global culture is essentially calculated and artificial, posing technical problems with technical solutions and using its folk motifs in a spirit of detached playfulness. Affectively neutral, a cosmopolitan culture reflects a technological base made up of many overlapping systems of communications bound by a common quantitative and technical discourse, manned by an increasingly technical intelligentsia, whose 'culture of critical discourse' replaces the social critique of its earlier humanistic counterparts (see Gouldner, 1979).

Memory, Identity and Cultures

Eclectic, universal, timeless and technical, a global culture is seen as pre-eminently a 'constructed' culture, the final and most imposing of a whole series of human constructs in the era of human liberation and mastery over nature. In a sense, the nation too was just such a construct, a sovereign but finite 'imagined community'.

Nations were 'built' and 'forged' by state elites or intelligentsias or capitalists; like the Scots kilt or the British Coronation ceremony, they are composed of so many 'invented traditions', whose symbols we need to read through a process of 'deconstruction', if we are to grasp the hidden meanings beneath the 'text' of their discourse. The fact, therefore, that a global culture would need to be constructed, along with global economic and political institutions, should occasion no surprise; nor should we cavil at the eclecticism with which such a cosmopolitan culture is likely to make use of bits and pieces of pre-existing national and folk cultures.[4]

Let us concede for the moment that nations are, in some sense, social 'constructs' and 'imagined' communities. Is it because of this 'constructed' quality that they have managed to survive and flourish so well? Are we therefore justified in predicting the same bright future for an equally well crafted 'global culture'?

To answer affirmatively would require us to place the whole weight of demonstration on the common characteristic of human construction and imagination, at the expense of those characteristics in which nations and national cultures differ markedly from our description of the qualities of a global culture. The obstinate fact is that national cultures, like all cultures before the modern epoch, are *particular*, *timebound* and *expressive*, and their eclecticism operates within strict cultural constraints. As we said at the outset, there can in practice be no such thing as 'culture', only specific, historical cultures possessing strong emotional connotations for those who share in the particular culture. It is, of course, possible to 'invent', even manufacture, traditions as commodities to serve particular class or ethnic interests. But they will only survive and flourish as part of the repertoire of national culture, if they can be made continuous with a much longer past that members of that community presume to constitute their 'heritage'. In other words, 'grafting' extraneous elements must always be a delicate operation; the new traditions must evoke a popular response if they are to survive, and that means hewing close to vernacular motifs and styles. That was the instinct which guided most nationalists and helped to ensure their lasting successes. The success of the nineteenth-century British Coronation ceremony or the Welsh Eisteddfoddau owed much to the ability of those who revived them to draw on much older cultural motifs and traditions, memories of which were still alive; though in one sense 'new', these revivals were only able to flourish because they could be presented, and were accepted, as continuous with a valued past (see Hobsbawm and Ranger, 1983).

If cultures are historically specific and spatially limited, so are those images and symbols that have obtained a hold on human imagination. Even the most imperialist of those images — emperor,

Pope or Tsar — have drawn their power from the heritage of Roman and Byzantine symbolism. It is one thing to be able to package imagery and diffuse it through world-wide telecommunications networks. It is quite another to ensure that such images retain their power to move and inspire populations, who have for so long been divided by particular histories and cultures, which have mirrored and crystallized the experiences of historically separated social groups, whether classes or regions, religious congregations or ethnic communities. The meanings of even the most universal of imagery for a particular population derives as much from the historical experiences and social status of that group as from the intentions of purveyors, as recent research on the national reception of popular television serials suggests (see Schlesinger, 1987).[5]

In other words, images and cultural traditions do not derive from, or descend upon, mute and passive populations on whose *tabula rasa* they inscribe themselves. Instead, they invariably express the identities which historical circumstances have formed, often over long periods. The concept of 'identity' is here used, not of a common denominator of patterns of life and activity, much less some average, but rather of the subjective feelings and valuations of any population which possesses common experiences and one or more shared cultural characteristics (usually customs, language or religion). These feelings and values refer to three components of their shared experiences:

1. a sense of continuity between the experiences of succeeding generations of the unit of population;
2. shared memories of specific events and personages which have been turning-points of a collective history; and
3. a sense of common destiny on the part of the collectivity sharing those experiences.

By a collective cultural identity, therefore, is meant those feelings and values in respect of a sense of continuity, shared memories and a sense of common destiny of a given unit of population which has had common experiences and cultural attributes.[6]

It is in just these senses that 'nations' can be understood as historic identities, or at least deriving closely from them, while a global and cosmopolitan culture fails to relate to any such historic identity. Unlike national cultures, a global culture is essentially memoryless. Where the 'nation' can be constructed so as to draw upon and revive latent popular experiences and needs, a 'global culture' answers to no living needs, no identity-in-the-making. It has to be painfully put together, artificially, out of the many existing folk and national identities into which humanity has been so long divided. There are no 'world memories' that can be used to *unite* humanity; the most global experiences to date — colonialism and the World Wars — can only serve to remind us of our historic cleavages. (If it is argued that nationalists suffered selective amnesia in order to construct their nations, the creators of a global culture would have to suffer total amnesia, to have any chance of success!)

The central difficulty in any project to construct a global identity and hence a global culture, is that collective identity, like imagery and culture, is always historically specific because it is based on shared memories and a sense of continuity between generations.

To believe that 'culture follows structure', that the techno-economic sphere will provide the conditions and therefore the impetus and content of a global culture, is to be misled once again by the same economic determinism that dogged the debate about 'industrial convergence', and to overlook the vital role of common historical experiences and memories in shaping identity and culture. Given the plurality of such experiences and identities, and given the historical depth of such memories, the project of a global culture, as opposed to global communications, must appear premature for some time to come.

'Ethno-history' and Posterity

If it proves difficult to envisage a point of departure for this project in common human experiences and memories, the universal stumbling-block to its construction is not far to seek. That ubiquitous obstacle is embodied in the continued presence of pre-modern ties and sentiments in the modern epoch. Indeed, just as a 'postmodern' era awaits its liberation from the modern industrial world, so the latter is still weighed down by the burden of pre-modern traditions, myths and boundaries. I have argued elsewhere that many of today's nations are built up on the basis of pre-modern 'ethnic cores' whose myths and memories, values and symbols shaped the culture and boundaries of the nation that modern elites managed to forge. Such a view, if conceded, must qualify our earlier acceptance of the largely 'constructed' quality of modern nations. That nationalist elites were active in inculcating a sense of national-ity in large sections of 'their' populations who were ignorant of any national affiliations, is well-documented (see Kedourie, 1960; Breuilly, 1982). It does not follow that they 'invented nations where none existed', as Gellner had once claimed, even where they used pre-existing materials and even when nations are defined as large, anonymous, unmediated, co-cultural units (see Gellner, 1964, Chapter 7; also Gellner, 1983, Chapter 5).

Nationalists, like others, found themselves constrained by accepted cultural traditions, from which they might select, and by popular responses, which they hoped to channel, if not manipulate. But their room for cultural manoeuvre was always limited by those cultural traditions and popular, vernacular repertoires of myth, memory, symbol and value. For nationalists, the 'nation-to-be' was not any large, anonymous, co-cultural unit. It was a community of history and culture, possessing a compact territory, unified economy and common legal rights and duties for all members. If 'nationalism creates nations' in its own image, then its definition of the nation was of a piece with its aspirations for collective autonomy, fraternal unity and distinctive identity. The identity and unity that was sought was of and for an existing historic culture-community, which the nationalists thought they were reviving and returning to a 'world of nations'. It depended, therefore, in large measure on the rediscovery of the community's 'ethno-history', its peculiar and distinctive cultural contribution to the worldwide fund of what Weber called 'irreplaceable culture values'. This was the nationalist project, and it is one that has by no means run its course, even as signs of its super-session by wider projects are on the horizon. In fact, it can be argued that nationalist and post-nationalist projects feed off each other, and are likely to do so for some time to come.

In fact, the success of the nationalist project depended not only on the creative skills and organizational ability of the intelligentsia, but on the persistence, antiquity and resonance of the community's ethno-history. The more salient, pervasive and enduring that history, the firmer the cultural base it afforded for the formation of a modern nation. Once again, these are largely subjective aspects. It is the salience of that history in the eyes of the community's members, and the *felt* antiquity of their ethnic ties and sentiments, which give an ethno-history its power and resonance among wide strata. It matters little whether the communal events recounted happened in the manner purveyed, or if heroes acted nobly as tradition would have us believe; the Exodus, William Tell, Great

Zimbabwe, derive their power not from a sober historical assessment, but from the way events, heroes and landscapes have been woven by myth, memory and symbol into the popular consciousness. For the participants in this drama, ethno-history has a 'primordial' quality, or it is power-less (A.D. Smith, 1988).[7]

Why do such myths and memories retain their hold, even today, to fuel the nationalist project? There is no single answer; but two considerations must take priority. The first is the role of ethno-history, its myths, values, memories and symbols, in assuring collective dignity (and through that some measure of dignity for the individual) for populations which have come to feel excluded, neglected or suppressed in the distribution of values and opportunities. By establishing the unity of a submerged or excluded population around an ancient and preferably illustrious pedigree, not only is the sense of bonding intensified, but a reversal of collective status is achieved, at least on the cognitive and moral levels. It is the start of a moral and social revolution through the mobilization of hidden collective energies, or *Kräfte*, to use Herder's prophetic term (see Barnard, 1965).

The second consideration is even more important. With the attenuation of the hold of traditional cosmic images of another, unseen existence beyond the everyday world, the problem of individual oblivion and collective disintegration becomes more pressing and less easily answered. Loss of social cohesion feeding off an increasing sense of individual meaninglessness, in a century when the old 'problem of evil' has been posed in unparalleled ways, drives more and more people to discover new ways of understanding and preserving 'identity' in the face of annihilation. For many, the only guarantee of preservation of some form of identity is in the appeal to 'posterity', to the future generations that are 'ours', because they think and feel as 'we' do, just as our children are supposed to feel and think like each of us individually. With the dissolution of all traditional theodicies, only the appeal to a collective posterity offers hope of deliverance from oblivion (see A.D. Smith, 1970; Anderson, 1983: Chapter 1).

It was in the eighteenth century that the quest for a terrestrial collective immortality was first firmly voiced, and not just for the philosopher. Poets, sculptors, painters and architects recorded and celebrated ancient and modern heroes whose *exempla virtutis* ensured the immortality of themselves and their communities, notably Sparta, Athens and ancient Rome, but equally of modern nations — England, France, Italy, Germany, America (see Rosenblum, 1967: Chapter 2; Abrams, 1985). The same century witnessed the birth of national*ism*, the ideological movement, and the demand to revive or build nations on the Anglo-French model, which would act as modern communities of history and destiny, to keep alive the sacred memory of individuals and families in the march of the nation through history. By placing that memory in the lap of the nation, posterity and a transcendent purpose would restore meaning and identity to individuals liberated by secularism. To this day, the serried monuments to the fallen, the ceaseless ritual of remembrance, the fervent celebration of heroes and symbols across the globe, testify to the same impulse to collective immortality, the same concern for the judgment and solace of posterity.

Vernacular Mobilization and Cultural Competition

There are also more specific reasons for the continuing hold of national cultures with their ethnic myths and memories in an increasingly interdependent world.

Perhaps the most common way in which nations have been, and are being, formed is through processes of 'vernacular mobilization' and 'cultural politicization'. Where ethnic communities (or *ethnie*) lack states of their own, having usually been incorporated in wider polities in an earlier epoch, they risk dissolution in the transition to modernity, unless an indigenous intelligentsia emerges, strong enough to mobilize wider sections of 'their' community on the basis of a rediscovered ethno-history and vernacular culture. The success of the intelligentsia largely hinges on their ability to discover a convincing cultural base, one that can find a popular response, at least among educated strata. The intelligentsia are populist to the extent that they make use of (some) popular culture and a living communal history, even where they stop short of mobilizing actual peasants. The important task is to convince immediate followers, and enemies outside, of the cultural viability of the nation-to-be. The richer, more fully documented, the ethno-history, the more widely spoken the vernacular tongue and the more widely practised the native customs and religion, the less difficult will it be to convince others, friends and enemies, of the actuality of the 'nation'; for it can be made to 'flow' coterminously with the demotic *ethnie* and seem its reincarnation after a long period of presumed death. Conversely, the scantier the records of ethnohistory and less widely spoken the vernacular and practised the customs, the harder will it be to convince others of the viability of the national project, and the more it will be necessary to find new ways of overcoming doubt and hostility. Hence the appeal to lost epics and forgotten heroes — an Oisin or Lemminkainen — to furnish a noble pedigree and sacred landscape for submerged or neglected communities (see Hutchinson, 1987; Branch, 1985: Introduction).

To create the nation, therefore, it is not enough simply to mobilize compatriots. They must be taught who they are, where they came from and whither they are going. They must be turned into co-nationals through a process of mobilization into the vernacular culture, albeit one adapted to modern social and political conditions. Only then can the old-new culture become a political base and furnish political weapons in the much more intense cultural competition of a world of nations. Old religious sages and saints can now be turned into national heroes, ancient chronicles and epics become examples of the creative national genius, while great ages of achievement in the community's past are presented as the nation's 'golden age' of pristine purity and nobility. The former culture of a community which had no other end beyond itself, now becomes the talisman and legitimation for all manner of 'national' policies and purposes, from agricultural villagization to militarism and aggrandisement. Ethnicity is nationalized (see Seton-Watson, 1977: Chapters 2–4; A.D. Smith, 1986: Chapter 8).

Though the intelligentsia tend to be the prime beneficiaries of the politicization of culture, other strata share in the realization of the national project. Peasants and workers are not immune, even if they are rarely prime movers, particularly where a marxisant 'national communism' holds sway. On the whole, it is the nationalist motifs which tap peasant energies most effectively, particularly where a foreign threat can be convincingly portrayed, as when China was invaded by Japan (see Johnson, 1969; A.D. Smith, 1979: Chapter 5). Because of this 'multi-class' character, the national project retains a popularity that is the envy of other ideological movements; for it appears to offer each class not just a tangible benefit, but the promise of dignity and unity in the 'super-family' of the nation (see Nairn, 1977: Chapter 9; Horowitz, 1985: Chapter 2).

One other reason for the continuing power of the national idea today needs to be remembered. This is the accentuation of that idea and of the several national cultures across the globe by their competition for adherents and prestige. I am not simply referring here to the way in which such cultures have become interwoven with the rivalry of states in the international arena. The cultures themselves have been thrown into conflict, as communities in their struggle for political rights and recognition have drawn upon their cultural resources — music, literature, the arts and crafts, dress, food and so on — to make their mark in the wider political arena, regionally and internationally, and continue to do so by the use of comparative statistics, prestige projects, tourism and the like. These are veritable 'cultural wars', which underline the polycentric nature of our interdependent world, as each community discovers afresh its 'national essence' in its 'irreplaceable culture values' (Weber, 1968, Vol. 1: Chapter 5).

Vernacular mobilization; the politicization of cultures; the role of intelligentsia and other strata; and the intensification of cultural wars: here are some of the reasons, briefly sketched, why national cultures inspired by rediscovered ethno-histories, continue to divide our world into discrete cultural blocks, which show little sign of harmonization, let alone amalgamation. When we add the sharply uneven nature of the distributions of both a 'rich' ethno-history and economic and political resources between nations and *ethnie* today, the likelihood of an early 'super-session' of nationalism appears remote. Feeding on each other, ethnic nationalisms seem set to multiply and accentuate national and ethnic boundaries and the uneven distribution of cultural and economic resources, at least in those areas where there remain a multitude of unsatisfied ethnonational claims. If the various regional inter-state systems appear strong enough (for how long?) to contain conflicting ethnonationalist movements, even in Africa and Asia, the number and intensity of current and potential ethnic conflicts hardly suggests a global diminution of the power of nationalism or the hold of national cultures in the next few decades.

Lingua Franca and Culture Areas
From the standpoint of both global security and cosmopolitan culture, this is a bleak conclusion. There is, however, another side to the overall picture, which may over the longer term help to mitigate some of the worst effects of intensified and proliferating ethno-national conflicts. I refer to the growing importance of the lingua franca and of various 'culture areas'.

The fact that certain languages — English, French, Russian, Arabic, Swahili and Chinese — have achieved regional or even global coverage and recognition, would not in itself lead us to predict a convergence of cultures, let alone a transcendence of nationalism. None of these widely spoken languages have achieved the transterritorial and transcultural corporate identity that medieval Latin and Arabic possessed. In that period, there were few rival written languages extending throughout the social scale of particular ethnic communities, except perhaps other sacred languages (Greek, Hebrew, Armenian in the West and Near East). The situation now is very different. Many 'low' cultures with purely spoken languages and dialects have been turned into literary 'high' cultures of mass, public education involving all social classes. Hence, the national identities that have emerged today are qualitatively different from the loose 'lateral' corporate identities of medieval clergy, ulema and aristocrats (see Armstrong, 1982: Chapter 3). This means that, in and of themselves, the rise of the lingua franca in various parts of the world, while affording a possibility for wider transterritorial cultures, cannot ensure their emergence. Other factors have to enter the field, which can then make use of the new linguistic and communications opportunities.

Paradoxically, it is a form of nationalism itself, coupled with political goals of regional peace and prosperity, which may afford a basis for the rise of regional, if not global, cultures. I have in mind the so-called 'Pan' nationalisms, defined as the attempt to unify in a single political community several, usually contiguous, states on the basis of common cultural characteristics or a 'family of cultures'. Historical examples of such nationalisms have included Pan-Turkism, Pan-Arabism, Pan-Africanism and to a lesser degree Pan-Latin Americanism.

From a narrow political standpoint, none of these movements was a success, where 'success' means unification of separate states into a 'super-state'; and those who measure Pan-Europeanism in similar circumscribed terms are fond of invoking these negative precedents. But we need not adopt so strictly political a standpoint. Judged in terms of other dimensions — cultural, economic, philanthropic — Pan nationalisms have some achievements to their credit. Pan-Arabism may not have prevented internecine wars among Arabs, but it has inspired inter-Arab development projects and broader cultural and philanthropic links, and the same was true, on a lesser scale, in the case of Pan-Turkism (see Landau, 1981). Above all, Pan nationalisms, by reminding burgeoning states and nations of a wider cultural heritage to which they are joint heirs, help to counteract the fissiparous tendencies of minority ethnic nationalisms and the rivalries of territorial state nationalisms. Even if the economic motivations and political will are insufficient to overcome conflicts, they keep alive the broad desire to negotiate differences within culture areas and create wider regional alignments and institutions.

It is in this context that we should view postwar attempts to create wider and deeper regional alignments in the western half of Europe. It is not a question of creating unity in or through diversity. Rather, the European 'family of cultures' consists of overlapping and boundary-transcending cultural and political motifs and traditions — Roman law, Renaissance humanism, Enlightenment rationalism, romanticism, democracy — which have surfaced in various parts of the continent at different times and in some cases continue to do so, creating or recreating sentiments of recognition and kinship among the peoples of Europe. It is on this basis, that a Pan-European movement, a loose form of 'Pan' nationalism, has been attempting to guide the desire for greater economic co-operation and union, and the political will to avoid the disastrous wars of the first half of this century, in the direction of a broad 'political community', though not necessarily a United States of Europe, let alone a 'super-state' (or 'super-nation') of Europe (see however Galtung, 1973).

Though the will to co-operation among European states is mainly economic in content, it is also based on cultural assumptions and traditions. Though individual national cultures remain distinctive and vibrant, there are also broader European cultural patterns which transcend national cultural boundaries to create an overlapping 'family' of common components. Democratic ideals and parliamentary institutions; civil rights and legal codes; Judeo-Christian traditions of ethics; the values of scientific enquiry; artistic traditions of realism and romanticism; humanism and individualism: these are some of the cultural patterns which straddle many of Europe's national cultures, to create a syndrome of repeated elements and form a culture area of overlapping components. Some of these components have been institutionalized; others remain at the level of belief and value, of underlying cultural assumption, as legitimations of choice and action.

It would be misleading to think of such 'culture areas' as unities in diversity or diversity within a unified framework. Perhaps such unities are and will be created in the political and economic spheres. But they bear only a partial relationship to the realities of culture areas and lingua franca. They are willed, constructed, institutional unities; whereas a culture area, with or without its lingua franca, is a product of long-term historical circumstances, often undirected and unintentional and unanticipated, which are no less powerful because they remain inchoate and uninstitutionalized. Islamic, Russian or European identities and sentiments are no less potent than the social and political institutions that 'express' them officially.

Conclusion

Such culture areas are, of course, a far cry from the ideal of a global culture which will supersede the many national cultures that still divide the world so resoundingly. Their loose patchwork quality and mixture of cultures do not as yet offer a serious challenge to the still fairly compact, and frequently revived, national cultures. There are, it is true, signs of partial 'hybridization' of national cultures, which were of course never monolithic in reality. At the same time, immigration and cultural mixing can produce powerful ethnic reactions on the part of indigenous cultures, as has occured in some western societies (see Samuel, 1989, Vol. II).

As this example illustrates, we are still far from even mapping out the kind of global culture and cosmopolitan ideal that can truly supersede a world of nations, each cultivating its distinctive historical character and rediscovering its national myths, memories and symbols in past golden ages and sacred landscapes. A world of competing cultures, seeking to improve their comparative status rankings and enlarge their cultural resources, affords little basis for global projects, despite the technical and linguistic infrastructural possibilities.

At the same time, the partial mixing of cultures, the rise of lingua franca and of wider 'Pan' nationalisms, though sometimes working in opposed directions, have created the possibility of 'families of culture' which portend wider regional patchwork culture-areas.

Such culture-areas may perhaps serve as models in the more long-term future for even broader inter-continental versions. Even in such distant scenarios, it is hard to envisage the absorption of ethno-national cultures, only a diminution in their political relevance. So attenuated a cosmopolitanism is unlikely to entail the supersession of national cultures.

Notes

1. This was a common neo-evolutionist theme in the 1960s; see Parsons (1966) and Smelser (1968). It was already presupposed in the work of 'communications theorists' such as Deutsch and Lerner; see also Nettl and Robertson (1968).

2. The Hegelian theory of 'history-less peoples' also played a part in their more specific analyses of particular nations, especially in the writings of Engels; see Davis (1967) and Cummins (1980).

3. I have brought together different phases of twentieth-century western culture in this sketch, in particular, the modernist trends of the 1960s, the 'postmodern' reactions of the 1960s and 1970s, and the technical 'neutrality' of the mass computer revolution of the 1980s. Of course, these trends and phases overlap: Stravinsky's pastiche dates from the early 1920s, while 'modernism' still exerts profound influences till today. The main point is that this Western image of 'things to come' is composed of several contradictory layers.

4. For the idea that nations should be conceived as sovereign but limited 'imagined communities', see Anderson (1983). His analysis, which gives pride of place to the 'technology of print capitalism' and the 'administrative pilgrimages' of provincial (read 'national' today) elites (to Washington, Moscow, Brussels?), could indeed shed light on the chances, and obstacles, to the rise of wider 'regional' cultures today.

5. Schlesinger (1987) discusses the work of Mattelart, Stuart Hall, Morley and others, which demonstrate the ways in which popular responses to the cultural products of American 'cultural imperialism' vary according to ethnic group and social class, lending support to the arguments for the historical specificity of imagery.

6. This is a necessarily curtailed discussion of the concept of collective cultural identity, which needs to be distinguished from the 'situational' analysis of individual identity, on which see Okamura (1981); see A.D. Smith (1986, Chapters 1-2).

7. This should not be construed as an argument for 'primordialism', the view that ethnicity and nationality are somehow 'givens' of human existence and/or history. For a discussion of the issues involved, see the essays by Brass and Robinson in Taylor and Yapp (1979); cf. also A.D. Smith (1984).

References

Abrams, Ann U. (1985) *The Valiant Hero: Benjamin West and Grand-Style History Painting*. Washington DC: Smithsonian Institution Press.

Anderson, Benedict (1983) *Imagined Communities: Reflections on the Origins and Spread of Nationalism*. London: Verso Editions and New Left Books.

Armstrong, John (1982) *Nations before Nationalism*. Chapel Hill: University of North Carolina Press.

Balsdon, J.V. (1979) *Romans and Aliens*. London: Duckworth.

Barnard, F.M. (1965) *Herder's Social and Political Thought: From Enlightenment to Nationalism*. Oxford: Clarendon Press.

Branch, Michael (ed.) (1985) *Kalevala: The Land of Heroes* (translated by W.F. Kirby). London: The Athlone Press, and New Hampshire: Dover.

Breuilly, John (1982) *Nationalism and the State*. Manchester: Manchester University Press.

Connor, Walker (1984) *The National Question in Marxist-Leninist Theory and Strategy*. Princeton: Princeton University Press.

Cummins, Ian (1980) *Marx, Engels and National Movements*. London: Croom Helm.

Davis, Horace B. (1967) *Nationalism and Socialism: Marxist and Labor Theories of Nationalism*. London and New York: Monthly Review Press.

Esman, Milton J. (ed.) (1977) *Ethnic Conflict in the Western World*. Ithaca: Cornell University Press.

Fedoseyev, P.N. et al. (1977) *Leninism and the National Question*. Institute of Marxism-Leninism, CC CPSU, Moscow: Moscow Progress Publishers.

Fisera, V.C. and Minnerup, G. (1978): 'Marx, Engels and the National Question', pp. 7–19 in E. Cahm and V.C Fisera (eds), *Socialism and Nationalism*, Vol. I. Nottingham: Spokesman.

Galtung, J. (1973) *The European Community: A Superpower in the Making*. London: George Allen and Unwin.

Gans, Herbert (1979) 'Symbolic Ethnicity', *Ethnic and Racial Studies* 2(1): 1–20.

Gellner, Ernest (1964) *Thought and Change*. London: Weidenfeld and Nicolson.

Gellner, Ernest (1983) *Nations and Nationalism*. Oxford: Basil Blackwell.

Glazer, N. and Moynihan, D.P. (eds) (1975) *Ethnicity: Theory and Experience*. Cambridge, MA: Harvard University Press.

Goldhagen, Eric (ed.) (1968) *Ethnic Minorities in the Soviet Union*. New York: Praeger.

Gouldner, Alvin (1979) *The Rise of the Intellectuals and the Future of the New Class*. London: Macmillan.

Hobsbawm, Eric and Ranger, Terence (eds) (1983) *The Invention of Tradition*. Cambridge: Cambridge University Press.

Horne, Donald (1984) *The Great Museum*. London and Sydney: Pluto Press.

Horowitz, Donald (1985) *Ethnic Groups in Conflict*. Berkeley, Los Angeles and London: University of California Press.

Hutchinson, John (1987) *The Dynamics of Cultural Nationalism; The Gaelic Revival and the Creation of the Irish Nation State*. London: George Allen and Unwin.

Johnson, Chalmers (1969) 'Building a Communist Nation in China', in R.A. Scalapino (ed.) *The Communist Revolution in Asia*. Englewood Cliffs, NJ: Prentice-Hall.

Kedourie, Elie (1960) *Nationalism*. London: Hutchinson.

Kilson, Martin (1975) 'Blacks and Neo-Ethnicity in American Political Life' pp. 236–66 in N. Glazer and D.P. Moynihan (eds), *Ethnicity: Theory and Experience*. Cambridge, MA: Harvard University Press.

Landau, Jacob (1981) *Pan-Turkism in Turkey*. London: C. Hurst.

Nairn, Tom (1977) *The Break-up of Britain*. London: New Left Books.

Nettl, J.P. and Robertson, Roland (1968) *International Systems and the Modernisation of Societies*. London: Faber.

Okamura, J.Y. (1981) 'Situational Ethnicity', *Ethnic and Racial Studies* 4(4): 452–65.

Parsons, Talcott (1966) *Societies: Evolutionary and Comparative Perspectives*. Englewood Cliffs, NJ: Prentice-Hall.

Richmond, Anthony (1984) 'Ethnic Nationalism and Post-industrialism', *Ethnic and Racial Studies* 7(1): 4–18.

Rosenblum, Robert (1967) *Transformations in Late Eighteenth Century Art*. Princeton: Princeton University Press.

Said, Abdul and Simmons, Luiz (eds) (1976) *Ethnicity in an International Context*. New Brunswick: Transaction Books.

Samuel, Raphael (ed) (1989) *Patriotism: The Making and Unmaking of British National Identity, Vol. II: Minorities and Outsiders*. London and New York: Routledge.

Schlesinger, Philip (1987) 'On National Identity: Some Conceptions and Misconceptions Criticised', *Social Science Information* 26(2): 219–64.

Seton-Watson, Hugh (1977) *Nations and States: An Inquiry into the Origins of Nations and the Politics of Nationalism*. London: Methuen.

Smelser, Neil J. (1968) *Essays in Sociological Explanation*. Englewood Cliffs, NJ: Prentice-Hall.

Smith, Anthony D. (1970) 'Modernity and Evil: Some Sociological Reflections on the Problem of Meaning', *Diogenes* 71: 65–80.

Smith, Anthony D. (1979) *Nationalism in the Twentieth Century*. Oxford: Martin Robertson.

Smith, Anthony D. (1981) *The Ethnic Revival in the Modern World*. Cambridge: Cambridge University Press.

Smith, Anthony D. (1984) 'Ethnic Myths and Ethnic Revivals', *European Journal of Sociology* 25: 283–305.

Smith, Anthony D. (1986) *The Ethnic Origins of Nations*. Oxford: Basil Blackwell.

Smith, Anthony D. (1988) 'The Myth of the "Modern Nation" and the Myths of Nations', *Ethnic and Racial Studies* 11(1): 1–26.

Smith, G.E. (1985) 'Ethnic Nationalism in the Soviet Union: Territory, Cleavage and Control', *Environment and Planning C: Government and Policy* 3: 49–73.

Taylor, David and Yapp, Malcolm (eds) (1979) *Political Identity in South Asia*. London and Dublin: Centre of South Asian Studies, SOAS, Curzon Press.

Tcherikover, Victor (1970) *Hellenistic Civilisation and the Jews*. New York: Athenaeum.

Weber, Max (1968) *Economy and Society* (edited by G. Roth and C. Wittich). New York: Bedminster Press.

Anthony D. Smith teaches Sociology at the London School of Economics. His latest book is *The Ethnic Origins of Nations* (Blackwell, 1986).

The Dream of a Secular Ecumene: The Meaning and Limits of Policies of Development

Friedrich H. Tenbruck

Forty years ago, development aid emerged as the recognized duty of some, the legitimate claim of others, and as a global task for all. Within forty years, the policies of development have thoroughly transformed the world by setting off a process of decolonialization, by deciding the fate of groups and by establishing a relationship between states on a client basis. Over the last forty years, a world-wide process of development came into being informed by scientific disciplines and under the watchful eyes of the public.

After forty years, differences in the level of development continue to represent historical dynamite, a political threat, and a human, even a moral and religious, challenge. Rational and humanitarian demands still confront us with the task of overcoming under-development. But today, this task is posed in quite a novel way because two limits are coming into view that have previously been overlooked.

For one, we have to recognize in all seriousness that the aim of all these efforts, the elimination of underdevelopment, lies in an uncertain future. The initial optimism which envisaged the goal close at hand has turned into a routine focused on singular, immediate endeavours. This realistic attitude came to become more convincing the more activities increased and were improved. What remains undecided is whether these endeavours, even if they prove successful in individual cases, will in the end eliminate underdevelopment permanently. In this respect, policies of development are sustained by hope and faith.

But we cannot rest content with the resolve to do our best. The problem of development poses itself anew once we take into account that the task of development cannot even remotely be accomplished.

Theory, Culture & Society (SAGE, London, Newbury Park and New Delhi), Vol. 7 (1990), 193–206

If development aid has so far merely served as an instrument of modernization then the realization that this aim cannot be reached will require of us a humane and ethical decision. Are we providing development aid as brotherly charity in order to alleviate misery, or to support, in piecemeal fashion, promising one-off projects, or is it payment on account to maintain the belief in modernization which cannot be fulfilled? Do we want to support the winners or compensate the losers?

All these questions have so far remained submerged under such general concepts as 'policy of development' and 'development aid' which suggest that it is only a case of providing the best means to achieve given ends. The difficulties inherent in this task remain unacknowledged, morally and factually, when we just assume that these ends are desirable and achievable. This diminishes our responsibility because our efforts are to be judged solely in relation to the success of development. The simplisitic alternative: 'development — yes or no?' represses the conflict of values that inheres in all our actions.

From the beginning, there was a comprehensive idea underlying the programme of the elimination of underdevelopment. One not only aimed to remedy underdevelopment but hoped to reduce rivalries, tensions and conflicts. One anticipated that uniform would mean joint development, leading to peaceable solidarity. Twenty years ago already, the encyclica *Populorum Progressio* stated poignantly that development 'is now the new name for peace'; it is an expectation pointing beyond the end of war and towards the fraternal commonality of interests and of understanding.

The New Message

It is for these reasons that we have to establish the limits of our ideas of development. There are some logical errors with which to start. If inequality is not conducive to peace it does not follow that equality is. While uniform development helps to resolve some problems of co-existence it may also create new ones. Because our ideas about development do not take this possibility into account they may turn into dangerous illusions. As long as we regard development as the solution to all our problems of co-existence we are prone to overlook, and thereby possibly exacerbate, other kinds of problems that cannot be remedied through development alone.

Even the concept 'developing countries' is deceptive because it hides some central facts. By suggesting an objective account it turns into a source of confusions, misunderstandings and contradicitions. What defines a developing country is simply the absence of certain criteria of development; at its most basic, a low GNP serves as an index of poverty. This serves the opinion that developing countries are such because of existing conditions. This is an erroneous view, however.

No country is a developing one just because it is less developed than others. There have always been 'rich' and 'poor' countries but never 'developing' ones, even though differentials between them may have been greater before than they are now. Even forty years ago, there were no 'developing countries' and no 'underdevelopment'. These terms surfaced only gradually in American political language and literature; they achieved wider circulation through international organizations (such as the International Bank for Reconstruction and Development, the United Nations, UNESCO) and through the rise of scientific disciplines that aimed to cater for these concerns.

The intention, or at least the hope, to improve the earthly lot of people was not unfamiliar to Christian missionaries and even to colonialism; the American conception was also influenced by the evolutionism of the nineteenth century with its faith in the general nature of problems of development. But it represented a revolutionary step to turn development aid into a global task and therefore into a regular duty together with a justified claim. In this way, the vision of the One World was created that since then has come to dominate thought and action irrespective of existing differences.

The new message did not just recognize differences in the level of development or establish development programmes; it rather turned uniform development into the expected norm that had not been realized, i.e. prevented, in the case of certain nations. In this way, countries that had previously been regarded as poor or undeveloped now were seen as 'underdeveloped' and as having been left behind expected development. Only in this way did we get the terms 'underdevelopment', 'underdeveloped countries', which transposed existing conditions into an anomaly which had to be corrected as rapidly as possible and which thereby turned it into a stigma for those concerned, one which was toned down through the new linguistic convention: 'developing countries'. Even though it may be difficult to notice it today, all related terms are value-laden because they proceed from the assumption of a uniform development as a valid and expected norm.

The idea of a global accord gave rise to the concept of developing countries, and the putting into effect of this accord produced its reality. Developing countries became a reality to the extent to which the alleviation of underdevelopment acquired the obviousness of a task in perpetuity. Most of the terms that keep the reality of developing countries in front of our eyes (such as development aid, service, minister) emerged with those institutions, activities and disciplines that were established for the realization of development policies in reference to their aim, i.e. uniform and collective development.

Idealistic Origins

Developing countries are the result of policies that regarded uniform development not only as a desirable or humanitarian goal, but as an achievable task. This led to the optimistic conviction that this task could be accomplished promptly and evenly just like any other technical problem, as long as there was enough good will, expertise and other forms of investment. Once that belief vanished it was the turn of the social sciences to uncover the underlying causes of 'underdevelopment' together with the unrecognized preconditions for the desired course of development. In this way, more and more disciplines were called on for the solution to problems of development; they then formed and expanded their own specialist areas in order to cope with the increasing demands for knowledge by institutionalized development policies.

Education has been of particular importance here. On the basis of the world-wide recommendations of Unesco it introduced, in schools and elsewhere, an awareness of the community of fate, of peace, and of the development of the One World. Since then, generations of children have grown up with the vision of a just world order as an ideal. It is therefore not surprising that art, literature, theatre, and magazines discovered a market for certain relevant issues. After all, membership of the fraternal community of development had become a part of our existential self-understanding, and the fight against underdevelopment the individual contribution to the salvation of humanity.

Whether the division of the world into developed and underdeveloped countries can be overcome remains to be seen. The same applies to the question whether development aid is the appropriate means towards this desired development. Until now, this path has largely allowed the governments of receiving countries to concentrate their power and to widen the activities of the state without, on the whole, benefiting the population. There is even cause for worry that reliance on foreign aid results in permanent pauperization. It is further to be questioned whether 'development' is a culturally neutral process which can be steered and speeded-up according to plan. But these and other presuppositions cannot easily be raised because they question obligations, aims and expectations that have long been taken for granted. For this reason it is necessary to uncover the underlying assumptions which inhibit a clear view of the facts.

The One World understands itself as a solidaristic community of free nations with the obligation to work for uniform, collective development. It did not arise out of itself from unco-ordinated processes but is evidently a willed and intended operation. It is based on a vision which was then regarded as the only possible, or at least appropriate, order and was declared and pursued as such. However correct it may be that this vision appeared plausible and acceptable it is also the case that these were responses to a novel idea. Today, however, we see the realization of this idea as the result of an unstoppable, anonymous process that would sooner or later have led to the same result. There is no longer any reference to the idealistic origins of the One World.

This view corresponds to our current mode of thinking that chooses to see historical developments as inevitable results of social circumstances and processes; it is in total harmony with the current thinking about development which sees the One World as the outcome of a natural evolutionary process. In this way, historical processes are redefined as necessary ones outside the influence of 'ideas' which, in any case, merely articulate what is happening anyhow if they are to have any influence at all. As such, the One World is the result of inevitable processes, most notably scientific, technological and economic progress, which accelerated and forced the growing interdependence of countries.

This conception is not convincing. These supposedly inevitable processes were if not initiated then, at least, decisively accelerated by the realization of this new idea. Even if they had otherwise been unstoppable they still would not have added up to the characteristic order which was attributed to the One World. The growing interlinking of the world would have been dealt with quite differently by the Axis powers had they won the War. But the world would also look differently now had England and France emerged as super-powers (out of their own strength or because of the renewed move by America into isolationism) or if Russia had been able to become a global power. Most probably, 'decolonialization' would sooner or later have occurred in any case; but such a statement of course leaves open the historically decisive, specific sets of circumstances surrounding this process. It is the forced tempo, the global programme, the general scheme which gave decolonialization its characteristic form and which produced the concrete situations, relationships, forces, and expectations that define the uniqueness of our historical situation.

America's Sense of Mission
The novel idea of a correct order could only emerge within the orbit of cultures that regarded themselves as based on a universal message directed at the whole of humanity and in this sense called upon to spread it worldwide. Such conceptions acquired strength only in some world religions with a corresponding missionary character or, in some instances, in secular philosophies such as the late Stoa where, however, it remained restricted to educated circles. Only in these few cases was it possible to overcome the normal self-understanding of cultures that all regard themselves, as long as it was at all tenable, as the only true and valid form of existence without having any interest in missionary efforts.

From a historical perspective it becomes clear fairly quickly that the idea of the One World could only spring from the ground of Christendom. It was such Christian conceptions as the Creation, the universality of the children of God and of brotherhood which, together with the chiliastic promise arising in the Middle Ages of the — however preliminary — salvation of the Kingdom of God on earth, that provided the medium for the growth of the idea of a secular ecumene as a this-worldly Coming True. Only in the context of secular remnants of this Christian theology of history could the idea of an equal and common development of humanity as the fulfil-ment of history be announced and welcomed.

These conceptions acquired their historical dynamic from the French Revolution with its ideas of liberty, equality and fraternity which beat the rhythm to the progression towards human happiness and self-determination. From them sprang, in the nineteenth century, the ideologies of political progress, liberalism and socialism which provided different paths towards the same goal, the global community. Initially, the concept of progress included all aspects of life but it gradually narrowed to mean the improvement of our material conditions and opportunities. It thereby came under the pressure of its own promise of the eventual fulfilment of history, i.e. the secure, and therefore ahistorical happiness of future mankind. This devaluation of the present to a permanent stepping-stone increasingly revealed the other face of the idea of progress as labour, effort, and sacrifice in the name of future happiness. Eventually, evolutionary theories reduced 'progress' to a smooth development but at the same time elevated it into something necessary and natural that should have taken place in history had it not been prevented by unnatural circumstances.

Nowhere was this cast into the belief in progress as cohesively as in the USA that started out from that belief and missionary zeal and held on to it without interruption. It was decisive here that the USA regarded their democracy as the universal prescription for progress. They considered their own history as the universal paradigm for the reliable interplay of independence, democracy and progress, and inferred this paradigm into all foreign ones. Even still today, as American foreign policy shows, every independence movement is seen as the spontaneous rising of a people to achieve American-style democracy, something all people naturally desire with their hearts and minds. With this conviction the USA entered the First World War and withdrew disappointedly from the peace process when they did not find their vision accepted. In 1945, however, the conditions were right for America to present a new order to the world, something they wished to do on the basis of their faith in their own mission. The One World, in which underdevelopment was to be overcome through a policy of development, was thus an idea which came to fruition in the USA after a long prehistory.

The programme itself found acceptance by developing countries; without their co-operation the whole enterprise would have been no more than a one-directional charitable action on the part of industrial countries. Rather than involving whole nations, this acceptance came from small indigenous groups who had been educated in Europe or had in some other way come into contact with European ideas. In this respect, and thanks to its pre-eminence, the USA was in a better position than the old colonial powers who had been unable to put forward plans for a global order on account of their differences and rivalries. But America at the same time profited from European expansion and colonization which had contributed essentially to modern ideas of liberty, equality, self-determination and progress spreading around the globe. But by now also, small educated elites had formed in the colonies who provided the leaders of liberation movements and the future governing elite in independent areas. It is only through their assent that a cultural consensus came into being that made possible the realization of a policy of development.

We underplay the significance of events if we reduce them to such formulae as 'development', 'modernization', 'cultural change'. Europe not only transformed the world economically and technologically and through colonization, it also exported its ideas. It is part of the genesis of the modern world that European ideas and ideologies travelled around the world in complex ways. Just as the ideas of 1789 crossed Europe and evoked mighty social and national movements, so they crossed the globe, supplemented by later ideologies. They not only created certain expectations concerning development but also led people to an awareness of their collective fate and gave rise to national, social, nativist and chiliastic movements. These ideas are now being turned back against their source in the form of demands for equality and redistribution.

Just as in the case of 'progress' so in that of 'development' too are we ongoingly concerned with concrete tasks as they surface, for example, in the context of development aid as more or less obvious and pressing projects. This is the rational side of the concept where we are dealing with identifiable tasks that have to be dealt with for humanitarian or pragmatic reasons. This plausible, concrete front hides, however, a comprehensive vision of reality that is unnoticeably imposed on thought and action through the concept of 'development'. As the mismatch of effort and results makes clear, development aid on the whole does not pursue practically solvable tasks even though it connects with them in particular instances. The idea of development calls forth constant help and planning and every failure only serves to increase this pressure. But even successes won't be sufficient for as long as they do not bring about a state of equality which itself represents only the starting point for further collective development. Once the idea of development takes a hold it pushes beyond single, concrete, obvious tasks into the wider realm of history. It inescapably entails the vision of an end-point of a society in an ahistorical future.

Marxism has justifiably been accused of having nothing much to say about the communist society that was to become a reality with the withering away of the state. But this is unavoidable if one conceives of history as a meaningful whole with a goal because once the goal has been reached, history comes to an end. This position is unknown in premodern civilizations which considered unexpected changes and difficulties as the fate of mankind, and which therefore conceived so often of 'a new heaven and earth' where all human needs could be satisfied. This is also the case with the original Christian understanding of the contrast between an aimlessly uniform process here on earth and the purposive realization of a heavenly plan for salvation. With the idea of progress, however, history acquires an inner-worldly goal and therefore also an end-point. The reproach levelled against Marxism applies to all theories of progress in basically the same way because they necessarily converge on a vision of an ahistorical future. It of course also applies to the notion of the world as a community of development which is oriented towards a goal in history.

Just as in Marxism history merges into an ahistorical epoch when all needs can be satisfied without giving rise to conflict, so the vision of development, too, anticipates an ahistorical epoch in which there is only 'development' without anything actually 'happening'. This is because 'development' stands for an empty sequence of future 'developments' which can be anticipated as 'improvements' only because we know nothing specific about them. The expectation that 'only development provides for our needs' gives birth to the belief that 'development solves all problems without causing new ones'. The only problems engendered by development that have been recognized are so far only the tangible threats to our survival, such as ecological destruction, over-population, the arms race; but even they are quickly relativized as 'undesired by-products' which can themselves be remedied through more development.

National Cultures and Global Civilization

It is the lack of historical consciousness which evidences the vacuity and limitations of the programme of development. Just as we are observing an increasingly powerful historical transformation of the world we expect to find at the end an ahistorical, that is unproblematic, state of co-existence which is to be achieved through development as a permanent process. This vision hides from view the fact that we can never escape history with its surprises, uncertainties and challenges. It thins out history to a universal society that no longer recognizes historical situatedness and problematics; in particular, it overlooks all those aspects that threaten the universal scheme because of their concrete individuality.

Wherever the vision of an inner-worldly fulfilment of the history of mankind has become triumphant, there the existence of nations and national cultures disturbed the dream of a secular ecumenicity. The vacuity (and limitations) of this vision become apparent in the almost total absence of any serious reflections concerning the fate of these historical givens in the developmental process. The question where development as a cultural process is leading to does not form part of this thinking. Where reference is made to this issue at all it tends to be in the form of a joyous anticipation of exchange, interaction, cross-fertilization and the blossoming of individual cultures, or it indulges in the opposite direction in dreams of a global culture; quite often there is not even any distinction made between these two radically different results. It was not even possible within this conception of development to ask the question concerning the fate of individual cultures.

Lenin had already posed this unsolvable puzzle for Marxism; 'just as mankind can arrive at the classless society only through the transitional period of the dictatorship of the suppressed classes, so it can arrive at the inevitable fusion of all nationalities only through the transitional period of the complete liberation, i.e. the freedom to become independent, of all suppressed nations'. This 'fusion' is 'inevitable' because history, as an inner-worldly event, will come to an end in the secular ecumenicity of mankind. But this requires the elimination of individual cultures as historical forces — to use Jacob Burckhardt's expression. For this reason, 'fusion' is regarded as inevitable in Marxist thought just as it is in Western historical thought. Here, too, history comes to an end in the vision of a secular ecumenel; here, too, 'fusion' is inevitable even though it does tend to shift vaguely between 'dissolution into a unitary global civilization' and 'completion through the flowering of national cultures'. To speak practically, for forty years Unesco, in particular, has very effectively been spreading the ideology of uniform and collective development. But its zeal appears as naive, if not already duplicitous, in view of the fact that the Third World continues to demand development while at the same time being more and more insistent on retaining its cultural identity.

What comes into view here is a global theme that comes into existence only through development activities, or which at least is made continuously more acute through them. This is so because what we perceive as development inescapably amounts to the multi-sided opening, interpenetration and mingling of cultures. This process endangers cultural identity in East and West and thus not just in the developing countries. The question that is now facing us is whether we see before us a unitary global culture or the flowering of individual cultures. There are many signs, though, that things will take a different course because all cultures find themselves enmeshed in a global struggle for their self-determination. As our eyes are riveted on the universal trend the question confronts us as to which cultures will survive this process. Not solely but especially at this point does the future, conceived of as development, reveal itself as a dangerous mirage that suggests the end of history which, however, never comes to be. It is therefore of pressing importance that we recognize behind that ahistorical mirage the historical constellation of a global struggle over culture that is engendered by development as surely as it is denied by the ideology of development.

Global Cultural Struggle

Even though world politics has, as we hope, come to eschew war, conquest and force this has, quite irrespective of grey and marginal areas, changed only the forms and means of conflict. Behind this domestication, in fact, lurks its intensification. This is because in contrast to earlier epochs where only a few cultures clashed at their geographic borders, modern developments through their universal presence and penetration now bring all cultures into a network of interrelationships. The unavoidable flip-side of this development is the confrontation of cultures whose continued self-affirmation is at risk. The more we push on with uniform and collective development the more it will have to acquire the tacit traits of a global cultural struggle; the latter will be more significant for future history than the noticeable progress in development that is the focus of all efforts.

Together with this, the foundations for legitimacy and loyalty have changed fundamentally. The well-known decrease in state sovereignty is only one part of this change. Previously, power holders legitimized themselves by convincing their followers; today they have to demonstrate their acceptance by world opinion. This applies as much to politics as it does to religion and other forces. Through this, the loyalties of the most varied political elites become internationalized as can be observed especially — but not exclusively — in the developing countries, above all in the newly independent nations of Africa. They have absorbed European science and education and their elites to some extent European culture and language, too. With the transition to an industrial organization of life the relationship of the people to their own culture and history is put into question as well. In this sense, the liberation of colonial countries together with the acceleration of modernization has only increased their dependence on developed countries, especially in relation to culture. As a consequence, the concern with cultural identity has already come supersede that of development in a number of cases.

They look towards the United States of America and the Soviet Union not just because these are superpowers which represent their interests on a global scale; they are also vast centres of cultural prestige which form the transmission belt for cultural development. Whether intended or not, this brings us to the point of the Americanization and Russification of their respective spheres of influence — which, as history shows, is something that only gets noticed once it has been completed. In this respect we have to expect the gradual colonization of the older European cultures whose individuality would in the end be levelled out and absorbed. Just as Latin became dominant in the Imperium Romanum and eventually abolished all native languages in the West, so today it is English and Russian which are advancing to the status of the lingua franca of the cultural elites in their particular spheres of influence; in certain respects, they are already the linguistic medium for the sciences and are penetrating in various ways into political and everyday language. The ideology of development — inherent in a seemingly objective terminology — makes us blind to the fact that history proceeds by the formation and dissolution of peoples, languages, cultures, nations, states, and will continue to do so more than ever in our era of global development. The expansion of European cultures has resulted in the ubiquitous co-presence and interpenetration of all cultures. Development has enhanced global migrations and dislocations of people and has moreover forced individual cultures into worldwide efforts of presenting and exporting their music, literature and religion, their ideas, world-views and lifestyles abroad. Yet what we presently perceive as a manifest increase in multi-cultural conjunctures will historically prove a contest over the preservation, survival, domination, dissolution and extinction of cultures.

This brings into focus the novel predicament of cultures in an age of electronic mass media with their pervasive global presence. Whereas the media formerly relied on language and were therefore geared primarily to national audiences, they now can by their reliance on sounds and pictures easily jump across linguistic and cultural frontiers and thereby become the direct bearers of cross-cultural images and messages. American television, for example, does not merely cater to private demands for light or serious entertainment, but serves as a powerful carrier of American culture. It does lead to disorientation and frustration in the homes of Bedouins or African tribes as they fail to come to grips with an illusory reality; in the West it is already bringing about an ongoing habitualization into the folklore of American history and the forms of life and cultural patterns of the 'American way of life'. It can be foreseen that other cultures will join the battle of the airwaves and also use the media of entertainment for the purposes of cultural messages and missions. Generally, individual cultures are losing their autonomy as they are being drawn into the network of electronic mass media that are instrumental in creating cross-cultural audiences, movements, issues, images and lifestyles. Conversely, all sorts of ideas — religious, political, moral or aesthetic — must now strive after a global hearing, recognition and respresentation, and therefore tend to get organized on a cross-cultural, global, missionary scale.

All this adumbrates a global cultural struggle with an uncertain outcome. The One World inevitably calls forth the contest and struggle or cultures for their survival, and consequently the fate of peoples, nations and languages. In the long-term this will determine which course, of courses, the process of development is going to take and what its outcome will be.

There lies a lesson in all this for the social sciences. In the wake of ideologies of development they have been concentrating on aggregate data, abstract factors, structural variables and artificial constructs, thereby losing sight of those social forces and formations which by their rise and fall, by their dissolution and recomposition largely shape and make history. Instead of perfecting general theories of society which anyway can never reproduce social reality, the social sciences must reconsider the historical role of individual cultures, peoples, nations, languages, religions and similar concrete social formations.

Note

This article is a shortened version of the original which was published in Italian and German in *Annali di Sociologia/Sociologisches Jahrbuch* 3 (1987).

Friedrich H. Tenbruck is Professor of Sociology at the University of Tübingen. His most recent books are *Die unbewaltigten Sozial-wissenschaften* (1984) and *Die kulturellen Grundlagen der Gesellschaft* (1989)

Nationalism, Globalization and Modernity

Johann P. Arnason

Introduction

It would be an understatement to say that the theory and practice of nationalism have not kept in step. A failure to progress beyond classical models and a preference for reductionistic versions of them have been characteristic of otherwise different perspectives on the modern world, but the discrepancy between the historical role and the theoretical understanding of nationalism is particularly striking. For the analysis of modern capitalism, the divergent but not essentially incompatible approaches initiated by Marx and Weber have remained indispensable points of reference; although the alternative paradigm of industrial society has never reached a comparable level, there is a distinctive problematic that can be traced back to Spencer and Durkheim; and despite the relative neglect of patterns and processes of state formation, studies in this area can build on — and must come to terms with — the conceptual foundations laid by Weber and recast by Norbert Elias. In all three cases, the confrontation with new historical experiences has underlined both basic shortcomings and unexhausted possibilities of the dominant theoretical models. There is no comparable background to theories of nationalism. The impact of the latter on the modern world has, of course, been far too conspicuous to be ignored, but the interest it has aroused among historians has not been matched by social theorists.

As I shall try to show, new theories of modernity have so far not done much to change the situation. Conversely, some theorists and historians of nationalism have tried to break new ground but their efforts have been undermined by obsolete conceptual frameworks and corresponding images of modernity. An alternative line of argument will be explored in the third section of the paper; with regard to their interpretive scope and explanatory potential, the most influential theories of modernity leave much to be desired, but they can also be read as provisional formulations of underlying perspectives that

Theory, Culture & Society (SAGE, London, Newbury Park and New Delhi), Vol. 7 (1990), 207–236

have yet to be fully articulated. One of the latter, the idea of globalization, is particularly relevant to the analysis of nationalism. Some of its implications will be discussed in the last two sections of the paper. The aim is not to develop — not even to sketch — a new theory of nationalism, but only to clarify some points that should be on the agenda for such a theory.

Theories of Modernity

The emergence — or re-emergence — of modernity as a dominant theme in social theory might seem a promising development. If the explicit focus on modernity is a reaction against implicit conceptions of it and against the reductionistic theories to which they gave rise, nationalism should find its place in the more complex vision that is now taking shape. The following discussion will explore some paths towards this goal. But although it will take note of the major attempts to construct a new theory of modernity, their relevance to our present purpose is limited; on the whole, they are less concerned with nationalism than with other previously underestimated aspects of the modern world.

Habermas's theory of modernity, grounded in a more general theory of communicative action, is a case in point. It contains no specific analysis of nationalism, but there is an allusion to nationalist doctrines as examples of 'the second generation of ideologies developed on the basis of bourgeois society' (Habermas, 1981: Vol.I, 519). Ideologies of this type respond to the problems and conflicts of an evolving modern society, but they remain rooted in a pre-modern context, inasmuch as they operate with 'totalizing conceptions of order', and when the credibility of the latter is irreversibly undermined by the modernizing process, the result is a 'fragmented consciousness' rather than a new form of ideological discourse. Within this frame of reference, there is no place for nationalism as a flexible — but by no means totally manipulative — substratum of successive and alternative ideologies. On the other hand, the distinctive characteristics and developmental trends of the modern state are analysed in terms of the general relation between system and life-world. On this level of analysis, the fact that the modern state is — or tends to become — a nation-state can be disregarded. It is true that Habermas has on other occasions had more to say about nations and nationalism, and that the overall thrust of his comments is clear: the nation is a specifically modern form of collective identity; its main historical role is to mediate between particularistic and universalistic orientations of modern society, and shifts in the balance between these two tendencies can lead to changes in the structure of national consciousness (cf. particularly Habermas, 1987: 159–79). But these observations have not been incorporated into the more systematic theory of modernity.

A more differentiated image of modernity does not ipso facto guarantee a better understanding of nationalism. In contrast to Habermas, Agnes Heller and Ferenc Feher have proposed a model which distinguishes between several different logics of modernity — those of capitalism, industrialism, and democracy — and rejects the idea of a common denominator (Heller, 1982; Feher and Heller, 1983). While this view is in principle less restrictive, it has so far not proved more receptive to the problematic of nationalism. The main reason is obvious: if the plurality of basic trends is reduced to the three logics, the dynamics of state formation and inter-state competition are thereby relegated to an even more derivative role than in the Habermasian scheme. The implicit refusal to regard them as the fourth (and not necessarily the last) dimension also blocks the analysis of nationalism; although the relationship of the latter to the modern state is neither simple nor stable, it is — as we shall see — a key element in a more complex structure.

Among recent contributions to the debate, the work of Anthony Giddens stands out as laying by far the strongest emphasis on the nation-state and its decisive role in the modernizing process. *The Nation-State and Violence* (Giddens, 1985) can be read as a comprehensive theory of modernity, with a thematic centre indicated by the title. This far-reaching change of focus still leaves open some questions concerning nationalism. Giddens rightly warns against conflating the nation, the nation-state and nationalism, but instead of treating the analytical separation as the first step towards an account of their interrelations, he tends to reify it by reducing nationalism to its psychological component. As various authors (some of whom will be discussed later) have shown, nationalism presupposes the image of the nation as a manifest, latent or desired form of collective identity and relates it to the nation-state as a co-evolving or anticipated form of political organization; at the same time, the reference to the nation is always an active and selective interpretation, and the political projection co-determines the process of state formation. Rather than a simple link between pre-existent patterns of culture and power, nationalism is thus a vehicle of their mutual determination and joint transformation. Some of

Giddens's formulations show both a certain awareness of this problematic and a preference for a psychological definition: 'By "nationalism" I mean a phenomenon that is primarily psychological — the affiliation of individuals to a set of symbols and beliefs emphasizing communality among the members of a political order' (Giddens, 1985: 116). Despite the reference to cultural symbols and political orders, the primacy of the psychological dimension is thus taken for granted, and this reductionist tendency reasserts itself after an apparent change of direction. Giddens lists four themes which ought to be of prime importance to theories of nationalism: the association with the nation-state; the ideological characteristics (related to both class domination and the 'historicity' of modern societies), i.e. 'the controlled use of reflection upon history as a means of changing history' (Giddens, 1985: 212); the psychological dynamics manifested in 'a range of sentiments and attitudes; and the particular symbolic content' (Giddens, 1985: 215–16). This agenda is then summed up in another definition: 'Nationalism is the cultural sensibility of sovereignty, the concomitant of the co-ordination of administrative power within the bounded nation-state' (Giddens, 1985: 219). To speak about a cultural *sensibility*, rather than a cultural *interpretation*, is to short-circuit the psychological and the cultural aspect; and the reference to a *concomitant*, rather than a *co-determinant*, minimizes the impact of culture on the political sphere. The constitutive role of culture is further obscured by an attempt to define the nation in purely objective terms as 'a collectivity existing within a clearly demarcated territory which is subject to a unitary administration, reflexively monitored both by the internal state apparatus and those of other states' (Giddens, 1985: 116). The hesitant approach to nationalism and the failure to explore its relations to the nation and the nation-state are thus clearly linked to a more general underestimation of cultural factors.

Interpretations of Nationalism

On the other hand, some recent work on nationalism is guided by an explicit reference to modernity as the proper context of analysis. Edward A. Tiryakian and Neil Nevitte argue that a reconceptualization of nationalism is one of the most important prerequisites for a comparative analysis of modernity (Tiryakian and Nevitte, 1985). On this view, the understanding of nationalism has been blocked by an excessive preoccupation with economic and technological aspects of the modernizing process, common to Marxists and non-Marxists. The alternative approach, however, turns out to be a more flexible version of the same basic assumptions: 'we understand by modernity a set of innovative adaptations to the social, cultural and physical environment which social actors adopt voluntarily' (Tiryakian and Nevitte, 1985: 59). The idea of 'adaptive upgrading' as the core component of modernization and as a cultural orientation that can be internalized by social actors is thus retained. Given this conceptual background, the main reason for paying more attention to nationalism is its importance in regard to political innovations; as I will try to show, the failure to break with an entrenched image of modernity thus weakens the case for a new approach to nationalism.

Tiryakian and Nevitte set themselves three interconnected tasks: to spell out the 'voluntaristic and dynamic attributes' that should be included in the concept of the nation; to clarify the relationship between nation and nation-state; and to develop a new typology of nationalism. On all three levels, they advocate a return to the classics — particularly Marcel Mauss and Max Weber — as a remedy for the shortcomings of contemporary sociology. Mauss is credited with several fundamental insights: No objective criteria of nationhood can be separated from the ongoing self-definition of the nation; from an evolutionary point of view, the national form of social integration represents a step beyond tribal or ethnic groups as well as beyond traditional empires; on the other hand, we can distinguish between more or less balanced and perfect cases of national integration; finally, the process of national unification culminates in the modern democratic state (in other words: nationality and citizenship complement each other).[1] A more simplifying interpretation of Weber highlights the themes which he shares with Mauss. He shows that national solidarity, although dependent on objective preconditions, is never fully and unequivocally determined by them, and that the self-determinative and self-articulating aspects of nationhood are most manifest in the striving for a political expression: 'A nation essentially strives for achieving or redeeming political autonomy; a nation is fundamentally a political community, and thus the concept of nation is intrinsically linked to that of political power' (Tiryakian and Nevitte, 1985: 64).[2] The amalgamation of Mauss and Weber paves the way for a return to Parsons. If nationhood is above all a matter of intersubjective solidarity and integration, rather than objective structures, it can be subsumed under the Parsonian category of societal community (Tiryakian and Nevitte, 1985: 67), and the close links between nation and state illustrate the interpenetration of the societal community and the polity. This line of argument may serve to correct some imbalances in Parsons's concrete analyses, but it does not question his main presuppositions.

If the 'creation and maintenance of culture' (Tiryakian and Nevitte, 1985: 65) and the quest for political autonomy are fundamental and consubstantial characteristics of the nation, rather than separate processes which need a co-ordinating instance, the problematic of nationalism is thereby simplified in advance. It can now be defined as 'the making of claims in the name, or on behalf of the nation' (Tiryakian and Nevitte, 1985: 67), and it becomes comparable to other forces that help to advance modernity through collective action. The typology constructed on this basis boils down to a rather elementary dichotomy. One kind of nationalism identifies the national community with the political centre of the nation-state, another sides with the periphery against the centre (or at the very least, against exclusionary practices of the latter); the greater diversity of the second type is due to a wider range of choice between defensive and offensive orientations.

A similar — but more acute — tension between a rediscovered problematic and a received paradigm is characteristic of Ernest Gellner's *Nations and Nationalism*. The stated aim of this book is to develop a theory of nationalism 'which shows it in its general forms if not in its details, to be a necessity' (Gellner, 1983: 129). The necessity in question turns out to be a mixture of functional and historical determinants. But for our present purposes, Gellner's preliminary definition of nationalism is no less interesting than his theoretical conclusions. He begins by underlining the political aspect: the claim that the state as a political unit should coincide with the nation as a cultural unit is the most obvious and universal expression of nationalism. In other words: nationalism presupposes a specific interpretation of political power and its place in social life, it generates sentiments and attitudes which facilitate or prevent the identification with existing structures of power, and it gives rise to movements which strive to implement its principles. Since a shared culture is a necessary — if not a sufficient — condition for the existence of the national community, the core idea of nationalism can be understood as 'the definition of political units in terms of cultural boundaries' (Gellner, 1983: 11). In contrast to the approach favoured by Tiryakian and Nevitte, the fusion of cultural and political unity — or at least a movement towards it — is not built into the concept of the nation. Rather, the convergence of two initially separate processes — state formation and the constitution of national identities — is regarded as the aim and achievement of nationalism. Since neither the project nor the result is predetermined by past history, the analysis of nationalism as an autonomous historical force becomes more important than the understanding of the supposedly more primordial phenomenon of national identity. 'It is nationalism which engenders nations, and not the other way round' (Gellner, 1983: 55). It is nationalism that adds to collective identity and cultural heritage the 'voluntaristic properties' highlighted by Tiryakian and Nevitte, and it can only do so by simultaneously giving them a political expression. Only some of the groups endowed with a distinctive and shared culture emerged as nations in this most complex sense.

If nationalism is to be understood as a specifically modern and unprecedentedly close relationship between culture and power, a more detailed examination of the two poles and of the possibilities inherent in their respective structures would seem necessary. But Gellner does not follow this road. His clarification of the concept of culture does not go beyond a reference to 'a system of ideas and signs and associations and ways of behaving and communicating' (Gellner, 1983: 7) and the more specific thesis that a difference in language entails a difference in culture, whereas linguistic homogeneity does not preclude further cultural differentiation. As to the problematic of the state, the well-known Weberian definition is accepted as a starting-point, and some modifications are suggested. The monopoly of legitimate violence must be seen more clearly as a characteristic of the modern Western state, rather than a universal feature; it is both a part and a general precondition of a complex division of labour; finally, another — and, as the discussion of nationalism will show, even more important — monopoly must be added: that of legitimate education. There is no discussion of the more general concept of power.

This apparent lack of interest is, of course, a logical consequence of Gellner's theory of nationalism. The necessary 'general forms' to which he refers are not the result of any intrinsic trends or essential interrelations of culture and politics; rather, they are determined and imposed by developments in the economic and technological sphere. The key to nationalism is to be found in the dynamics and demands of industrial society. 'In brief, the mutual relationship of a modern culture and state is something quite new, and springs, inevitably, from the requirements of a modern economy' (Gellner, 1983: 140). The latter 'depends on mobility and communication between individuals, at a level which can only be achieved if those individuals have been socialized into a high culture, and indeed into the same high culture' (1983: 140). A comprehensive and constantly changing division of labour cannot function without an adequate cultural medium of interaction; to ensure the standardization and diffusion of the cultural pattern, a centralized state is needed; but the state also depends on the cultural context which generates the necessary commitment and identification on the part of its citizens.

But this functionalist image of modernity does not explain why the demand for a new form of cultural integration should have led to the development of nationalism. The functional logic operates within and is specified by a historical context; 'a world that inherited both the political units and the cultures, high and low, of the preceding age' (Gellner, 1983: 52). The progress towards cultural homogenization takes place on the basis of multiple pre-constituted units and in such a way that the consolidation of larger and more integrated units creates new obstacles to global homogeneity. And there is a further twist to Gellner's argument. Because he defines nationalism in terms of a desired unity of cultural and political units and an effort to bring it about, he is less interested in the kind of unity that grows out of a gradual fusion and generates nationalism, rather than the other way round. In the case of the earliest nation-states, a process of cultural unification — limited but genuine — accompanied the centralization of power and thus created a basis on which a closer relationship between culture and power could develop. Gellner's starting-point is, by contrast, the tension between the new social need for homogeneity and the historical obstacles to it; if this tension is experienced as a disadvantage by specific social groups, nationalism is the logical response. Among situations of this type, Gellner singles out three recurrent patterns of conflict, determined by the relationship between three components of industrial society: power, education, and shared culture (capital, an 'overrated category' according to Gellner, is subordinated to educational resources). If a monopoly of power is combined with a monopoly of high culture, and if those who are thus excluded are also underprivileged with regard to education, the result is what Gellner calls the 'classical Habsburg form of nationalism'; if a shared high culture with relatively high standards of education lacks political unity and is in that sense underprivileged with regard to other cultural units, the attempt to correct the imbalance gives rise to 'unificatory nationalism' of the German or Italian type; finally, there is the 'diaspora nationalism' of culturally distinctive and economically specialized communities which are not only barred from access to political power, but scattered across political frontiers (Greeks, Jews and Armenians are the most conspicuous cases).

For many earlier historians of nationalism, the classic example of its Western version and the beginning of its worldwide diffusion was the new kind of national consciousness which matured in and through the French Revolution: 'the moment when the nation, ceasing to be dependent on the state which had created it, wanted to make the state dependent on itself' (Morin, 1984: 130). Gellner's typology links the Western model to Germany and Italy, rather than France. There is a similar shift in his discussion of Habsburg nationalism. The more concrete the description becomes, the better it fits southeastern Europe rather than Czech or Hungarian nationalism. Apart from the difficulty of explaining the two latter cases in terms of underprivileged groups struggling for access to education and power, a more specific aspect is obscured by Gellner's argument: the reference to earlier states which had — after a complex and in some ways original development — lost their independence but retained at least a symbolic continuity within the framework of the Habsburg empire. And in both cases, modern nationalism inherited — albeit in different ways and with different consequences — the problematic of states which had been characterized by tensions between a multinational structure and a dominant ethnic component. The failure to do justice to this central European pattern reflects the same conceptual shortcomings as the neglect of the French paradigm. Gellner's explanatory model has no place for the process of state formation as an autonomous variable, following its own logic and functioning well in advance of the transition to industrial society. In the functionalist image of modernity, the state appears only as a complement to the division of labour and as a backdrop to its cultural medium. A crucial determinant of the modern world is thus downgraded and its interaction with other historical forces correspondingly simplified; neither its significance for the development of nationalism in general nor its impact on specific types of nationalism can be properly evaluated.

Although Gellner has more to say on the cultural preconditions of nationalism than on the political ones, he arrives at similarly reductionistic conclusions. His typology is only concerned with the correlations between cultural differences and differences in access to education and power. At this level, the contents of specific cultural patterns are irrelevant to the problematic of nationalism. No systematic connection is made between the 'varieties of nationalist experience' and the diversity of traditional experiences and interpretations of identity. John Armstrong's seminal work on 'nations before nationalism' (Armstrong, 1982) highlights the strength and complexity of the traditional background; another case in point is Gellner's own analysis of Islam — 'the most protestant of the great monotheisms' (Gellner, 1983: 79) and its very distinctive contribution to modern nationalism, but this argument is not integrated into his general theory. A further consequence of the decision to abstract from cultural contents should at least be briefly noted: The nationalist fusion of culture and power interacts with other images and interpretations of power that are characteristic of or remain active within the modern world, and since the resultant constellations cannot be analysed without allowing for the role of varying interpretive contents, this line of differentiation is excluded from Gellner's typology. The relationship between nationalism and democracy depends to a significant extent on the cultural interpretations of power which prevail on both sides; the constitutive imagery of particular nationalisms is more or less conducive to the perpetuation or reactivation of imperial projects: last but not least, the rise of totalitarian domination was facilitated in different ways by different types of nationalism. Gellner's ambition is to develop a general theory of nationalism, and he explicitly refuses to concern himself with the historical explanation of its most extreme forms, but although the mutation of nationalism into fascism only took place under very specific circumstances, its global impact on the modern world was such that the general theory ought to include an analysis of its preconditions.

A promising first step — the location of nationalism in the field of relations between culture and power — is thus overshadowed by functionalist preconceptions and by the classificatory framework in which they are reflected. An attempt to continue the initial argument along non-functionalist lines would involve a stronger emphasis on the autonomy of both politics and culture. There is, however, a prima-facie reason for beginning with culture: nationalism defines and justifies power in terms of culture, rather than the opposite, and even a theory which wants to demystify this claim must first come to grips with it. Anthony D. Smith's most recent work on nations and nationalism spells out some consequences of this approach. It is easy to show that nationalism as movement and ideology remains dependent on the nation as a cultural form, and although the latter may lend itself to strategies of manipulation and mobilization, it also sets limits to them. Most importantly, the nation presupposes and remains dependent on an earlier form of collective identity: 'Put simply, modern nations are not as "modern" as modernists would have us believe. If they were, they could not survive'; in other words, they 'require ethnic cores if they are to survive' (Smith, 1986: 212). As neither past nor present experience suggests that modern nations can transcend ethnicity (as Smith rightly stresses, the case of the United States is certainly not a counter-example), the first task of a theory of nationalism is to clarify the concept of an ethnic group (or *ethnie*, as Smith prefers to call it). Although Smith does not use this expression, his analysis could be summed up in terms of a double paradox of ethnicity. On the one hand, the ethnic community transcends the bond of kinship, but it can only do so by generalizing and sublimating it through a myth of common descent and a corresponding sense of solidarity. On the other hand, this double-edged relationship to the cultural model of kinship is based on a combination of several factors. The most salient of them are a shared history, a distinctive shared culture, and an association with a specific territory. Although their relative weight varies, a comparative analysis of ethnic survival leaves no doubt about the particular significance of religion. More precisely, it is the identification of an ethnic community with a salvationist religion that appears to secure survival more effectively than anything else. The tension between the particularistic closure of the *ethnie* and the universalistic potential of the religion can be neutralized in various ways. But in the most general terms, it seems appropriate to describe the apparent solidity and durability of the ethnic bond as the superstructure of a more problematic basis — an intermediary position between kinship and religion, dependent on both but also on the capacity to subordinate them to the ethnic imperative.

To stress the indispensability of ethnic foundations is not to deny all novelty to modern nations. Smith explains the formation of nations as a response to the 'triple revolution' — in economic integration, administrative control, and cultural co-ordination — which marks the advent of modernity. The impact of this global structural change on the ethnic core is twofold. On the one hand, it is subordinated to new forms of social integration: the nation becomes a 'territorially centralized, politicized, legally and economically unified unit bound by a common civic outlook and ideology' (Smith, 1986: 152). On the other hand, the fusion and stabilization of these innovations is impossible without the active involvement of the ethnic substratum: 'the "nation" must take over some of the attributes of pre-existing *ethnie* and assimilate many of their myths, memories or symbols, or invent ones of its own' (Smith, 1986: 152). The 'civic' and the 'ethnic' component are thus interdependent and equally fundamental aspects of the modern nation, but they can also give rise to conflicting definitions of nationhood and types of nationalism (on this view, nationalism is the theoretical and practical articulation of the process which leads to the formation of nations). The civic model of the nation was a Western invention, and its world-wide diffusion is comparable to that of some other products of Western civilization, but the ethnic element also left its mark on the earliest Western nations, although it became more pronounced in later stages of development and other parts of the world.[3]

Smith's main contention is clearly formulated and convincingly argued: the formation of nations is not simply a part of the modernizing process; it is co-determined by the ethnic antecedents, and the latter can even enter into conflict with the more distinctively modern factors. But it remains to be seen how this argument is combined with a more comprehensive theory of modernity. At this point, Smith returns to a functionalist perspective; his explanatory model rests on the claim that the triple revolution made the formation of nations 'desirable' (Smith, 1986: 131). Both the traditional and the modern ingredients of nationhood had integrative functions to fulfil, and it was their simultaneous activation in response to societal needs that generated the tension between them. This reassertion of a functionalist image of modernity prevents Smith from developing his argument in another direction. If nations and nationalism can only be understood as changing mixtures of modern and pre-modern elements, this might be a special — and particularly obvious — case of a more general pattern: the permanent and co-constitutive presence of tradition within modernity. We could, in other words, try to use the problematic of nations and nationalism as a new key to the interpretation of modernity, rather than subordinating it to a pre-existent model. This suggestion will seem more plausible if we link it to some other focal points of the debate.

Pointers to an Alternative

The three above-mentioned theories of nationalism are, as I have tried to show, all open to the same objection: the reluctance to question a received image of modernity limits their interpretive and explanatory scope. On the other hand, each of them centres on a specific idea which would lend itself to other uses. Tiryakian and Nevitte draw attention to the integrative properties of the nation; if we are to avoid transfiguring them into a 'societal community' and thus conflating them with an integrative core of society in general, we need a comparative analysis of contrasts and connections between the nation and other forms of integration. Gellner interprets nationalism as a new and distinctive link between culture and power; although the nation represents the cultural pole of the relationship, its formation presupposes the political one as well. This line of argument can be continued more effectively if the cultural and political determinants of modernity are not collapsed into the division and organization of labour. Finally, Smith's discussion of the relationship between *ethnie* and nations highlights both the need for a more general reconsideration of the distinction between tradition and modernity and the impossibility of tackling this problem within a functionalist framework.

But as I argued in the first section of the paper, current theories of modernity are characterized by a lack of interest in or a limited grasp of nationalism. There is thus no ready-made conceptual framework for the three suggested lines of enquiry. We can, however, try to relate them to some observable shifts and trends in the recent history of social theory. From this point of view, concrete proposals for a new image of modernity are less important than the general direction indicated by the break with the old one; while the former will no doubt be superseded by more complex models, the latter is a long-term perspective that has yet to be fully articulated. If we look for a common denominator of new approaches to the question of modernity, three changes — interconnected in principle but unequally developed and sometimes isolated in practice — stand out as particularly important. For our present purposes, it will be convenient to describe them as globalization, pluralization and relativization. Within the limits of this paper, neither the antecedents in classical theory nor the new aspects added by recent analyses can be discussed in detail; I shall confine myself to a brief clarification of the three concepts.

1. The term *globalization* can be used to refer both to a historical process and to the conceptual change in which it is — belatedly and still incompletely — reflected. Globalization in the first and broadest sense is best defined as 'the crystallization of the entire world as a single place' (Robertson, 1987a: 38) and as the emergence of a 'global-human condition' (Robertson, 1987b: 23). But the interpretations of the process have proved at least as prone to reductionism as the theories which were consciously or unconsciously adapted to the more limited horizon of the nation-state. Globalization theory is thus still faced with the task of transcending partial perspectives and constructing a frame of reference which would correspond to the brief description quoted above. In this context, world system theory can perhaps be regarded as a special case of globalization theory — open to the charge of economic reductionism, but still constituting a challenge to less developed versions. Wallerstein's work has led to a systematic transformation of the Marxian perspective which has yet to be matched by neo-Durkheimian or neo-Weberian variants of globalization theory.

2. By *pluralization* I mean the growing awareness of several interdependent but mutually irreducible components of modernity, and of the discrepancies and tensions between them. The historical reference is both to a plurality which has always been constitutive of the modern world, although it was temporarily obscured by one-dimensional theories, and to the various processes which transformed the original constellation. It is not enough to multiply characteristics and criteria of the modern condition or the modernizing process; the decisive step is, rather, the idea of different 'logics', i.e. patterns of basic relations and long-term developments that can enter into conflict with each other and give rise to divergent or even mutually exclusive paradigms of modernity. Both the Habermasian dichotomy of system and life-world (with their respective patterns of rationalization) and the three-dimensional model proposed by Feher and Heller can be regarded as moves in this direction, but they can also be criticized from the standpoint of a more radical pluralism. The neglect of nationalism is one of many consequences of the premature closure of the conceptual scheme.

3. An analysis in terms of different aspects and changing relationships between them necessarily leads to a *relativization* of the image of modernity — not only in the sense that it undermines the idea of a unified project or a paradigmatic model, but also — and more importantly — because of its implications for the distinction between tradition and modernity. If the structure of modernity lends itself to variations which depend on the historical context, it is by the same token open to a partial determination by the traditional background. The diversity of cultural traditions is thus reflected in the configurations of modernity as well as in the roads to it. This does not mean that the unity which can no longer be guaranteed by an idea or a project of modernity is restored on the level of particular traditions. It is more frequently the case that internal tensions and conflicts of the tradition are reactivated in a new context. And the synthesis of tradition and modernity should be seen as a matrix of further changes, rather than a stable model (the transformations of Japanese society after its breakthrough to modernity are a particularly striking example). The theoretical expressions of this new perspective are as varied as those of the other two. At one end of the spectrum, S.N. Eisenstadt proposes to redefine the Western paradigm of modernity as a new 'great tradition', comparable to the universal religions, and to explain non-Western variants in terms of fusions and conflicts with other traditions. At the other, Alain Touraine argues that all modern societies are combinations of modern structures and modernizing processes, and that the second component can never be deduced from the first; there is no endogenous unfolding of modernity, only changing forms of dependence on non-modern bases and forces of development.

There are some obvious points of contact between these perspectives and the interpretations of nationalism discussed in the second section of this paper. The emphasis on national integration must be qualified in the light of globalization theory; in the context of the global situation, the nation and the nation-state intersect and conflict with other forms of integration. If nationalism is (as Gellner suggests) to be understood as a link between initially separate and fundamentally autonomous processes in the cultural and the political sphere, this is already a first step towards a pluralization of the overall image of modernity. Finally, if a pre-modern foundation (such as the *ethnie* analysed by Smith) turns out to be essential to the very modernity of nations, this conclusion should raise some further questions about the distinction between tradition and modernity. But on the other hand, the connections between the theoretical perspectives are too complex and far-reaching for them to be used separately in relation to specific themes. Each of them needs further clarification in the light of the others. Globalization theory specifies the framework within which the two other approaches have to be located; conversely, pluralization and relativization are necessary correctives against simplified models of global unity.

This interdependence has to some extent been acknowledged. Robertson's globalization theory is in principle open to the other two perspectives: 'the insistence on heterogeneity and variety in an increasingly globalized world is, as I have said, integral to globalization theory' (Robertson, 1987b: 22). This would seem to apply to the intrinsic heterogeneity of the modern world no less than to the additional variety derived from different civilizational backgrounds. But a more concrete synthesis could only be the outcome of a more explicit dialogue with the theories that have given first priority to pluralization or relativization, and some formulations of globalization theory suggest a rather restrictive view of this task. References to 'a single place with systemic properties', to be 'treated in terms of what we call a "voluntaristic" world system theory', and involving 'the problem of global order, in addition to, or perhaps even instead of the old problem of social and societal order' (Robertson and Lechner, 1985: 103) are unmistakably indicative of a Parsonian approach, transferred from an artificially isolated and unified society to the global condition. If we accept that theories of both society and modernity have — as a result of pluralizing and relativizing approaches — moved away from models of systemic closure, the premises of globalization theory will have to be reconsidered in the light of these developments. Conversely, some advocates of pluralization and relativization try to link their theses to the international context, but miss the specific perspective of globalization. For example, Eisenstadt argues that the various levels of interaction between civilizations give rise to several world systems (economic, political and ideological), but the character of the global framework within which they interact remains unclear.

Despite the implicit convergences, the emerging problematic is thus still a fragmented one, and a closer look at some classical arguments might help to bridge the gaps. As I shall try to show in the following section, Max Weber's work can — notwithstanding an apparent unconcern with globalization — still be used as a guide towards a combination of the three perspectives.

For the construction of post-functionalist images of society and modernity, all these perspectives are essential. Critics of functionalism have shown that its systemic models (at least the traditional, i.e. pre-Luhmannian ones) are idealized projections of bounded social units, such as the nation-state; the latter are secondary configurations, imposed on a more complex and open social field. Globalization, pluralization and relativization are complementary approaches to the modern structure of this field. A detailed analysis of their interconnections is beyond the scope of this paper; the following discussion will centre on the first perspective and treat the other two as subordinate parts of it. In general terms, a similar preference for pluralization or relativization would of course be equally justified. But with regard to nations and nationalism, there are good reasons for the present approach: inasmuch as globalization theory confronts the national phenomenon with a qualitatively different and more comprehensive form of integration, it constitutes a particular radical challenge to the traditional view.

Globalization and its Countercurrents

No theory of nationalism has ignored the integrative properties of the nation or their role in the modernizing process, but it has proved easier to recognize their importance than to place them in a proper context. Some major conceptual obstacles have already been alluded to. In particular, the effects of the 'functionalist persuasion' (J. Alexander), with which contemporary theorists of nationalism seem reluctant to break even when they reject its most systematic versions, are both obvious and far-reaching. In the last instance, it subordinates integrative relations to instrumental ones; the details of the connection depend on the systemic concepts into which the instrumentalist perspective is translated, most directly on the primacy of reproduction or adaptation. And if the distinctive logic of integration is emphasized more strongly (against the systemic point of view or within a more flexible version of it), the specificity of national integration is often overshadowed by more general principles. The Parsonian stance adopted by Tiryakian and Nevitte is a good example. The reasons for this shift from the particular to the general are not hard to find. As several critics of the sociological tradition (Elias, Giddens and Touraine, to mention only the most important ones) have convincingly argued, the nation-state, under-stood as the political expression of the nation, is the historical reality behind the more or less elaborated concept of society. The particular characteristics of national integration have thus been too system-atically sublimated into a general model of social integration for them to be thematized in their own right; and conversely, the general theory of social integration has been too universally dominated by the special case of the modern nation-state for a genuine compara-tive perspective to develop. The nation-state is, in other words, both presupposed and transfigured by the sociological tradition. This applies not only to those who were most concerned with social integration or most aware of the nation-state as a matrix of modernity. Solomon Bloom's interpretation of Marx (Bloom, 1941) shows to what extent Marx took the national and the international context (the latter in the literal sense of the interaction between nations and nation-states) for granted as a background to class struggles and capitalist development.

But the image of a 'world of nations', in which Bloom sums up this tacit dimension of Marxian theory, has another and even more important connotation. Nations and nation-states do not simply interact with each other; under modern conditions, they form — or tend to form — a *world*, i.e. a global context with its own processes and mechanisms of integration. The national form of integration thus develops and functions in a close connection and a more or less acute conflict with the global one. This brings us back to globaliza-tion theory and its research programme. To grasp its relevance to the analysis of nationalism, it is necessary to bear in mind that globalization is by no means synonymous with homogenization (which is not to say that it does not involve processes of partial homogenization). It should rather be understood as a new frame-work of differentiation. Robertson stresses the need to 'include individuals, societies, relations between societies and (in the generic sense) mankind as the major contemporary components or dimen-sions of the global-human condition' (Robertson, 1987b: 23), and he draws attention to the 'global valorization of particular identi-ties' (1987b: 21) which forms part of the overall process of globaliza-tion. Among the identities that are thus reinforced and reoriented by the global context, civilizational complexes and traditions are not the least important.

We can now define more precisely the contributions of globaliza-tion theory to the understanding of nations and nationalism. On the one hand, the differentiating impact of globalization strengthens or reactivates national identities, communities and projections. This process — national differentiation as the obverse of the constitution of a world society — has, of course, not gone unnoticed. The more sensitive Marxist approaches (cf. especially Bauer, 1924) throw some light on it; despite its functionalist premises, the same can be said about Gellner's analysis. But globalization theory can link such insights to a more explicit and adequate framework. On the other hand, the national level of integration complements, conditions and counteracts the global one. Within the 'world of nations', the nations have a more or less pronounced tendency to become worlds in their own right, and in this capacity, they also face the task of coming to terms with the other lines of differentiation which are built into the global condition. The phenomena of sub- or counter-globalization, centering on the nation and the nation-state, have been less thoroughly analysed than the first aspect. The following remarks should be read as an attempt to put them in perspective.

Theories of the global condition have so far been primarily concerned with its economic and political aspects, i.e. the capitalist world-economy and the internationalization of the European state system. On both levels, nations and nationalism can be related to the global context in three different ways. Inasmuch as they serve to consolidate and demarcate the units of which it is composed, it may seem plausible to treat them as functional supports of the international division of labour (Wallerstein) or subordinate by-products of interstate competition (Elias). But even within the limits of this relationship, the functionalist approach is inadequate. National identities and nationalistic perspectives can become the starting-point for different interpretations of the global situation; together with different civilizational traditions and conflicting currents in modern culture, they thus lend to the tendential singularity of the globalizing process a plurality of meanings. This factor always accompanies the subordination of national units to the global socio-cultural field, but its impact can — as the two other configurations show — go much further.

On the one hand, the periodic reappearance and partial success of imperial projects is no less characteristic of modern history than is the constitution of economic and political world systems. This part of the modern constellation might be seen as an attempt to re-impose a pre-modern pattern on the globalizing process, but under modern conditions. In the case of imperial projects which developed on the basis of nation-states, this is obvious; as to the dynastic empires which tried to adapt to a new historical environment, their ability or inability to mobilize nationalist currents was of crucial importance. Both the imperial and the national component were, of course, transformed by the connection. If the apologists of nineteenth-century imperialism could describe it as patriotism transfigured by universalistic ideals, there was a grain of truth in this claim: the association with imperialism shows that nationalism can give rise to or be translated into aspirations which go beyond the nation-state and the system of nation-states, and that developments in this direction add new aspects to the combination of tradition and modernity. Conversely, the adaptation to a world of nations calls for new approaches to the cultural definition and legitimation of imperial projects.

On the other hand, the national imagery and its institutional embodiment can also become the basis for strategies of withdrawal from the global context. It is one of the most intriguing facts about modern history that the most significant attempts of this kind have been linked to revolutionary transformations and universalistic ideologies. The idea of 'socialism in one country' marked a decisive step towards the conflation of a strategy of systemic change with one of withdrawal and isolation, and towards a corresponding fusion of socialism and nationalism, but because of the imperial character of the state with which it was first associated, the particularistic implications were more muted than they became in some later cases. The contribution of post-revolutionary states to the 'global valorization of particularity' is thus more adequately exemplified by Cambodia, North Korea and — above all — Albania. Their experience has shown the impossibility of total withdrawal, but also the possibility of a dissociation that is real enough to initiate a regressive mode of development and to lend some plausibility to the phantasm of an alternative world.

The relationship of nations and nationalism to the global background is thus a complex, ambiguous and changing one. But there is yet another and less obvious side to it. A detour through a classic text which at first sight has nothing to do with globalization theory might be the best way of bringing this aspect to light. In 'Science as a Vocation', Max Weber compared the conflicts between different value-orientations to the rivalry of national cultures (Weber, 1946: 129–56). The vision of an irreducible pluralism of value-orientations can be understood in the light of the analysis of 'world orders' which tend to become closed universes with their own totalizing logic (Weber, 1946: 323–59), but the direct comparison with national cultures is more puzzling. It is perhaps easier to understand if we assume a shared but tacit reference to globalization. Within the global context, the world orders — those, for example, of a modern capitalist economy, of sovereign states and state systems, or of a cognitive-instrumental reason based on the assumption of universal calculability and striving for an unlimited domination of nature — can develop more far-reaching aspirations and become more independent of each other than within the boundaries of more restrictive societal units. Each of them has its own distinctive forms and contents of internationalization; Weber's account implicitly presupposes this dimension. To the extent that the concept of world system is applicable to the globalization process, the appropriate frame of reference is thus a plurality of systems, rather than a single one. On the other hand, the nation and the national imagery internalize the global horizon. The image of the nation as a cultural totality, capable of imposing a new unity on the diverging 'life orders', is a response to the globalizing process and an attempt to neutralize the latter on its own ground, and the plurality of such responses is — up to a point — comparable to the plurality of the orders. Both the unifying and the fragmenting tendencies must be understood in relation to the global-human condition.

If globalization and differentiation are inseparably linked, the first of our three theoretical perspectives leads directly to the second. The above considerations have already touched upon the problematic of pluralization; a theory which wants to relate nations and nationalism to the global condition must also locate them in the field of a multi-dimensional and multi-directional modernity. It is true that national forms and ideals of integration may obscure the links between globalization and pluralization; they lend added strength — both real and imaginary — to the boundaries which more localized social units try to impose on a global and pluralized social field. But from another point of view this distinctive contribution makes it all the more necessary to consider nations and nationalism in relation to other dimensions of modernity. This is not simply a matter of interactions between mutually external forces. More importantly, the national imagery and its nationalist articulations constitute themselves by relating to various other aspects of a broader context, and the different ways of doing so are reflected in their self-definitions as well as in their impact on the overall patterns of modernity. The most obvious case in point is the connection with the modern state: nationalism defines and defends the nation in relation to the state as a given, desirable or recoverable form of political organization, and even in the rare and extreme case of a purely cultural nationalism, supposedly capable of transcending political divisions, the project must involve an explicit devaluation of the state. Apart from this central point of reference, a theory of nationalism would have to deal with more selective and flexible relations to other components of modernity. But cultural definitions of the nation do not only situate it with regard to other socio-cultural significations; an important part of the history of nationalism consists in the assimilation of the nation to other interpretive categories, more clearly defined or more attuned to specific purposes. The identification of national *grandeur* with a revolutionary project is an example of this; another is the idea of the 'proletarian nation', which substitutes nation for class as the subject of collective action, but at the same time draws on the idea of the class struggle to legitimize the shift. On a different and less ideologically charged level, the modern idea of individuality has functioned as a model or at least a necessary point of reference for interpretations of the national phenomenon. Defenders of nationalism as a principle of legitimation and organization have tried to strengthen their case by comparing the equal right of nations to self-determination to the mutual recognition of autonomous individuals; a closer but more ambivalent relationship is envisaged by those who think of nationality as an 'inner, inseparable property of the person', and conclude that 'it is impossible to stand in a moral relationship to this person without recognizing the existence of what is so important to him' (Solovyev, quoted in Kamenka, 1973: 9). Theorists of nationalism have often been guided by the idea that 'nations are the great corporate personalities of history' and that 'their differences in character and outlook are one of the main factors shaping the course of events' (Kohn, 1946: 329). Among other things, the notion of a national character became the starting-point for the most systematic Marxist analysis of the national question (Bauer, 1924). On the other hand, those who wanted to liberate the national imaginary from the restrictions of nineteenth-century nationalism condemned the latter because of its tendency to think of nations as individuals writ large (Jünger, 1932).

But the nation is not only a component of modernity. If its

interpretive constitution involves a pre-existent ethnic core, it is also a changing combination of tradition and modernity, and the cultural interpretations which serve to situate the nation within a pluralized world should be seen against this background. In this way, the perspective of pluralization converges with that of relativization, in the sense of a recognition of the presence and ongoing reactivation of tradition within modernity. Another look at Max Weber's work and the questions he left open — or saw no reason to ask — may help to understand the relationship between the two approaches and their common links to globalization theory.

Weber's analysis of conflicting cultural spheres is, as we have seen, a pioneering and still relevant contribution to the theory of pluralization. But contrary to some recent interpretations, the 'world orders' which he distinguishes are not reducible to a modern pattern of differentiation; they are, rather, co-determined — albeit not all to the same degree — by traditional patterns of meaning and orientation. This is most obvious in the case of religion. With the transition from the traditional to the modern world, it loses its central position and much of its integrative capacity, but it remains a constitutive part of the modern constellation — not only as an increasingly irrational and marginal haven of retreat from other spheres, but also as an implicit model for the logic of the dominant orders, whose development is to a considerable extent shaped by the necessity to occupy the place and assume the roles left vacant by religion. This link to the traditional background is reinforced by specific patterns of meaning in other spheres. In Weber's model, the pluralization and relativization of modernity thus go hand in hand, and the significance of the synthesis is easier to understand if we relate it to another connection which Weber did not spell out. His comparative analysis of civilizations is, first and foremost, an inventory of the socio-cultural structures and forces which obstructed or facilitated the emergence of modern capitalism. If we locate capitalist development within the field of tensions constituted by multiple and conflicting 'world orders', the logical next step would be a comparison of the civilizational patterns — Occidental and Oriental — as matrices of differentiation. Weber touches upon this theme — the reflection of different civilizational contexts in different patterns of the separation and interaction of cultural spheres — on various occasions, but there is no systematic discussion of it. Weber's failure to explore this problematic is easy to understand. He was interested in the Western road to a modernity dominated by capitalism and in the obstacles to a comparable break-through in societies dominated by other traditions; the complementary question of modifications of modern patterns (including, in particular, patterns of pluralization) in other parts of the world, caused by the enduring or reactivated impact of other civilizational complexes, was not yet on the agenda. Later developments brought it to the fore, but they have also shown that the phenomena in question — the reconstitution of traditions and identities — can only be understood in relation to the globalizing process.

The third theoretical perspective — the relativizing one, in the sense defined above — can thus be linked to the first in a way which highlights the potential contribution to the theory of nations and nationalism. A comparative study would analyse the various transitions from *ethnie* to nation in the light of different civilizational legacies and corresponding roads to modernity. Such an approach would be incompatible with the Eurocentric distinction between the original nationalisms of the West and the derivative nationalisms which resulted from its impact on the rest of the world. But this point must be discussed in connection with some other typological distinctions.

Towards a Typology of Nationalism

As soon as it is admitted that the nation has to be analysed as an interpretive construct, rather than an objective structure, the theory of the nation becomes inseparable from that of nationalism. The theorists who focus on integrative structures may still try to defend the primacy of the nation, but for the two other approaches discussed in the second section of the paper, this claim is much less acceptable; Gellner argues that nationalism creates nations, rather than the other way around, and Smith's analysis points to a similar conclusion — nationalism is obviously involved in the transition from *ethnie* to nation. And since the perspectives of globalization, pluralization and relativization all relate the interpretive constitution of the nation to broader contexts, they strengthen the case for a primacy of nationalism. On the other hand, nationalism finds expression in conflicting ideologies and movements, and the nation appears as a common but disputed background. There are, in other words, good reasons to distinguish between nationalism and the nation, but the latter should be regarded as a co-constituted horizon, rather than a pre-existent condition. Gellner's thesis can thus be taken one step further: nationalism generates nations, but in a way that endows them with a certain autonomy in regard to the generative contexts.

For these reasons, a theory of nationalism is a more appropriate frame of reference than a theory of the nation, and because of the extraordinary diversity of its object, it must begin with a simplifying typological scheme. In the present context, we must limit ourselves to a brief reconsideration of three typological distinctions, widely used in the literature on nationalism but open to some objections on the basis of new insights into the relationship between nationalism and modernity. Each of them can be related to one of the three theoretical perspectives discussed above, but it can also be shown that the perspective of globalization has a more comprehensive bearing on all of them.

Analysts of nationalism have often distinguished between a Western and an Eastern type. The former is said to be more solidly grounded in social and political realities, whereas the latter compensates for its weakness in this respect by emphasizing cultural unity and specificity, and by attributing to the culture in question a more or less mythical continuity. Eastern nationalism thus tends to regard the nation-state as the natural expression of a pre-existent unity which can also serve to de-legitimize social and political conflicts; it is, in other words, more conducive to anti-democratic attitudes than the Western type. Despite its prima-facie plausibility, the distinction has proved very difficult to define in precise terms. Hans Kohn used it to explain the contrast between Germany and Western Europe (Kohn, 1946); later authors have often moved the boundary further to the East.[4] On the other hand, some descriptions of Eastern nationalism stress its affinity with Fascist ideologies and movements, and since it seems clear that the first Fascist mutation of nationalism took place in France (Sternhell, 1983), this raises some questions about the contrast between West and East. Finally, it can be shown that nationhood and nationalism depend on both political and cultural factors and that different types can be explained in terms of different proportions between these components. The supposedly Western and Eastern types are, on this view, complementary sides and alternative directions of every nationalism.

The geographical division has thus proved untenable. But if we relate the underlying question more directly to globalization theory, the distinction can perhaps be reformulated. The differences that were first perceived in terms of West and East were partly caused by different positions within the global context and the most basic distinctions of the latter kind reflect a fundamental ambivalence in the relationship between the two forms of integration. Nations, nation-states and nationalisms function, on the one hand, as links to the global context and components of its various levels and, on the other hand, as a real and imaginary counterweight to the globalizing process. While the second aspect is never completely absent, its strengthening can, as we have seen, give rise to defensive as well as offensive strategies. Its impact on the national imagery is obviously conducive to a de-contextualization and essentialization of the nation. This can be justified on cultural, racial or territorial grounds; the attempts to draw a line between Western and Eastern nationalism have usually singled out one or the other of those aspects. But although images of national essence draw on different sources and emphasize different contents, they converge in their response to the globalizing process; if the two types of nationalism are to be reduced to an intrinsic duality of nationalism, the global context is thus essential to the understanding of the latter.

The second distinction has to do with successive patterns, rather than geographically separate types. The liberal or 'Risorgimento' nationalism which developed in the aftermath of the French revolution and became one of the formative forces of nineteenth-century Europe is often contrasted to the 'integral nationalism' which was more characteristic of a later era of imperialist expansion and international conflicts (for this version of the typology, cf. particularly Alter, 1985). It is tempting to reinterpret this dichotomy in the light of the pluralizing perspective described above. Liberal nationalism relates the nation to other aspects of modernity in such a way that it becomes a general framework for their unfolding and thereby loses some of its specific content. The nation-state, envisaged as a necessary focus of national identity, allows a more or less continuous development of a capitalist-industrial economy and the corresponding social conflicts; furthermore, it permits and circumscribes the progress of the democratic counterweight to capitalism. By contrast, integral nationalism (particularly in its Fascist version) affirms the primacy of the nation and the nation-state at the expense of the historical forces with which they were previously associated in a more balanced way. The consequences of the change were not the same for industrialism, capitalism and democracy (their developmental logic could be instrumentalized, reoriented, or suppressed), but the overall pattern is clear; the attitudes and doctrines in question could perhaps be more adequately described as exclusivistic nationalism. The label 'integral', first used as a self-definition and later adopted as a typological concept, stresses the totalizing claims rather than the conflictual context in which they are embedded.

But integral — or exclusivistic — nationalism must also be seen as a response to the globalizing process. Its most extreme forms culminated in imperial projects which aimed at a restructuring of the global context. This double background — the ultimately self-destructive project of bringing not only the structural differentiation of modernity, but also its de-centering global expansion under control — helps to explain another aspect of the phenomenon in question: the need for interpretive reinforcements which would make the nation more capable of assuming the role of a supreme value and an exclusive focus of integration. The additional contents which are thus grafted onto the imaginary signification of the nation can be more or less disruptive of its relation to the nation-state. In the light of historical experience, this applies most obviously to the notion of a racial community. But other ways of transfiguring the national imperative — the identification with religious or imperial traditions, or the appropriation of a suitably revised universalistic ideology — have had some similar consequences with regard to the nation-state and its adaptation to an international state system.

The third distinction is both geographical and historical. One of the most influential analysts of nationalism distinguished between the formative age of nationalism in Europe and the subsequent era of a 'pan-nationalism' which was the result of a world-wide diffusion of Western ideas (Kohn, 1968); a more detailed typology allows for several successive waves of nationalism (Morin, 1984: 129–38), but the underlying diffusionist assumptions remain unchanged. As I have already suggested, they would have to be revised in the light of the third theoretical perspective. The relativizing approach would not ignore the role of Western models, but it would pay more attention to the specific orientations and connotations which non-Western nationalisms have inherited from or acquired through interaction with their respective civilizational backgrounds. Both the borrowings and the endogenous transformations, however, take place against the background and under the impact of globalization.

Obviously, non-Western nationalisms vary in content as well as strength and originality. The most appropriate starting-point for a comparison with the West is the case which combines the strongest and most lasting influence of nationalism with the most spectacular breakthrough to modernity and the most successful transition from a peripheral to a central role. For an analysis of the relationship between nationalism and modernity, the development of Japanese society before and after 1868 is of unique importance, and its context is so distinctive that there is a strong prima-facie case for placing Japanese nationalism in a typological category of its own. This is what Masao Maruyama (1969: 1–25 and 135–56) tried to do in his theory of ultra-nationalism. His main emphasis was on the ability of Japanese nationalism to impose from the outset a restrictive and particularistic project of modernity, and to protect it against radical and universalistic challenges. Ultra-nationalism is thus primarily defined in terms of its structural (and structuring) properties. But its historical dimension is no less relevant. If the reference to an ethnic core always serves to impose on history a more or less mythical vision of continuity, ultra-nationalism could draw on several aspects of the Japanese tradition which were particularly conducive to an extreme version of this pattern.[5]

Further typological categories and combinations are beyond the scope of this paper. But it is worth noting that our reconsideration of the three most frequent distinctions has highlighted some sources of variety and change: the differentiating impact of globalization, the changing relations between different aspects of modernity, and the reactivation of different traditions. Although the argument has not gone beyond tentative formulation, it would seem to throw some light on the question posed at the beginning of the paper. If the task of the theory of modernity is to analyse a global, complex and open structure, nations and nationalism are not simply a neglected component which should be granted equality with others. Because of their ambiguity and diversity, as well as their ability to influence the constitution and development of other factors, they are a counter-example to the interpretations which try to construct a single overall logic or a *set* of separate and unequivocal logics. The problematic of nationalism is, in other words, a particularly useful corrective against over-systematized versions or short-circuiting applications of the theory of modernity, and a test case for the emerging new approaches.

Notes

1. The general theory of integration is not the only frame of reference for Mauss's analysis of the nation. There is also the more specific emphasis on the Western tradition and its unique contributions to the idea of the nation. If Western Europe became, as Mauss puts it, an 'empire of nations' the prehistory of this process can be

traced back to the Aristotelian distinction between *ethnos* and *polis*, and one of the essential intermediary phases was the development of Roman law (Mauss, 1969: 571-639).

2. This reading of Weber neglects — among other things — his interpretation of national solidarity as an obverse of the rivalry between political units, and as a way of transfiguring the struggle for power: as Weber sees it, the concept of nation means 'above all, that it is *proper* to expect from certain groups a specific sentiment of solidarity in the face of other groups'; thus 'the naked prestige of power is transformed into other special forms of prestige, and especially into the idea of the "nation" ' (Weber, 1968: 922).

3. On the different contributions of state-centred and culture-centred processes to the formation of modern nations, cf. also Eugen Lemberg (1964).

4. For a particularly extreme and simplistic version of the dichotomy, cf. John Plamenatz, 'Two Types of Nationalism', in Kamenka (1973: 22-37).

5. For a more detailed discussion of this aspect, cf. J.P. Arnason, (1987a, 1987b) 'The Modern Constellations and the Japanese Enigma'.

References

Alter, Peter (1985) *Nationalismus*. Frankfurt: Suhrkamp.

Armstrong, John (1982) *Nations before Nationalism*. Chapel Hill: University of North Carolina Press.

Arnason, J. (1987a) 'The Modern Constellations and the Japanese Enigma Part I', *Thesis Eleven*, 17: 4-39.

Arnason, J. (1987b) 'The Modern Constellations and the Japanese Enigma, Part II', *Thesis Eleven*, 18: 56-84.

Bauer, Otto (1924) *Die Nationalitätenfrage und die Sozialdemokratie*. Wien: Wiener Volksbuchhandlung.

Bloom, Solomon (1941) *The World of Nations*. New York: Oxford University Press.

Feher, Ferenc and Heller, Agnes (1983) 'Class, Democracy, Modernity', *Theory & Society* 12(2): 211-44.

Gellner, Ernest (1983) *Nations and Nationalism*. Oxford: Blackwell.

Giddens, Anthony (1985) *The Nation-State and Violence*. Cambridge: Polity Press.

Habermas, Jürgen (1981) *Theorie des kommunikativen Handelns*, 2 Volumes, Frankfurt: Suhrkamp.

Habermas, Jürgen (1987) *Eine Art Schadensabwicklung*. Frankfurt: Suhrkamp.

Heller, Agnes (1982) *A Theory of History*. London: Routledge & Kegan Paul.

Jünger, Ernst (1932) *Der Arbeiter. Herrschaft und Gestalt*. Hamburg: Hanseatische Verlagsanstalt.

Kamenka, Eugene (1973) *Nationalism: The Nature and Evolution of an Idea*. Canberra: Australian National University Press.

Kohn, Hans (1946) *The Idea of Nationalism*. New York: Macmillan.

Kohn, Hans (1968) *The Age of Nationalism*. New York: Harper & Row.

Lemberg, E. (1964) *Nationalism*, 2 Vols. Reinbek: Rowohlt.

Maruyama, Masao (1969) *Thought and Behaviour in Japanese Politics*. London: Oxford University Press.

Mauss, Marcel (1969) *Oeuvres*, Vol. 3. Paris; Editions de Minuit.

Morin, Edgar (1984) 'Pour une théorie de la nation', pp. 129-38 in E. Morin (ed.), *Sociologie*. Paris: Fayard.

Robertson, Roland (1987a) 'Globalization and Societal Modernization: A Note on Japan and Japanese Religion', *Sociological Analysis* 47(S), 35–43.

Robertson, Roland (1987b) 'Globalization Theory and Civilization Analysis', *Comparative Civilizations Review* 17: 20–30.

Robertson, Roland and Lechner, Frank (1985) 'Modernization, Globalization and the Problem of Culture in World System Theory', *Theory, Culture & Society*, 2(3): 103–18.

Smith, Anthony (1986) *The Ethnic Origins of Nations*. Oxford: Blackwell.

Sternhell, Zeev (1983) *Ni droite ni gauche: L'idéologie fasciste en France*. Paris: Seuil.

Tiryakian, Edward and Nevitte, Neil (1985) 'Nationalism and Modernity', pp. 57–86 in Edward Tiryakian and Ronald Rogowski (eds), *New Nationalisms of the Developed West*. London: Allen & Unwin.

Weber, Max (1946) *From Max Weber*, ed. Hans Gerth and C. Wright Mills. New York: Oxford University Press.

Weber, Max (1968) *Economy and Society*, three volumes. New York: Bedminster Press.

Johann Arnason teaches Sociology at La Trobe University, Bundoora, Victoria, Australia.

Cosmopolitans and Locals in World Culture

Ulf Hannerz

There is now a world culture, but we had better make sure that we understand what this means. It is marked by an organization of diversity rather than by a replication of uniformity. No total homogenization of systems of meaning and expression has occurred, nor does it appear likely that there will be one any time soon. But the world has become one network of social relationships, and between its different regions there is a flow of meanings as well as of people and goods.[1]

The world culture is created through the increasing interconnectedness of varied local cultures, as well as through the development of cultures without a clear anchorage in any one territory. These are all becoming sub-cultures, as it were, within the wider whole; cultures which are in important ways better understood in the context of their cultural surroundings than in isolation. But to this global interconnected diversity people can relate in different ways. For one thing, there are cosmopolitans, and there are locals.

The cosmopolitan–local distinction has been a part of the sociological vocabulary for close to half a century now, since Robert Merton (1957: 387ff.) developed it out of a study, during the Second World War, of 'patterns of influence' in a small town on the eastern seaboard of the United States. At that time (and certainly in that place), the distinction could hardly be set in anything but a national context. The cosmopolitans of the town were those who thought and who lived their lives within the structure of the nation rather than purely within the structure of the locality. Since then, the scale of culture and social structure has grown, so that what was cosmopolitan in the early 1940s may be counted as a moderate form of localism by now. 'Today it is international integration that determines universality, while national culture has an air of provincialism', the Hungarian author George Konrad writes in his *Antipolitics* (1984: 209).

Theory, Culture & Society (SAGE, London, Newbury Park and New Delhi), Vol. 7 (1990), 237–251

What follows is above all an exploration of cosmopolitanism as a perspective, a state of mind, or — to take a more processual view — a mode of managing meaning. I shall not concern myself here with patterns of influence, and not so very much with locals. The point of view of the latter I will touch upon mostly for purposes of contrast. My purpose is not so much to come up with a definition of the true cosmopolitan, although I may have an opinion on that as well, but merely to point to some of the issues involved.

The Cosmopolitan Perspective: Orientation and Competence
We often use the term 'cosmopolitan' rather loosely, to describe just about anybody who moves about in the world. But of such people, some would seem more cosmopolitan than others, and others again hardly cosmopolitan at all. I have before me an old cutting from the *International Herald Tribune* (16 October 1985) about travel and trade (the latter fairly often illicit) between Lagos and London. The article quotes reports by flight attendants on the route, claiming that Lagos market women board London-bound planes with loose-fitting gowns, which enable them to travel with dried fish tied to their thighs and upper arms. The dried fish is presumably sold to their countrymen in London; on the return trip, the women carry similarly concealed bundles of frozen fish sticks, dried milk, and baby clothes, all of which are in great demand in Lagos. London is a consumer's (or middleman's) paradise for Nigerians. About 1 percent of the passengers on the London-bound flights have excess baggage, and about 30 percent of those travelling in the opposite direction.

Is this cosmopolitanism? In my opinion, no; the shopping trips of Lagosian traders and smugglers hardly go beyond the horizons of urban Nigerian culture, as it now is. The fish sticks and the baby clothes hardly alter structures of meaning more than marginally. And much of that involvement with a wider world which is characteristic of contemporary lives is of this kind, largely a matter of assimilating items of some distant provenience into a fundamentally local culture.

Historically we have been used to think of cultures as distinctive structures of meaning and meaningful form usually closely linked to territories, and of individuals as self-evidently linked to particular such cultures. The underlying assumption here is that culture flows mostly in face-to-face relationships, and that people do not move around much. Such an assumption serves us well enough in delineating the local as an ideal type.

Yet as collective phonemena cultures are by definition linked primarily to interactions and social relationships, and only indirectly and without logical necessity to particular areas in physical space. The less social relationships are confined within territorial boundaries, the less so is also culture; and in our time especially, we can contrast in gross terms those cultures which are territorially defined (in terms of nations, regions, or localities) with those which are carried as collective structures of meaning by networks more extended in space, transnational or even global. This contrast, too — but not it alone — suggests that cultures, rather than being easily separated from one another as the hard-edged pieces in a mosaic, tend to overlap and mingle. While we understand them to be differently located in the social structure of the world, we also realize that the boundaries we draw around them are frequently rather arbitrary.

Anyway, such a view of the present in cultural terms may help us identify the cosmopolitan. The perspective of the cosmopolitan must entail relationships to a plurality of cultures understood as distinctive entities. (And the more the better; cosmopolitans should ideally be foxes rather than hedgehogs.)[2] But furthermore, cosmopolitanism in a stricter sense includes a stance toward diversity itself, toward the coexistence of cultures in the individual experience. A more genuine cosmopolitanism is first of all an orientation, a willingness to engage with the Other. It is an intellectual and aesthetic stance of openness toward divergent cultural experiences, a search for contrasts rather than uniformity. To become acquainted with more cultures is to turn into an *aficionado*, to view them as art works. At the same time, however, cosmopolitanism can be a matter of competence, and competence of both a generalized and a more specialized kind. There is the aspect of a state of readiness, a personal ability to make one's way into other cultures, through listening, looking, intuiting and reflecting. And there is cultural competence in the stricter sense of the term, a built-up skill in manoeuvring more or less expertly with a particular system of meanings and meaningful forms.

In its concern with the Other, cosmopolitanism thus becomes a matter of varieties and levels. Cosmopolitans can be dilettantes as well as connoisseurs, and are often both, at different times.[3] But the willingness to become involved with the Other, and the concern with achieving competence in cultures which are initially alien, relate to considerations of self as well. Cosmopolitanism often has a narcissistic streak; the self is constructed in the space where cultures mirror one another.

Competence with regard to alien cultures itself entails a sense of mastery, as an aspect of the self. One's understandings have expanded, a little more of the world is somehow under control. Yet there is a curious, apparently paradoxical interplay between mastery and surrender here. It may be one kind of cosmopolitanism where the individual picks from other cultures only those pieces which suit himself. In the long term, this is likely to be the way a cosmopolitan constructs his own unique personal perspective out of an idiosyncratic collection of experiences. But such selectivity can operate in the short term, situationally, as well. In another mode, however, the cosmopolitan does not make invidious distinctions among the particular elements of the alien culture in order to admit some of them into his repertoire and refuse others; he does not negotiate with the other culture but accepts it as a package deal. Even this surrender, however, is a part of the sense of mastery. The cosmopolitan's surrender to the alien culture implies personal autonomy vis-à-vis the culture where he originated. He has his obvious competence with regard to it, but he can choose to disengage from it. He possesses it, it does not possess him. Cosmopolitanism becomes proteanism. Some would eat cockroaches to prove the point, others need only eat escargots. Whichever is required, the principle is that the more clearly the alien culture contrasts with the culture of origin, the more at least parts of the former would even be seen with revulsion through the lens of the latter, the more conspicuously is surrender abroad a form of mastery at home.

Yet the surrender is of course only conditional. The cosmopolitan may embrace the alien culture, but he does not become committed to it. All the time he knows where the exit is.

Cosmopolitanism and the Varieties of Mobility

Of course, cosmopolitans are usually somewhat footloose, on the move in the world. Among the several cultures with which they are engaged, at least one is presumably of the territorial kind, a culture encompassing the round of everyday life in a community. The perspective of the cosmopolitan may indeed be composed only from experiences of different cultures of this kind, as his biography includes periods of stays in different places. But he may also be involved with one culture, and possibly but not usually more, of that other kind which is carried by a transnational network rather than by a territory. It is really the growth and proliferation of such cultures and social networks in the present period that generates more cosmopolitans now than there have been at any other time.

But being on the move, I have already argued, is not enough to turn one into a cosmopolitan, and we must not confuse the latter with other kinds of travellers. Are tourists, exiles, and expatriates cosmopolitans, and when not, why not?

In her novel *The Accidental Tourist* (1985), Anne Tyler has a main character who makes his living churning out travel books for anti-cosmopolitans, people (mostly business travellers) who would rather not have left home; people who are locals at heart.[4] These are travel guides for Americans who would want to know what restaurants in Tokyo offer Sweet'n'Low, which hotel in Madrid has king-size Beauty-rest mattresses, and whether there is a Taco Bell in Mexico City.

Another contemporary writer, Paul Theroux (1986: 133), continuously occupied with themes of journeys and the cosmopolitan experience, comments that many people travel for the purpose of 'home plus' — Spain is home plus sunshine, India is home plus servants, Africa is home plus elephants and lions. And for some, of course, travel is ideally home plus more and better business. There is no general openness here to a somewhat unpredictable variety of experiences; the benefits of mobility are strictly regulated. Such travel is not for cosmopolitans, and does little to create cosmopolitans.

Much present-day tourism is of this kind. People engage in it specifically to go to another place, so the cosmopolitanism that could potentially be involved would be that of combinations of territorially based cultures. But the 'plus' often has nothing whatsoever to do with alien systems of meaning, and a lot to do with facts of nature, such as nice beaches. Yet this is not the only reason why cosmopolitans nowadays loathe tourists, and especially loathe being taken for tourists.

Cosmopolitans tend to want to immerse themselves in other cultures, or in any case be free to do so. They want to be participants, or at least do not want to be too readily identifiable within a crowd of participants, that is, of locals in their home territory. They want to be able to sneak backstage rather than being confined to the frontstage areas. Tourists are not participants; tourism is largely a spectator sport. Even if they want to become involved and in that sense have a cosmopolitan orientation, tourists are assumed to be incompetent. They are too likely to make a nuisance of themselves. The local, and the cosmopolitan, can spot them from a mile away. Locals evolve particular ways of handling tourists, keeping a distance from them, not necessarily exploiting them but not admitting them into local reciprocities either. Not least because cosmopolitanism is an uncertain practice, again and again balancing at the edge of competence, the cosmopolitan keeps running the risk of being taken for a tourist by locals whose experience make them apply this label increasingly routinely. And this could ruin many of the pleasures of cosmopolitanism, as well as pose a threat to the cosmopolitan sense of self.

The exile, also shifted directly from one territorial culture to another, is often no real cosmopolitan either, for his involvement with a culture away from his homeland is something that has been forced on him. At best, life in another country is home plus safety, or home plus freedom, but often it is just not home at all. He is surrounded by the foreign culture but does not often immerse himself in it. Sometimes his imperfections as a cosmopolitan may be the opposite of those of the tourist: he may reluctantly build up a competence, but he does not enjoy it. Exile, Edward Said has argued, is an unhealable rift, a discontinuous state of being, a jealous state:

> With very little to possess, you hold on to what you have with aggressive defensiveness. What you achieve in exile is precisely what you have no wish to share, and it is in the drawing of lines around you and your compatriots that the least attractive aspects of being an exile emerge: an exaggerated sense of group solidarity as well as a passionate hostility toward outsiders, even those who may in fact be in the same predicament as you. (Said, 1984:51)

The French intellectuals who escaped to New York during the Second World War, as portrayed by Rutkoff and Scott (1983), were mostly exiles of this sort. Their New York, with its own academy and its own revue, was a sanctuary where they sustained the notion that France and civilization were just about interchangeable terms. Among them, nonetheless, were individuals who seized the opportunity to explore the city with all their senses. Claude Lévi-Strauss (1985: 258ff.), in a charming memoir included in *The View from Afar*, has described his New York, of antique shops, department stores, ethnic villages, museums of everything from art to natural history, and a Chinese opera performing under the first arch of the Brooklyn Bridge.

So now and then exiles can be cosmopolitans; but most of them are not. Most ordinary labour migrants do not become cosmopolitans either. For them going away may be, ideally, home plus higher income; often the involvement with another culture is not a fringe benefit but a necessary cost, to be kept as low as possible. A surrogate home is again created with the help of compatriots, in whose circle one becomes encapsulated.

The concept of the expatriate may be that which we will most readily associate with cosmopolitanism. Expatriates (or ex-expatriates) are people who have chosen to live abroad for some period, and who know when they are there that they can go home when it suits them. Not that all expatriates are living models of cosmopolitanism; colonialists were also expatriates, and mostly they abhorred 'going native'. But these are people who can afford to experiment, who do not stand to lose a treasured but threatened, uprooted sense of self. We often think of them as people of independent (even if modest) means, for whom openness to new experiences is a vocation, or people who can take along their work more or less where it pleases them; writers and painters in Paris between the wars are perhaps the archetypes. Nevertheless, the contemporary expatriate is rather more likely to be an organization man; so here I come back to the transnational cultures, and the networks and institutions which provide their social frameworks.

Transnational Cultures Today

The historian James Field (1971), surveying the development in question over a longer period, writes of 'Transnationalism and the New Tribe', but one may as well identify a number of different tribes, as the people involved form rather separate sets of social relationships, and as the specialized contents of these cultures are of many kinds. Transnational cultures today tend to be more or less clearcut occupational cultures (and are often tied to transnational job markets). George Konrad emphasizes the transnational culture of intellectuals:

> The global flow of information proceeds on many different technical and institutional levels, but on all levels the intellectuals are the ones who know most about one another across the frontiers, who keep in touch with one another, and who feel that they are one another's allies . . .

We may describe as transnational those intellectuals who are at home in the cultures of other peoples as well as their own. They keep track of what is happening in various places. They have special ties to those countries where they have lived, they have friends all over the world, they hop across the sea to discuss something with their colleagues; they fly to visit one another as easily as their counterparts two hundred years ago rode over to the next town to exchange ideas. (1984: 208-9)

Yet there are transnational cultures also of bureaucrats, politicians, and business people and of journalists and diplomats, and various others (see e.g. Sauvant, 1976). Perhaps the only transnational culture in decline is that of hereditary royalty. These cultures become transnational both as the individuals involved make quick forays from a home base to many other places — for a few hours or days in a week, for a few weeks here and there in a year — and as they shift their bases for longer periods within their lives. Wherever they go, they find others who will interact with them in the terms of specialized but collectively held understandings.

Because of the transnational cultures, a large number of people are nowadays systematically and directly involved with more than one culture. In human history, the direct movement between territorial cultures has often been accidental, a freak occurrence in biographies; if not an expression of sheer personal idiosyncracy, then a result of war, political upheaval or repression, ecological disaster.

But the transnational and the territorial cultures of the world are entangled with one another in manifold ways. Some transnational cultures are more insulated from local practices than others; that of diplomacy as compared with that of commerce, for example. The transnational cultures are also as wholes usually more marked by some territorial culture than by others. Most of them are in different ways extensions or transformations of the cultures of western Europe and North America. If even the transnational cultures have to have physical centres somewhere, places in which, or from where, their particular meanings are produced and disseminated with particular intensity, or places to which people travel in order to interact in their terms, this is where such centres tend to be located. But even away from these centres, the institutions of the transnational cultures tend to be organized so as to make people from western Europe and North America feel as much at home as possible (by using their languages, for one thing). In both ways, the organization of world culture through centre-periphery relationships is made evident.

It is a consequence of this that western Europeans and North Americans can encapsulate themselves culturally, and basically remain metropolitan locals instead of becoming cosmopolitans, not only by staying at home in their territorial cultures. Like Ann Tyler's 'accidental tourists', they can also do so, to a fairly high degree if not completely, in many of the transnational cultures. For those who are not western Europeans or North Americans, or who do not spend their everyday lives elsewhere in occidental cultural enclaves, involvement with one of the transnational cultures is more likely in itself to be a distinctive cultural experience.

The real significance of the growth of the transnational cultures, however, is often not the new cultural experience that they themselves can offer people — for it is frequently rather restricted in scope and depth — but their mediating possibilities. The transnational cultures are bridgeheads for entry into other territorial cultures. Instead of remaining within them, one can use the mobility connected with them to make contact with the meanings of other rounds of life, and gradually incorporate this experience into one's personal perspective.

Cosmopolitanism and Cultures of Critical Discourse

The readiness to seize such opportunities and cosmopolitanize is no doubt often a very personal character trait. On the other hand, different transnational cultures may also relate in different ways to these opportunities. Here and there, and probably especially where the occupational practices themselves are not well insulated from the cultures of varied local settings, the development of competences in alien cultures has appeared too important to be left to chance and to personal whim; in the last few decades, we have seen the rapid growth of a culture shock prevention industry. Cross-cultural training programmes have been developed to inculcate sensitivity, basic *savoir faire*, and perhaps an appreciation of those other cultures which are of special strategic importance to one's goals (from the occidental point of view, particularly those of Japan and the oil-rich Arab world). There is also a burgeoning do-it-yourself literature in this field.[5] Sceptics, of course, may dismiss these programmes and this literature as a 'quick cosmopolitan fix'. They would be inclined to doubt that course work for a couple of days or weeks, or a characteristically unsubtle handbook genre, can substitute for the personal journey of discovery. And they may be committed to the notion that cosmopolitans, as such, should be self-made men.

Some transnational cultures, on the other hand, may have a kind of built-in relationship to that type of openness and striving toward mastery that I have referred to above. George Konrad, in the statement which I have already quoted, proposes that intellectuals have a particular predilection toward making themselves at home in other cultures. This is more true in some instances than others; the French academia in its New York exile, we have seen, tended to keep to itself. Nonetheless, it may be worth considering the possibility that there is some kind of affinity between cosmopolitanism and the culture of intellectuals.

When locals were influential, Robert Merton (1957: 400) found in his classic study, their influence rested not so much on what they knew as on whom they knew. Cosmopolitans, in contrast, based whatever influence they had on a knowledge less tied to particular others, or to the unique community setting. They came equipped with special knowledge, and they could leave and take it with them without devaluing it.

Not surprisingly, there has been more attention given to such people recently.[6] They are 'the new class', people with credentials, decontextualized cultural capital. Within this broad social category some would distinguish, as Alvin Gouldner (1979) has done, between intelligentsia and intellectuals. This is hardly necessary for my purposes here; in any case, according to Gouldner, they share a 'culture of critical discourse'.

Certainly these are a type of people who now stand a particularly good chance of becoming involved with the transnational cultures. Their decontextualized knowledge can be quickly and shiftingly recontextualized in a series of different settings. (Which is not to say that the transnational cultures consist of nothing but such knowledge — they may well evolve their own particularisms as well, of the kind which are elsewhere the special resource of locals: biographical knowledge of individuals, anecdotal knowledge of events and even of the constellations of locales which form the settings of these cultures.) What they carry, however, is not just special knowledge, but also that overall orientation toward structures of meaning to which the notion of the 'culture of critical discourse' refers. This orientation, according to Gouldner's (1979: 28ff.) description, is reflexive, problematizing, concerned with metacommunication; I would also describe it as generally expansionist in its management of meaning. It pushes on relentlessly in its analysis of the order of ideas, striving toward explicitness where common sense, as a contrasting mode of meaning management, might come to rest comfortably with the tacit, the ambiguous, and the contradictory.[7] In the end, it strives toward mastery.

Obviously it cannot be argued that such an orientation to structures of meaning is in any way likely to show a particularly close fit with those alien cultures in themselves which the cosmopolitan desires to explore. These are probably as full of contradictions, ambiguities, and tendencies toward inertia as any other local culture, including that in which the cosmopolitan himself originates. Yet as a mode of approach, it seems to include much of that openness and drive toward greater competence which I have suggested is also characteristic of cosmopolitanism. It is not a way of becoming a local, but rather of simulating local knowledge.

The special relationship between intellectuals and cosmopolitanism, if there is one, could also be described in another way, hardly unrelated to what I have just said. Intellectuals in the narrower sense are involved in a particular way with what we might see as the centre-periphery relationships of culture itself. Kadushin (1974: 6), in his study of American intellectuals, has suggested that each culture has certain central 'value concepts' which give meaning to experience and action, and that most members of society manipulate these concepts easily enough because they tend to be defined essentially in their concrete applications rather than through abstract formulations. Intellectuals, however, have the special task of finding the relationship between value concepts, and tracing the application of these concepts over time. Such concepts, Kadushin notes, are for example 'rights of man', 'justice', or 'freedom of speech'.

In their enquiries, the intellectuals traffic between the core of culture and the peripheral, ephemeral facts of everyday life. If they are vocationally in the habit of doing so, they would appear to have an advantageous point of departure for explorations of other cultures as well, when the opportunity of cosmopolitanism presents itself. And this advantage is surely not lost when different cultures in fact turn out to have central value concepts in common; George Konrad's transnational intellectuals, forming alliances across frontiers, tend to get together precisely over such shared concerns.

The Cosmopolitan at Home

This has mostly been a sketch of the cosmopolitan abroad. Much of the time, even cosmopolitans are actually at home. Yet what does that mean in their case?

Perhaps real cosmopolitans, after they have taken out membership in that category, are never quite at home again, in the way real locals can be. Home is taken-for-grantedness, but after their perspectives have been irreversibly affected by the experience of the alien and the distant, cosmopolitans may not view either the seasons of the year or the minor rituals of everyday life as absolutely natural, obvious, and necessary. There may be a feeling of detachment, perhaps irritation with those committed to the local common sense and unaware of its arbitrariness. Or perhaps the cosmopolitan makes 'home' as well one of his several sources of personal meaning, not so different from the others which are further away; or he is pleased with his ability both to surrender to and master this one as well.

Or home is really home, but in a special way; a constant reminder of a pre-cosmopolitan past, a privileged site of nostalgia. This is where once things seemed fairly simple and straightforward. Or it is again really home, a comfortable place of familiar faces, where one's competence is undisputed and where one does not have to prove it to either oneself or others, but where for much the same reasons there is some risk of boredom.

At home, for most cosmopolitans, most others are locals. This is true in the great majority of territorially based cultures. Conversely, for most of these locals, the cosmopolitan is someone a little unusual, one of us and yet not quite one of us. Someone to be respected for his experiences, possibly, but equally possibly not somebody to be trusted as a matter of course. Trust tends to be a matter of shared perspectives, of 'I know, and I know that you know, and I know that you know that I know'. And this formula for the social organization of meaning does not necessarily apply to the relationship between local and cosmopolitan.

Some cosmopolitans are more adept at making it apply again. *'Wenn jemand eine Reise tut, dann kann er 'was erzählen'*, the saying goes, and there are those who make a speciality out of letting others know what they have come across in distant places. So the cosmopolitan can to some extent be channelled into the local; and precisely because these are on the whole separate spheres the cosmopolitan can become a broker, an entrepreneur who makes a profit. Yet there is a danger that such attempts to make the alien easily accessible only succeeds in trivializing it, and thereby betraying its nature and the character of the real first-hand encounter. So in a way the more purely cosmopolitan attitude may be to let separate things be separate.

Despite all this, home is not necessarily a place where cosmopolitanism is in exile. It is natural that in the contemporary world many local settings are increasingly characterized by cultural diversity. Those of cosmopolitan inclinations may make selective use of their habitats to maintain their expansive orientation toward the wider world. Other cosmopolitans may be there, whether they in their turn are at home or abroad, and strangers of other than cosmopolitan orientations. Apart from the face-to-face encounters, there are the media — both those intended for local consumption, although they speak of what is distant, and those which are really part of other cultures, like foreign books and films. What McLuhan once described as the implosive power of the media may now make just about everybody a little more cosmopolitan. And one may in the end ask whether it is now even possible to become a cosmopolitan without going away at all.

Conclusion: the Dependence of Cosmopolitans on Locals, and their Shared Interests

To repeat, there is now one world culture. All the variously distributed structures of meaning and expression are becoming interrelated, somehow, somewhere. People like the cosmopolitans have a special part in bringing about a degree of coherence, and because they have this part they have received closer attention here. If there were only locals in the world, world culture would be no more than the sum of its separate parts.

As things are now, on the other hand, it is no longer so easy to conform to the ideal type of a local. Some people, like exiles or migrant workers, are indeed taken away from the territorial bases of their local culture, but try to encapsulate themselves within some approximation of it; yet it is a greater number who, even staying home, find their local cultures less pervasive, less to be taken for granted, less clearly bounded toward the outside. If that other kind of world culture were ever to come about, through a terminal process of global homogenization, locals would become extinct; or, seen differently, through the involvement with the one existing culture, everybody would be the same kind of local, at the global level.

Here, however, today's cosmopolitans and locals have common

interests in the survival of cultural diversity. For the latter, diversity itself, as a matter of personal access to varied cultures, may be of little intrinsic interest. It just so happens that this is the principle which allows all locals to stick to their respective cultures. For the cosmopolitans, in contrast, there is value in diversity as such, but they are not likely to get it, in anything like the present form, unless other people are allowed to carve out special niches for their cultures, and keep them. Which is to say that there can be no cosmopolitans without locals.

Notes

1. The first version of this paper was presented at the First International Conference on the Olympics and East/West and South/North Cultural Exchanges in the World System, in Seoul, Korea, 17–19 August 1987. The paper has been prepared as part of the project 'The World System of Culture' in the Department of Social Anthropology, University of Stockholm. The project has been supported by the Swedish Research Council for the Humanities and Social Sciences (HSFR).

2. Anthropologists are thus not necessarily very cosmopolitan; many of them are one-tribe people. On hedgehogs and foxes, see Berlin (1978).

3. The dilettante, remember, is 'one who delights'; someone whose curiosity takes him a bit beyond ordinary knowledge, although in a gentlemanly way he refrains from becoming a specialist (cf. Lynes, 1966).

4. There is, of course, also a film based on this novel.

5. See for example the volume *Do's and Taboos Around the World*, issued by the Parker Pen Company, which describes its goals:

> Ideally, this book will help each world traveler grow little invisible antennae that will sense incoming messages about cultural differences and nuances. An appreciation and understanding of these differences will prevent embarrassment, unhappiness, and failure. In fact, learning through travel about these cultural differences can be both challenging and fun. (Axtell, 1985: foreword)

6. See also for example Randall Collins's (1979: 60ff.) contrast between 'indigenous' and 'formal' production of culture.

7. On common sense, see for example Geertz (1975), and Bourdieu's (1977: 164ff.) discussion of the 'doxic mode'.

References

Axtell, Roger E. (1985) *Do's and Taboos Around the World*. New York: Wiley.

Berlin, Isaiah (1978) *Russian Thinkers*. New York: Viking.

Bourdieu, Pierre (1977) *Outline of a Theory of Practice*. Cambridge: Cambridge University Press.

Collins, Randall (1979) *The Credential Society*. New York: Academic Press.

Field, James A., Jr. (1971) 'Transnationalism and the New Tribe', *International Organization* 25: 353–62.

Geertz, Clifford (1975) 'Common Sense as a Cultural System', *Antioch Review* 33: 5-26.

Gouldner, Alvin W. (1979) *The Future of the Intellectuals and the Rise of the New Class*. London: Macmillan.

Kadushin, Charles (1974) *The American Intellectual Elite*. Boston: Little, Brown.

Konrad, George (1984) *Antipolitics*. San Diego and New York: Harcourt Brace Jovanovich.

Lévi-Strauss, Claude (1985) *The View from Afar*. New York: Basic Books.

Lynes, Russell (1966) *Confessions of a Dilettante*. New York: Harper & Row.

Merton, Robert K. (1957) *Social Theory and Social Structure*. Glencoe, IL: Free Press.

Rutkoff, Peter M., and Scott, William B. (1983) 'The French in New York: Resistance and Structure', *Social Research* 50: 185-214.

Said, Edward W. (1984) 'The Mind of Winter: Reflections on Life in Exile', *Harper's Magazine* (September): 49-55.

Sauvant, Karl P,. (1976) 'The Potential of Multinational Enterprises as Vehicles for the Transmission of Business Culture', in Karl P. Sauvant and Farid G. Lavipour (eds), *Controlling Multinational Enterprises*. Boulder, CO: Westview.

Theroux, Paul (1986) *Sunrise with Seamonsters*. Harmondsworth: Penguin.

Tyler, Anne (1985) *The Accidental Tourist*. New York: Knopf.

Ulf Hannerz is head of the Department of Social Anthropology at the University of Stockholm. He is author of *Exploring the City: Inquiries Toward an Urban Anthropology* (Columbia University Press, 1980).

Conflicts of Culture in Cross-border Legal Relations: The Conception of a Research Topic in the Sociology of Law

Volkmar Gessner and Angelika Schade

1. The Problem

Cross-border contacts between private persons or organizations which have legal implications are occurring more and more frequently worldwide. In Europe we will witness further substantial growth once the EC's single internal market comes into operation. With regard to the law itself, cross-border legal relations are governed by private international law, by internationally unified law and, in the EC countries, by the Treaties of Rome and legislation resulting from harmonization within the Community. A sociological typology of such cases, however, is virtually unknown even though it must be presumed that cross-border social action differs from the interactions taking place within a society or (legal) culture.

Whereas problems in the development of international law have become part of the established canon of research in jurisprudence, hardly any attention has been paid to the *social action* of the groups such law is aimed at. If this were to be systematically researched, this would provide the basis for a proper conception of international law with regard to private relations. Multinational corporations have been the only object to be examined with regard to the legal provisions under which they operate and their contribution to the development of international business law (cf. Grossfeld, 1980). On the other hand sociological research has yet to be carried out into how business-people establish agreements or conduct disputes with their counterparts in other countries. It is precisely the fact that such situations are relatively weakly regulated by legal norms when compared with transactions taking place within a single country which directs sociology, and the sociology of law, in particular to concentrate on the structures created by the business world (norms,

Theory, Culture & Society (SAGE, London, Newbury Park and New Delhi), Vol. 7 (1990), 253–277

institutions, professions) aimed at conflict avoidance and reso-lution. In non-business affairs, too, everyday interactions occur across borders which can generate conflicts (under family law or compensation law, for example) which may have to be managed without the 'infrastructure' which is so helpful to the business world.

Having previously dealt with or compared purely national phenomena the sociology of law is now directing its attention to how definitions of the situation are made in processes occurring directly between the parties involved in cross-border relations or when people make use of advisory, negotiating, conciliation or arbitration facilities. It is also looking specifically at anomic situations which may arise out of a lack of sufficient normative guidance of either a legal or cultural nature. Both of these objects of interest are derived from the assumption that a latent cultural conflict exists in cross-border legal relations (cf. the conceptualization in den Hollander, 1955). Cultural conflicts have been thematized most fully to date in the sociology of deviance (summarized in von Trotha, 1985), which tackles the *intra*cultural relativity of social orders in a differentiated modern society. If, in theoretical approaches to modernization, the state of normlessness is associated with social change, this is frequently combined with a diagnosis of the permissive society of our times and the escalation of criminality (cf. the critique of this in Pearson, 1985: 15ff.). Yet the investigations conducted to date suggest that anomie in cross-border legal relations has somewhat abated, with many mechanisms and bodies (such as insurance schemes, conciliation bodies, courts of arbitration) contributing, together with a more flexible attitude on the part of domestic courts dealing with foreign matters, to the reduction of such conflicts. This leads on to the question of what legal mechanisms exist for avoiding such cultural conflicts and how far the parties to cross-border relations have recourse to the law at all. This in turn brings us to the broader question of the extent to which law, as a social institution, structures social reality and, leading on from this, how the relation-ship between culture and society can be formulated in theoretical terms (cf. Featherstone, 1985: 3; Haferkamp, 1989). It is also an open question as to how far the hypothesis of the normative structuring of society can be empirically refuted, given that many surveys conducted by sociologists of law conclude that the scope of legal control is extremely limited (cf. Griffiths, 1979; Gessner and Höland, 1989). Up to now, however, legal theory '. . . has made a paradigm of the closed system, and private international law prefers to define away any awareness of the plurality and ambiguities of the international legal world' (verbal communication from Flessner).

2. The Thematization of the Cultural Conflict in World Society

The political and economic dimensions of cross-border social interaction have been thematized for the most part by *theories of international relations* (see Rittberger and Wolf, 1987), *international systems theories* (cf. von Beyme et al., 1987), *world systems theories* (cf. Wallerstein, 1974) and associated research (Hopkins and Wallerstein, 1982).

Whereas the theory of international relations and international systems theory long harboured the predominant notion that only governments and their representatives could be considered relevant actors in the international system, the situation today also favours the *recognition of individuals, groups and organizations as actors with a structuring role in the international system* (cf. Singer, 1987: 214f.;[1] Czempiel, 1981; Sauvant, 1987: 69ff.). Rittberger and Wolf (1987: 4) point out that the 'new' concept of international politics ought to include all sequences of interrelated actions across national or societal boundaries in so far as they involve '. . . the making or enforcement of decisions concerning the apportionment of values in different spheres of life'. Especially in the fields of information and communication, trade and finance, it is quite evident that in this latter sense actions by non-state parties must also be classed as 'political'. Hence what non-state actors do is of particular interest to political science in the field of *cross-border economic and business relations*.

Just as political analysis now places some stress on the significance of cross-border interactions[2] between private individuals and businesses, we similarly believe it is important that the sociology of law should also seek to analyse such interactions and not just investigate the particular laws of nations within the international system. Interactions between private individuals or organizations are becoming more and more frequent and hence are to be regarded as not just relevant in economic and political terms but also with regard to broader cultural and social factors.

The *theory of world society*[3] starts out from a position that worldwide interaction is now an established phenomenon, albeit with various discontinuities (Senghaas, 1988). In order for interactions involving parties from different cultures to succeed, the awareness has to be reached that each country has its own particular quantity of things it needs to learn (Luhmann, 1971: 7). According to Luhmann, one associates with the idea of the world society a situation in which everyone '. . . is able — having achieved a normal amount of learning — to pursue his/her own objectives as a stranger among strangers'. This, says Luhmann (1971: 9) is the result of harmonization of the intersubjective formation of expectations on all levels, or of the 'de facto correspondence in the horizon within which (corresponding or non-corresponding) expectations are constituted', the 'expectation that others' horizons of expectation will correspond to one's own' and 'the expectation that others will expect their horizons to be identical with those of others'. To put it more concisely, world-wide interaction is possible because a common basis of expectations exists. Although the concept of world society does thematize problems of intercultural communication, the theory nevertheless operates on a very high level of abstraction, making it difficult to formulate hypotheses which would be suitable for guiding research. The concept seems rather more to act as a stimulus for macrosociological research (Senghaas, 1988). Nevertheless Luhmann (1971: 10ff.) also puts forward a thesis on the structures of expectation in the world society which could serve as a guide to microsociological enquiry. He submits that there is a *predominance of 'cognitive, adaptive expectations showing willingness to learn'* and a *decline in 'normative, prescriptive expectations with moral pretensions'*. The difference between these modes of expectation, says Luhmann, lies in how they react to disillusionment in its strict, neutral sense. Even if disillusionment occurs, normative expectations will be maintained and means of persuasion or applying sanctions will be resorted to, whereas cognitive expectations are implicitly willing to learn and if necessary change. For solving problems, says Luhmann, these modes of expectation arise depending on the situation involved: 'There is a greater tendency to adopt a normative attitude to situations where no immediate, clear, secure opportunity to learn exists, and to adopt a cognitive stance when there is no prospect of help for one's expectations.' Senghaas, too, stresses *the growing cognitive networking of the world*. In his enquiry regarding the growth of interdependence he does refer to the role of law, particularly international law, but he mentions it only in passing — '. . . in this century in particular, international law has made great progress in this respect [of the civilizing process]' (Senghaas, 1988: 27) — and does not go into further detail.

Robertson and Lechner (1985), enquiring into culture's standing in world-systems theory, posit that cultural pluralism is a constitutive characteristic of the system of the modern world. However, that is to prompt the question of whether cultural pluralism really has been accepted and internalized to such an extent that cultural differences no longer produce anomie and conflicts (cf. den Hollander, 1955: 166). Is it not rather the case that cultural pluralism demands effort on our behalf to deal with it properly? One possibility, which is seen by Habermas (1982), is that the legal system will intervene and, by expanding the scope of its procedural, strategic rationality to cover more and more aspects of life, will destroy developing forms of communicative rationality. Communicative relations would then be objectified because systems rationality would endeavour to overcome the danger of anomie. As it did so, the initiative would be taken away from social actors, and systemic control would induce indifference and the fragmentation of consciousness in place of anomie. The question which needs to be posed here, though, is whether the necessity for intercultural communication and/or negotiation does not also clear a path for communicative rationality in the legally structured sphere. We can only find this out with the help of microsociological research.

Since the end of the 1960s, a new branch of research carrying the title of 'intercultural communication' has become established (cf. Mauviel, 1987), among the aims of which is to investigate transnational relations among private persons or organizations, and which makes use of an amalgam of predominantly psychological, sociological, anthropological and linguistic hypotheses. Intercultural communication is defined as the communication process occurring — whether verbally or non-verbally — between members of different cultural groups in different situational contexts (Samovar and Porter, 1976; Prosser, 1978). Though there is a long history of investigations concerning *culture* and *communication*, it is the *linking of the two areas of research* which is relatively new. Research into intercultural communication has primarily been inspired by practical problems, i.e. problems of intercultural behaviour in a situation where cultures come into contact, whether it be in matters of foreign affairs, business or some other area. The key problems in the field of intercultural communication are 'miscommunication' or 'misunderstandings' attributable to differences of culture (Mauviel, 1987; Rehbein, 1985: 7ff.).

The development of *theories of intercultural communication*[4] has also now made progress, though the overall picture is still rather a heterogeneous one — as rightly observed by Loenhoff (1988: 1; cf. also the complaint on the 'aparadigmatic' state of the theory in Gudykunst, 1983: 14) — in as far as the problems of intercultural communication dealt with remain bound to the concrete situation in each particular case, thus making generalizations and theory development more difficult. A further problem which arises when it comes to researching cross-border legal relations is that *juridical interaction* has not so far been thematized within the context of the theory of intercultural communication, one exception being a recent article by Joan B. Kessler (1988) dealing with communicative problems between lawyers and clients from different cultural backgrounds.

The focus of discussion on intercultural communication lies particularly on conflicts: on how they emerge, how they are coped with, and what approaches are taken to them[5] (cf. Nadler et al., 1985; Ting-Toomey, 1985; Cushman and Sanderson-King, 1985). As a form of social action, *conflict* is partly determined by culture, according to Stella Ting-Toomey (1985: 72) and others. Intercultural misunderstandings, and hence possible conflict, occur when two individuals coming from different cultures give a different expression to or differently interpret the same symbolic action. In an intercultural context, then, there is more to conflict than merely divergent interests. An already complex situation is exacerbated by ambiguities, lack of awareness and/or the misunderstanding of cultural behavioural standards, of language or of relational dimensions such as confidentiality or status.

The first aspect of an analysis of intercultural conflict is to investigate the *cultural context* in which particular episodes of conflict occur. A useful point of reference here is the notion of *cultural constraints.*[6] In situations where cultural constraints are low, tolerance towards anyone or anything different and towards adverse tensions tends to be higher, that is to say the actors benefit from the open confrontation of ideas. Conversely, in situations with high cultural constraints the conflict threshold level tends rather to be lower, that is, preventive strategies are typically resorted to.

An examination of conflicts and their relationship with culture also needs to take heed of the specific *conditions under which conflicts probably arise.* Intercultural tensions and misunderstandings occur if any of the participants in intercultural communication implicitly or explicitly acts in violation of others' expectations. Where cultural constraints are low, a relatively high level of insecurity and risk prevails in the intercultural interaction. Conversely, if there is a high degree of cultural constraint the prevailing level of insecurity and risk is relatively low. The potential for conflict between strangers is relatively greater in situations with low cultural constraints than in those with high constraints. To put it another way, the danger of committing an error of interaction is greater when there are no specific rules governing and guiding the various episodes of interaction (Ting-Toomey, 1985: 78f.).

Another matter of importance in the relationship between conflict and culture is that of the *attitude and strategies adopted towards conflict* (Ting-Toomey, 1985; Nadler et al., 1985: 92ff.; Cushman and Sanderson-King, 1985: 122ff.). In a context with low cultural constraints, the conflicting parties will probably take up direct confrontational stances, whilst in a context with high constraints the predominant attitude is best described as one of circumventing or avoiding conflict.

A number of authors (including Nadler et al., 1985; Harnett and Cummings, 1980[7]) see *intercultural negotiation* as playing an increasingly important role in the present-day world (cf. also the many practical handbooks on 'How to do business in . . .', Fox, 1988). In a conflict situation, communication acts as the means by which conflict is given a social definition, as the instrument for exerting influence in conflicts, and as a medium which allows either those involved or third parties to prevent, cope with or actually solve conflicts. Negotiation is the process by which participants communicate with one another as they seek to identify behavioural alternatives and endeavour to achieve outcomes which are both individually and mutually advantageous.

Long-drawn out relationships and negotiations, especially characteristic of international organizations, can lead to the development of a common, *third culture*. Useem et al. (1963: 169) define this 'as the behaviour patterns created, shared, and learned by men of different societies who are in the process of relating their societies, or sections thereof, to each other'.

In their view there are already many societal interfaces where such a third culture had developed. The examples they cite are the United Nations, the European common market, the ecumenical movement among the Christian churches, international student exchanges, the international communities in the sciences and the arts, and the diplomatic community. In their understanding of the expression, this third culture is not merely a mutual accommodation or amalgamation of two separate, parallel cultures, but the birth of something new as far as behaviour, lifestyles, world views, etc. are concerned (Useem et al., 1963: 170).

Empirical assessments of international organizations which are developing a common culture show they have attained a generally increased significance (cf. Senghaas-Knobloch, 1969: 59ff.). Evidence is also available for the fact that processes by which contact is nurtured within these organizations have become more extensive (Senghaas-Knobloch, 1969: 171). Finally, attitude surveys have been conducted which show that it is only after a certain time has elapsed that transnational contacts lead to a differentiation of conceptual images (Senghaas-Knobloch, 1969: 169). There is a lack of additional research in this area, however, particularly as far as intercultural legal contact is concerned.

The *sociology of culture* which has been in the ascendancy again since the end of the 1970s (witness the special issues of the *Kölner Zeitschrift für Soziologie und Sozialpsychologie*) has once again focused interest on cultural conflict. Friedrich H. Tenbruck, for example, has explicitly cited the cultural problems arising when two cultures impinge on each other as a research task for the sociology of culture (1979: 416). Extensive research has already been conducted on the problems faced by or associated with guest workers in particular (cf. Heckmann, 1981, with many further references; Ansay and Gessner, 1974), and a broad field has developed to deal with the social-work aspects of intercultural education (cf., for example, the periodical *Ausländerkinder* [immigrant children]). Here too, though, once one leaves the guest-worker area, one will find that there are virtually no transcultural studies dealing with cross-border phenomena.

Parallel to these trends, in the field of law itself recent years have seen the development of *research in legal culture* (see *Zeitschrift für Rechtssoziologie*, 1985), in which attention is drawn by the sociology of law to phenomena involving societies' cultural identities. Such identity in the sense of legal culture is said to be best described in terms of elements such as styles of legislation, of court proceedings and of adjudication, the status of the legal professions and public officials, their ways of acting, and the level of acceptance of legally prescribed norms (cf. Blankenburg, 1988). A negative point here is that research tends to confine itself — as has already been noted for the sociology of law in general — to comparing legal cultures without examining what happens when those cultures collide, that is to say with the part played by various legal background features in cross-border legal relations. Nevertheless one must give credit to the researchers into legal culture for having pointed out the relevance of culture as a factor in explaining legal phenomena (cf. Lewis, 1985: 291), even if its significance when set against formal legal rules has yet to be determined. An especially important achievement of the legal culture researchers in this regard has been to make it clear that even if one makes the assumption — a reductionist assumption, they believe — that economic motives represent the predominant structural principle, one must still take account of the fact that even they are ultimately shaped by cultural characteristics.

3. The Legal Point of View

In contrast to the sociological literature, most writing within the field of law assumes a uniformity of business practices, and hence also of legal needs, in all countries around the world (Goldstajn, 1973; Berman and Kaufman, 1978).

The line generally taken is that trading conventions and the autonomous regulations of various institutions concerned with international business (General Terms & Conditions, Uniform Customs of the International Chamber of Commerce, INCOTERMS, ECE standard conditions), the judgments made by international courts of arbitration, and also to no small degree by international agreements (the Hague Convention on uniform law for the international sale of goods, and on contracts for such transactions, Vienna agreement on unified commercial law) have all encouraged the development of a common private law covering world trade, although this then comes face to face with variations in public business law from country to country. This approach goes on to say that if and in so far as success is also achieved in harmonizing that public business law (by means of the GATT and EC), cross-border business relations would then take place on a uniform legal basis.

It is possible, therefore, that the theses on the difficulties involved in intercultural communication put forward by sociological research cannot be applied to the sphere of international trade. It may be that there is now a sufficient amount of uniform law — especially since UN Commercial Law came into effect on 1 January 1988 — and, on top of that, such a variety of standard clauses and conventions (marine and overland transport, credit terms, payment systems) that these have displaced much of the effect of cultural differences. Two examples from within the EC are the agreement reached in 1968 on the courts' spheres of jurisdiction and the enforcement of court decisions in civil and commercial cases, as well as the 1980 agreement on the law of obligations. There are also a number of EC directives designed to achieve greater uniformity in private law, either serving as a basis for conforming legislation in member countries or directly being given the force of law (see Müller–Graff, 1987; Reich, 1987). Apart from unification measures taken via guidelines and directives, that is, apart from secondary Community law, private legal relations are also directly impinged upon by primary Community law (cf. Reich, 1987). The Single Internal Market now being planned for is currently giving rise to a great deal of effort in unifying public business law for the entire EC area.

New types of actor (for example, consumers, real-estate purchasers, tourists) which the unified law has not yet catered for, as well as cross-border legal relations outside the business field (family relationships, environmental damage), though outside the ambit of a *lex mercatoria* (Schmitthoff, 1964; Langen, 1981; Horn and Schmitthoff, 1982), are at least covered by private law. So even here there is no need for anyone to be uncertain as to which law should apply.

This picture, although referred to in the literature on law, does not properly reflect life in practice.

(a) If anything, the unification of law so far achieved applies more to marginal areas (Schlechtriem, 1987: 35). It is still fragmented at present in the area of private law and (to use the metaphor in Kötz, 1986: 12) has only created tiny islands of unified law in a sea of national legislation. This also applies to the EC, for the Community Private Law is anything but completely comprehensive as yet. It is 'fractional, isolated, lacks any systematic overall concept, is random and unduly involved' (Müller-Graff, 1987: 39). Efforts to also unify public international business law are confined to the EC, and even there they are only half way to fruition.

(b) Even in the cases where unified law applies, it is frequently contractually excluded (this is recommended by the leading German handbook for practitioners: cf. Sandrock, 1980: 491). Nor has unified law brought about the slightest unification in judicial practice in the signatory countries (Honnold, 1987; Kötz, 1986; Kramer, 1988).

(c) At least as far as any party referred to a law which is alien to it is concerned, private international law represents an 'insecure solution' (Langen, 1969: 359). Domestic judges are said to lack competence in matters of international trade (Berman and Kaufman, 1978).

There can be no question, then, of the parties to cross-border legal relations having anything approaching the same orientation to norms as their counterparts in strictly national affairs would by observing the laws of their own country. It is impossible to tell from the available literature whether there is a complete lack of such norm orientation, meaning that actors find themselves in anomic situations, or whether its place is taken by cognitive patterns of action. Both of these alternatives would appear to occur in practice.

In the sphere of significant, long-term business agreements, at any event, there is some evidence of forms of action which conform to the cognitive model. One feature in particular which we would interpret in this way is the great interest devoted by legal literature to consensual processes in the shape of negotiations and arbitration procedures. An immediate example one can cite are comparative legal studies of the dogmatic aspects in the renegotiation of contractual obligations (acts of God, frustration of contract, the *rebus sic stantibus* clause) which seek to lend more flexibility to cross-border business dealings (Horn, 1985).

The situations described here are not so unusual that the principle of contractual fidelity would necessarily have to be abandoned. However, law literature evidently expects the parties to cross-border contracts to be highly flexible and willing to learn. It therefore leaves the way clear for cognitive expectations (which are 'adapted to reality in the case of disappointment', Luhmann, 1972: 42).

Other, more radical propositions are based on a 'pluralistic theory of the derivation of law' (Steiner and Vagts, quoted in Schanze, 1986: 30ff.). International business law, in this view, is continually produced and changed by the 'consensual regulation of economic affairs' (Schanze, 1986: 30ff.), which means the task of creating greater order is accomplished by non-state actors. Cross-border legal relations, it is also posited, do not follow legally prescribed models. Since, at the most, they are negotiated 'under the shadow of the law', they are really the result of lawyers' efforts to pre-empt possible legal liabilities by drafting exclusion clauses and the like. Neither unified law nor private international law, they say, would be able to prevent the adjustment and renegotiation of the wording of contracts. It seems, though, that the predominant opinion in the relevant legal literature is not prepared to shift very far from normative structures to become closer to cognitive ones (Sandrock, 1988).

Where there is no dispute, however, is over the great part played by conciliation procedures in the event of contractual problems (cf. the contributions by Horn, Glossner, Mezger, Herrmann and Barrigan Mercantorio in Horn, 1985; also Bartels, 1983: 119ff.); that is, by procedures which permit a commonly accepted solution to be found for the future while removing the precise legal position from consideration. This too is, of course, our typical cognitive model of action.

On the other hand, *anomic* situations are indicated by reports that unified law is still largely a matter with which people are unfamiliar in practice (Piltz, 1987: 46; Basedow in Schlechtriem, 1987: 74; Fallon, 1988) or that it at least leads to divergent interpretations from case to case. The complaint has in any case always been voiced about private international law that even lawyers have difficulty in giving expert information on foreign law. Lay people are generally in the dark as to their legal positions, which they cannot therefore use as an orientation for their actions. The same applies to public legislation and regulations which, apart from being mostly inscrutable to foreigners, in many cases bear no proper relation to cross-border legal conditions (cf. Müllender, 1989).

One contribution which comes very close to the theses put forward by sociological theories of communication, even if it is almost alone in the legal literature, is an article by von Mehren (1969) on the misunderstandings arising in cross-border dealings as a result of cultural differences. A number of practical handbooks which all have the stereotyped title of 'How to do business in . . .' can also be regarded as indications of anomic situations.

Finally, many complaints are made of anomic conditions outside the area of business relations, in fields such as the enforcement of compensation claims (Chernobyl, Sandoz), tourism, work done in foreign countries or, above all, disputes in mixed nationality families.

4. Conclusions on the Development of the Research Topic of 'Cultural Conflicts and Legal Interaction'

The approaches to the subject taken by sociology and the study of law paint differing pictures of cross-border legal relations. While the sociologists place emphasis on cultural conflict and regard intercultural negotiation in the developing 'world society' which is characterized by pronounced interdependences as an important phenomenon, jurists predominantly devote their efforts to discussing the unification and harmonization of the law as models for solving the problems arising out of cross-border legal contracts. Although phenomena of differing legal cultures and value conceptions are recognized in the study of law too, there is nevertheless a belief that the associated conflict situations can be resolved by *legal* developments. In the case of divergent value conceptions, for example, the idea is put forward that an international *ordre public* should be developed (cf. Horn, 1980). One reason for such a narrowed perspective could be that there is a lack of empirical legal surveys in this field. In cases where they do exist, such as the examination of investment agreements in international business law (Schanze, 1986), the role of negotiations is properly thematized. Looking at it from the opposite side, sociological work on the subject, if it deals with the law at all, usually does so marginally and instead places intercultural communication and resulting conflicts at the centre of attention. Yet because the conflicts of culture build up within a framework given a prior structure by the law, the hypotheses put forward by researchers on intercultural communication do have to be specified anew in the sphere of legal interaction.

4.1 Negotiations

We work on the premise that the cross-border phenomena which intensify to produce conflicts or interdependences and structures of cooperation and reliance can be traced back to what actors themselves do. What we are particularly interested in is the portion of reality which those actors plan, actively shape and communicatively convey to others. We do not by any means wish to deny that part of reality — interdependence in Elias's sense of the expression — which develops behind actors' backs without their being able to comprehend it, but this is not our specific focus of attention. We follow what has been termed the 'negotiated order approach', as was developed by Strauss (1978) above all, treating actors as themselves the creators of social structures. The negotiated order approach views the interplay of negotiations and structures in such a way that, although structures do exert their influence on negotiations, it is also ultimately revealed by closer research into negotiations how present structures can be attributed to the negotiations of the past and are hence what might be termed consolidations and sedimentations of negotiation processes.

A further fundamental consideration is that norms in interactions are not accorded the status of absolute prescriptions for action and sources of orientation, but it is taken to be important for actors to be able to specify their expectations in a manner which is appropriate to the situation. In other words, we assume that actors make use of creative, constructive and adaptive abilities in their interactions: interactions are guided by 'everyday theories' which have recourse to all kinds of funds of knowledge and typifications, especially typifications of expectations (cf. Matthes, 1976: 53f.). Interaction, then, does not consist in the enforcement of norms, and the main determinants of action are these expectations which actors themselves have created or selected.[8]

We accept that cross-border contacts and communication do also occur according to normative premises, that is to say that they are predicated upon stabilized structures which transcend factual conditions. However, communication problems also possess a certain degree of autonomy: 'They are not identical with structural problems, nor with the degree to which structures are realized' (Luhmann, 1980: 99). Norms depend on being cited and on being activated on the right occasions in communication processes occurring in the real world, that is, on being thematized in real situations. In legal matters, though, there are also thematization thresholds which need to be overcome. It is a worthwhile exercise, in our view, to subject these thresholds to empirical examination.

In contrast to the normative paradigm, the interactive paradigm stresses the part played by spontaneity, by creativity, which is said to manifest itself at all times in social action and to develop by way of role-taking (cf. Wilson, 1973). Yet it is apparent from problems of intercultural communication that, because parties to interaction are unaccustomed to each other, role-taking may not necessarily be possible. In the absence of typical patterns of behaviour, roles in such situations have to be developed 'from scratch'. This may occur via the development of a common (third) culture. An interesting point in this regard is Macaulay's thesis (cf. 1985: 467ff., now modified however: cf. Galanter et al., 1989), which he developed with reference to the legal culture of the USA. Macaulay proposes that long-term business relations are not based upon the law, and indeed hardly on contractual agreements, but on business cultures derived from reciprocal strategic considerations which favour the continuation of a mutually beneficial relationship:

> Contract planning and contract law, at best, stand at the margin of important long-term continuing business relations. Business people often do not plan, exhibit great care in drafting contracts, pay much attention to those that lawyers carefully draft, or honor a legal approach to business relationships. There are business cultures defining the risks assumed in bargains, and what should be done when things go wrong. . . . There are relatively few contract cases litigated, and those that are have special characteristics. . . . At best, formal legal procedures usually are but a step in a larger process of negotiation. (Macaulay, 1985: 467)

Macaulay's explanation for this limited relevance of the law in business dealings is the existence of relational sanctions which arise whenever transactions occur in a setting of continual interrelationships and interdependences. There is evidently a great interest in maintaining such persistent relationships as long as they are generally satisfactory. So it is, then, that potential conflicts are suppressed or ignored, or that compromises are arrived at in order to keep these relationships alive. Accordingly, social networks and systems of communication are formed.

4.2 On the Concept of Anomie

Since Durkheim (1911), the absence, insufficiency or inappropriateness of the legal and/or moral regulation of particular spheres of collective life has been defined as social anomie. Anomie also arises whenever regulations, though they do exist, no longer correspond to the level of development of collective organizations. There is no need in this context to go into the reformulation of the concept undertaken by Merton (1949) in order to explain deviant behaviour. It is important, however, to discuss how normlessness is regarded by sociological theory as it currently stands.

Many authors with concerns ranging from 'micro' to 'macro' convey the impression in the various approaches they are pursuing that society is not actually ordered by norms. Normlessness is then no longer understood as a sign of crisis as it was by Durkheim. Indeed, symbolic interactionism places its emphasis — as discussed above — on the continual reinterpretation of action structures by the actors themselves. Systems theory points out how norms valid for society in its entirety are petering out in view of the increased significance of partial systems which control themselves (cf., for example, Willke, 1983; Rosewitz and Schimank, 1988). Do such new perspectives or do changes taking place within society mean that the concept of anomie has had its day?

Part of the answer to this question must undoubtedly be yes. The problem of the intensity of control and the enforcement of norms which are appropriate to society is described differently today from how it was in Durkheim's time (cf. Preuss, 1988). Yet a quite modern conception of anomie can be made, as a state in which social integration is lacking (Habermas, 1982), as a problem of central or de-central controllability (Mayntz, 1988), as a lack of commonly shared knowledge (Habermas, 1982; Haferkamp, forthcoming), or as a situation in which institutionalized typifications have to be created (Berger & Luckmann, 1969).

Deficiencies in the application of norms (whether because it is too weak or too strong) are still considered according to our current knowledge to carry serious consequences as an aggregate state of society, and hence to be of considerable sociological relevance. The sphere of cross-border legal relations would appear to be in exactly that aggregate state at present, which makes it a promising field of enquiry precisely because such enquiries can draw upon and complement current discussions. The best concept for drawing together the sociological interest in this phenomenon remains that of anomie.

The interactive paradigm and the concept of a 'third' culture suggest that various situations could arise as a result of anomie in the sphere of cross-border social relations. The actors in such relations (business people, chambers of commerce, etc., law firms, courts of arbitration, the European Court of Justice, signatory countries in systems of unified law) have created systems of cultural and/or legal norms in partial areas. The expectations made here are normative, yet they admit of cognitive elements to allow adjustments to cater for frequent changes in conditions (movements in the world economy, political crises, measures affecting a country's trade). Structures of expectation are then created which differ from the 'home cultures' of those involved, which develop different institutions and which place particularly high demands on actors' personal accomplishments ('Ich-Leistungen' in Dreitzel, 1972: 118 and passim). These high demands exclude many potential participants, or lead to anomic reactions among newcomers or those who only participate sporadically. The typical actor here is the large organization concluding major contracts, say, for the extraction and delivery of raw materials or for the construction of a turnkey project. Its behaviour is hardly now attributable to any kind of cultural identity. It receives the advice of international banks and large law firms which use quasi-universal business language and which thrash out any differences on the level of interests rather than that of values, world-views or social norms.

It is this 'third culture' of international business and economic relations which has led the legal literature to its across-the-board neglect of the cultural elements in cross-border legal relations. Because of its large normative content, this 'third culture' is receptive to legal control even though it does not necessarily need it given its competence in regulating itself (cf. evidence of the limited practical need for legal unification in Kötz, 1986: 8f.; Kramer, 1988: 25ff.). Problems of anomie hardly crop up among insiders, and the predominant structural principle is *economic rationality*.

Apart from that, cross-border interactions also occur — to an extent which we are as yet unable to quantify — which would be regarded as legal relations in a domestic context but which take place in both a legal and a sociological no-man's-land. The only literature we are aware of in the field of law which takes up this precarious situation is the article by von Mehren already mentioned (1969: 255): 'To operate effectively in transactions involving more than one legal system requires a kind of insight and feel that perhaps relatively few lawyers have . . . The parties may hold different conceptions of "contract" even though both understand the terms of the agreement.'

Concurring entirely with the theory of anomie, von Mehren expects deviant modes of behaviour to occur in cross-border legal relations ('behaviour that would be most exceptional if they were operating solely within their own society'). Day-to-day newspaper reports on the frequency of criminal offences in international trade would appear to confirm this assumption. It is said that one form of reaction to a lack of norm orientation is the formation of subcultures practising deviant behaviour (Dreitzel, 1972: 324). Further types of reaction resulting from *cultural predisposition* are named by role theory as withdrawal from the interaction situation, the staging of conflicts, and the attempt to attain emancipation via an autonomous orientation (Dreitzel, 1972: 324). Examples from the sphere of cross-border contact can be found for all these forms of reaction:

Withdrawal	— Avoiding dealings with people or organizations in other countries, and journeys abroad
	— Avoiding contact with migrant workers, or 'foreigners-go-home' political views
	— Avoiding, or divorce from, marriage to foreigners
Conflict-staging	— Debt-service moratorium by third-world countries
	— Abduction of children from their country of residence by a parent
Emancipation	— Formulation of autonomous norms (*lex mercatoria*)
	— Renegotiation of contracts
	— Marriage contracts between partners of different nationalities.

That one of the forms of reaction should be emancipation demonstrates that a cognitive response to the lack of norm orientation is by all means consistent with anomie theory. The (role-theoretical) theory of anomie describes the conditions under which 'planned action interrelations' come about (Haferkamp, forthcoming: 165ff.), that is to say, in which social structures are created — cognitively — by the actors concerned themselves in learning processes. This may make the anomie situation in cross-border 'legal' relations an ideal field in which to pursue processes of 'establishing common knowledge' (Haferkamp, forthcoming: 105ff.). Common knowledge is in fact a precondition for actors to relate to each other in what they do. It is the foundation on which a third culture is built, without having to be as comprehensive as that culture. It is possible for it to relate simply to the situation at any given moment, manifesting itself in shared definitions of the situation and the convergence of 'differences of perspective' between the participants in intercultural communication.

4.3 The Formation of Structures

The structures described above frequently no longer carry any signs of how they originated, yet this is something one has to know before a proper assessment of their social effects can be made. Just as the dimensions of a tennis court, the height of the net and size of the racquets are geared to a Central European physical build (meaning that a Japanese person has less chance from the outset), legal procedures governing cross-border relations may have been given dimensions over which one of the cultures involved has exerted a dominant influence.

There have been hypotheses for some time claiming the existence of differing initial conditions for the establishment of legal structures, particularly with regard to dealings touching upon the law of nations and its institutions. These hypotheses apply to North–South trade, indeed also to the North–South divide within the EC (Guibentif, 1988). The following questions can be developed on the formation of structures:

(a) Is there a greater tendency for conflicts of culture to be alleviated or exacerbated by the dominance of the English language and Anglo-Saxon legal methods in international contractual agreements and arbitration proceedings?

(b) What structural effects result from the fact that large American law firms are extending their operations to more and more countries around the world?

Certainly it is true that not all the structures in cross-border legal relations originated autonomously. We have already spoken of attempts to establish norms by the state, and even outside the areas of family and probate law, there will be no denying a certain amount of significance to the courts at the domestic level in any particular country. In this context the discrimination hypothesis needs to be reformulated to the effect that whichever (legal) culture is *foreign in the given situation* may be placed at a disadvantage.

Nevertheless one must expect there to be a certain relationship of tension between discrimination hypotheses and those proposing the (increasing) cognitive structuring of 'world society'. To the extent that the willingness to learn is institutionalized, the idea of discrimination can no longer be consistently sustained, for

(a) the German courts are prepared to a certain extent to apply foreign law and even foreign cultural norms;

(b) should the renegotiation of contracts become the general rule, this ought to be of particular benefit to contractual parties from the Third World.

Finally, the problem of anomie will also be of significance in researching the infrastructures of cross-border legal relations in that, whatever advisory, negotiating, conciliation and arbitration bodies are set up, an important source for the derivation of norms exists apart from the actors who are directly involved, with the result that particularized norm cycles are set in motion. These are not only distinct from unstructured fields of interaction but also from those areas which suffer from orientation deficiencies because the norms enforced by the state are either too involved or are not acceptable in practice. We would position these three different fields of interaction as follows on a hypothetical scale:

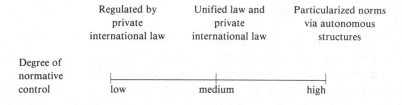

Regulated by private international law	Unified law and private international law	Particularized norms via autonomous structures

Degree of normative control

low   medium   high

Notes

This essay is dedicated to Hans Haferkamp who would have been fifty and Ulrich Drobnig who was sixty. It was translated by Neil Johnson.

1. Such relations which pertain between private persons or organizations are frequently described as transnational rather than international (cf. Singer, 1987: 215f.).

2. Czempiel (1981: 22) uses this term to describe 'sequences of actions with a meaningful link between them, which gain durability, consistency and the backing of a consensus from the fact that the actions concerned are typically in accordance with expectations'. For a similar definition, cf. the concept of planned action interrelations in Haferkamp (forthcoming: 165ff.).

3. The term 'world society' is intended to fulfil an analytical purpose and not to describe the actual state of the world as such, for this would be to assume the existence of systemic relationships which do not exist on that scale. Those dealing with the theory of world society nevertheless find it useful to construct ideal types and then to investigate how far these are at odds with reality (cf. Senghaas, 1988 and others).

4. Cf. the various contributions in Gudykunst (1983). The theoretical perspectives which have evolved are: (a) codes and code systems; (b) constructivism; (c) various

philosophical perspectives; (d) mathematical models; (e) relationship development; (f) rhetorical theory; (g) rules perspectives; (h) systems perspectives; cf. also Loenhoff's (1988) attempt to achieve a generalization.

5. Cf. Loenhoff (1988: 24): 'Theory builders are faced with the greatest task here, their chief difficulty consisting of gaining a conceptual grasp of the true specifics of intercultural communication. It is, however, apparent from the search for a suitable paradigm that the "conflictual communication model" allows a better approach to be made to the problems of intercultural communication, refraining as it does from seeing the basis of all communicative understanding in a real consensus and emphasizing as it does the pragmatic and situational dimension in communication which, in principle, is always an uncertain matter.'

6. 'The term "cultural constraints" can . . . be divided into three types: cultural cognitive constraints, cultural emotional constraints, and cultural behavioural constraints' (Ting-Toomey, 1985: 74).

7. These authors believe that, because of increased interdependence, scarce resources and the problem of cost which alternative solutions to conflicts entail, the significance of intercultural negotiations is continually growing.

8. Cf. Haferkamp (1980: 20): 'Behavioural representations are generated and instructions and plans are followed in a constructive process which cannot take place without formative ability. However, whenever it is expected of anyone that they should form something, they are also allowed enough leeway by the other participants in carrying out the detailed work, especially if unforeseen circumstances arise.'

References

Ansay, Tuğrul and Gessner, Volkmar (1974) *Gastarbeiter in Gesellschaft und Recht.* Munich: Beck.

Bartels, Martin (1983) *Vertragsanpassung und Streitbeilegung.* Bremen: Diss.

Berger, Peter L. and Luckmann, Thomas (1969) *Die gesellschaftliche Konstruktion der Wirklichkeit.* Frankfurt: Fischer.

Berman, Harold J. and Kaufman, Colin (1978) 'The Law of International Commercial Transactions (Lex Mercatoria)', *Harvard International Law Journal* 19: 221–75.

Beyme, Klaus von et al. (eds) (1987) *Politikwissenschaft. Eine Grundlegung. Band III: Aussenpolitik und Internationale Politik.* Stuttgart: Kohlhammer.

Blankenburg, Erhard (1988) 'Zum Begriff "Rechtskultur" ', paper prepared for presentation at the 24th Meeting of the German Sociological Association in Zurich, 4–7 October 1988.

Cushman, Donald P. and Sanderson-King, Sarah (1985) 'National and Organizational Cultures in Conflict Resolution: Japan, the United States, and Yugoslavia', in William B. Gudykunst et al. (eds), *Communication, Culture and Organizational Processes.* Beverly Hills: Sage.

Czempiel, Ernst-Otto (1981) *Internationale Politik.* Paderborn: Schöningh.

Dreitzel, Hans Peter (1972) *Die gesellschaftlichen Leiden und das Leiden an der Gesellschaft.* Stuttgart: Enke.

Durkheim, Emile (1911) *De la division du travail social.* Paris: Alcan.

Fallon, Marc (1988) 'Problematik der grenzüberschreitenden Verbraucherstreitsachen' in der EWG', *Europäische Zeitschrift für Verbraucherrecht*: 229–54.

Featherstone, Mike (1985) 'The Fate of Modernity: An Introduction', *Theory, Culture & Society* 2(3): 1–5.

Fox, William F. (1988) *International Commercial Agreements*. Deventer, Netherlands: Kluwer.

Galanter, Marc et al. (1989) *The Transformation of American Business Disputing*. Unpublished manuscript.

Gessner, Volkmar and Höland, Armin (1989) 'Orientations théoriques de la sociologie du droit empirique en République fédéral', *Droit et Société* 11/12.

Goldstajn, Aleksandar (1973) 'The New Law Merchant Reconsidered', pp. 171–85 in Fritz Fabricius (ed.), *Law and International Trade — Festschrift für Schmitthoff*. Frankfurt: Athenäum.

Griffiths, John (1979) 'Is Law Important?', *New York University Law Review*: 339–74.

Grossfeld, Bernhard (1980) 'Multinationale Unternehmen als Anstoss zur Internationalisierung des Wirtschaftsrechts', *Wirtschaft und Recht* 32: 106–21.

Gudykunst, William B. (ed.) (1983) *Intercultural Communication Theory. Current Perspectives*. Beverly Hills: Sage.

Guibentif, Pierre (1988) 'Rechtskulturelle Aspekte der Effektivität des Rechts der Europäischen Gemeinschaft', lecture at the 24th Meeting of the German Sociological Association in Zurich, 4–7 October 1988.

Habermas, Jürgen (1982) *Theorie des kommunikativen Handelns*, Vol. 2. Frankfurt: Suhrkamp.

Haferkamp, Hans (1980) *Herrschaft und Strafrecht. Theorien der Normentstehung und Strafrechtsetzung*. Opladen: Westdeutscher Verlag.

Haferkamp, Hans (ed.) (1989) *Social Structure and Culture*. Berlin & New York: de Gruyter.

Haferkamp, Hans (forthcoming) *Soziales Handeln. Theorie sozialen Verhaltens und sinnhaften Handelns, geplanter Handlungszusammenhänge und sozialer Strukturen*. Opladen: Westdeutscher Verlag.

Harnett, Donald L. and Cummings, L.L. (1980) *Bargaining Behavior: An International Study*. Houston: Dame Publications.

Heckmann, Friedrich (1981) *Die Bundesrepublik: Ein Einwanderungsland?* Stuttgart: Klett–Cotta.

Hollander, A.N.J. den (1955) 'Der "Kulturkonflikt" als soziologischer Begriff und als Erscheinung', *Kölner Zeitschrift für Soziologie und Sozialpsychologie* 7: 161–87.

Honnold, John O. (1987) 'Uniform Words and Uniform Application. The 1980 Sales Convention and International Juridicial Practice', pp. 115–46 in Peter Schlechtriem (ed.), *Einheitliches Kaufrecht und nationales Obligationenrecht*. Baden-Baden: Nomos.

Hopkins, Terence K. and Wallerstein, Immanuel (1982) 'Grundzüge der Entwicklung des modernen Weltsystems. Entwurf für ein Forschungsvorhaben', in Dieter Senghaas (ed.), *Kapitalistische Weltökonomie*. Frankfurt: Suhrkamp.

Horn, Norbert (1980) 'Die Entwicklung des Internationalen Wirtschaftsrechts durch Verhaltensrichtlinien — Neue Elemente eines internationalen ordre public', *RabelsZ* 44: 423–54.

Horn, Norbert (ed.) (1985) *Adaptation and Renegotiation of Contracts in International Trade and Finance*. Antwerp: Kluwer.

Horn, Norbert and Schmitthoff, Clive M. (eds) (1982) *The Transnational Law of Commercial Transactions*. Antwerp: Kluwer.

Kessler, Joan B. (1988) 'The Lawyer's Intercultural Communication Problems with Clients from Diverse Cultures', *Northwestern Journal of International Law & Business* 9: 64–79.

Kötz, Hein (1986) 'Rechtsvereinheitlichung — Nutzen, Kosten, Methoden, Ziele', *RabelsZ* 50: 1–17.

Kramer, Ernst A. (1988) *Europäische Privatrechtsvereinheitlichung — Institutionen, Methoden, Perspektiven*. Europa-Institut der Universität des Saarlandes.

Langen, Eugen (1969) 'Vom Internationalen Privatrecht zum Transnationalen Handelsrecht', *Neue Juristische Wochenschrift*: 358–60.

Langen, Eugen (1981) *Transnationales Recht*. Heidelberg: Verlag Recht und Wirtschaft.

Lewis, Philip S.C. (1985) 'Lawyers and Legal Culture', *Zeitschrift für Rechtssoziologie* 2: 291–8.

Loenhoff, Jens (1988) 'Modelle interkultureller Kommunikation. Verständigungsbedarf im globalen System', paper prepared for presentation at the 24th Meeting of the German Sociological Association in Zurich, 4–7 October 1988.

Luhmann, Niklas (1971) 'Die Weltgesellschaft', *Archiv für Rechts- und Sozialphilosophie* 57: 1–35.

Luhmann, Niklas (1972) *Rechtssoziologie*. Reinbek: Rowohlt.

Luhmann, Niklas (1980) 'Kommunikation über Recht in Interaktionssystemen', *Jahrbuch für Rechtssoziologie* 6: 99–112.

Macaulay, Stewart (1985) 'An Empirical View of Contract', *Wisconsin Law Review*: 465–82.

Matthes, Joachim (1976) 'Handlungstheoretisch-interaktionistisch-phänomenologisch orientierte Theorien', in M. Rainer Lepsius (ed.), *Zwischenbilanz der Soziologie. Verhandlungen des 17. Deutschen Soziologentages*. Stuttgart: Enke.

Mauviel, Maurice (1987) 'La communication interculturelle: constitution d'une nouvelle discipline', *Cahiers de sociologie économique et culturelle* 7: 45–66.

Mayntz, Renate (1988) 'Funktionelle Teilsysteme in der Theorie sozialer Differenzierung', in Renate Mayntz et al. (eds), *Differenzierung und Verselbständigung — Zur Entwicklung gesellschaftlicher Teilsysteme*. Frankfurt and New York: Campus.

Mehren, Arthur T. von (1969) 'The Significance of Cultural and Legal Diversity for International Transactions', pp. 247–58 in Ernst von Caemmerer et al. (eds), *Ius Privatum Gentium, Festschrift für Max Rheinstein*. Tübingen: Mohr.

Merton, Robert K. (1949) *Social Theory and Social Structure*. New York: Free Press.

Müllender, Bernd (1989) 'Schilda kennt keine Grenzen', *Die Zeit* 19 (5 May): 28.

Müller-Graff, Peter-Christian (1987) Privatrecht und europäisches Gemeinschaftsrecht', pp. 17–52 in Peter-Christian Müller-Graff and Manfred Zuleeg, *Staat und Wirtschaft in der EG*. Baden–Baden: Nomos.

Nadler, Lawrence B. et al. (1985) 'Culture and the Management of Conflict Situations', in William B. Gudykunst et al. (eds), *Communication, Culture and Organizational Processes*. Beverly Hills: Sage.

Pearson, Geoffrey (1985) 'Lawlessness, Modernity and Social Change: A Historical Appraisal', *Theory, Culture & Society*, 2(3): 15–35.

Piltz, Burghart (1987) 'Praktische Erfahrungen in Deutschland mit der Anwendung der Haager Einheitlichen Kaufgesetze', in Peter Schlechtriem (ed.) *Einheitliches Kaufrecht und nationales Obligationenrecht*. Baden-Baden: Nomos.

Preuss, Ulrich K. (1988) 'Entwicklungsperspektiven der Rechtswissenschaft', *Kritische Justiz*: 361–76.

Prosser, Michael H. (1978) *The Cultural Dialogue. An Introduction to Intercultural Communication*. Boston: Houghton Mifflin.

Rehbein, Jochen (1985) 'Einführung in die interkulturelle Kommunikation', in Jochen Rehbein (ed.) *Interkulturelle Kommunikation*. Tübingen: Gunter Narr.

Reich, Norbert (1987) *Förderung und Schutz diffuser Interessen durch die Europäischen Gemeinschaften*. Baden-Baden: Nomos.

Rittberger, Volker and Wolf, Klaus Dieter (1987) 'Problemfelder internationaler Beziehungen (aus politologischer Sicht)', in Deutsches Institut für Fernstudien (ed.), *Problemfelder internationaler Beziehungen*. Tübingen.

Robertson, Roland and Lechner, Frank (1985) 'Modernization, Globalization and the Problem of Culture in World-Systems Theory', *Theory, Culture & Society* 2(3): 103–17.

Rosewitz, Bernd and Schimank, Uwe (1988) 'Verselbständigung und politische Steuerbarkeit gesellschaftlicher Teilsysteme', in Renate Mayntz et al. (eds), *Differenzierung und Verselbständigung — Zur Entwicklung gesellschaftlicher Teilsysteme*. Frankfurt & New York: Campus.

Samovar, Larry and Porter, Richard L. (1976) 'Communicating Interculturally', in Larry Samovar and Richard L. Porter, *Intercultural Communication. A Reader*. Belmont: Wadsworth.

Sandrock, Otto (ed.) (1980) *Handbuch der internationalen Vertragsgestaltung*, Vol. 1. Heidelberg: Verlagsgesellschaft Recht und Wirtschaft mbH.

Sandrock, Otto (1988) 'Internationales Wirtschaftsrecht durch "konsensuale Wirtschaftsregulierung"?', *Zeitschrift für das gesamte Handelsrecht und Wirtschaftsrecht*: 66–87.

Sauvant, Karl P. (1987) 'Die Institutionalisierung der internationalen Zusammenarbeit', in Klaus von Beyme et al. (eds), *Politikwissenschaft. Eine Grundlegung. Band III: Aussenpolitik und Internationale Politik*. Stuttgart: Kohlhammer.

Schanze, Erich (1986) *Investitionsverträge im internationalen Wirtschaftsrecht*. Frankfurt: Metzner.

Schlechtriem, Peter (1987) 'Bemerkungen zur Geschichte des Einheitskaufrechts', pp. 27–36 in Peter Schlechtriem (ed.), *Einheitliches Kaufrecht und nationales Obligationenrecht*. Baden-Baden: Nomos.

Schmitthoff, Clive M. (1964) 'Das neue Recht des Welthandels', *Rabels Zeitschrift*: 47–77.

Senghaas, Dieter (1988) *Konfliktformationen im internationalen System*. Frankfurt: Suhrkamp.

Senghaas-Knobloch, Eva (1969) *Frieden durch Integration und Assoziation. Literaturbericht und Problemstudien*. Stuttgart: Klett.

Singer, Marshall R. (1987) *Intercultural Communication. A Perceptual Approach*. Englewood Cliffs, NJ: Prentice-Hall.

Strauss, Anselm (1978) *Negotiations. Varieties, Contexts, Processes, and Social Order*. San Francisco: Jossey Bass.

Tenbruck, Friedrich H. (1979) 'Die Aufgaben der Kultursoziologie', *Kölner*

Zeitschrift für Soziologie und Sozialpsychologie 36: 399–421.

Ting-Toomey, Stella (1985) 'Toward a Theory of Conflict and Culture', in William B. Gudykunst et al. (eds), *Communication, Culture, and Organizational Processes*. Beverly Hills: Sage.

Trotha, Trutz von (1985) 'Kultur, Subkultur, Kulturkonflikt,' in Günther Kaiser et al. (eds), *Kleines Kriminologisches Wörterbuch*, 2nd edn. Heidelberg: C.F. Müller.

Useem, John et al. (1963) 'Men in the Middle of the Third Culture', *Human Organization* 22: 169–79.

Wallerstein, Immanuel (1974) *The Modern World System*. New York: Academic Press.

Willke, Helmut (1983) *Entzauberung des Staates*. Königstein: Athenäum.

Wilson, Thomas P. (1973) 'Theorien der Interaktion und Modelle soziologischer Erklärung', pp. 54–79 in Arbeitsgruppe Bielefelder Soziologen (ed.), *Alltagswissen, Interaktion und gesellschaftliche Wirklichkeit*. Opladen: Westdeutscher Verlag.

Volkmar Gessner is a Director at the Zentrum für Europäische Rechtspolitik at the University of Bremen.

Angelika Schade is a Research Associate at the Zentrum für Europäische Rechtspolitik at the University of Bremen.

The *Big Bang* and the Law: The Internationalization and Restructuration of the Legal Field

Yves Dezalay

To a great extent, the Western nation-states have been a construction of the legislators. While it is true that the history of the relation between the lawyers and state power has not always been trouble-free, this professional grouping has always regarded itself as invested with a certain public authority and responsibility. Their view extends beyond civil matters into the very institutions of the state, which are not only to provide the best guarantee of preserving the state's quasi-monopoly as regards the management of conflict, but are also accountable for the formation of social relations.

How have the lawyers, who for centuries have tied their fate to that of the nation-states,[1] accommodated themselves to the opening of frontiers which has accompanied the placing in question of a certain number of state prerogatives? Dissociated from the nation-state, which gave it its authority and historical legitimacy, is the law condemned to become merely a technique, just one more management tool like all the others? Will the 'high priests of the law', well used to treading the corridors of power and to fashioning wise compromises between hallowed regulations and the exigencies of politics, be able to adjust to the displacement of centres of power at this time of internationalization and deregulation? In putting themselves at the service of the market, and becoming entrepreneurial service providers who are more interested in economic return than justice, aren't these new mercenaries ('hired guns') in the employ of capital squandering the stock of legitimacy and credibility built up by their 'gentleman lawyer' predecessors? In a word, doesn't the surrender of certain royal prerogatives in favour of the market mean that the lawyers are themselves paradoxically proclaiming the 'end of law'?

Theory, Culture & Society (SAGE, London, Newbury Park and New Delhi), Vol. 7 (1990), 279–293

At first sight, it is nothing of the kind. On the contrary, the market for legal services has undergone an unprecedented expansion,[2] and the lawyers are poised to become a scarce resource (Hampton, 1988). Moreover, this sudden change in fortunes is accompanied by a recovery of prestige. Some continental jurists even think that the breaking down of national frontiers and the concomitant decline of state interventionism constitute a great chance for social renewal. Some leading liberal lawyers, like Ripert (1949), had previously accused the welfare state of precipitating the decline of the law. Their heirs now celebrate the opening of a critical attack against the state as a whole, and they predict that the 1990s will truly be the decade of the jurists. According to them, the law is in the process of emancipating itself from the supervision of the state, so that it will be able to recover its real purpose: the regulation of a market economy to which the states themselves must submit (Cohen-Tanugi, 1985, 1988).

This renewal of the law — or at least the new prosperity of the lawyers — has not been without cost. There has been a radical reorientation. The ideal of social law has been killed off, replaced by the *lex mercatoria*: the transnational law of market relations. Like a phoenix, the law is continuously reborn out of its own ashes. The old look has gone, the law has a modern face even at the same time as its new ideas derive their legitimacy from the legal tradition. But these new lawyers, who develop the mechanisms which can structure and regulate international finance, are after all doing much the same as their predecessors, who focused their legal talents on the territorial ambitions of rulers picking over the remains of the feudal system. The functionary wants to be paid, and so stays with the Prince; but prosperity and even survival can depend on knowing when to leave the protection of one patron for another. The recent infatuation with Brussels, shown by continental and even North American Lawyers (Tutt, 1988), indicate that the old tendencies are still with us.

These changes that we are seeing have very considerable significance for the sociology of law and, more widely, for the sociology of the professions.

In the first place, outmoded schemes of legal thinking do not easily survive concrete demonstrations of the recomposition of the juridical field as it accompanies and even facilitates the internationalization of financial markets[3] fed by new technology and the ambitions it has aroused. It is no coincidence that, throughout

Europe, the *legal big bang* followed straight after the *financial big bang*.[4] Second, it should be said that juridical innovations do not appear fully formed in the mind of the legislator — even if professional mythologies might pretend otherwise. Most often, especially when the juridical innovations are important, as is the case here, they have been provoked, anticipated by a refiguration of the field in which the professionals say what the law is and put it into practice. Thus redefinition of the law comes through redefinition of and by the professionals who operate the new definitions. Next, the play of professional and inter-professional (Abbott, 1988) competition, in a context where strategies are as diverse as resources, tends to favour the kind of permanent recomposition of the professional field which allows it to be both autonomous and closely symbiotic with the economic world (Dezalay, 1986, 1989a). When economic or political power changes hands, it is always the case that professional diversity will ensure a ready supply of those who can speak the new language and who are eager to take those opportunities that come their way. The financial predators who are restructuring the economic terrain do not have to look far before they are surrounded by all the legal talent that they need.

The analysis of the globalization of the market in legal services throws new light on to the old question of the autonomy or, if one prefers, the singularity, of national juridical cultures. This globalization is for the most part an Americanization. Arriving in Europe and the Far East, in the wake of their multinational clients, North American professional firms soon realized that here were potential markets that they were well able to exploit (Labaton, 1988; Rice, 1989c). The Wall Street law firm, invented over a century ago in response to the demands of American finance and industry, has become a model for similar developments everywhere, as the local lawyers, in a struggle for survival, feel that they also must adopt the model of the *corporate law firm* (Campbell-Smith, 1985). Such changes are not limited to business law alone. These foreign professional practices only thrive if they set off, domino-fashion, a complete remodelling which gradually extends throughout the complete ensemble of structures and expectations which characterize a legal culture. It would be wrong, however, to think of this as a simple matter of colonization. The metamorphosis in European legal practice could not have occurred if it had not also been powered from the inside by a new generation of lawyers, pure products of an academic meritocracy, whose ambitions would be realized only by a new deal which would do away with the self-reproducing habits and privileges of the gentleman lawyers. The unscrupulous ambition of the *yuppie lawyers*, supported by a good technical command of the law, makes them the perfect auxiliaries to today's *robber barons*, the financial predators who have already transformed the financial landscape of the new decade.

New Rules for International Commerce

Even if these newcomers are often denounced by their elders as vulgar legal entrepreneurs who pay more attention to their *bottom line*[5] than to their civic or professional responsibilities, they are careful not to forget where their primary duties lie. Completely at the service of their clients' interests, they are working towards the construction of increasingly more sophisticated juridical mechanisms for the framing and regulation of international economic exchange. Perhaps this is the shape of the future; in any event, it is clear that these strategies function both to protect their professional monopoly and to respond to the marketing imperatives of an epoch in which the major economic actors are themselves searching for new rules of engagement.[6]

Contemporary advances in the law pertaining to international trade are both numerous and convergent: codes of conduct, like those which have been adopted, under the aegis of the United Nations, for international enterprises, the harmonization of accounting procedures (OPA), the rise of international commercial arbitrage. These developments that are so many signs of the business community's 're-regulation', are in themselves very different from the welfare-state model of regulation they aim to supplant. Traders, and economic actors in general, need regularities and securities because they are the basis of conventions, institutional forms, and the harmony between them. We can see at this point that a thorough understanding of how legitimate social rules are reproduced can be crucial for the explanation of how contradictory tendencies can spring up in the field of business law. On the one hand, we can see all the signs of a 'banalization of legal services' which have become just one sector of financial services among others, and which are just as subject to the logic of profit and competition; on the other hand, the legal practitioners, and often their clients, are very much concerned with contributing in a pure kind of way to the development of the law itself, their struggles are about principles, and there is active involvement in national and international discussion about the redefinition and reinterpretation of legal rules. What is at stake here as we approach the end of the century, both for the agents of economic power and for their professional auxiliaries, is not just the management of conflict, it is control over the circuits which produce and interrelate the basic rules and institutions governing economic activity (Boyer, 1986).

In general, transnational economic relations require an array of basic rules if they are to remain stable, and as the international economic arena becomes more dense the greater is the need for this clarity and stability. For a long time now, the 'Atlantic ruling class' (Van der Pijl, 1984) has accepted and welcomed the existence of national bureaucracies which have in various ways been pushed towards the little recognized task of normative homogenization and control (Picciotto, 1988). Only the very largest multinationals are able to profit from the disparities between different national legislative regimes; for the vast majority of economic actors, a general set of rules for the economic field is what is required.

But things have changed, and we are now faced with the delocalization of capital markets and the spread of international exchange relations which are outside of state regulation, especially as regards taxation and the surveillance of work conditions. The deregulation of markets ratifies and activates the process of delocalization: powerless to stop this phenomenon, governments only think of using it to advantage by attracting floating capital to their own currencies. Additionally, the renewal of the financial establishment, and the arrival on the scene of new kinds of players who both profit from and intensify the new situation, increases international deregulation and disequilibrium. Corporate raiders and 'white knights' who buy up organizations, courtesy of junk bonds, and then carve them up, do not have the same scruples as the heirs of paternalistic capitalism about questioning established conventions whether they are about such things as salaries, or suppliers, or even shareholders. In fact they thrive on this. In accelerating the breaking down of the old order, they make both possible and urgent the construction of the new norms which the markets need if they are to prosper.

It is therefore significant that behind such public figures as Carl Icahn (Chairman of TWA and a host of other companies) one can spot the serried ranks of grey suited experts: international lawyers, corporate tax accountants, financial advisors, and management consultants. These new professionals present themselves as appointed to the noble task of modernizing and rationalizing the management of organizations. Their real ambition is to occupy a strategic and intermediary position as much relating to internal transactions in the field of economic power as to those that mesh with the field of political power — a position — which was previously the privilege of the business financiers, the bankers who saw themselves as the business elite. Profiting from the lack of involvement of the politicians, and from the absence of wider social forces, the international and multi-professional networks — which may be informal, uncontrolled, even chaotic to a degree, and without any legitimacy other than that based on technical expertise, and without any motive other than profit, even if it does go by the rather more modest name of the professional fee — constituted by these new functionaries actually serve to provide some regulation of economic activity.

This new international market in consultancy has experienced a phenomenal growth as a consequence of the obsolescence of many of the established governmental mechanisms for the framing of economic activity. It has become the crucible in which the new rules and institutions of international capitalism are formed. It is not just a coincidence that the globalization of the market in services to commerce and industry followed on from the globalization of capital. The same goes for the legal 'big bang' which followed on from that in the City. These new flows of economic exchange could not be sustained without the expert assistance of the professional brokers who diagnose and evaluate commercial enterprises, establishing financial and legal structures in the process,[7] and even unhesitatingly lending a hand in the reorganization of production (Dezalay, 1989a). At the same time, the inherent logic of the situation, as the economic game rules change in accordance with their expert evaluations, impels these apostles of the new economic order to consolidate and legitimize their power. Their proliferation, therefore, constitutes a motive force, and is the best indicator of the importance of the process of homogenization of global economic space. The long-term cultural significance of this should not obscure the material benefit which directly accrues to these brokers. For this excites the appetites and ambitions which vitalize the new market in commercial services. This is especially the case for lawyers, who have been seen traditionally as experts in both the analysis and construction of procedural forms of social relations — even if they are not exactly alone in this field.

New Forms of Competition and the Acceleration of Change

The juridicization of the new commercial order leads toward the re-introduction of competition and market imperatives within the world of the law (Rice, 1989b). The expansion of economic activity and of demands upon the law results in a general splitting apart of national professional standards which all regulated and even excluded untrammelled competition within the law (Karpik, 1988). The opening and expansion of the market in legal services has unleashed a process of homogenization and of interconnection between national legal systems which until now have strongly preserved their own identities. The breaking down of barriers favours the strongest performers — in this case, the great North American firms — and forces the others to align themselves on their model if they wish to survive.[8]

The tribulations of 'mixed practice' in the UK, or of the profession of '*avocat-conseil*' in France, will therefore be only local episodes in a restructuring of the market for professional services to commerce and industry. This restructuring will affect all the developed economies and throw national boundaries into question just as much as the division of tasks and profits among the different categories of professionals: lawyers, accountants, stockbrokers, management consultants, and so on. Each of these experts, whose skills are as much in competition as complementary, aspire to occupy the privileged position of advisor to economic power. Since the turn of the century when they became the right hands of such unscrupulous magnates as J.P. Morgan or J.D. Rockefeller, that place has been occupied by *lawyers* on Wall Street. Their continental counterparts have never been in that position, but the more ambitious among them look forward to the single European market of 1992.[9]

Unfortunately for them, they are not the only contenders. Apart from the major Wall Street firms who at present seem to have a virtual monopoly as far as big business[10] is concerned, there are plenty of new firms that are attacking the less prestigious but far larger market for legal and financial services to small and medium-sized enterprises. Old established firms of accountants now purvey themselves as audit specialists or financial engineers. Supported by the structures which have been developed through the formidable market penetration of the major accounting firms, these newcomers make no secret of their desire to take business from European law firms,[11] who thus find themselves caught in a crossfire.

The pre-eminence of North American firms in the field of international law and the generalization of the model of the corporate
lawyer within European legal culture could incline us toward an
interpretation in terms of relations of power: a dominant economy
exports and imposes its legal technology, in the same way as its
manufactured products, its language and its culture. This reading is
doubtless too simple and makes too little of the internal logic of the
professional field. The domination of lawyers in the sphere of
business law is above all the effect of a historical interlude. A
century before their European colleagues, American lawyers had
become legal entrepreneurs, creating 'law factories' so as to provide
a better service for their clients. The success of the American model
is primarily that of a concentration and division of juridical labour
appropriate and adequate to the expansion of industrial capitalism
(Gawalt, 1984). Their headstart has enabled the Wall Street lawyers
and investment bankers to be at the forefront of the process of the
internationalization of capital, and at the same time to be considerable beneficiaries of it (Labaton, 1988; Rice, 1989c). It is also
across the Atlantic, therefore, that we can see the first signs of an
imploding juridical system, due to the combined effect of a multi-
plication of producers and a transformation in demand. The model
of the *law firm*, fashioned in response to commercial demand, has
tended to evolve at the same time as the market in legal services. The
quantitative increase in business and production has caused a
qualitative change: market imperatives have invaded the terrain of
the law. The explosion of the market in legal services has overflown
the internal control mechanisms dealing with competition and
concentration; the result has been the emergence of the 'mega-law
firms' (Galanter and Palay, 1988) which no longer hesitate to engage
in relentless competition for both clients and staff. In spreading well
beyond their original territory, these 'mega-firms' have clearly
helped to accelerate the diffusion of the phenomenon of the
commercialization of legal practice. But the conditions were ripe for
this to happen.

A New Generation of Entrepreneurial Lawyers
The conjunction which can be observed, throughout the West,
between postwar demographic trends and the spread of superior
education to the middle classes, has contributed in no small measure
to the development of what lawyers now offer and to the definition of professional excellence. Traditionally, the training and

recruitment of lawyers, even in countries with a codified legal system, followed a quasi-aristocratic model of reproduction based on apprenticeship, social selection, and a rigorous politics of *numerus clausus* (Abel, 1988). The spread of the academic model encouraged a more meritocratic logic where good manners and social connections lost their importance in favour of technical competence (Dezalay et al., 1989). Over the last twenty years, the major Western countries have seen the emergence of a new kind of lawyer, distinguished from their predecessors as much by their appetite for success as by the resources that they are able to mobilize: they rely less on social connections and the reciprocal granting of favours, classical characteristics of the insulated world of the law, and present themselves more as technical experts who are sure of their competence and quite ready to put it into practice. As a result of this, the law comes to resemble less and less a club for 'gentlemen', and more and more a business like any other.[12]

This change in attitudes goes together with a redefinition of the clientele. The growth and, especially, the qualitative transformation that has come over corporate legal departments — often the ones to bear the brunt of media attention as such affairs as Bhopal and the Amoco–Cadiz would indicate — reflects a modification in behaviour with regard to having recourse to the law. American-style litigiousness has crossed the Atlantic. Individuals, and commercial organizations even more, are increasingly willing to go to court to settle their conflicts, or rather, to put pressure on their trading partners in order to negotiate from a more advantageous position.[13]

The fierce battles in which the OPA (Rice, 1989a; Waller, 1989) have been involved are typical of these new forms of tactically aggressive recourse to the law. We can see here one of the effects of the breaking apart, under the impact of various critical changes, of local networks of business leaders, who would formerly have ensured that their conflicts were not aired in public since this might have endangered the long-term personal relationships on which the satisfactory conduct of business depended (Bourdieu and Saint-Martin, 1978). The disappearance of the model of the business notable coincides with the decline of the patrician lawyer disdainful of ideas like marketing. The aggression and technique of new generations of 'yuppie lawyers' is more suited to the unscrupulous predators who henceforth will take the front of the financial and economic stage.

Commercial Litigation under the Law of the Market

It appears today that the restructuration of the legal field around the axis of commercial justice is irreversible. It is difficult to say what the long-term effects of this will be. At the very most one can point to certain dynamics and contradictions within the system as it is currently developing. The drawing together of various juridical systems can be contrasted to their diversification, against which can be seen the breaking down of national judicial systems in the face of possible unification. Where society has a fast and a slow lane, the same follows for justice. The old principle of one equal justice for all[14] is increasingly breached by the autonomization, even the quasi-privatization of a system of business justice which has become global.

Clearly, the courts profit from this surge in litigation, but they are not the only ones; alternative forums for the resolution of conflicts — notably the various forms of arbitration, or new forms of para-judicial mediation (*rent-a-judge*, *mini-trials*, etc.) — which allow the business community to take control over the management of differences between its members, have progressed to the equivalent of recourse to state jurisdiction, if not beyond it. The success of these different forms of 'private justice' is moreover such that the judicial authorities are attracted by the idea of going for a strategy similar to the one adopted by the monetary authorities in the face of the rapid development of euro-money: the deregulation of their jurisdictions, so as to attract a clientele which otherwise might escape them. To struggle against the development of private justice, there are those therefore who would advocate that state justice should privatize itself, giving to the parties the possibility of choosing their judge, their law, and avoiding any adverse publicity (Dezalay, 1989c). It is a question here of establishing a sort of justice *à la carte* (accurately referred to as the 'multi-door courthouse'). The judicial monopoly over the resolution of conflict (more theoretical than real now, especially in the business sector) is replaced by a situation where judges and jurisdictions are in their turn placed in competition with other modes of conflict resolution. The litigant goes shopping and chooses between different models, in practice ending up with one particular blend rather than another. Furthermore, even when the parties decide to submit themselves to a judge, this does not actually mean that this figure will pass a judgement on their difference. Only a small minority of cases will actually go their full term. In most cases, it is a question of a tactical recourse which functions as an added argument in the parallel negotiations between the parties. Galanter (1983) has proposed the neologism 'litigociation' to describe this multi-layered involvement in both the judicial process and private negotiation.

This irruption of competition within the sphere of justice[15] is not only related to the growth of supply and demand in the market for legal services. At the same time as this market has been opened to new producers and new clients, it has also tended to merge into the even larger market for professional expertise in general, and this is where juridical products come into competition with other forms of professional facilitation ('*investissements de forme*': Eymard-Duvernet and Thévenot, 1983). The increased competition within the field of consultancy, then, rebounds upon the lawyers. The last decades have seen management education flourish, and this has thrown a whole series of experts in *marketing, personnel management, financial engineering*, etc., onto the labour market. The pursuit of success by these newcomers, both as individuals and as representatives of new forms of knowledge, has been largely responsible for clearing away the old management practices of their predecessors together with the structures of sociability connected to them, whether these latter were formal, as with organized patronage, or informal, as with the membership of country clubs or the like. If yesterday's worthies have partially disappeared from the economic scene (or at least have been converted into experts), the new service professionals, whether bankers, accountants or consultants[16] now present themselves in the mediating role of intermediary between economic agents. As a result of this, the networks that they make up, their techniques and their rationalities are all involved in the framing and regulation of the contemporary forms of production and exchange. Thus it is that the law and its practitioners no longer have the monopoly over the formal regulation of social relations.

The incursion of these new techniques and these new professionals into the formerly secure territory of the lawyers does not, however, mean the end of the law. Quite the opposite in fact, for by a paradoxical effect, already demonstrated by Weber when he analysed the instrumentalization of the law, this external competition leads to the reinforcement of the technicality and specificity of the law. Faced with this competition on the terrain of negotiation and mediation between economic actors, the commercial lawyers safeguard a certain primacy by falling back to judicial and jurisprudential strategies. The strategies of judicial harrying, for example, perfected by Skadden Arps on behalf of the corporate raiders, and now exported to Europe, can be described as aggressive, if not excessive. Such developments contribute not only to the prosperity of lawyers but also to the durability of the law, and to its revalorization within the field of power, from which it cannot stray far without endangering its very existence. It is certainly true that these new lawyers and the mechanisms that they are perfecting are very different from preceding generations of jurists with their concern for social justice. But the law is no different from other social institutions which only endure by transforming themselves in the wake of political changes. The law, especially as it relates to business, is at the forefront of things now. The question we cannot answer is how long things will remain thus.

Notes

This article was translated by Roy Boyne.

1. The German example is probably the most conclusive here. Jurists had provided much of the underpinning of Bismarck's regime, and for a long time were virtually treated as civil servants (Rueschemeyer, 1973). In any event, it can be said that the relationship with the state is one of the keys to the social history of the professions (Rueschemeyer, 1986; Burrage, 1989).

2. Growth rates have been of the order of 30 percent per annum, even 50 percent in the specialized area of corporate restructuring.

3. As Doreen McBarnet (1984) has written, if the law corresponds to the interests of capital this is not because of some kind of structurally determined automatism, but because of the incessant practical everyday work of practitioners who are seeking to satisfy their own and their clients' interests.

4. 'The demolition of barriers between trading, stockbroking and advising, which happened on October 27, 1986 . . . led to a year-long expansion in legal work, with the lawyers barely able to cope . . . . The change for the lawyers has come rather from the new international element, added regulation and new tactics. Internationalisation calls for knowledge of other countries' laws . . . . It makes it cost-efficient to open branches across the world . . . . The increasing complexity of the transactions themselves and the habits brought into London by the new entrants, especially from the U.S., have added to the lawyer's load.' (Hampton, 1988; see also Dezalay, 1989b; *The Economist*, 1989).

5. *The American Lawyer*, which presents itself as the organ and mouthpiece of this new generation, publishes a hit-parade of the biggest deals and the best paid lawyers every month. Quite a few of them pride themselves on having passed the million dollars a year mark.

6. Note that the *Financial Times* revives the old dream of the *Lex mercatoria* in the title of A.H. Herman's (1989) article: 'Need of trans-national law for trans-national mergers'.

7. Bourdieu has suggested (1986) that the degree of formalism of social relations is

a function of the distance that separates the protagonists. One business lawyer has said 'The field of discussion between the representatives of Siemens and Plessey is necessarily juridical' (Jézégabel, 1989). The opposite of this is that the need for the law is rather less in an epoch when business affairs were almost treated as family matters. In this regard, we can recall what the chairman of Lazards, Lord Poole, said after the 1974 crash: 'I never lost any money, because I never lent money to anyone I didn't go to school with' (cited in Charman, 1989).

8. 'City solicitors in London are increasingly drawing comparisons between themselves and their counterparts in the US. Practices of some of the leading firms have already come to resemble those of their transatlantic cousins, though there are important differences' (Campbell-Smith, 1985). Changes in the French Bar are less advanced; but the direction is the same. In an editorial, entitled, '*Attachez vos ceintures*' ('Fasten your safety-belts') the Paris Bar defends the idea of one great profession with the argument that 'only a regrouping of the two professions, giving rise to the French *lawyer*, will be able to face up to domestic and international competition' (La lettre de la Conférence, No. 24, January, 1988).

9. This is particularly true for those French advocates who are hoping, in effect, that the new era will put into question the existing positions of privilege within the field of economic power, especially those which relate to the control of public institutions. But the importance of the Common Market dynamic should not be over-estimated. The imminence of the Single European Market which is often invoked to explain and justify the radical transformations within the professions, which are the order of the day in France, the United Kingdom, and even Germany, only actually confirm and accelerate the process of evolution, as much internal as external, which has come in the wake of the crises of the seventies. The best proof of this is that not only are these transformations not specific to Europe, but they manifested themselves first of all in the US where they are besides much more developed (Galanter and Palay, 1988).

10. This seems to apply especially to the more glamorous cases involving the OPA and privatizations; see especially the well-known case of the Générale de Belgique (cf. Rozen, 1988; also Pollock, 1989).

11. It has been suggested that we are now past the time of the 'Republic of letters' and that we have entered the 'empire of numbers' (ATH, 1985).

12. 'Competition was very much a gentlemanly affair. . . . Protected by their captive relationships, the established practices had no reason to fear competitive assaults and were not, in turn, moved to encroach on their competitors' turf. Blessed with virtual monopolies in their respective markets, [the law firms] focused instead on practice standards, on establishing self-indulgent compensation systems, and on perfecting the mystique and the mannerisms of elite professionals' (Stevens, 1987: 8–9).

13. For a discussion of conflicts at work in this light, see Leadbeater (1989).

14. A principle which hardly corresponds in any event to the historical reality of dual justice (cf. Dezalay, 1987).

15. Placed under conditions of competition, justice and judges are no longer untouchable. One sign of this, among others, can be seen in the list of 'worst judges' published by *The American Lawyer*.

16. These different activities tend, in any event, to merge into each other especially for the multinational firms (Stevens, 1981, 1985) which provide the whole array of services to the business community. The great law firms seem also to want to orient

themselves toward this global strategy of the 'multinational supermarket' (Labaton, 1988; Rothfeld, 1989).

References

Abbott, A. (1988) *The System of the Profession: An Essay on the Division of Expert Labour.* Chicago: University of Chicago Press.

Abel, R. (1988) *The Legal Profession in England and Wales.* Oxford: Basil Blackwell.

ATH (1985) *L'empire des chiffres.* Paris: Fayard.

Bourdieu, P. (1986) 'La force du droit: éléments pour une sociologie du champ juridique', *Actes de la recherche en sciences sociales* 64.

Bourdieu, P. and Saint-Martin, M. (1978) 'Le patronat', *Actes de la recherche en sciences sociales* 20–21.

Boyer, R. (1986) *Capitalismes fin de siècle.* Paris: PUF.

Burrage, M. (1989) 'Revolution as a Starting Point for the Comparative Analysis of the French, American and English Legal Professions', in R. Abel and P. Lewis (eds), *Lawyers in Society, Vol. 3: Comparative Theories.* Berkeley: University of California Press.

Campbell-Smith, D. (1985) 'The Legal Profession: Facing up to the Global Challenge', *Financial Times* (15 July).

Charman, P. (1989) 'The Hardest of Sells', *The Times* (21 March).

Cohen-Tanugi, L. (1985) *Le droit sans l'État.* Paris: PUF.

Cohen-Tanugi, L. (1988) 'La décennie du droit', *L'express* (16 December).

Dezalay, Y. (1986) 'From Mediation to Pure Law: Practice and Scholarly Representation within the Legal Sphere. La restructuration du champ des professionnels de la restructuration des enterprises', *International Journal of the Sociology of Law* 14.

Dezalay, Y. (1987) 'The Forum should fit the Fuss: the Economics of Negotiated Justice', paper presented to the Amherst Seminar, 4 December.

Dezalay, Y. (1989a) 'Le droit des faillites: du notable à l'expert', *Actes de la recherche en sciences sociales* 76–77.

Dezalay, Y. (1989b) 'Putting Justice into Play on the Global Market: Law, Lawyers, Accountants and the Competition for Financial Services', presentation to Law and Society Annual Meeting, Madison, Wisconsin, 9 May.

Dezalay, Y. (1989c) 'Negotiated Justice as a Renegotiation of the Division of Labour within the Field of Law: the French Case', in C. Meschievitz and K. Plett (eds), *Beyond Disputing: Exploring Legal Cultures in Five European Countries.* Baden-Baden: Nomos.

Dezalay, Y., Sarat, A. and Silbey, S. (1989) 'D'une démarche contestaire à un savoir méritocratique. Esquisse d'une histoire sociale de la sociologie juridique américaine', *Actes de la recherche en sciences sociales* 78.

The Economist (1989) 'Big Bang for the City's Law Firms' 9 September.

Eymard-Duvernet, F. and Thévenot, L. (1983) *Les immobilisations de forme pour l'usage de la main d'oeuvre.* Paris: INSEE.

Galanter, M. (1983) 'Mega-law and Mega-lawyering in the Contemporary US', in R. Dingwall, and P. Lewis (eds), *The Sociology of the Professions.* London: Macmillan.

Galanter, M. and Palay, T. (1988) *The Growth of Law Firms*. Madison: Institute of Legal Studies.

Gawalt, G. (ed.) (1984) *The New High Priests: Lawyers in Post-Civil War America*. Westport: Greenwood Press.

Hampton, C. (1988) 'A Breath-taking Growth Rate', *Financial Times* (20 October).

Herman, A.H. (1989) 'Needs of Trans-national Law for Trans-national Mergers', *Financial Times* (28 March).

Jézégabel, M. (1989) 'Avocats d'affaires contre "lawyers" ', *Dynasteurs* (16 December).

Karpik, L. (1988) 'Lawyers and Politics in France, 1814–1950: the State, the Market, the Public', *Law and Social Inquiry* 13(4).

Labaton, S. (1988) 'US Law Firms Expand to Reach Global Clientele', *New York Times* (12 May).

Leadbeater, C. (1989) 'The Law Finds Fresh Advocates in Industry', *Financial Times* (18 May).

McBarnet, D. (1984) 'Law and Capital: the Role of Legal Form and Legal Actors', *International Journal of the Sociology of Law* 12.

Picciotto, S. (1988) 'The Control of Transnational Capital and the Democratization of the International State', *Journal of Law and Society* 15(1).

Pollock, E. (1989) 'US Law Firms, Catching 1992 Fever, Bet They'll Gain Edge in United Europe', *Wall Street Journal* (26 September).

Rice, R. (1989a) 'Growing Use of Law in Attack and Defence', *Financial Times* (13 July).

Rice, R. (1989b) 'Lawyers Come Face to Face with Competition', *Financial Times* (17 July).

Rice, R. (1989c) 'US Firms Pioneer the Route to Global Practices', *Financial Times* (25 September).

Ripert, F. (1949) *Le déclin du droit*. Paris: LGDJ.

Rothfeld, C. (1989) 'Law Firms Are Moving Rapidly into New Businesses', *New York Times* (9 June).

Rozen, M. (1988) 'Take-over à l'Américain' *The American Lawyer*.

Rueschemeyer, D. (1973) *Lawyers and Their Society*. Cambridge, Mass.: Harvard University Press.

Rueschemeyer, D. (1986) 'Comparing Legal Professions Cross-nationally: from a Professions-centred to a State-centred Approach', *American Bar Foundation Research Journal* 3.

Stevens, M. (1981) *The Big Eight*. New York: Collier.

Stevens, M. (1985) *The Accounting Wars*. New York: Collier.

Stevens, M. (1987) *Power of Attorney: the Rize of the Giant Law Firm*. New York: McGraw-Hill.

Tutt, N. (1988) 'Bar sans frontières in Brussels', *New Law Journal* (30 September).

Van der Pijl, K. (1984) *The Making of an Atlantic Ruling Class*. London: Verso.

Waller, D. (1989) 'The UK takeover scene: a crucial role for lawyers', *Financial Times* (13 July).

Yves Dezalay is a Research Fellow at the Centre Nationale de la Recherche Scientifique, Vaucresson.

Disjuncture and Difference in the Global Cultural Economy

Arjun Appadurai

The central problem of today's global interactions is the tension between cultural homogenization and cultural heterogenization. A vast array of empirical facts could be brought to bear on the side of the 'homogenization' argument, and much of it has come from the left end of the spectrum of media studies (Hamelink, 1983; Mattelart, 1983; Schiller, 1976), and some from other, less appealing, perspectives (Gans, 1985; Iyer, 1988). Most often, the homogenization argument subspeciates into either an argument about Americanization, or an argument about 'commoditization', and very often the two arguments are closely linked. What these arguments fail to consider is that at least as rapidly as forces from various metropolises are brought into new societies they tend to become indigenized in one or other way: this is true of music and housing styles as much as it is true of science and terrorism, spectacles and constitutions. The dynamics of such indigenization have just begun to be explored in a sophisticated manner (Barber, 1987; Feld, 1988; Hannerz, 1987, 1989; Ivy, 1988; Nicoll, 1989; Yoshimoto, 1989), and much more needs to be done. But it is worth noticing that for the people of Irian Jaya, Indonesianization may be more worrisome than Americanization, as Japanization may be for Koreans, Indianization for Sri Lankans, Vietnamization for the Cambodians, Russianization for the people of Soviet Armenia and the Baltic Republics. Such a list of alternative fears to Americanization could be greatly expanded, but it is not a shapeless inventory: for polities of smaller scale, there is always a fear of cultural absorption by polities of larger scale, especially those that are near by. One man's imagined community (Anderson, 1983) is another man's political prison.

This scalar dynamic, which has widespread global manifestations, is also tied to the relationship between nations and states, to

Theory, Culture & Society (SAGE, London, Newbury Park and New Delhi), Vol. 7 (1990), 295–310

which I shall return later in this essay. For the moment let us note that the simplification of these many forces (and fears) of homogenization can also be exploited by nation-states in relation to their own minorities, by posing global commoditization (or capitalism, or some other such external enemy) as more 'real' than the threat of its own hegemonic strategies.

The new global cultural economy has to be understood as a complex, overlapping, disjunctive order, which cannot any longer be understood in terms of existing center-periphery models (even those that might account for multiple centers and peripheries). Nor is it susceptible to simple models of push and pull (in terms of migration theory) or of surpluses and deficits (as in traditional models of balance of trade), or of consumers and producers (as in most neo-Marxist theories of development). Even the most complex and flexible theories of global development which have come out of the Marxist tradition (Amin, 1980; Mandel, 1978; Wallerstein, 1974; Wolf, 1982) are inadequately quirky, and they have not come to terms with what Lash and Urry (1987) have recently called 'disorganized capitalism'. The complexity of the current global economy has to do with certain fundamental disjunctures between economy, culture and politics which we have barely begun to theorize.[1]

I propose that an elementary framework for exploring such disjunctures is to look at the relationship between five dimensions of global cultural flow which can be termed: (a) ethnoscapes; (b) mediascapes; (c) technoscapes; (d) finanscapes; and (e) ideoscapes.[2] I use terms with the common suffix scape to indicate first of all that these are not objectively given relations which look the same from every angle of vision, but rather that they are deeply perspectival constructs, inflected very much by the historical, linguistic and political situatedness of different sorts of actors: nation-states, multinationals, diasporic communities, as well as sub-national groupings and movements (whether religious, political or economic), and even intimate face-to-face groups, such as villages, neighborhoods and families. Indeed, the individual actor is the last locus of this perspectival set of landscapes, for these landscapes are eventually navigated by agents who both experience and constitute larger formations, in part by their own sense of what these landscapes offer. These landscapes thus, are the building blocks of what, extending Benedict Anderson, I would like to call 'imagined worlds', that is, the multiple worlds which are constituted by the historically situated imaginations of persons and groups spread around the globe (Appadurai, 1989). An important fact of the world we live in today is that many persons on the globe live in such imagined 'worlds' and not just in imagined communities, and thus are able to contest and sometimes even subvert the 'imagined worlds' of the official mind and of the entrepreneurial mentality that surround them. The suffix scape also allows us to point to the fluid, irregular shapes of these landscapes, shapes which characterize international capital as deeply as they do international clothing styles.

By 'ethnoscape', I mean the landscape of persons who constitute the shifting world in which we live: tourists, immigrants, refugees, exiles, guestworkers and other moving groups and persons constitute an essential feature of the world, and appear to affect the politics of and between nations to a hitherto unprecedented degree. This is not to say that there are not anywhere relatively stable communities and networks, of kinship, of friendship, of work and of leisure, as well as of birth, residence and other filiative forms. But it is to say that the warp of these stabilities is everywhere shot through with the woof of human motion, as more persons and groups deal with the realities of having to move, or the fantasies of wanting to move. What is more, both these realities as well as these fantasies now function on larger scales, as men and women from villages in India think not just of moving to Poona or Madras, but of moving to Dubai and Houston, and refugees from Sri Lanka find themselves in South India as well as in Canada, just as the Hmong are driven to London as well as to Philadelphia. And as international capital shifts its needs, as production and technology generate different needs, as nation-states shift their policies on refugee populations, these moving groups can never afford to let their imaginations rest too long, even if they wished to.

By 'technoscape', I mean the global configuration, also ever fluid, of technology, and of the fact that technology, both high and low, both mechanical and informational, now moves at high speeds across various kinds of previously impervious boundaries. Many countries now are the roots of multinational enterprise: a huge steel complex in Libya may involve interests from India, China, Russia and Japan, providing different components of new technological configurations. The odd distribution of technologies, and thus the peculiarities of these technoscapes, are increasingly driven not by any obvious economies of scale, of political control, or of market rationality, but of increasingly complex relationships between money flows, political possibilities and the availability of both low and highly-skilled labor. So, while India exports waiters and chauffeurs to Dubai and Sharjah, it also exports software engineers to the United States (indentured briefly to Tata-Burroughs or the World Bank), then laundered through the State Department to become wealthy 'resident aliens', who are in turn objects of seductive messages to invest their money and know-how in federal and state projects in India. The global economy can still be described in terms of traditional 'indicators' (as the World Bank continues to do) and studied in terms of traditional comparisions (as in Project Link at the University of Pennsylvania), but the complicated technoscapes (and the shifting ethnoscapes), which underlie these 'indicators' and 'comparisions' are further out of the reach of the 'queen of the social sciences' than ever before. How is one to make a meaningful comparison of wages in Japan and the United States, or of real estate costs in New York and Tokyo, without taking sophisticated account of the very complex fiscal and investment flows that link the two economies through a global grid of currency speculation and capital transfer?

Thus it is useful to speak as well of 'finanscapes', since the disposition of global capital is now a more mysterious, rapid and difficult landscape to follow than ever before, as currency markets, national stock exchanges, and commodity speculations move megamonies through national turnstiles at blinding speed, with vast absolute implications for small differences in percentage points and time units. But the critical point is that the global relationship between ethnoscapes, technoscapes and finanscapes is deeply disjunctive and profoundly unpredictable, since each of these landscapes is subject to its own constraints and incentives (some political, some informational and some techno-environmental), at the same time as each acts as a constraint and a parameter for movements in the other. Thus, even an elementary model of global political economy must take into account the shifting relationship between perspectives on human movement, technological flow, and financial transfers, which can accommodate their deeply disjunctive relationships with one another.

Built upon these disjunctures (which hardly form a simple, mechanical global 'infrastructure' in any case) are what I have called 'mediascapes' and 'ideoscapes', though the latter two are closely related landscapes of images. 'Mediascapes' refer both to the distribution of the electronic capabilities to produce and disseminate information (newspapers, magazines, television stations, film production studios, etc.), which are now available to a growing number of private and public interests throughout the world; and to the images of the world created by these media. These images of the world involve many complicated inflections, depending on their mode (documentary or entertainment), their hardware (electronic or pre-electronic), their audiences (local, national or transnational) and the interests of those who own and control them. What is most important about these mediascapes is that they provide (especially in their television, film and cassette forms) large and complex repertoires of images, narratives and 'ethnoscapes' to viewers throughout the world, in which the world of commodities and the world of 'news' and politics are profoundly mixed. What this means is that many audiences throughout the world experience the media themselves as a complicated and interconnected repertoire of print, celluloid, electronic screens and billboards. The lines between the 'realistic' and the fictional landscapes they see are blurred, so that the further away these audiences are from the direct experiences of metropolitan life, the more likely they are to construct 'imagined worlds' which are chimerical, aesthetic, even fantastic objects, particularly if assessed by the criteria of some other perspective, some other 'imagined world'.

'Mediascapes', whether produced by private or state interests, tend to be image-centered, narrative-based accounts of strips of reality, and what they offer to those who experience and transform them is a series of elements (such as characters, plots and textual forms) out of which scripts can be formed of imagined lives, their own as well as those of others living in other places. These scripts can and do get disaggregated into complex sets of metaphors by which people live (Lakoff and Johnson, 1980) as they help to constitute narratives of the 'other' and proto-narratives of possible lives, fantasies which could become prologemena to the desire for acquisition and movement.

'Ideoscsapes' are also concatenations of images, but they are often directly political and frequently have to do with the ideologies of states and the counter-ideologies of movements explicitly oriented to capturing state power or a piece of it. These ideoscapes are composed of elements of the Enlightenment world-view, which consists of a concatenation of ideas, terms and images, including 'freedom', 'welfare', 'rights', 'sovereignty', 'representation' and the master-term 'democracy'. The master-narrative of the

Enlightenment (and its many variants in England, France and the United States) was constructed with a certain internal logic and presupposed a certain relationship between reading, representation and the public sphere (for the dynamics of this process in the early history of the United States, see Warner, 1990). But their diaspora across the world, especially since the nineteenth century, has loosened the internal coherence which held these terms and images together in a Euro-American master-narrative, and provided instead a loosely structured synopticon of politics, in which different nation-states, as part of their evolution, have organized their political cultures around different 'keywords' (Williams, 1976).

As a result of the differential diaspora of these keywords, the political narratives that govern communication between elites and followings in different parts of the world involve problems of both a semantic and a pragmatic nature: semantic to the extent that words (and their lexical equivalents) require careful translation from context to context in their global movements; and pragmatic to the extent that the use of these words by political actors and their audiences may be subject to very different sets of contextual conventions that mediate their translation into public politics. Such conventions are not only matters of the nature of political rhetoric (viz. what does the aging Chinese leadership mean when it refers to the dangers of hooliganism? What does the South Korean leadership mean when it speaks of 'discipline' as the key to democratic industrial growth?).

These conventions also involve the far more subtle question of what sets of communicative genres are valued in what way (newspapers versus cinema for example) and what sorts of pragmatic genre conventions govern the collective 'readings' of different kinds of text. So, while an Indian audience may be attentive to the resonances of a political speech in terms of some key words and phrases reminiscent of Hindi cinema, a Korean audience may respond to the subtle codings of Buddhist or neo-Confucian rhetorical strategy encoded in a political document. The very relationship of reading to hearing and seeing may vary in important ways that determine the morphology of these different 'ideoscapes' as they shape themselves in different national and transnational contexts. This globally variable synaesthesia has hardly even been noted, but it demands urgent analysis. Thus 'democracy' has clearly become a master-term, with powerful echoes from Haiti and Poland to the Soviet Union and China, but it sits at the center of a variety of ideoscapes (composed of distinctive pragmatic configurations of rough 'translations' of other central terms from the vocabulary of the Enlightenment). This creates ever new terminological kaleidoscopes, as states (and the groups that seek to capture them) seek to pacify populations whose own ethnoscapes are in motion, and whose mediascapes may create severe problems for the ideoscapes with which they are presented. The fluidity of ideoscapes is complicated in particular by the growing diasporas (both voluntary and involuntary) of intellectuals who continuously inject new meaning-streams into the discourse of democracy in different parts of the world.

This extended terminological discussion of the five terms I have coined sets the basis for a tentative formulation about the conditions under which current global flows occur: *they occur in and through the growing disjunctures between ethnoscapes, technoscapes, finanscapes, mediascapes and ideoscapes*. This formulation, the core of my model of global cultural flow, needs some explanation. First, people, machinery, money, images, and ideas now follow increasingly non-isomorphic paths: of course, at all periods in human history, there have been some disjunctures between the flows of these things, but the sheer speed, scale and volume of each of these flows is now so great that the disjunctures have become central to the politics of global culture. The Japanese are notoriously hospitable to ideas and are stereotyped as inclined to export (all) and import (some) goods, but they are also notoriously closed to immigration, like the Swiss, the Swedes and the Saudis. Yet the Swiss and Saudis accept populations of guestworkers, thus creating labor diasporas of Turks, Italians and other circum-mediterranean groups. Some such guestworker groups maintain continuous contact with their home-nations, like the Turks, but others, like high-level South Asian migrants tend to desire lives in their new homes, raising anew the problem of reproduction in a deterritorialized context.

Deterritorialization, in general, is one of the central forces of the modern world, since it brings laboring populations into the lower class sectors and spaces of relatively wealthy societies, while sometimes creating exaggerated and intensified senses of criticism or attachment to politics in the home-state. Deterritorialization, whether of Hindus, Sikhs, Palestinians or Ukranians, is now at the core of a variety of global fundamentalisms, including Islamic and Hindu fundamentalism. In the Hindu case for example (Appadurai and Breckenridge, forthcoming) it is clear that the overseas movement of Indians has been exploited by a variety of interests both within and outside India to create a complicated network of finances and religious identifications, in which the problems of cultural reproduction for Hindus abroad has become tied to the politics of Hindu fundamentalism at home.

At the same time, deterritorialization creates new markets for film companies, art impressarios and travel agencies, who thrive on the need of the deterritorialized population for contact with its homeland. Naturally, these invented homelands, which constitute the mediascapes of deterritorialized groups, can often become sufficiently fantastic and one-sided that they provide the material for new ideoscapes in which ethnic conflicts can begin to erupt. The creation of 'Khalistan', an invented homeland of the deterritorialized Sikh population of England, Canada and the United States, is one example of the bloody potential in such mediascapes, as they interact with the 'internal colonialisms' (Hechter, 1974) of the nation-state. The West Bank, Namibia and Eritrea are other theaters for the enactment of the bloody negotiation between existing nation-states and various deterritorialized groupings.

The idea of deterritorialization may also be applied to money and finance, as money managers seek the best markets for their investments, independent of national boundaries. In turn, these movements of monies are the basis of new kinds of conflict, as Los Angelenos worry about the Japanese buying up their city, and people in Bombay worry about the rich Arabs from the Gulf States who have not only transformed the prices of mangoes in Bombay, but have also substantially altered the profile of hotels, restaurants and other services in the eyes of the local population, just as they continue to do in London. Yet, most residents of Bombay are ambivalent about the Arab presence there, for the flip side of their presence is the absence of friends and kinsmen earning big money in the Middle East and bringing back both money and luxury commodities to Bombay and other cities in India. Such commodities transform consumer taste in these cities, and also often end up smuggled through air and sea ports and peddled in the gray markets of Bombay's streets. In these gray markets, some members of Bombay's middle-classes and of its lumpenproletariat can buy some of these goods, ranging from cartons of Marlboro cigarettes, to Old Spice shaving cream and tapes of Madonna. Similarly gray routes, often subsidized by the moonlighting activities of sailors, diplomats, and airline stewardesses who get to move in and out of the country regularly, keep the gray markets of Bombay, Madras and Calcutta filled with goods not only from the West, but also from the Middle East, Hong Kong and Singapore.

It is this fertile ground of deterritorialization, in which money, commodities and persons are involved in ceaselessly chasing each other around the world, that the mediascapes and ideoscapes of the modern world find their fractured and fragmented counterpart. For the ideas and images produced by mass media often are only partial guides to the goods and experiences that deterritorialized populations transfer to one another. In Mira Nair's brilliant film, *India Cabaret*, we see the multiple loops of this fractured deterritorialization as young women, barely competent in Bombay's metropolitan glitz, come to seek their fortunes as cabaret dancers and prostitutes in Bombay, entertaining men in clubs with dance formats derived wholly from the prurient dance sequences of Hindi films. These scenes cater in turn to ideas about Western and foreign women and their 'looseness', while they provide tawdry career alibis for these women. Some of these women come from Kerala, where cabaret clubs and the pornograpic film industry have blossomed, partly in response to the purses and tastes of Keralites returned from the Middle East, where their diasporic lives away from women distort their very sense of what the relations between men and women might be. These tragedies of displacement could certainly be replayed in a more detailed analysis of the relations between the Japanese and German sex tours to Thailand and the tragedies of the sex trade in Bangkok, and in other similar loops which tie together fantasies about the other, the conveniences and seductions of travel, the economics of global trade and the brutal mobility fantasies that dominate gender politics in many parts of Asia and the world at large.

While far more could be said about the cultural politics of deterritorialization and the larger sociology of displacement that it expresses, it is appropriate at this juncture to bring in the role of the nation-state in the disjunctive global economy of culture today. The relationship between states and nations is everywhere an embattled one. It is possible to say that in many societies, the nation and the state have become one another's projects. That is, while nations (or more properly groups with ideas about nationhood) seek to capture or co-opt states and state power, states simultaneously seek to capture and monopolize ideas about nationhood (Baruah, 1986; Chatterjee, 1986; Nandy, 1989). In general, separatist, transnational movements, including those which have included terror in their methods, exemplify nations in search of states: Sikhs, Tamil Sri Lankans, Basques, Moros, Quebecois, each of these represent imagined communities which seek to create states of their own or carve pieces out of existing states. States, on the other hand, are everywhere seeking to monopolize the moral resources of community, either by flatly claiming perfect coevality between nation and state, or by systematically museumizing and representing all the groups within them in a variety of heritage politics that seems remarkably uniform throughout the world (Handler, 1988; Herzfeld, 1982; McQueen, 1988). Here, national and international mediascapes are exploited by nation-states to pacify separatists or even the potential fissiparousness of all ideas of difference. Typically, contemporary nation-states do this by exercising taxonomical control over difference; by creating various kinds of international spectacle to domesticate difference; and by seducing small groups with the fantasy of self-display on some sort of global or cosmopolitan stage. One important new feature of global cultural politics, tied to the disjunctive relationships between the various landscapes discussed earlier, is that state and nation are at each's throats, and the hyphen that links them is now less an icon of conjuncture than an index of disjuncture. This disjunctive relationship between nation and state has two levels: at the level of any given nation-state, it means that there is a battle of the imagination, with state and nation seeking to cannibalize one another. Here is the seedbed of brutal separatisms, majoritarianisms that seem to have appeared from nowhere, and micro-identities that have become political projects within the nation-state. At another level, this disjunctive relationship is deeply entangled with the global disjunctures discussed throughout this essay: ideas of nationhood appear to be steadily increasing in scale and regularly crossing existing state boundaries: sometimes, as with the Kurds, because previous identities stretched across vast national spaces, or, as with the Tamils in Sri Lanka, the dormant threads of a transnational diaspora have been activated to ignite the micro-politics of a nation-state.

In discussing the cultural politics that have subverted the hyphen that links the nation to the state, it is especially important not to forget its mooring in the irregularities that now characterize 'disorganized capital' (Lash and Urry, 1987; Kothari, 1989). It is because labor, finance and technology are now so widely separated that the volatilities that underlie movements for nationhood (as large as transnational Islam on the one hand, or as small as the movement of the Gurkhas for a separate state in the North-East of India) grind against the vulnerabilitities which characterize the relationships between states. States find themselves pressed to stay 'open' by the forces of media, technology, and travel which had fueled consumerism throughout the world and have increased the craving, even in the non-Western world, for new commodities and spectacles. On the other hand, these very cravings can become caught up in new ethnoscapes, mediascapes, and eventually, ideoscapes, such as 'democracy' in China, that the state cannot tolerate as threats to its own control over ideas of nationhood and 'peoplehood'. States throughout the world are under siege, especially where contests over the ideoscapes of democracy are fierce and fundamental, and where there are radical disjunctures between ideoscapes and technoscapes (as in the case of very small countries that lack contemporary technologies of production and information); or between ideoscapes and finanscapes (as in countries, such as Mexico or Brazil where international lending influences national politics to a very large degree); or between ideoscapes and ethnoscapes (as in Beirut, where diasporic, local and translocal filiations are suicidally at battle); or between ideoscapes and mediascapes (as in many countries in the Middle East and Asia) where the lifestyles represented on both national and international TV and cinema completely overwhelm and undermine the rhetoric of national politics: in the Indian case, the myth of the law-breaking hero has emerged to mediate this naked struggle between the pieties and the realities of Indian politics, which has grown increasingly brutalized and corrupt (Vachani, 1989).

The transnational movement of the martial-arts, particularly through Asia, as mediated by the Hollywood and Hongkong film industries (Zarilli, forthcoming) is a rich illustration of the ways in which long-standing martial arts traditions, reformulated to meet the fantasies of contemporary (sometimes lumpen) youth populations, create new cultures of masculinity and violence, which are in turn the fuel for increased violence in national and international politics. Such violence is in turn the spur to an increasingly rapid and amoral arms trade which penetrates the entire world. The worldwide spread of the AK-47 and the Uzi, in films, in corporate and state security, in terror, and in police and military activity, is a reminder that apparently simple technical uniformities often conceal an increasingly complex set of loops, linking images of violence to aspirations for community in some 'imagined world'.

Returning then to the 'ethnoscapes' with which I began, the central paradox of ethnic politics in today's world is that primordia, (whether of language or skin color or neighborhood or of kinship) have become globalized. That is, sentiments whose greatest force is in their ability to ignite intimacy into a political sentiment and turn locality into a staging ground for identity, have become spread over vast and irregular spaces, as groups move, yet stay linked to one another through sophisticated media capabilities. This is not to deny that such primordia are often the product of invented traditions (Hobsbawm and Ranger, 1983) or retrospective affiliations, but to emphasize that because of the disjunctive and unstable interplay of commerce, media, national policies and consumer fantasies, ethnicity, once a genie contained in the bottle of some sort of locality (however large) has now become a global force, forever slipping in and through the cracks between states and borders.

But the relationship between the cultural and economic levels of this new set of global disjunctures is not a simple one-way street in which the terms of global cultural politics are set wholly by, or confined wholly within, the vicissitudes of international flows of technology, labor and finance, demanding only a modest modification of existing neo-Marxist models of uneven development and state-formation. There is a deeper change, itself driven by the disjunctures between all the landscapes I have discussed, and constituted by their continuously fluid and uncertain interplay, which concerns the relationship between production and consumption in today's global economy. Here I begin with Marx's famous (and often mined) view of the fetishism of the commodity, and suggest that this fetishism has been replaced in the world at large (now seeing the world as one, large, interactive system, composed of many complex sub-systems) by two mutually supportive descendants, the first of which I call production fetishism, and the second of which I call the fetishism of the consumer.

By production fetishism I mean an illusion created by contemporary transnational production loci, which masks translocal capital, transnational earning-flows, global management and often faraway workers (engaged in various kinds of high-tech putting out operations) in the idiom and spectacle of local (sometimes even worker) control, national productivity and territorial sovereignty. To the extent that various kinds of Free Trade Zone have become the models for production at large, especially of high-tech commodities, production has itself become a fetish, masking not social relations as such, but the relations of production, which are increasingly transnational. The locality (both in the sense of the local factory or site of production and in the extended sense of the nation-state) becomes a fetish which disguises the globally dispersed forces that actually drive the production process. This generates alienation (in Marx's sense) twice intensified, for its social sense is now compounded by a complicated spatial dynamic which is increasingly global.

As for the fetishism of the consumer, I mean to indicate here that the consumer has been transformed, through commodity flows (and the mediascapes, especially of advertising, that accompany them) into a sign, both in Baudrillard's sense of a simulacrum which only asymptotically approaches the form of a real social agent; and in the sense of a mask for the real seat of agency, which is not the consumer but the producer and the many forces that constitute production. Global advertising is the key technology for the worldwide dissemination of a plethora of creative, and culturally well-chosen, ideas of consumer agency. These images of agency are increasingly distortions of a world of merchandising so subtle that the consumer is consistently helped to believe that he or she is an actor, where in fact he or she is at best a chooser.

The globalization of culture is not the same as its homogenization, but globalization involves the use of a variety of instruments of homogenization (armaments, advertising techniques, language hegemonies, clothing styles and the like), which are absorbed into local political and cultural economies, only to be repatriated as heterogeneous dialogues of national sovereignty, free enterprise, fundamentalism, etc. in which the state plays an increasingly delicate role: too much openness to global flows and the nation-state is threatened by revolt — the China syndrome; too little, and the state exits the international stage, as Burma, Albania and North Korea, in various ways have done. In general, the state has become the arbiter of this *repatriation of difference* (in the form of goods, signs, slogans, styles, etc.). But this repatriation or export of the designs and commodities of difference continuously exacerbates the 'internal' politics of majoritarianism and homogenization, which is most frequently played out in debates over heritage.

Thus the central feature of global culture today is the politics of the mutual effort of sameness and difference to cannibalize one another and thus to proclaim their succesful hijacking of the twin Enlightenment ideas of the triumphantly universal and the resiliently particular. This mutual cannibalization shows its ugly face in riots, in refugee-flows, in state-sponsored torture and in ethnocide (with or without state support). Its brighter side is in the expansion of many individual horizons of hope and fantasy, in the global spread of oral rehydration therapy and other low-tech instruments of well-being, in the susceptibility even of South Africa to the force of global opinion, in the inability of the Polish state to repress its own working-classes, and in the growth of a wide range of progressive, transnational alliances. Examples of both sorts could be multiplied. The critical point is that both sides of the coin of global cultural process today are products of the infinitely varied mutual contest of sameness and difference on a stage characterized by radical disjunctures between different sorts of global flows and the uncertain landscapes created in and through these disjunctures.

Notes

A longer version of this essay appears in *Public Culture* 2 (2), Spring 1990. This longer version sets the present formulation in the context of global cultural traffic in earlier historical periods, and draws out some of its implications for the study of cultural forms more generally.

1. One major exception is Fredric Jameson, whose (1984) essay on the relationship between postmodernism and late capitalism has in many ways, inspired this essay. However, the debate between Jameson (1986) and Ahmad (1987) in *Social Text* shows that the creation of a globalizing Marxist narrative, in cultural matters, is difficult territory indeed. My own effort, in this context, is to begin a restructuring of the Marxist narrative (by stressing lags and disjunctures) that many Marxists might find abhorrent. Such a restructuring has to avoid the dangers of obliterating difference within the 'third world', of eliding the social referent (as some French postmodernists seem inclined to do) and of retaining the narrative authority of the Marxist tradition, in favor of greater attention to global fragmentation, uncertainty and difference.

2. These ideas are argued more fully in a book I am currently working on, tentatively entitled *Imploding Worlds: Imagination and Disjuncture in the Global Cultural Economy*.

References

Ahmad, A. (1987) 'Jameson's Rhetoric of Otherness and the "National Allegory" ', *Social Text* 17: 3–25.

Amin, S. (1980) *Class and Nation: Historically and in the Current Crisis*. New York and London: Monthly Review.

Anderson, B. (1983) *Imagined Communities: Reflections on the Origin and Spread of Nationalism*. London: Verso.

Appadurai, A. (1989) 'Global Ethnoscapes: Notes and Queries for a Transnational Anthropology', in R.G. Fox (ed.), *Interventions: Anthropology of the Present*.

Appadurai, A. and Breckenridge, C.A. (forthcoming) *A Transnational Culture in the Making: The Asian Indian Diaspora in the United States*. London: Berg.

Barber, K. (1987) 'Popular Arts in Africa', *African Studies Review* 30(3).

Baruah, S. (1986) 'Immigration, Ethnic Conflict and Political Turmoil, Assam 1979-1985', *Asian Survey* 26 (11).

Chatterjee, P. (1986) *Nationalist Thought and the Colonial World: A Derivative Discourse*. London: Zed Books.

Feld, S. (1988) 'Notes on World Beat', *Public Culture* 1(1): 31-7.

Gans, Eric (1985) *The End of Culture: Toward a Generative Anthropology*. Berkeley: University of California.

Hamelink, C. (1983) *Cultural Autonomy in Global Communications*. New York: Longman.

Handler, R. (1988) *Nationalism and the Politics of Culture in Quebec*. Madison: University of Wisconsin.

Hannerz, U. (1987) 'The World in Creolization,' *Africa* 57(4): 546-59.

Hannerz, U. (1989) 'Notes on the Global Ecumene', *Public Culture* 1(2): 66-75.

Hechter, M. (1974) *Internal Colonialism: The Celtic Fringe in British National Development, 1536-1966*. Berkeley and Los Angeles: University of California.

Herzfeld, M. (1982) *Ours Once More: Folklore, Ideology and the Making of Modern Greece*. Austin: University of Texas.

Hobsbawm, E. and Ranger, T. (eds) (1983) *The Invention of Tradition*. New York: Columbia University Press.

Ivy, M. (1988) 'Tradition and Difference in the Japanese Mass Media', *Public Culture* 1(1): 21-9.

Iyer, P. (1988) *Video Night in Kathmandu*. New York: Knopf.

Jameson, F. (1984) 'Postmodernism, or the Cultural Logic of Late Capitalism', *New Left Review* 146 (July-August): 53-92.

Jameson, F. (1986) 'Third World Literature in the Era of Multi-National Capitalism', *Social Text* 15 (Fall): 65-88.

Kothari, R. (1989) *State Against Democracy: In Search of Humane Governance*. New York: New Horizons.

Lakoff, G. and Johnson, M. (1980) *Metaphors We Live By*. Chicago and London: University of Chicago.

Lash, S. and Urry, J. (1987) *The End of Organized Capitalism*. Madison: University of Wisconsin.

McQueen, H. (1988) 'The Australian Stamp: Image, Design and Ideology', *Arena* 84 Spring: 78-96.

Mandel, E. (1978) *Late Capitalism*. London: Verso.

Mattelart, A. (1983) *Transnationals and Third World: The Struggle for Culture*. South Hadley, MA: Bergin and Garvey.

Nandy, A. (1989) 'The Political Culture of the Indian State', *Daedalus* 118(4): 1-26.

Nicoll, F. (1989) 'My Trip to Alice', *Criticism, Heresy and Interpretation (CHAI)*, 3: 21-32.

Schiller, H. (1976) *Communication and Cultural Domination*. White Plains, NY: International Arts and Sciences.

Vachani, L. (1989) 'Narrative, Pleasure and Ideology in the Hindi Film: An Analysis of the Outsider Formula', MA thesis, The Annenberg School of Communication, The University of Pennsylvania.

Wallerstein, I. (1974) *The Modern World-System* (2 volumes). New York and London: Academic Press.

Warner, M. (1990) *The Letters of the Republic: Publication and the Public Sphere.* Cambridge, MA: Harvard.

Williams, R. (1976) *Keywords.* New York: Oxford.

Wolf, E. (1982) *Europe and the People Without History.* Berkeley: University of California.

Yoshimoto, M. (1989) 'The Postmodern and Mass Images in Japan', *Public Culture* 1(2): 8–25.

Zarilli, P. (Forthcoming) 'Repositioning the Body: An Indian Martial Art and its Pan-Asian Publics' in C.A. Breckenridge, (ed.), *Producing the Postcolonial: Trajectories to Public Culture in India.*

Arjun Appadurai teaches Anthropology and South Asian Studies at the University of Pennsylvania. He is author of *Worship and Conflict Under Colonial Rule* (1981) and editor of *The Social Life of Things* (Cambridge University Press, 1986).

Being in the World: Globalization and Localization

Jonathan Friedman

Introduction

From 1970 to 1980 the population of North American Indians increased from 700,000 to 1.4 million including the creation of several new tribes. The world network of stockmarkets are overcapitalized and lodged on the fluctuating brink of the threatening crash of 1990. The governments are there to stem disaster, by means of massive credit, whatever problem that may solve. In the Eastern bloc, large scale ethnic mobilization threatens the monolithic face of empire while presenting new and even less manageable problems. The same T-shirt designs from Acapulco, Mallorca or Hawaii; the same watch and computer clones with different names, even Gucci clones, the nostalgic turn in the tourist trade, catering to a search for roots, even if largely simulacra, and the western search for the experience of otherness. Ethnic and cultural fragmentation and modernist homogenization are not two arguments, two opposing views of what is happening in the world today, but two constitutive trends of global reality. The dualist centralized world of the double East–West hegemony is fragmenting, politically, and culturally, but the homogeneity of capitalism remains as intact and as systematic as ever. The cultural and by implication intellectual fragmentation of the world has undermined any attempt at a single interpretation of the current situation. We have been served everything from post-industrialism, late capitalism and post-modernism (as a purely cultural phenomenon expressive of an evolution of western capitalist society), to more sinister traditionalist representations of the decline of western civilization, of creeping narcissism, moral decay etc. For years there has been a rampaging battle among intellectuals concerning the pros and cons of postmodernity, while imperialism theorists have become addicted admirers of all sorts of social movements, and the development elites have shifted interests,

Theory, Culture & Society (SAGE, London, Newbury Park and New Delhi), Vol. 7 (1990), 311–328

from questions of development to those of human rights and democracy. And if the Fernand Braudel Center continues to analyse long waves, there has been a growing interest in older civilizations, their rise and fall, and in culture and identity. The intensive practice of identity is the hallmark of the present period. Rushdie's confrontation with fundamentalism highlights the volatile nature of this desperate negotiation of selfhood; the very consumption of modernist literature is suddenly a dangerous act. Global decentralization is tantamount to cultural renaissance. Liberation and self-determination, hysterical fanaticism and increasing border conflicts, all go hand in hand with an ever-increasing multinationalization of world market products. The interplay between the world market and cultural identity, between local and global processes, between consumption and cultural strategies, is part of one attempt to discover the logics involved in this apparent chaos.

Negotiating Selfhood and Consuming Desires

The aim of this discussion is to explore consumption as an aspect of broader cultural strategies of self-definition and self-maintenance. My use of the word 'cultural' is equivalent to 'specificity' as in a specific structure of desire expressed in a specific strategy of consumption that defines the contours of a specific identity space — such and such $\Sigma(a. . .n)$, a sum of products configured into an arrangement that expresses what I am. It is to be kept in mind that the currently conventional use of the concept culture to refer to maps, paradigms, or semiotic codes would yield results which are diametrically opposed to the aims that I have set out, since they imply the existence of a text-like reality that provides a recipe for the organization of social life and thought. On the contrary, from this perspective, maps, paradigms and semiotic codes are all abstractions from social products whether dress fashions or forms of discourse. As such they merely reflect the products from which they are abstracted, but cannot generate those products. Strategies of consumption can only be truly grasped when we understand the specific way in which desire is constituted. And we shall assume for the time being that the latter is a dynamic aspect of the formation of personhood or selfhood.

This argument parallels Bourdieu's modelling of the relation between *habitus* and practice, between the 'durably installed generative principle of regulated improvisation' (1977: 78) and specific strategies of consumption. But while Bourdieu seems to maintain a rationalist perspective on practice whereby it is ultimately reducible to the accumulation of cultural capital, i.e. of power, we have suggested that this is tantamount to economism and fails to take into account the non-rational constitution of desire. Thus the (not so) explicitly Veblenesque model of *La Distinction*, may tell us a great deal about the role of cultural differentiation in the definition of social position, a process whereby a particular 'class' determined *habitus* distinguishes itself in the cultural marketplace by identifying itself with a clearly defined set of products and activities, a lifestyle.

> Chacque condition est définie, inséparablement, par ses propriétés relationnelles qu'elle doit à sa position dans le système des conditions qui est aussi un *système de différences*, de positions différentielles, c'est-à-dire par tout ce qui la distingue de tout ce qu'elle n'est pas et en particulier de tout ce à quoi elle s'oppose: l'identité sociale se définit et d'affirme dans la différence. (Bourdieu, 1979: 191)

But this kind of model cannot account for the more spectacular aspects of capitalist consumption in general, based on the desire for new identities and accompanying strategies that render any particular set of consumer based distinctions obsolete after relatively short periods of stability.[1] Campbell's insightful analysis of the relation between modern individualism, romanticism and consumerism supplies a larger frame necessary to any understanding of strategies of consumption that display an instability that cannot be grasped in the terms set out by Bourdieu.

> The dialectic of conventionalization and romanticization is the personally concrete expression of the dialectic of class and capitalist reproduction in general, a dynamic contradiction between distinction and revolution, between other directed and self-directed images, between dandy and bohemian. (Friedman, 1989: 129)

The common ground in these approaches to consumption is the explicit connection between self-identification and consumption. The former may be a conscious act, a statement about the relation between self and world, or it may be a taken for granted aspect of everyday life, i.e. of a pre-defined identity. It is from this point of departure that it is possible to envisage consumption as an aspect of a more general strategy or set of strategies for the establishment and/or maintenance of selfhood. Other practices of cultural self-constitution, ethnic, class, gender, religious paint and clothed bodies, produce and consume specific objects, and construct life spaces. These are higher order modes of channelling consumption to specific ends. The latter is a means of identification.

The Struggle for Authenticity

Every social and cultural movement is a consumer or at least must define itself in relation to the world of goods as a non-consumer. Consumption within the bounds of the world system is always a consumption of identity, canalized by a negotiation between self-definition and the array of possibilities offered by the capitalist market. The old saying, 'you are what you eat', once a characterization of a vulgar ecological view of humanity, is strikingly accurate when it is understood as a thoroughly social act. For eating is an act of self-identification, as is all consumption. Proteins and calories aside, consumption, the libidinous half of social reproduction is a significant part of the differential definition of social groups and individuals. The act of identification, the engagement of the person in a higher project, is in one sense an act of pure existential authenticity, but to the degree that it implies a consumption of self-defining symbols that are not self-produced but obtained in the market place, the authenticity is undermined by objectification and potential decontextualization.[2] Thus while engagement authenticates, its consumption de-authenticates. The only authentic act inside of such a system is an act that encompasses both the authentic and its commodification, i.e. an engaged cynicism, a distanciation that is simultaneously at one with the world.

La sape

Les sapeurs of the Peoples Republic of the Congo and other similar groups, recruit their members primarily from the lower ranks of the partially employed if not lumpenproletariat inhabiting Brazzaville and the second largest city of Pointe Noire. The dominant ethnic group is Bakongo, significant in so far as this former ruling group of southerners which identifies itself as the most civilized, i.e. western, group in the Congo, has been politically displaced by the Mbochi of the North. The latter represent a region which was very much outside of direct French administration and which did not undergo the commercialization and concentrated missionary activity of the South. As such Bakongo consider them to be backward if not barbarian, at least at a certain level of discourse, since in reality relations between north and south are more complex. *Les sapeurs* progress through a system of age grades which begins in Brazzaville with the acquisition of European ready-to-wear imports, and which then takes them to Paris where they accumulate, by any means available, famous designer clothes from France and highest ranked Italy at tremendous expense. An occasional return to Brazzaville — Paris in the Congo, centre in the periphery, the only endroit not to have had its name Africanized by the revolutionary national government — to perform the *danse des griffes*, with the great name labels that are sown into the lapels of a jacket and displayed accordingly as part of the ritual of status.

It should be kept in mind, here, that such activities are an extreme form of a more general cultural strategy. In Brazzaville there are two kinds of coke, one produced locally under licence and consumed in bottles, and another more expensive, imported in cans from Holland. The consumption of coke in Brazzaville is locally significant! To be someone or to express one's position is to display the imported can in the windshield of one's car. Distinction is not simply show, but is genuine 'cargo' which always comes from the outside, a source of wellbeing and fertility and a sign of power. So in terms of western categories it might appear as the ideal type of the kind of Veblenesque ranking outlined in Bourdieu's *La Distinction*, but it is, in reality, much more than that. A Congolese can identify everyone's social rank in a crowd by their outward appearance. It is only by gaining some insight into the relation between local structures of desire and identity and the political and economic context that one can understand why a European professor of physics complained that she gained her prestige not from her academic position but from the fact that she invested all her savings in the acquisition of a fleet of taxis.

At one level *la sape* seems to be a commentary on modern consumerism. The French word is derived from the verb *se saper* which means the art of dressing elegantly, connoting the flâneur of our own society, the other-directed dandy (Campbell, 1987; Friedman, 1989). La SAPE in its Congolese version is an institution, *société des ambianceurs et personnes élégantes*. But this is no cynical statement on hyperconsumerism, no punk parody of middle-class ideals. While the dandy may have been other-directed, his practice of self-identification was very much a question of the manipulation of appearances. And while the borderline narcissism involved in this may have been such that the dandy was relatively bound to the 'gaze of the other' for his own well-being, this entire world of activity occurred and occurs again today in a larger universe in which appearance and being are quite distinct from one another, i.e. where there is, in principle, at least, a 'real person' beneath the surface. Such is not the case for the Congolese, where, tendentially, appearance and being are identical — you are what you wear. Not because, 'clothes make the man' but because clothes are the immediate expression of the degree of life-force possessed by a person, and life-force is everywhere and always external. Consumption of clothing is encompassed by a global strategy of linkage to the force that provides not only wealth but also health and political power. Congolese medicine is very much focused on methods of maintaining or increasing flows of cosmic force to the body in order to maintain good health and defend the person against witchcraft. Western medicines like any powerful substances are not symbols for but aspects of God. Similarly clothing is not a symbol of social position but a concrete manifestation of such position.

The strategy of self-definition in *la sape* is in no sense cynical, nor is there a distancing, on the part of the participants, from the commodity as such, since the commodity is not 'as such' in this kind of strategy. Consumption is a life and death struggle for psychic and social survival and it consumes the entire person. If there is a fundamental desperation at the bottom of this activity it is perhaps related to the state of narcissistic non-being generated by a social crisis of self-constitution.

> Comment ferai-je pour arriver en France?
> Comment y arriverai-je?
> La France pays de bonheur.
> Comment y arriverai-je?
> Peut-être y arriverai-je, si Dieu le veut
> Peut-être y arriverai-je?
> J'y vais doucement,
> Comment y arriverai-je?
> (from *Kua Kula* by J. Missamou, translated in Gandoulou, 1984: 195)

As a striving after well-being in a more general sense, and so-called Cargo cults or any millenarism whose goal it is to overcome a lack in the present via the importation of life-force from the outside: 'l'aventure', as it is called, the great move to Paris, initiating the *sapeur* into the higher category, 'parisien', might be understood as the expression of a millenarian wish, as indicated in the above verses. But this dream is immediately destroyed by the realities of Paris for the Congolese. Living in squalor and eeking out a bare subsistence, all and any cash is channelled into the instalment purchase of the great names in menswear, from shirts and socks, to trousers, suits and shoes. If consumption for us consists in the construction of life-spaces for ourselves, for *la sape* it consists in the constitution of prestige, precisely without the lifestyle which such garments are meant to manifest. Thus it must be that the satisfaction gained does not lie in the lifestyle experience, but in the constitution of self for others, the appearance of 'les grands', the powerful elites. And this strategy of acquisition is not simply a rational manipulation of appearances.

Nous sommes devenus comme des drogués qui ne pouvons renoncer à tout cela. (Gandoulou, 1984: 61)

The organization of *la sape* is such that immigrants, 'parisiens', attempt to accumulate 'la gamme' the set of famous name haut couture that is necessary to make the 'descente' to Brazzaville where the 'danse des griffes' must be performed to demonstrate the famous labels acquired. The latter is accomplished by sewing the labels onto the jacket lapel where they can be exhibited for others. It is noteworthy that the word 'gamme' means scale, indicating the ranked nature of prestige consumption. This enormously cosmopolitan strategy has its immediate effects in the production of a clear status demarcation.

quand l'aventurier parle de 'paysan', ou de *ngaya*, il désigne à la fois le Brazzavillois qui n'adhere pas au système de valeurs des Sapeurs-Aventuriers, notamment à la sape. (Gandoulou, 1984: 152)

La sape is not a Congolese invention at odds with the very fabric of that society. On the contrary it is a mere exaggeration of a strategy of prestige accumulation, but one which fundamentally negates its internal logic. It is thus a formula for success and a potential threat to the real power structure. While, as we have argued, the actual strategies of consumption are generated by a form of identity very different from that to be found in the modern West, the political implications have a clear historical parallel in European history.

the different ranks of people are too much confounded: the lower orders press so hard on the heels of the higher, if some remedy is not used the Lord will be in danger of becoming the valet of his Gentleman. (Hanway, 1756: 282–3)

But if the outcome of this confrontation ran in favour of the new consumers and a democratization of consumption, in the Congo the same kind of activity poses a more structural threat since no such democratization is in the offing. On the contrary, lumpen-proletarian dandyism is not a cheap imitation of the real thing, but a consumption of the highest orders of status, that, as such, strikes at the heart of elite status itself from the bottom of society.

> Le scandale éclate dès qu'il s'agit de jeunes désoevrés, d'aventuriers qui, dans l'outrance qu'ils apportent par voie d'esthétisme et de dandysme, se placent en vis-à-vis, se posent hors catégorie. Ils imitent ceux qui ont réussi, et ce faisant on aurait pu s'attendre à ce qu'ils soient acceptés, a ce qu'ils s'intègrent convenablement dans la société Congolaise. (Gandoulou, 1984: 188)

The European consumer revolution created a major threat to a system of class status which was previously impervious to imitation, but it resulted in a vast system of ranking in which the 'originals', *la haute couture*, are the unassailable centre in the clothing of social position. *La sape*, on the other hand, is thus a very expensive assault on the rank order of society and not merely on its symbolism. European dandyism was an individualistic affair, a practical manipulation of status symbols and rules of etiquette. The dandy's strategy was to subtly pass into the higher ranks. *La sape* is, in its systematic age-rank grading and explicit discourse of prestige, a subversion of the cultural classification of a political order. And it is logical that it is the product not of a western revolt against fashion, but of a Third World hypermodernity in which fashion is not merely representative but constitutive of social identity.

The special kind of consumption that we have described here cannot be separated out as a distinct sphere of activity separate, from the more general strategies that characterize modern Congolese society as an international phenomenon. The *sapeur* is not a flâneur because he is, in structural terms, authentic, i.e. his identity is univocal. The outward appearance that he appropriates is not a mere project to fool the public to appear as something other than himself. It is his very essence. It is this quality that renders it exotic to the westerner, for whom this apparent narcissism ought to be openly cynical, even in its desperation. But the point is that the narcissist whose identity partakes of a larger cosmology of lifeforces is an authentic clothing freak and not a trickster.[3]

If *la sape* is a specific expression of a more general praxis of consumption, the latter is in its turn an expression of a praxis of self-identification and self-maintenance which defines the nature of power, well-being and sickness. Over and above the seven official churches, there are ninety-five sects in Brazzaville, whose principle functions are therapeutic. Even the churches are very much engaged in what is called 'traditional medicine'. And there is clearly no undersupply of patients. Nor is it unusual for practitioners to don the white attire of western doctors and to flaunt western equipment and even medicines where possible. This is not mere status seeking, nor a recognition of a supposed superiority (in a scientific sense) of western technique, but a real identification with higher and thus more powerful forms and substances. It would appear that cults increased dramatically in the 1970s after having declined in the 1960s wave of modernism. There is certainly evidence that a large percentage of the population is not 'well' and needs the source of life-force and protection from witchcraft that can be provided by the cult groups.

Even business enterprises make use of such 'magical' sources:

> On fétiche contre moi pour ne pas avoir (que j'aie) de clients en particulier X. Moi aussi je dois féticher contre lui — c'est tout à fait normal. — shipper

> Pour réussir ici, il faut chercher un moyen d'attirer les clients (le fétiche). Savoir travailler ne suffit pas — tailor

> Je fétiche seulement pour me protéger et protéger mon affaire. Je n'ai jamais féticher contre l'oncle (bien que sa famille l'accuse de sorcellerie) — bar owner (all quoted in Devauges, 1977: 150).

There is a common core in these different domains of practice. There is an appropriation of modernity by means of a set of trans-formed traditional practices, transformed by the integration of the Congo into the French franc zone of the world economy. In all of this there is the invariant core whereby the maintenance and accumulation of self is dependent upon access to external life-force coming from the gods, ancestors (also gods), from Europe, the heavenly source of such force. If the flow of force is disturbed, frag-mentation ensues, witchcraft and conflict abound and 'fetishism' and cultism reach epidemic proportions, a massive and desperate attempt to survive.

The Ainu[4]
The Ainu are a well-known ethnic minority of Japan, traditionally described by anthropologists in the general category of hunters and

gatherers, primarily inhabiting the northern island of Hokkaido. When discussing the present situation it is usually claimed that Ainu culture has largely disappeared and they exist as a poorly acculturated and economically and politically marginal minority. Recent historical work would, however, indicate that the Ainu were at one time a hierarchical society with a mixed economy and that their present status, including the image of the hunter/gatherer is a product of the long and painful integration of Hokkaido into the Meiji state. For the Japanese the Ainu do not have ethnic status, simply because no such status exists. All the inhabitants of the territory of Japan, Nihonjin, are variations of the Wajin people, some more developed than others. Ainu, as other deprived groups, are simply outcasts, a social and not a cultural definition. Their position can only be changed in Japanese official ideology via a fuller integration into the larger economy and society. They must, in other words, enter modernity as the Japanese define it. There are many Ainu who attempt to do this, who deny their Ainu identity and attempt to become Japanese, which, of course, would imply consuming Japanese. This strategy has not been generally successful, primarily because of discrimination against Ainu, for if, officially, Ainu are as Wajin as any other Japanese, they are still outcasts, i.e. their social position, their aboriginal Japanese status, functions as effectively as any ethnic stigmatization. Of the Ainu 60 percent depend on welfare to a greater or a lesser degree. As their lands were lost to the Japanese, they most often work for others, in agriculture and related industries, and in tourism and service sectors. The unemployment rate is 15.2 percent.

During the 1970s an Ainu cultural movement developed, whose aim has been to gain recognition as a separate ethnic group. There is no interest in political autonomy, but rather, acceptance on equal terms with the majority population. While this might appear simple for the western observer, it is a very serious problem for a state whose very legitimacy is threatened by the existence of multiethnicity. The Ainu strategy is decidedly ethnic. They have established schools for the teaching of language and traditions to those who have lost them, and, not least, for their children. But they do much more than that. In several areas they have established traditional village structures for the expressed purpose of producing traditional handcrafted goods and having tourists come and witness their traditional lifestyle. Although Ainu live in Japanese houses today, they have built traditional Ainu houses, *chise*, where important village activities, such as teaching of history and language, traditional dance, weaving and woodcarving, occur on a weekly basis. Many ritual activities are also held here, and it is usual to advertise their occurrence in order to get tourist attendance and newspaper coverage. Tourists are invited not only to buy Ainu products, but to see how they are made, even to learn how they are made and to experiment in making them themselves. They can also hear about Ainu mythology, ritual and history, taste Ainu food and live in Ainu homes, especially when the few boarding houses are full.

Tourist production and display has become a central process in the conscious reconstruction of Ainu identity. It emphasizes the distinctive content of Ainu ethnicity for Japanese tourists in a context where such specificity is officially interpreted as a mere variation of Japanese culture and not a separate identity. The presentation of Ainu selfhood is a political instrument in the constitution of that selfhood.

> My personal opinion is that the Ainu people have come to realize that in order to become a complete human being, an 'Ainu', one cannot repress one's origins. Instead one has to let it come into the open and that is exactly what is happening among the Ainu people today. They are eager to know about olden times, values, things, everything. They have been starving, mentally for so many years now. There is nothing to stop their enthusiasm now. (Interview with Ainu leader, in Sjöberg, 1990)

One might suspect that placing that identity on the market would have a de-authenticating effect, but here again, as in the obverse case of the Congolese, commodification is encompassed by the larger authenticating project.

> Every Ainu man is a 'Kibori man'. We make carvings because we cannot stop. It is in our blood. If we can make a profit, well we do not think there is anything wrong with this. (Interview in Nibutani 1988, from Sjöberg, 1990)

The entire tourist project of the Ainu can be seen from this perspective, i.e. a manifestation via a commodity form of a larger constitutive process of cultural identity, one that must, of course, be manifested for others if it is to have any real existence. It is in defining themselves for the Japanese, their significant Other, that they establish their specificity.

> They are arranging Ainu food festivals, where people can taste our food. *We have our own specialties you know.* The food is cooked in a traditional way and the people use traditional cooking utensils when they prepare the food. Now to be able to eat Ainu food we cannot use our land to cultivate imported crops only. We have to have areas where we can cultivate our own cereal. . . . Our food festivals are very popular and people come from all over Nihon to visit and eat. They say our food is very tasty and they will recommend their friends to come here and eat. *As a matter of fact we already have restaurants in Sapporo, Asahikawa and Hakodate.* (Interview with Ainu leader, in Sjöberg, 1990)

While food festivals, publicized rituals, courses in handicrafts and the sale of Ainu products in self-consciously organized villages-for-tourists creates a public image for the Ainu, it is also instrumental in recreating or perhaps creating a traditional culture. The demand for land to grow Ainu crops, the revival of a great many rituals and other activities, the renaissance of Ainu history and language — cannot be dissociated from the tourist based strategy.

> the tourist villages forthwith shall function as research centers for the investigation of cultural and traditional varieties of the Ainu way of life. The vision is that the villages shall serve as information centers, with possibilities to provide lectures in various traditionally based activities. (Interview with Ainu leader, in Sjöberg, 1990)

The Ainu would appear to be as extreme as the *sapeurs* in their strategy even if their contents are diametrically opposed to one another. Just as we might suspect the apparent hyperconsumptionism of the latter, the former's orientation to the tourist market would seem to be nothing short of cultural suicide. And this is not simply a western intellectual position.

The Hawaiian cultural movement, for example, is adamantly anti-tourist. Their struggle for the revival of a traditional way of life is part of a struggle for sovereignty which might enable Hawaiian culture to be realized on the ground. It is a movement that began in the 1970s as an attempt to re-establish cultural identity and rights to land which would enable them to practise that culture after more than a century of social disintegration and cultural genocide resulting from the forcible integration of the islands into an expanding American hegemony. Following the decline of the Hawaiian monarchy's autonomy a coup d'etat made over the islands to the American missionary–planter class in 1892. The massive import of foreign plantation workers from Asia made the already dwindling Hawaiian population a minority in their own land. Their culture and language were forbidden and stigmatized. As most Hawaiians by the mid-twentieth century were 'part-Hawaiians' they often chose to identify as part-Chinese, part-Filipino, part-White. As Hawaii became thoroughly Americanized, Hawaiian cultural identity largely disappeared until the end of the 1960s when, as we have argued elsewhere, the decline of American and Western hegemony in the world system led to a decline of modernist identity in general. The fragmentation of the world system is expressed at one level in the resurgence of local cultural identities, ethnicities and sub-nationalisms. The Hawaiian movement is very much part of this process. And since the tourist industry has been the absolutely dominant force in Hawaii following the demise of the plantation economy, an industry which does not express Hawaiian strategies, but which has done more to displace them than any previous colonial economy, the movement defines itself in strong opposition to that industry.

Contemporary Hawaiians do not feel a need to advertise their local culture. It has already been thoroughly advertised and continues to be depicted in the media, controlled by an enormous industry specialized in imaging and commodifying all aspects of Hawaiian tradition. Hawaiians are acutely aware of the potential de-authenticating power of commodification. The constitution of Hawaiian identity excludes tourism and especially the objectification of Hawaiianess implied by tourist commercialization. Western intellectual sympathies are congruent with Hawaiian attitudes. Hawaiians do not wish to be consumed as domesticated exotica, and the West has produced a massive amount of critical literature on so-called consumer culture. Both we and the Hawaiians would appear to share a similar cynicism with respect to the commercial product. But then both the Hawaiians and ourselves confront such products as externalities. The Ainu control the production of their culture-for-others. Their aim is not simply to sell commodities but to present their identity as they conceive it, in order to have it recognized by the larger world. They experience their products as extensions of themselves.

Transformations of Being-in-the-world and Global Process
Congolese consume modernity to strengthen themselves. The Ainu produce traditional goods in order to create themselves. The former appropriate otherness while the latter produce selfhood for others. Hawaiians produce selfhood for themselves. In more concrete

terms, the *sapeurs*, at the bottom of a hierarchy of ranked well-being defined as imported lifeforce, desperately struggle to appropriate the latter via the accumulation of what appear to us as the signs of status, but which for them are the substance of life. The verb *se jaunir* is often used of the *sapeurs* referring to the use of bleach to lighten the skin but also to the more general whitening effect of status mobility. For the Congolese, identity is very much outside of the body, outside of the society. To realize oneself is to become *un grand*, and the latter is manifested in its highest form in the best of the West, the most modern and latest design and the least accessible. To obtain a Volvo or Saab in this franc zone monopoly would truly be a status coup. The practice of identity here is the accumulation of otherness.

The Ainu, unlike the Congolese, have no sovereignty, but are an oppressed minority whose ethnicity is officially denied. They are described as abject descendants of a proto-Wajin people which has since evolved into a great modern nation. If certain Bakongo are bent on being Parisians, their Ainu counterparts are striving to become Ainu. If *la sape* is about becoming 'modern' for one's own people, the Ainu movement is about becoming Ainu for modern Japanese. The contrast is one of symmetrical inversion: consumption of modernity vs. production of tradition, other-centred vs. self-centred, pilgrimage to Paris vs. struggle for land rights. The contrast in strategies of identity, I would suggest, is not simply a question of cultural difference, but of global position. Bourdieu might perhaps be invoked here in referring to the way in which different conditions of existence generate different structures of habitus. The specific properties of these different strategies is, of course, clothed in cultural specificity, but I think it might well be argued that the strategies themselves can be accounted for by the particular local/global articulations within which they emerge. This does not imply that local cultural strategies are not crucial, but that to understand the strategies themselves it is necessary to account for their historical emergence. Congolese society was totally integrated as an already hierarchical system based on monopoly over imported prestige goods into a colonial system which was completely compatible with the former while becoming the major source of local wealth and welfare. It is important to note here that while Congolese society was radically transformed throughout contact and colonialization, the resultant product contains essential aspects of clanship and personhood which represent a continuity with the past, and which generate strategies expressive of a 'non-modern' organization of existence. The Ainu were defeated and their land expropriated as the result of the unification of the formerly fragmented political systems of that island group. Their political autonomy disappeared in their integration as a stigmatized lower caste in the new nation state. Hawaiians were also defeated, culturally, socially and demographically, by British and especially American colonial expansion. While the process here cannot be compared with that of the Ainu, the results were such that Hawaiians became a stigmatized minority in their own land, access to which they all but lost, along with their traditions and language. For both the Ainu and Hawaiians, as opposed to the Congolese, 'traditional' culture is experienced as external, as a past which has been lost and must be regained. They are both integrated into a larger modern society that is not their own. This fundamental rupture has not occurred in the Congo.

I would argue, then, that the differences among the above strategies cannot be accounted for by simply referring to different stable cultural paradigms as Sahlins has been wont to argue. On the contrary, a consideration of the historical material would seem to imply that radical changes have indeed occurred. The early literature on contact Hawaii indicates that the consumption of Western goods by the chief class was an all-consuming pastime. Before 1820 American merchants engaged in the China trade,

descended upon the islands in a swarm, bringing with them everything from pins, scissors, clothing, and kitchen utensils to carriages, billiard tables, house frames, and sailing ships, and doing their utmost to keep the speculating spirit at a fever heat among the Hawaiian chiefs. And the chiefs were not slow about buying; if they had not sandalwood at hand to pay for the goods, they gave promissory notes. (Kuykendall, 1968: 89)

Lists of items imported include fine broadcloth, chinese silks, cashmere, ladies dresses, and there is an escalation of types and 'qualities'.

Everyone that comes brings better and better goods, and such as they have not seen will sell when common ones will not. (Bullard, 1821-3)

While such goods are very much monopolized by the chiefs in what appears as a kind of status competition a number of western and Chinese goods find there way into the lower ranks (Morgan

1948: 68). The image of the enthusiastic accumulation of Western and Chinese goods is reminiscent of Central Africa. Even the adoption of European names, the identification with what is conceived as the source of power or *mana* is common to both. Thus the description from the period 1817–19 of the Hawaiian king's men might ring true for many other parts of the globe.

> The soldiers around the King's house had swords and muskets with bayonets. Some of them wore white shirts, some waistcoats, and some were naked. (Morgan, 1948: 68)

Early contact Hawaii provides a model of the accumulation of western identity via acts of consumption of both goods and names. Chiefs attempt to identify as closely as possible with the *mana* which is embodied in such imports and which as such is simultaneously an accumulation of status (in our terms). But the disintegration of the Hawaiian polity and the marginalization of the Hawaiians in the colonial setting, produce the kind of rupture, referred to above, whereby a separate identity emerges in conditions of stigmatized poverty.

> The household is living at a poverty level. . . . Compared with this standard budget, the Hawaiian is high on food, particularly with the addition of payments on back food debts, low on household operation, and fortunately situated with no rent to pay. The tent shelter, in the midst of a sea of rubbish, is a shack that is neither beautiful nor probably, very healthful. Clothes from the dump heaps may not be a good quality, but at least they are free and enable their wearers to be conventionally dressed for the most part. (Beaglehole, 1939: 31)

> Informant has bought no clothes for himself for many years. When he has need to dress up he wears suits made for him 20 years ago, the material of which is so good that it simply will not wear out. . . . Prestige is acquired in this neighborhood by having a laundry van call each Monday morning.
> All the hats and clothes of the women are home-made. (Beaglehole, 1939: 32–3)

Hawaiians in the early part of this century a minority, in a multi-ethnic society, develop a sense of their own culture of generosity, of reciprocal feasting, of egalitarianism, and the extended family, as they are increasingly integrated into the larger society. Food as the stuff of social relations among Hawaiians acquires a special value, while things imported and the trappings of modernity lose very much of their function.

> With their decreasing use, Hawaiian foods have increasingly become enveloped

with that luscious haze which overhangs the golden age of Hawaiian glory. Thus, in one poor Hawaiian family, in which there is little food for many mouths, whenever there is not enough food to go around, the old Hawaiian mother requests her children to pretend they are eating the delicacies which the old Hawaiians love. The family thus fills its stomach on the golden age if not on the golden foods. Again, another older Hawaiian is fond of attributing the degeneration of the modern Hawaiian to his love of strange and exotic foods. . . . This informant attributes his own vigor to the fact that he prepares his own foods himself. (Beaglehole, 1939: 38)

Here we find the core of a developing ethnicity, a strategy of self-production and consumption which appears to be the foundation of modern Hawaiian identity and a strategy for cultural rebirth. This self-directedness is not something intrinsically Hawaiian but the specific product of the global transformation of the local society.

Conclusion

For several years now there has been an ongoing reconceptualization of processes of production and especially consumption as more than simply material aspects of subsistence. Following a line of argument that began with the recognition that goods are building blocks of life-worlds, we have suggested, as have others, that they can be further understood as constituents of selfhood, of social identity. From this point of view, the practice of identity encompasses a practice of consumption and even production. If we further assume a global historical frame of reference it is possible to detect and even to account for the differences among broad classes of strategies of identity and therefore of consumption and production as well as their transformations in time. This is the case, at least, to the extent that the different strategies of identity, which are always local, just as their subsumed forms of consumption and production, have emerged in interaction with one another in the global arena.

Notes

1. One might even seriously question the validity of Bourdieu's differential model as applied to his own empirical data, where diametrically opposed categories are often represented by statistical differences of a more indeterminate nature; 49 percent vs. 42 percent and where most of the defined categories of style correlated to 'class' linger in the 50 percent range at best. Could it be that cultural identification is not so clearly linked to social position and that whatever linkages there are result from other kinds of systemic processes.

2. The most common example is the tourist industry's capacity to commodify ethnicity, making once powerful symbols of cultural identity available to an international market.

3. 'Seeking a Master'. At the post-office I met a young man who attended the Lycée Technique in Brazzaville. He was from the Teke region to the north and lived in town with his maternal uncle. He demonstrated an unusually enthusiastic interest in developing a stable relation to me and expressed the hope of being able to come to Sweden after only a few minutes of conversation. He conveyed in no uncertain terms his interest in becoming my client or subordinate, a dependent for whom I would be responsible. The strategy is not reducible to subordination. It implies, for a student with a possible career, a connection that might enable him to establish his own clientele. Tapping into a source of social lifeforce is crucial: it explains why both Swedish and even American cars are ranked well above the more accessible French products, and why Sweden, origin of the major Protestant mission, is associated with 'heaven'.

4. The material from the Ainu is based on the very important, but as yet unpublished, doctoral thesis of K. Sjöberg (1990) which deals with Ainu cultural identity today and which provides a brilliant analysis of the historical relationships between Ainu and Japanese.

References

Beaglehole, E. (1939) *Some Modern Hawaiians*. Honolulu: University of Hawaii, Research Publications No. 19.

Bourdieu, P. (1977) *La Distinction*. Paris: Minuit. (English translation *Distinction*, London: Routledge, 1984.)

Bourdieu, P. (1979) *Outline of a Theory of Practice*. Cambridge: Cambridge University Press.

Bullard, C.P. (1821–23) 'Letterbook of Charles B. Bullard, Supercargo for Bryant and Sturgis at Hawaiian Islands and Canton, 20 March 1821–11 July 1823', typescript, Hawaiian Mission Children's Society Library, Honolulu.

Campbell, C. (1987) *The Romantic Ethic and the Spirit of Modern Consumerism*. Oxford: Blackwell.

Devauges, R. (1977) *L'Oncle, le Ndoki et L'entrepreneur: La petite entreprise congolaise à Brazzaville*. Paris: Orstom.

Friedman, J. (1989) 'The Consumption of Modernity', *Culture and History* 4: 117–29.

Gandaoulou, J.D. (1984) *Entre Paris et Bacongo*. Paris: Centre George Pompidou.

Hanway, J. (1756) 'Essay on Tea' in *A Journal of Eight Days' Journey*. London.

Kuykendall, R.S. (1969) *The Hawaiian Kingdom*. Honolulu: University of Hawaii Press.

Morgan, T. (1948) *Hawai'i: A Century of Economic Change 1778–1876*. Cambridge, MA: Harvard University Press.

Sjöberg, K. (1990) 'Mr Ainu', unpublished PhD thesis, Department of Anthropology, University of Lund.

Jonathan Friedman is Professor of Anthropology at Lund University, Sweden.

AIDS as a Globalizing Panic

John O'Neill

In the present context of HIV/AIDS knowledge, marked as it is by
the absence of a vaccine discovery, it falls to the social and health
sciences broadly conceived to devise institutional responses to AIDS
that will contain both the illness and our social responses to it. Here,
of course, 'containment' is sought on two levels and it may be that a
considerable fiction is involved in hoping that the HIV virus is, so to
speak, *virus sociologicus*. While it is doubtful that the virus can
learn sociology, it is certainly true that sociology cannot remain
ideologically ignorant of virology. But this in turn means that the
social sciences in general are obliged to rethink themselves before
they can be adapted ready-made to the new limitations which
HIV/AIDS imposes not only upon our sexual conduct but upon a
range of professional behavior where contact with AIDS is
involved. This is especially the case since the professionalization of
the social sciences, like that of the medical sciences, has proceeded in
terms of an ideological demarcation between factual knowledge and
moral knowledge that, while honored by hardline scientists of either
ilk, is in fact breached by developments in the bio-technological
sciences that have reopened the frontier of ethico-legal enquiry. The
social sciences no longer have any neutral ground in these matters,
and this is particularly the case with those who suffer from AIDS
since they oblige us to reconceive our social policies and our moral
values regarding trust and community.

Although AIDS is a relatively recent phenomenon, and despite
the complexity of the virological and epidemiological dimensions
of the HIV virus, it may be said that we have acquired a considerable knowledge of it in the short span of little over five years
research (Royal Society of Canada, 1988; Spurgeon, 1988; Fee
and Fox, 1988; Altman, 1987; *Daedalus*, 1989; New England
Journal of Public Policy, 1988; *The Milbank Quarterly*, 1986;
Ornstein, 1989). Indeed, AIDS has moved quickly through a cycle

Theory, Culture & Society (SAGE, London, Newbury Park and New Delhi), Vol. 7
(1990), 329–342

of first stage of relative ignorance, followed by intensive research and discovery, to a plateau where we are waiting for the break-through which would permit us to counteract the HIV virus by means of a vaccine. This state of affairs has only been achieved through a considerable pace of biomedical research (*Scientific American*, 1988; *Daedalus*, 1989) and the involvement of govern-mental health agencies from the federal to municipal level, including hospitals, clinics, gay community organizations, AIDS workshops, hotlines and pamphleteering, in addition to a constant reportage of AIDS information in newspapers and on television. AIDS has even generated its own art forms in theatre, film and folk art (Crim, 1988; Watney, 1987). All these activities, then, have combated social ignorance with social awareness. As a new stage of conscience-raising, AIDS awareness is now projected to recruit even pre-adolescent children. The cardinal virtues of contemporary sexual citizenship are exemplified in our awareness of the practices of contraception and abortion, as well as the achievement of copulation and the avoidance of AIDS. It should be observed that by the same token a great deal of secular faith is involved in the assumption that 'awareness' — which varies from sect-like membership to glancing through myriad minor pamphlets — will alter sexual conduct to any great extent. 'Safe' sex is not so easily institutionalized if only because the concept of 'sex' is itself not to be understood outside of any extraordinary range of social behavior where 'excitement' may preclude 'safety' in any form.

I want to argue that, despite what we already know about HIV and AIDS, any further development in our knowledge and the pedagogies to be devised in public education programs is confronted with the phenomenon I shall call *socially structured carnal ignorance*. Here, what I have in mind is a number of factors that determine bodily conducts as necessarily, wilfully and desirably matters of 'unknowing', of 'spontaneity', of 'passion', of 'desire', or of 'fun', 'phantasy'. In short, we use our clothing, eating, drinking and sexual behavior to achieve relationships and end-expe-riences that may be considered moral or immoral, rational or non-rational, competitive or communal, safe or risky. It is not our task to pursue the cultural, class, and gender and age variations that operate here, although these operate upon the social structure of carnal knowledge and ignorance (O'Neill, 1985a). Nor have we to recount the historical and ideological shifts in the codes that dress our bodily conduct, provided we do not overlook them. It must suffice to articulate with regard to AIDS the following elements that condition a structure of ignorance which in turn generates the fear of AIDS upon which so much public energy is expended:

1. the carrier may not be known to him/herself due to the latency period of up to eight years;
2. the range of risk behaviors may not be known to potential victims;
3. the HIV carrier may not be known to him/herself;
4. the pursuit of epidemiological knowledge regarding the HIV virus may conflict with the civil rights affording non-knowledge of persons' behavior and associations; and
5. the code of civil rights may guarantee non-knowledge of persons or ways that prevent or conflict with medical, police, educational, employment practices of testing and identification of 'AIDS persons'.

In turn, within the general population carnal ignorance may be valued in such experiences and settings as: (a) sex; (b) drugs; (c) alcohol; (d) at parties; (e) at concerts, clubs; and (f) on the street, in alleys, in cars. The specific behavioral codes defining these experiences where reason 'goes on holiday', so to speak, will vary according to membership in a variety of settings and practices shaped by: (a) age group; (b) sexual ideology, e.g., consumptive rather than reproductive sex; (c) sexual identification, i.e., homosexual, lesbian, bisexual and/or heterosexual; (d) religious beliefs; (e) ethnicity; and (f) socio-economic class, i.e., level of education, income and professional ideology.

There exists an enormous bias in the social sciences against the study of the ways in which our ignorance, misinformation and deception is socially structured. For this reason our enlightenment with regard to sexual behavior proceeds much more slowly than the deliverance promised to us by our present rationalist bias towards knowledge. If we are to make any progress in devising sexual pedagogies to respond to sexually transmitted diseases (STD), specific empirical and ethnographic data on the social structure of carnal ignorance, as I have outlined it, must be gathered (Rubin, 1984; Crawford, 1977). In part, such information is already available in material collected from the standpoint of the sociology of attitudes, beliefs and opinions. What can be said, however, is that those who are least educated and most socio-economically underprivileged in virtue of class, racial and colonial status, will bear the brunt of prostitution, drugs and HIV-infected births in the urban areas of the world which constitute a 'fourth world' of social problems wherever they are situated.

With these remarks in mind, I shall turn now to the development of a framework for the study of AIDS which sets national and local concerns in the context of the global political economy (Law and Gill, 1988). From this standpoint, AIDS must be considered as one of a number of panics of a political, economic, financial and 'natural' sort to which the global order responds with varying strategies of crusade, sentimentality or force. By a *globalizing panic* I understand any practice that traverses the world to reduce the world and its cultural diversity to the generics of coca-cola, tourism, foreign aid, medical aid, military defense posts, tourism, fashion and the international money markets (O'Neill, 1988a). Since these practices are never quite stabilized, their dynamics include deglobalizing tendencies which will be reinscribed by the global system as threats to the 'world order'. Some nations may consider themselves to be the prime agents in this world order, while others can only maintain an aligned status, or else are allowed to enjoy a toy nationality, like that of Canada, which can be appealed to in order to supply neutrality functions on behalf of the world order. The globalizing panics that confirm the world order rely heavily upon the media and television, newspapers, magazines, films and documentaries to specularize the incorporation of all societies in a single global system designed to overcome all internal division, if not to expand into an intergalactic empire. Such a vision is confirmed, for example, by the performance of chemical experiments under the gravity-free conditions of space flight which may enhance the future discovery of an AIDS vaccine. Thus sexual practices that would not be tolerated within the social system of the space capsule nevertheless provide ideological justification for global medicine's quest for a perfect experimental environment. Furthermore, the relatively ghettoized sexuality of gays and black and Hispanic IV drug users finds its projection in the starry heaven of the heroes of all-American science, war and medicine. Meantime, this medicine is largely unavailable to the poor in the United States and the so-called Third World whose infants are ravaged by disease and death amidst populations that are continuously uprooted by famine, flood and warfare. By the same token, media images from this part of the world are exploited on behalf of the promise of the global order whose own political economy is largely responsible for the natural disasters that ravage the third world.

The sexual economy, which must be treated as the framework for any grasp of the political economy of AIDS, is subject to every other sub-system of the global economy and national political economy. It is so when it appears most disengaged because its disengagement celebrates the processes of disenfranchisement elsewhere in the society, i.e. the degradation of gendered economies, of family and of church authority, as well as of any politics grounded in these communities. When the general will is sexualized, politics is privatized; when politics is privatized, the general will is idiotized. The politics of desire is the desire politics of a global economy which entirely escapes articulation in the speechlessness of sexualized desire. Meantime in the West, the postmodern insistence on cultural fragmentation implodes all differences and reduces everything to shifts in fashion and its constant revision of the spatio-temporal order of global capitalism which itself remains class and colonial in nature and cannot be thought in terms of the shibboleths of sexism, racism or anti-humanism which it has outlawed at the same that it is the principle source of these very phenomena because reformism on these issues is anything but revolutionary.

It might be argued that postmodernism celebrates a phantasmatic economy of sex and power while remaining tied to the market for global rock, drugs and fashion and to the concert politics whose evanescent sentimentality reflects and deepens the global exploitation (O'Neill, 1988b). From this standpoint, postmodernism is the 'classless' culture of a globalizing economy that exports its industrial basis whenever labor is cheapest while dividing its internal economy into rich and poor service sectors. In these sectors activities are neither community nor self-building. Here the political economy of the signifier without sign (family, class, race, gender) is operative. Since there is nothing at the center of a doughnut or of a dress, variety is everything. Since money has no absolute value, variety is the only norm. In this culture, those who look for signs are traditionalists, semantic fools, or semiotic idiotics — they are out of style, out of touch. Nothing looks worse on television than nationalism, fundamentalism and anti-colonialism with their murders, their starving children, their destruction and immolation. The same is true of the images of domestic poverty, urban decay, illiteracy and alienation that are floated without any attempt to implicate the class system. To be 'it' is to be 'out' in the game of global circulation.

The global economy is concerned equally with the promotion of individualism and its sexualized erasure. Its primary politics are those of corporate identity which, in turn, conscripts an aggressive individuality pitted against his-or-her own nature and community. The active, young, calculating, realistic and hedonistic recruits to corporate capitalism and its cosmopolitan culture are the idols of global media culture. They move like gods and goddesses amidst the debris of urban crime and desolation, cocaine colonialism and the life and death struggles of high-tech medicine, war and 'communication'. To this end, global culture is perfectly 'uni-sexual', i.e., it is a same-sex-culture whose technological infra-structure is indifferent, benign or emancipated with respect, to its male and female protagonists. (O'Neill, 1985a: ch. 4). In turn, this monoculture refigurates itself as 'difference' by means of its agonistic pursuits of profit, sex, drugs, peace, health, justice and progress. Here winners are 'hyper-men', a caste which includes 'executive' women who have proven they can be winners within the agonistic culture of global high technology and corporate capitalism. That is why it is important that females not be excluded from the business and social science professions and especially that they not be excluded from the police and military forces. Global capitalism is 'unisexual' and it offers every prosthetic and thera-peutic aid to the monobodies required to service its way of life. Against this promise, AIDS may be understood to constitute a potential global panic on two fronts; namely (a) a *crisis of legitimation* at the level of global unisexual culture; and (b) a *crisis of opportunity* in the therapeutic apparatus of the welfare state and the international medical order. AIDS threatens to produce a *crisis of cultural legitimation* because it tempts highly committed individuals to withdraw from the unisexual culture of global capitalism and to renounce its specific ideologies that (a) sex is the most intimate expression of freedom and choice in the market society; (b) sex is consumptive and not necessarily productive; (c) sex is genderless, unfamilied, classless and homeless; (d) sexual repairs are available through the biomedical and psychiatric services of the therapeutic state; and (e) all high risk behavior on behalf of global capitalism will be supported by its prophy-lactic and prosthetic technologies whose ultimate aim is to immunize its members against the environment of their own risk behavior.

The experience of AIDS panics the sexual culture of global capitalism in several ways. In the first place, it has 'disappointed' those who were most committed to its ideology of sexual freedom. To its credit, the gay community has learned that its sexuality cannot be played out in the anonymous intimacy and extraordinarily high rates of casual contact which were enjoyed in the bath houses. This re-evalution has taken effect precisely because gays in fact constituted a quasi-community marked by levels of literacy and organizational skills beyond what can be found in the IV drug alleys (Brandt, 1988; Altman, 1988). However, 'heterosexuals' have been tempted to turn against the gay community in a number of ways that threaten to degrade the civil rights achievable in capitalist democracies. Business, educational and medical institutions have all been strained by the fear of AIDS. At the heart of these delegitimizing strains in the social order is the immediate lack of any vaccine against HIV which would, as it were, immunize the society against its own responses to what I shall call *AFRAIDS*. Short of a vaccine, AIDS constitutes a panic both on the individual life level and on a collective level where AFRAIDS threatens to undermine the order of civil liberties. To the extent that panic spreads, especially where AFRAIDS or the fear of AIDS, generates secondary fundamentalist and revisionist panics, the sexual economy of global capitalism is threatened with a crisis of legitimation. The AIDS panic, however, strikes most deeply into the legitimation process when it prompts the general population in a rationalized industrial society to question the probability value of scientific knowledge with demands for absolute certainty or for the immediate availability of drugs such as AZT where the experimental controls and clinical tests properly required may be short-circuited by the clamor for immediate reduction of suffering, 'fast-tracking' hope despite the necessarily cautious pace of research. Here modern medical knowledge is particularly exposed since rational experiment, placebo practices, and the ethico-legal issues in patient consent reveal the costs as well as the benefits of our commitment to the industrial order. This order is threatened less by proposals to ghettoize AIDS patients, however politically crude such a suggestion may be, than by any loss of commitment to the protocols of the medicalization of health and happiness (O'Neill, 1986). As things stand, there is a considerable need to attempt some realignment between community based medicine, corporate research and national medical research.

At the very worst, the AIDS panic threatens the liberal order of global capitalism with a 'rebarbarization' of its social bond. Hitherto, it was possible to sustain the global phantasy of a social order without deep commitment, as in the figure of the American Express man whose creditability lies in his credit and whose faith lies in the fiction of a card that would make him at home in the homeless world of global capitalism. Will the American Express Card guarantee immunity against foreign HIV tests, and even if it did, can we be sure that American Express will issue its precious cards at home to persons without a prior HIV test? Or will those who carry the American Express Card, having passed an HIV test, constitute a new biological order of eligible capitalists? However bizarre such questions may seem, they already have their counterpart in the experiment with AIDS-free singles clubs. What is extraordinary in such responses is that they threaten to return the capitalist order to a *purity rule*, that is, to return us to a social order founded upon a contagion model of social relations rather than on the present contract model of society that has been the engine of our extra-ordinarily globalizing history. If this were the ultimate consequence of the AIDS panic, global capitalism would have succeeded in rebarbarizing itself because of an unfortunate contingency in its sexual culture, rather than because of its other phantasied threats of interstellar barbarism.

AIDS presents *a crisis of opportunity* in the global culture of late capitalism precisely because its immediate features namely: (a) autotoxicity; (b) fatality; and (c) absence of vaccine renew demands upon the therapeutic state and its biomedical apparatus to provide interim care, socio-legal immunity and a vaccine. To do this, the social and health sciences have already been recruited to furnish ethical, economistic and pedagogical discourses, conferences, pamphlets, multi-disciplinary research and media treatments to the public. Here, the supply of AIDS 'knowledge' and pedagogy to the public whose fears demand it creates a perfect symbiosis between state power as knowledge, on the one hand, and knowledge as individual power/powerlessness, on the other hand. Individuals attempt to learn that only they can stop AIDS, or drinking/driving or waste, whereas these are cultural complexes produced by and (re)productive of the ideological and therapeutic culture in which they live. In this process individuals learn that

1. The state is the ultimate producer of knowledge/science.
2. The state is the ultimate producer of health, education and employment.
3. The state is the ultimate guarantor of civil liberties.
4. The state is the ultimate guarantor of all ideologies.
5. The state is the ultimate producer of the state and of society and of the individual.

It is important to see that whatever ways we devise to speak about our sexuality, sexual disease, sexual discrimination, sexual liberation, they are shaped by a pre-existing field of institutionalized discourses which have been devised by the church, the state and the socio-medical sciences with a concern for public and private welfare. These discourses contain both prescriptive and descriptive technologies to which different professional groups claim legitimate access and application in the complex of power-knowledge-pleasure that may be called the 'therapeutic state'. Thus the HIV/AIDS phenomenon enters into a highly structured field of discourse upon social policy, health and moral ideology that is contested by church, state, family, school and secular counter-cultural groups with varying degrees of progressive and fundamentalist beliefs in the possibility of social control of youth sexuality, drugs and family breakdown (Treichler, 1988a, 1988b). The danger exists that 'AIDS' will function as a pretext for a social backlash against the civil rights of gays, lesbians and the achievement of gender equality to the extent they are seen as the source of troubles plaguing groups marginalized by the larger global economy in which these movements function. For want of a comparable pedagogic effort from the national center, these marginalized groups will be educated by televangelism which itself adopts an extraordinary global mimetics in reporting and commenting upon the world sources of spiritual trouble (Luke, 1989; chapter 3). Social critics will be quick to pounce upon such degraded versions of the cultural hegemony of the family and religious values, as well as pointing to the danger of rightist political regression. However, some moral and cultural weight must be reassigned to the primary institutions upon which modern societies continue to depend unless they can envisage a social order whose fundamental bond is entirely an effect of secondary institutions. The pedagogical challenge this would involve quite exceeds anything we can reasonably expect in a postmodern age of collapsed narratives. At the same time, emancipatory ideologies of the absolute autonomy of the individual in all matters of sexuality and reproduction cannot be pursued outside of a framework of institution, law and morality which in turn require large allocations of public energy. They thereby raise the question — which we cannot consider here — of their own allocative position within the political economy of nation states. At this level, we must surely ask how this individualized sexual economy functions within the new global political economy.

The crises of global culture are at once extraordinarily nation state-building, at least with respect to the levels of the therapeutic apparatus of the state — and transnational on the economic and political level, depending upon shifts in the multinational corporate agenda. Of course, these two levels interact, so that global capitalism responds to its own trans-state activities through the nation state and even through a layer of 'international' agencies. Seen in this context, AIDS is again simultaneously a globalizing panic and a national state epidemic, mobilizing government health institutions from the municipal level all the way to the World Health Organization (Christakis, 1986, 1989). As a global panic, AIDS becomes a further charge upon the Third World, whereas *US AIDS* is principally an advanced economy, urban male (age 20–40 years) anal partner hazard, with drug users and bisexual males as secondary transmitters. US AIDS has benifited from the same trade routes as other sexually transmitted diseases. But gay sub-culture has been a highly articulate ideological element in North American society. The imperial dominance of American capitalism within the global system, of course, diffuses American 'life-style' ideologies through global mass culture, tourism, commercial and military travel.

Thus the global health system is only the promissory side of a world disease system. Each generates the other. Here, once again, there is a potential for a rebarbarization of the global order through quarantine orders, immunization control and racism — witness the construct of Afro-AIDS. The concept of Afro-AIDS is marvelously suited to project on to 'world history' so to speak, an Afro-origin for AIDS whereas the socio-economic conditions of blacks and Hispanics in the United States and its dependencies are clearly the principal source of American disease, crime and poverty. Similarly in Africa, where AIDS is a widespread heterosexual trouble, one must take into account shifts in marriage practices due to urban migration, poverty and a fragile medical infrastructure, before 'racializing' the disease (Fortin, 1987; Christakis, 1988). Yet the search for a Simian-based HIV, endorsed by the *Scientific American* (Essex and Kanki, 1988) inspires hopes of naturalizing a colonial and class history whose overwhelming dimensions cannot possibly be reduced by the bio-medical sciences. Since America's internal black population is the immediate source of virtually inorganizable and ineducable IV drug users, who are in turn viewed as the principal transmitters in the heterosexualization of AIDS, a third crisis looms within the US medical system inasmuch as so many millions of Americans are without any medical coverage but could hardly continue to be ignored should their deaths be attributable to AIDS. As we have said, AIDS as a global pandemic puts considerable stress on the international (world) health order.

The United States and Africa are the two epicenters of the AIDS pandemic, with respectively 204 and 150 cases per million, despite huge differences in socio-economic and socio-medical infrastructures. Yet these two centers cannot be treated in the same way, as though the one were the shadow of the other, nor can they be allowed to drift apart. In the meantime, the world medical order will have to reappraise its foundations built upon Western biomedicine and the colonial power of its corporate pharmacological institutions (Hunt, 1988; Ehrenreich and Ehrenreich, 1971; Navarro, 1976). National states will vary in their capacity to sustain the costs of AIDS where these are predicated upon a purely medical strategy that presupposes no state intervention with respect to high risk sexual and narcotic behavior. These countries may also take different stances upon American efforts to medicalize AIDS just as they may or may not co-operate with American efforts to 'police' the international order on such other issues as immigration or environmental pollution. Similarly, it may not be possible to impose allegedly international standards of medical and social science research across cultures whose definition of illness, community and knowledge are known to vary. To do so, embroils such research in counter charges of a medical imperialism with which colonial countries are already familiar (Christakis, 1986, 1989).

It is a conceit of the American political order that beyond its borders life is everywhere short, nasty and brutish — despite the fact that its own urban scene answers at least as well to such description as any foreign culture to which it is thought to apply. US AIDS intensifies the lethal content of American culture in unprecedented ways because it threatens to spill over the class wall which separates the rich from the poor, the suburbs from the inner city and family life from individual lifestyles that challenge it. By the same token, since this spillage has largely been a construct of the media coverage of AIDS, the state therapeutic complex has simultaneously achieved a considerable 'containment' of the epidemic as one that is by and large responsive to its administrative institutions without raising revolutionary changes to our fundamental ethical and political constitution. So long as we are able to muddle along in this fashion, we avoid the most catastrophic scenarios envisaged as an effect of the global ravage of AIDS. Here, of course, the ultimate breakdown would be in *the class system* as an immunological order and the destruction of the medical system predicated upon such an order. Short of such a conflagration, we may expect class politics to slide into caste politics in the hope of preserving the health of society by sacrificing its principle of charity to group preservation. To the extent that this scenario develops, the global order will have collapsed into a barbarous conflict of national biological elites each seeking to preserve its own purity whilst trying to eliminate the other as a possible contaminant (O'Neill, 1985b).

Note

This paper has benefited from earlier presentations at the Tenth International Summer Institute for Semiotics and Structural Studies, University of British Columbia, Vancouver, 13 August 1988 and the Theory Culture & Society Conference on Global Futures, The Burn, Aberdeen, 14 September 1988, as well as the Public Access series Counter-Talk: The Body, 25 October 1988.

References

Altman, Dennis (1987) *AIDS in the Mind of America*. New York: Anchor Press.

Altman, Dennis (1988) 'Legitimation through Disaster: AIDS and the Gay Movement', pp. 301–15 in Elizabeth Fee and Daniel M. Fox (eds), *AIDS: the Burdens of History*. Berkeley: California University Press.

Brandt, Allen M. (1988) 'AIDS: From Social History to Social Policy', pp. 147–71 in Elizabeth Fee and Daniel M. Fox (eds), *AIDS: the Burdens of History*. Berkeley: California University Press.

Christakis, Nicholas A. (1986) 'International Aspects of AIDS and HIV Infection' in *Confronting AIDS: Directions for Public Health, Health Care and Research*. Washington: National Academy Press.

Christakis, Nicholas A. (1988) 'The Ethical Design of an AIDS Vaccine Trial in Africa, *Hastings Center Report* 18(3): 31–7.

Christakis, Nicholas A. (1989) 'Responding to a Pandemic: International Interest in AIDS Control', *Daedalus* (spring): 113–34.

Crawford, Robert (1977) 'You are Dangerous to Your Health: the Ideology and Politics of Victim Blaming', *International Journal of Health Services* 7(4): 663–80.

Crim, Douglas (ed.) (1988) *AIDS: Cultural Analysis, Cultural Activism*. Cambridge, MA: MIT Press.

Daedalus (1989) Special issue 'Living with AIDS' (spring).

Ehrenreich, B. and Ehrenreich, J. (1971) *The American Health Empire: Power, Projects and Politics*. New York: Random House.

Essex, Max and Kanki, Phyllis J. (1988) The Origins of the AIDS Virus', *Scientific American* (October): 64–71.

Fee, Elizabeth and Fox, Daniel, M. (1988) *AIDS: The Burdens of History*. Berkeley: California University Press.

Fortin, Alfred, J. (1987) 'The Politics of AIDS in Kenya', *Third World Quarterly* 9(3): 907–19.

Hunt, Charles (1988) 'AIDS and Capitalist Medicine', *Monthly Review* (January): 11–25.

Law, David and Gill, Stephen (eds) (1988) *The Global Political Economy: Perspectives Problems and Policies*. New York: Harvester Press.

Luke, Timothy W. (1989) *Screens of Power: Ideology, Domination and Resistence in Informational Society*. Urbana: University of Illinois Press.

The Milbank Quarterly (1986) Special issue on 'AIDS: The Public Context of an Epidemic', 64 (supplement 1).

Navarro, Vincente (1976) *Medicine Under Capitalism*. New York: Prodist.

New England Journal of Public Policy (1988) Special issue on AIDS, 4(1).

O'Neill, John (1985a) *Five Bodies: The Human Shape of Modern Society*. Ithaca: Cornell University Press.

O'Neill, John (1985b) 'To Kill the Future?', *Bulletin of the Graduate School of International Relations* No. 3. Nigigata: International University of Japan.

O'Neill, John (1986) 'The Medicalization of Social Control', *Canadian Review of Sociology and Anthropology* 23(3): 350–64.

O'Neill, John (1988a) 'Techno-culture and the Specular Functions of Ethnicity', pp. 17–35 in I.H. Angus (ed.), *Ethnicity in a Technological Age*. Edmonton: University of Alberta.

O'Neill, John (1988b) 'Religion and Postmodernism: the Durkheimian Bond in Bell and Jameson', *Theory, Culture & Society* 5(2–3): 493–508.

Ornstein, Michael (1989) *AIDS in Canada: Knowledge, Behaviour and Attitudes of Adults*. Toronto: University of Toronto Press.

Royal Society of Canada (1988) *AIDS: A Perspective for Canadians*. Ottawa: Royal Society of Canada.

Rubin, Gayle (1984) 'Thinking Sex: Notes on For a Radical Theory of Politics of Sexuality', pp. 267–319 in Carole S. Vance (ed.), *Pleasure and Danger: Exploring Female Sexuality*. London: Routledge.

Scientific American (1988) 'What Science Knows about AIDS', 259 (4/October).

Spurgeon, David (1988) *Understanding AIDS: A Canadian Strategy*. Toronto: Key Porter Books.

Treichler, Paul A. (1988a) 'AIDS, Gender, and Biomedical Discourse: Current Contests for Meanings', in pp. 190–266 Elizabeth Fee and Daniel M. Fox (eds), *AIDS: the Burdens of History*. Berkeley: California University Press.

Treichler, Paul A. (1988b) 'Biomedical Discourse: an Epidemic of Signification', in D. Crim (ed.), *AIDS: Cultural Analysis, Cultural Activism*. Cambridge, MA: MIT Press.
Watney, Simon (1987) *Policing Desire: Pornography, AIDS and the Media*. Minneapolis: University of Minnesota Press.

John O'Neill is Professor of Sociology at York University, Toronto. His publications include *Five Bodies* (Cornell University Press, 1985).

The Two Faces of Sociology: Global or National?

Bryan S. Turner

Introduction

Since its formal inception in the first half of the nineteenth century, sociology has been, generally implicitly, located in a tension or contradiction between a science of particular nation-states and a science of global or universal processes. It developed ambiguously as a science of the specific societies of the industrial world and as a science of humanity. Although the vocabulary of sociology is typically couched at a sufficiently abstract level to suggest that it is a science of universal social processes ('action', 'structuration', 'norm' or 'social system'), in practice sociology has been developed to explain and understand local or national destinies. From a sociology of knowledge point of view, we might be surprised if this nationalistic purpose were absent. Paradoxically we might argue that the greater the sociologist, the more local the purpose, namely that sociology developed by brilliant insights into concrete issues of local capitalist development. I wish to explore these paradoxes through a commentary on certain classical sociologists, but the burden of this examination will focus on France and Germany up to the First World War.

Percy Bysshe Shelley once argued in his *A Defence of Poetry* in 1821 that poets were the 'hierophants of an unapprehended inspiration' because they possessed a superior imagination. Although I would not want to claim such heroic powers for sociologists, we should at least expect that sociology would reflect, if possible sooner rather than later, the major tensions and developments of given societies. Since the modern world is itself subject to the contradictory tensions of globalization and localization, secularization and fundamentalization, of modernization and post-modernization, we should expect to see these contradictions

Theory, Culture & Society (SAGE, London, Newbury Park and New Delhi), Vol. 7 (1990), 343–358

reflected in the conceptual apparatus of sociology itself. My purpose in this paper is therefore to examine the relationship between the emergence of a universalistic concept of citizenship and global notions of humanity and simultaneously to review the various ways in which sociology has been implicated in these global developments.

The Genesis of Sociology

Although the idea that sociology is a product of the French and industrial revolutions but mediated by the three principal ideologies of modern politics (namely conservatism, liberalism and socialism) is controversial (Nisbet, 1967), it does provide an initially useful paradigm for considering the argument that sociology embodies a tension between a global science of humanity and a 'local' discipline in the service of the nation-state. The problem is that, while sociology may have been a response to the universalistic implications of both revolutions, it became institutionalized, often within the context of the exponential growth of national higher education systems in the postwar period, under the auspices of the state. Is it a global science of humanity or implicitly the study of local structures of the national community? Writing of the Americanization of sociology, W.E. Moore (1966) deplored the decline of a tradition of European sociology which originally regarded the discipline as the study of humanity, and noted that the development of the world into a global system might bring about a revival of sociology with a global perspective. Moore identified a number of classical sociologists who clearly had a vision of a global science (Ibn Khaldun, Comte, Durkheim and Spencer), but curiously enough neglected to discuss Claude-Henri de Saint-Simon (1760–1825). From the vantage point of the emerging (re)unification of Europe and increasing awareness of modern globality (Robertson, 1987; Robertson and Chirico, 1985), Saint-Simon's commentary on the relationship between industrialism and human globalization has proved to be extraordinarily prescient.

As an individual, Saint-Simon was perfectly placed to experience the revolutionary implications of his own epoch. A member of the French aristocracy who served briefly in the French army during the American war of independence, he was subsequently arrested in 1793 and financially ruined by revolutionary change. His failure to secure public recognition led eventually to an unsuccessful suicide attempt in 1823 when he shot himself in the head seven times. He miraculously survived only to die two years later after an attack of gastro-enteritis. He left behind him a genuine following and a body of work which proved crucial for the foundation of both sociology and socialism because it directly influenced Durkheim (Gouldner, 1958; Lukes, 1973) and Marx (Rattansi, 1982).

In his philosophical works he advocated positivism as an antidote to metaphysical speculation, but the core of Saint-Simon's substantive sociology was dominated by the analysis of industrialism. In fact, Saint-Simon's conceptualization of social change anticipated Herbert Spencer's sociology because Saint-Simon wanted to draw a sharp contrast between militaristic and industrial systems. In the feudal systems of the Middle Ages, the clerical class enjoyed political and ideological dominance, because the Church was an institution which provided social cohesion. With the development of industrialism, militaristic virtues and monastic virtues of asceticism cease to be socially relevant as the social system turns from the production of war to the production of useful things, through the organization of the sciences and arts in the interests of humanity. The old style of militaristic politics is to be replaced by a system of co-operative administration in which the traditional parasitic classes will be replaced by the 'new' classes of engineers and industrialists. While Saint-Simon worked with an ideal–typical dichotomy of militaristic–theological and pacific–industrial systems, he recognized that in specific cases these two systems could overlap and continue to persist in given societies. Thus, in *De la réorganisation de la société européenne* which he published with Augustin Thierry in 1814, he criticized the militaristic dimension of England's social constitution which was combined with industrialism. In order to establish a European peace, it would be necessary to curtail this aggressive aspect of English social organization by uniting England and France under a common parliamentary system (Taylor, 1975: 130–36).

These features of Saint-Simonian sociology are relatively well known. Perhaps what is far more interesting is Saint-Simon's vision of an integrated system of European states, the international spread of industrialism and the emergence of a global culture. Saint-Simon's view of industrialism creating an international order which will undermine the legacy of provincialism is important from our point of view precisely because he saw an intimate connection between the growth of globalism and a change in the nature of social science. The scholars of Europe were already forming social bonds which would challenge the archaic forms of local consciousness, he argued in *L'Organisateur* of 1819. Sociology was to become the science of the new industrialism, while a religion of humanity would replace the decaying force of Catholicism. It is this aspect of Saint-Simon's teaching which struck Durkheim forcefully. An economic industrialism will not in itself be sufficient to create a new moral basis to European societies, which are in a state of disarray with the collapse of the moral authority of the papacy. In the *Nouveau christianisme* Saint-Simon sought the principles which would provide the notion of universal unity to bring the separate European nations into a morally coherent system. In his study of Saint-Simon, Durkheim fundamentally supported this normative feature of global socialism, but he thought internationally organized professional groups would be necessary to sponsor and carry these norms.

The notion that there are important, and at times paradoxical, relations between global industrialism, secularized Christianity, cosmopolitan sociology and socialism became a persistent feature of the legacy of classical sociology. Saint-Simon's ideas about positivism and sociology were taken up by August Comte (1798–1857) in his *Cours de philosophie* where in volume four in 1838 we find the first self-conscious reference to 'sociology'. Comte elaborated the idea of developing sociology as the pinnacle of the positive sciences and a universal religion as the cohesive force of contemporary sciences. Comte wrote to Czar Nicholas, the Grand Vizier of the Ottoman Empire and the head of the Jesuit order to encourage them to accept the new positive universalism. Again following Saint-Simon, Comte took the universalism and hierarchical authority of the Roman Catholic Church as models of organization for the new order. The new religion of Humanity would have rituals, saints and calendars like the old faith, but it would be revolutionized by the spirit of positivism (Kolakowski, 1968).

This simultaneous concern for a science of society and the unification of humanity (or at least as a first step the integration of a peaceful Europe) was further developed by Nemis Fustel de Coulanges and Durkheim who regarded the universalism of medieval Roman Catholicism as mid-way between the pantheism of Rome and the cosmopolitanism of the new industrial order. In the *The Elementary Forms of the Religious Life*, Durkheim argued that modern societies would have to discover a new set of universally significant moral bonds. These normative elements were necessary to curb the impact of utilitarianism individualism which was another feature of the new order of industrialism. Tragically Durkheim, in response to German nationalism and as a consequence of the devastation of the First World War on the young men of the Durkheim movement or school, came to see nationalist rituals and symbols, rather than professionalism, as the key feature of the new integrative system replacing Christianity. These nationalist senti- ments, especially in *Qui a voulu la guerre?* (1915) and *L'Allemagne au-dessus de tout* (1915) were also a reaction against the dangerous ideas of Heinrich von Treitschke on pan-Germanism. We can interpret Durkheim's sociology, especially his sociology of morals and education, as an attempt to provide French society with an analytical paradigm which would contribute to the restoration of social coherence, which Durkheim thought was threatened by the hedonistic materialism and anomie of rapid industrialization. In part, Durkheim's interest in the problems of social order in advanced societies under conditions of organic solidarity had been occasioned by the crisis of the Franco-Prussian war. The French defeat contributed to his sense of patriotism (Lukes, 1973: 41). While it is probably an exaggeration to assert that 'the *raison d'être* of his scientific research in sociology was the welding of France into a well organized and well integrated nation' (Mitchell, 1931: 87), it is clear that the idea of nationalism as a modern version of more traditional sources of the *conscience collective* runs throughout his work.

The involvement of many European intellectuals in the euphoria which embraced the opening of the First World War as a panacea for the crisis of European culture and as an antedote to cultural nihilism snuffed out much of the universalistic legacy of nineteenth- century positivism. But while the slaughter of 1914–18 made the prospects of international agreements look remote, over a longer period of time the twin themes of nationalism and cosmopolitanism were interwoven in Durkheim's sociology and that of his followers. In 1900 at the Exposition Universelle in Paris, Durkheim offered a lecture to a congress on problems of solidarity in modern societies in which he recognized the current force of national sentiment, but argued that there was also a new and broader social trend towards European solidarity and towards humanity (Hayward, 1959). The theme was also explored by Marcel Mauss in a deve- lopment of Durkheim's ideas in 'Sociologie politique: la nation et l'internationalisme' (Mauss, 1968-9, Vol. 3). In short, the theme of Saint-Simonian internationalism continued in Durkheimian sociology, despite the devastations of war.

German Universalism/German Parochialism

We can define modernization in terms of the emergence of concepts of internationalism and cosmopolitanism in so far as they break with the limitations, narrowness and provincialism of tradition. In this respect, universalism is bound up with the growth of the city, with trading corporations, with universities and with the emergence of a money economy. The project of modernization is about the conditions which give rise to the abstract citizen. The disappearance of status as the primary axis of social hierarchy and the development of notions of contract were critical processes which prepared the ground for the elaboration of modern notions of universalistic citizenship (Turner, 1986, 1988). It is perfectly appropriate therefore that Jürgen Habermas should claim in *The Philosophical Discourse of Modernity* that 'With Kant, the modern age is inaugurated' (Habermas, 1987: 260), and it is equally appropriate that the two essays which have drawn most attention in the recent discussions of modernity and postmodernity have been 'What is enlightenment?' and 'Idea for a universal history from a cosmopolitan point of view', which were both published in the *Berlinische Monatschrift* in 1784. As a theorist of modernity, Kant was interested in the developmental possibilities of a universalistic morality, which would function as an alternative to or replacement of (official) Christianity.

These 'political' writings show that Kant's critical writings on philosophical issues were not remote from the social and political issues of his time. On the contrary, they may be seen as responses to the erosion of the universalism of Christian morality against the background of the American and French revolutions. In this article on universal history, therefore, Kant reflected upon the global implications of the transition of human societies from barbarism to civil society — a theme common to Enlightenment philosophers and subsequently developed of course, via Ferguson and Hegel, by Marx into a historical materialism of world society. In order to understand this aspect of Kant's article, we should perhaps note that 'Idee zu einer allgemeinen Geschichte' can be translated as a 'general normative paradigm for world history', while 'im weltbürgerliche Absicht' could be plausibly rendered as 'from the standpoint of global citizenship'. In short, there is a parallel between Saint-Simon's vision of an integrated Europe in the context of an expanding humanity and Kant's essays on universal history, enlightenment and perpetual peace (Beck, 1988). This parallel or convergence is hardly surprising, given the fact that they were both responding to the (largely implicit) ideas of global citizenship in the French Revolution. Thus, Kant argued that, while necessity compelled humanity to surrender individual (natural) freedoms in order to form a civic union, the highest goal of Nature was the formation of a perfect human community. Such a global community could only be possible in a context of international regulation of states. This idea Kant recognized was 'fantastical' (from the perspective nationalistic objectives), but ultimately necessary, if humanity were to progress beyond the condition of perpetual war. The final solution to the Hobbesian state of nature was the creation of an international order of mutual regulation.

If Kant inaugurated the modern age, then according to Habermas, it was with Hegel (1770–1831) that modernity became a problem, because it was in Hegel's theory of the evolution of a world spirit that the constellation of rationality, consciousness of historical time and modernity became visible and self-consciously theorized. For Hegel 'the History of the World is nothing but the development of the Idea of Freedom' (Hegel, 1956: 456), through a series of dialetical struggles towards self-realization through the Greek world, the Roman period and the German world. For Hegel, religion, and in particular reformed Christianity, played a crucial part in the emergence of modern subjectivity and individualism. In the subjectivity of Christian spirituality, Hegel saw the origins of modern consciousness, but Christianity in modern times had become fragmented and could no longer function as a common morality and a universal vision. With the growing division of labour and the competitiveness of bourgeois society, civil society lacked coherence and this alienation had separated individuals from the common realm. A new civil religion was required to replace Christianity and to express the new level of universalism and freedom which was implicit in modern society. In common with his contemporaries, Hegel combined this view of Christianity with an idealization of the Greek polis as a period in which there was no fundamental alienation between the private individual and the public arena. In his later work, Hegel moved increasingly towards a secular view of political integration, believing that a civil religion might develop to provide the necessary integration for a developed social system (Plant, 1973).

It is well known that Hegelianism had entirely contradictory implications, and as a result divided early into conservative Right Hegelians and the so-called Young Hegelians of the left. On the one hand, Hegel's ideas justified the critique of Christianity as only a partial realization of the universal spirit of freedom and legitimized a revolutionary criticism of the particularities and limitations of modern times as an anticipation of a new leap into the future. On the other hand, Hegelianism provided a reconciliation of the present and the past, because modern institutions are the fullest realization of the course of history. Hegel's slogan 'the real is the rational' was taken to mean that what exists now (for example the Prussian state) is the embodiment of the highest form of rationality. This ambiguity permitted Popper to accuse Hegel of instigating the New Tribalism (Popper, 1945: 30), while other scholars have argued that there was nothing in the text of *Philosophie des Rechts* to justify such an assertion (Knox, 1940).

The fact is that we cannot understand the contradictory themes of German social philosophy without an understanding of the social structure of the German states in the period following the French Revolution. Before the Revolution, the German ruling classes and the court had looked towards France for a model of civilized taste and behaviour. This preference for French high culture had driven a major cultural wedge between the court, the middle classes and the peasantry. Germany was still a collection of small, divided and fragmented cities, principalities and states. In cultural terms, this produced a narrow small-town mentality which idealized the virtues of self-governing towns against the external threat of absolutism. The peculiarity of eighteenth-century Germany, however, was that this very localism also provided the roots of a rapid development of interest in global culture on the part of officials in the bureaucracy. The German state bureaucracy also typically included teachers and clergymen, and thus there was an audience for a more universalistic culture. This bureauratic state structure provided the institutional context for the development of the ideals of *Bildung*, of education on the part of the state employees of the middle classes. There was, however, no national cultural centre in the German states and 'it was in the absence of a national center and a national public that German literary aspirations came to focus on humanity as a whole' (Bendix, 1977: 126).

After the Revolution, the educated elites either looked towards England for a model of liberalism which might provide an alternative to revolutionary terror or they continued to develop notions about individual cultivation, self-education and aesthetic refinement as an alternative to practical politics. Their moral world view implied a criticism of the aristocracy whose culture was thought to be based on blood sports, heavy drinking and sexual immorality, without ever rejecting social inequality as such. The literature of the middle classes reflected their de facto reconciliation with the world in terms of the virtues of diligence, restraint and ethical refinement. These values of the *Bildungsburgertum* implied an ambiguity about power poltics because the educated middle classes feared revolutionary terror from below and authoritarian regulation from above. Hence they 'escaped' into self-cultivation. The development of 'character' was an alternative to political struggle. In Germany, in response to the violence of the French terror writers like Goethe embraced classical humanism and hoped for the development of an idealized global citizenry (*Weltbürgertum*). This context led Marx to observe that what France had achieved in the field of revolutionary politics, it was left to Germany to bring about in the sphere of philosophy. Hence in the *German Ideology* and the *Critique of Hegel's Philosophy of Right*, we see Marx attempting to transcend the limitations of German idealism through the development of a materialistic interpretation of world history, which would require Marxism to go beyond the constraints of a merely bourgeois conception of a universalistic civil society.

Marx and Weber on World History

Marx's legacy to Hegelian idealism is too well known to require elaboration (Avineri, 1968). The universal development of the absolute spirit became the historical development of the production of the material conditions of existence in which under capitalism the progressive character of historical development is momentarily lost in the alienation of labour from the means and objects of production. However, from the contradictions of capitalism the proletariat emerges as the universal class of historical change. However, if we look at Marx as a theorist of modernity, we can see the continuation of Kant and Hegel. For example 'Three aspects characterize capitalism according to Marx: the rationalization of the world, the rationalization of human action, and the universalization of inter-human contact' (Avineri, 1968: 162). Marx's view of capitalism was as a result paradoxical. Capitalism subordinated the majority of the population to a life of enforced misery, but capitalism also destroyed local tradition, provincial sentiments and the enchanted garden of magic and superstition. Through its universal impulse, capitalism made history into world-history. In the *German Ideology* Marx and Engels claimed that capitalism

> produced world history for the first time, insofar as it made all civilised nations and every individual member of them dependent for the satisfaction of his wants on the whole world thus destroying the formal natural exclusiveness of separate nations. (Marx and Engels, 1965: 75–6)

This view of the world dynamism of the capitalist economy was further illustrated by the notion that Asia was characterized by its stationariness and lack of global significance. Indeed, the Asiatic mode of production precluded the possibility of internal change (Turner, 1978). It was the British Empire with its railways, private property system, newspapers and competitive commodities which would start the revolution in Asia. Because the workers have no stake in the national economy, their interests are in reality cosmopolitan. Nationalism and patriotism are thus reactionary forces, which will wither away with the global development of capitalism. National sentiment is a bourgeois device to divide the global consciousness of the workers (Davis, 1965; Kolakowski, 1974).

Although Marx was overtly writing about the global expansion of a capitalist world-system, we can also interpret Marx as a theorist of modernity. This interpretation of Marx has been developed recently by Marshall Berman (1982) in *All That is Solid Melts into Air*. Berman wants to show that modernist writers and Marx converge, but also that the tensions and contradictions of modernism as an experience are produced by capitalism as analysed by Marx. Berman reads modernism from within a Marxist paradigm

> to suggest how its characteristic energies, insights and anxieties spring from the strives and strains of modern economic life: from its relentless and insatiable pressure for growth and progress; its expansion of human desires beyond local, national and moral bounds . . . the volatility and endless metamorphosis of all its values in the maelstrom of the world market; its pitiless destruction of everything. (Berman, 1982: 121)

Marx is certainly a brilliant theorist of modernity, especially in identifying the destructive economic origins of modern progress, and thus in describing the dark side (the blood and pain) of change. However, there remains the suspicion that Marx's account of modernization is inextricably a description of Westernization, and therefore that his view of global history is a general history of the West. In this respect, Marxism may share precisely the limitations conventionally associated with functionalist theories of development. Marx had little or no appreciation for the universalism, for example of Islam, and he characteristically regarded 'Asiatic societies' as uniformly stagnant. His account of the progress of world history in developmental stages — from barbarism to civil society — was the legacy of a Western Enlightenment. Even Marx's view of European history was inescapably shaped by the German experience of historical change. Thus Marx's version of Hegel's view of the world history was a strange combination of a global vision with a distinctive Orientalist perspective on the origins of rational capitalism. In this regard, there is little to separate Marx's account of capitalist accumulation in the West from Weber's perspective on the revolution force of Western rational capitalism in the *General Economic History*.

In Weber the globalization force of capitalism was translated into a theory of global rationalization. The combination of Protestant asceticism and Western rationalism has produced an irresistible force, which will slowly but surely convert the world into a regulated and organized social system within which there will be little room for tradition, magic or charisma. The de-mystification of the world will make everything in principle subject to rational calculation. Although many cultures have 'anticipated' such changes, only in post-Calvinistic Europe and in the Protestant cultures of North America has the full force of the spirit of instrumental rationalism come to full bloom.

Weber combined a vision of this global process towards a single-world rationality with a clear view of the fact that the social sciences had to serve a national German purpose. In his own research, there was a continuous commitment to German nationalist objectives. In the 1890s he condemned the use of Polish and other agricultural workers in East Prussia which he felt represented a long-term threat to the cultural integrity of Germany (Tribe, 1983). In his Freiburg address on 'The National State and Economic Policy' (Weber, 1980), it is clear that economics has a direct contribution to make to the creation of a strong German state. Weber's interest in the

Russian revolution was at least partly inspired by a traditional German fear of Cossack cavalry penetrating Germany via the flat plains of eastern Europe. Weber described the First World War as 'great and wonderful' (Käsler, 1988: 18), although he did not support the expansion of Germany via for example the annexation of Belgium. Weber's persistent and overt involvement in the national politics of German life obviously raises issues about the conventional interpretations of Weber's doctrine of value-neutrality. Without entering into this epistemological issue, it is important to keep in mind the fact that Weber's statements on the issue of sociology in relation to practical politics arose in the context of his confrontation with the Minister of Education concerning the autonomy of university professors in the Prussian university system (Weber, 1973). The value-neutrality doctrine is thus more a statement about university organization than about the conduct of sociological inquiry; it did not prohibit Weber from direct statements about army, foreign or domestic policy.

Intellectuals and the Sociology of Knowledge
It could be objected that my analysis so far has merely stated an obvious proposition about the sociology of knowledge, namely that sociologists might be expected to reflect national goals and objectives, especially during periods of social crisis. In contintental Europe, especially where a Germanic university system is in operation, university academics are essentially civil servants, whose research is expected in part at least, to follow governmental objectives and assumptions. In the Netherlands, for example, 'most faculty members consider it perfectly appropriate that the government should decide the role of university research in Dutch society' (Philips, 1986: 65). This situation means that the notion of 'academic freedom' will have very different meanings and implications in different university traditions and structures. In the context of government dominated university systems, it is hardly possible to see what Mannheim's notion, following Alfred Weber, of the 'free-floating intelligentsia' or 'socially unattached intellectuals' (*sozial freischwebende Intelligenz*) could mean (Mannheim, 1986). One would expect university-based academics-as-civil-servants to reflect national, indeed nationalistic goals. In so far as classical sociology developed a global vision of reality, it may be that this view depended more on marginalized and alienated Jewish scholars (Durkheim, Simmel, Benjamin, Adorno and so forth) than on any other social group.

Yet the 'calling' of a sociologist is also to wider and broader goals, which would include in principle a commitment to the universalistic character of the discipline, the global features of intellectual life, some notion of science as a set of practices and commitments over and above national and local objectives. The very sociology of knowledge which argues that sociological knowledge will be as determined by social processes as any other type of knowledge permits us to reflect self-consciously on the vocation of a sociologist to a global picture of a science of humanity in the context of the often covert strains towards a local or 'Little England' view of reality. Sociology should on these grounds reflect this bifurcation between a global view of sociology and a commitment to nationally-specified research targets.

While this observation is introduced as an 'optimistic' observation on the limitations and prospects of sociology as a global science of humanity, it has also to be recognized how frequently sociology and sociologists have served entirely local causes. In Germany, sociology adapted relatively successfully to Nazi conditions (Rammstedt, 1986); American sociology has been frequently co-opted to serve nationalistic foreign-policy objects, in the project Camelot affair; major sociology textbooks tend to exhibit local views of the content of the discipline (Coulson and Riddell, 1970); and very few major sociologists have written about sociological problems in an international, let alone a global context. For example, Parsons's sociology is overshadowed by the dilemma of his overt commitment to American democratic values (Holton and Turner, 1986) and his clear intention to write a general theory of action which would be relevant to the human commitment as such. Or to take a very different example, despite the global character of the analytical questions of Habermas's social philosophy, his comments on actual societies (which are in any case rather rare) tend to be parochial in their focus on Western capitalist societies (Habermas, 1979).

Conclusion: The Fin-de-siècle Crisis

We can expect a deluge of publications in the 1990s on fin-de-siècle everything. Martin Jay has to some extent paved the way prematurely perhaps with fin-de-siècle socialism (1988). There are certainly some interesting possible parallels between 1890 and 1990. There is our sense of impending doom, this time ecological rather than necessarily militaristic, although it would be foolhardy to preclude the possibility of an eco-military disaster. The greenhouse effect, the destruction of the ozone layer, the break-up of Eastern Europe, the Aids epidemic, fundamentalist revivals in the world religions, the greying of the industrial societies and world-wide religio-ethnic conflicts and communal violence offer a daunting picture of global catastrophe. Many versions of nihilism and/or cultural decadence are now on offer. The notion of the crisis of values, the rise of the masses and the isolation of the individual which was common in the 1890s may find a resonance today. Similarly recent studies of the 'end of organized capitalism' (Lash and Urry, 1987) might be compared (not with reference to their contents but to the scale of social change which they addressed) with Rudolf Meyer's *Der Capitalismus fin de siècle* of 1894. In our period, anxiety about the future has been summarized under the prefix 'post' as in postmodernism, postMarxism, postFordism. I am assuming that even this uncertainty will give way to greater doubts, involving a comparison of our end-of-century existence with an absolutist Baroque culture.

Perhaps the crisis which drove intellectuals at the end of the nineteenth century into sociology, socialism and internationalism might, however, also find an echo in our own epoch. Durkheim's reflections on Saint-Simon's vision of the necessity for European integration, an end to English aggression against the European continent and a new science of humanity might be a valuable point of departure for contemporary social sciences to begin to engage (once again) with the tensions between our local concerns with national issues and our vocation, albeit underdeveloped and ill-defined, for a global sociology of humanity. At the very least, it would be an intellectual tragedy if the nationalistic and parochial politics of the Anglo-American world of Thatcher and Bush were to obscure the real possibilities which are opening up with 1992 — possibilities which were not only anticipated but actually described by Henri Saint-Simon in his observations on the need for a European parliament in 1814.

References

Avineri, S. (1968) *The Social and Political Thought of Karl Marx*. Cambridge: Cambridge University Press.

Beck, L.W. (1988) *Kant, Selections*. New York: Macmillan.

Bendix, R. (1977) 'The Province and the Metropolis: the Case of Eighteenth-century Germany', pp. 119–49 in J. Ben-David and T.N. Clark (eds), *Culture and its Creators, Essays in Honor of Edward Shils*. Chicago and London, University of Chicago Press.

Berman, M. (1982) *All that is Solid Melts into Air, the Experience of Modernity*. London: Verso.

Coulson, M.A. and Riddell, D.S. (1970) *Approaching Sociology, a Critical Introduction*. London: Routledge & Kegan Paul.

Davis, H.B. (1965) 'Nations, Colonies and Social Classes; the Position of Marx and Engels', *Science & Society* 29: 26–43.

Gouldner, A.W. (1958) 'Introduction' to Emile Durkheim, *Socialism*. New York: Collier Books.

Habermas, J. (ed.) (1979) *Geistigen Situation der Zeit*, 2 volumes. Frankfurt: Suhrkamp.

Habermas, J. (1987) *The Philosophical Discourse of Modernity*. Cambridge: Polity Press.

Hayward, J.E.S. (1959) 'Solidarity: the Social History of an Idea in Nineteenth-century France', *International Review of Social History* 4: 261–84.

Hegel, G.W.F. (1956) *The Philosophy of History*. New York: Dover.

Holton, R.J. and Turner, B.S. (1986) *Talcott Parsons on Economy and Society*. London: Routledge & Kegan Paul.

Jay, M. (1988) *Fin-de-siècle Socialism*. London and New York: Routledge.

Käsler, D. (1988) *Max Weber, an Introduction to his Life and Work*. Cambridge: Polity Press.

Knox (1940) 'Hegel and Prussianism', *Philosophy* (January): 51–63.

Kolakowski, L. (1968) *Positivist Philosophy, from Hume to the Vienna Circle*. New York: Doubleday.

Kolakowski, L. (1974) 'Marxist Philosophy and National Reality', *Round Table* 253: 43–55.

Lash, S. and Urry, J. (1987) *The End of Organized Capitalism*. Cambridge: Polity Press.

Lukes, S. (1973) *Emile Durkheim, his Life and Work*. London: Allen Lane.

Mannheim, K. (1986) *Conservatism, a Contribution to the Sociology of Knowledge*. London: Routledge.

Marx, K. and Engels, F. (1965) *The German Ideology*. London: Lawrence & Wishart.

Mauss, M. (1968-9) *Ouevres*, 3 volumes. Paris.

Mitchell, M.M. (1931) 'Emile Durkheim and the Philosophy of Nationalism', *Political Science Quarterly* 46: 87–106.

Moore, W.E. (1966) 'Global Sociology: the World as a Singular System', *American Journal of Sociology* 71: 475–82.

Nisbet, R.A. (1967) *The Sociological Tradition*. London: Heinemann.

Philips, D. (1986) 'Americans in Holland', pp. 64–69 in D. Bok (ed.), *Harvard and Holland*. N.V. Indivers.

Plant, G. (1973) *Hegel*. London: Unwin University Books.

Popper, K. (1945) *The Open Society and its Enemies*. London: Routledge & Kegan Paul.

Rammstedt, O. (1986) *Deutsche Soziologie 1933-1945*. Frankfurt: Suhrkamp.

Rattansi, A. (1982) *Marx and the Division of Labour*. London: Macmillan.

Robertson, R. (1987) 'Globalization Theory and Civilization Analysis', *Comparative Civilizations Review*. 17: 20–30.

Robertson, R. and Chirico, A. (1985) 'Humanity, Globalization and Worldwide Religious Resurgence: A Theoretical Exploration', *Sociological Analysis* 46: 219–42.

Taylor, K. (1975) *Henri Saint-Simon 1760-1825, Selected Writings on Science,*

Industry and Social Organisation. London: Croom Helm.

Tribe, K. (1983) 'Prussian Agriculture — German Politics: Max Weber 1892-7', *Economy and Society* 12: 181-226.

Turner, B.S. (1978) *Marx and the End of Orientalism*. London: Allen & Unwin.

Turner, B.S. (1986) *Citizenship and Capitalism, the Debate over Reformism*. London: Allen & Unwin.

Turner, B.S. (1988) *Status*. Milton Keynes: The Open University Press.

Weber, M. (1973) 'The Power of the State and the Dignity of the Academic Calling in Imperial Germany', *Minerva* 4: 571-632.

Weber, M. (1980) 'The National State and the Economic Policy', *Economy and Society* 9: 428-49.

Bryan S. Turner is Professor of Sociology at the University of Essex. His latest books include *Nietzsche's Dance* (with G. Stauth) and *Status*.

The Globalization of Human Society as a Very Long-term Social Process: Elias's Theory

Stephen Mennell

> Previous bipolar figurations . . . were *de facto* regional in character. . . . Hence the victor in an elimination struggle was usually confronted, sooner or later, by outsider groups with a roughly equivalent or an even higher power ratio. In the present phase of the millennial elimination struggle, all possible actors are already on stage. (Elias, 1987b: 89–90)

Any attempt to pinpoint the exact beginning of a major social transformation such as globalization is likely to prove misleading. On the one hand it is true, as Peter Worsley (1984: 1) has strikingly written, that 'until our day, human society has never existed' — but only in the sense that never before have all the possible actors been on stage at once. On the other hand, some of the processes which in this century have made the human world one have been at work in human societies as long as the species *Homo sapiens* has existed.

In a sense, the potential for a single global human society has always existed, but the occasion has not arisen until now. Human beings have always remained one single species, capable of interbreeding, communicating (not, of course, without linguistic obstacles) and learning from each other. They have filled the globe without any further biological evolution. Plants, insects, fish, birds and other animals all divided into a great number of species no longer able to interbreed, each exploiting its distinctive capacities in a particular environment, and thus filling all the different niches of the planet which could offer a living. In contrast, the single human species adapted itself to widely varying conditions on earth by means not of biological but of *cultural* differentiation.

Humans filled the earth by learning from experience and by handing on

Theory, Culture & Society (SAGE, London Newbury Park and New Delhi), Vol. 7 (1990), 359–371

knowledge from one generation to another. They adapted themselves to new surroundings with the help of social transformations: that is, transformations in the form of social development, and without further evolutionary transformations breaking the biological unity of the species. (Elias, 1987c: 343)[1]

The long-term socio-cultural differentiation of human groups in varying degrees of competitive interdependence has been familiar to sociologists since the days of the Victorian social evolutionists. So have processes of integration into larger co-ordinated units, processes which are the other side of the coin from differentiation, the two running together in the long term, though with many complicated leads and lags over the shorter term.

These long-term processes in human history have always been a central concern in the work of Norbert Elias. In his early writings, particularly in the second volume of *The Civilising Process* (1939), he focused on what is in effect chronologically the middle part of the long-term story of globalization and its antecedents in one region of the world. That is to say, he dealt with state-formation in Western Europe and, more particularly relevant to present purposes, the formation of *systems of states* and the growth and development of inter-state balances of power in the region through warfare from the Middle Ages to the twentieth century. In his later work, he has been concerned to extend the story both backwards and forwards in time — backwards to the role of 'survival units' in human society from its earliest beginnings, and forwards to the dynamics of the nuclear balance between the global superpowers since the Second World War.[2]

Survival Units
The life of early humans may well have been, in Thomas Hobbes's famous phrase, 'poor, nasty, brutish and short', but it was never (as Hobbes also asserted) 'solitary'. The primal condition of society is not a war of every human being against every other; all the evidence is that humans have always lived in groups. The primal condition appears rather to have been one in which human *groups* had no protection against possible annihilation or enslavement by another, stronger, *group* than their own physical strength, weapons, and *collective* fighting capacity. In other words, people always lived together in groups which Elias calls survival units. He attributes to Marx the crucial insight into the first of the elementary functions which members of a group have to perform adequately if they are to survive as a group (Elias, 1987d: 227); the need to provide food and

other basic wherewithals of life. But there is a second essential function, that of controlling violence — whether in conflicts internal to the survival group or in conflicts between different survival groups. It is a mistake, Elias argues, to see the 'economic' function as more 'basic' than that of using and counteracting the use of violence. The two are inextricably linked in processes of social development, and indeed in the earliest and smallest survival units are performed by the same non-specialist people. Marx was right to point out that not until a food surplus was produced could there emerge a specialist class of warriors who took no direct part in the production of food. Nor for that matter could there be priests specializing in the deployment, development and transmission of knowledge. On the other hand, in the long run, a relatively high level of physical security is essential to the regular production of a food surplus. Moreover, as populations increased with sedentary agriculture, the more irreversibly 'locked in' to agricultural production did they become (Festinger, 1983: 81–2). The greater their dependence on grown as opposed to gathered food, the more dependent were agrarian survial units on defence against external marauders or the internally disruptive. An agrarian community was virtually defenceless against organized military bands, unless it could mobilize an army of its own. This, as Goudsblom (1989b: 89) has remarked, explains the apparent functional paradox of warrior-hood: '*the function of warriors was to fight against other warriors*'. Thus the connection between the emergence of economic surpluses on the one hand and specialist priests and warriors on the other is reciprocal, not causally one-sided, in a process through time.

A survival unit in which there has emerged a category of people specializing in the monopolization of violence, and no longer sharing directly in other tasks such as food production, can be spoken of as a state. In his later work, Elias has reviewed the archaeological evidence of the early development of the Sumerian city-states, finding in it support for the symbiotic connection between the monopolization of the means of violence and the monopolization of taxation that he had previously emphasized in European history (1939: Vol. II, 201–25), as well as for the advance hand in hand of the differentiation of social functions, the growth of large-scale administration and store-keeping centred on the temples, and the elaboration of defensive installations (1987d: 228–9).

Over the course of human development as a whole, the overall trend has been towards survival units larger and larger both in population and geographical extent. The trend is particularly clear if one looks at the largest survival units existing in each successive period. Taagepera (1978) has demonstrated quantitatively how, after the collapse of each of the great empires of the Old World, the next succeeding one managed to integrate a larger geographical area than its precursor. The European state-formation process, to the understanding of which Elias (1939, Vol. II) insightfully contributed in his discussion of such component processes as the 'elimination contest' between competing territorial magnates, the 'monopoly mechanism', the 'royal mechanism', and the transformation of private into public monopolies, is only one small and relatively local instance of the overall trend in world history towards bigger survival units incorporating more people and more territory. Elias recognizes that a full study of this tendency would have to deal with the great variety of competitive figurations in different continents at different stages of the development of society. Such a study would, for instance, have to show why it was that the war-leaders of sedentary populations organized as military–agrarian state-societies were eventually able to mobilize the military and economic resources to defeat recurrent invasions by migrant pre-state people, in the end quite decisively. The question is not as obvious as it may seem, and the process took longer than is sometimes appreciated. Only at the stage of development reached by European society in about the fifteenth and sixteenth centuries did the power ratios between state and pre-state societies become so great that the latter no longer posed any serious military danger to the former. Such a study would also have to look at the role of military power in state-formation processes in continents and periods beyond those Elias dealt with in the European case; such writers as McNeill (1982), Mann (1986) and Gellner (1988) have contributed more recently to this task.

Inter-state Tension Systems
Just as clear as the overall trend towards bigger survival units is the persistent differential in the use of violence within and between survival units. It is often overlooked that in Volume II of *The Civilising Process* Elias constantly draws attention to the contrast between the taming of impulses towards the use of violence *within* state-societies — a taming following from people's being *forced* to live in peace with one another (Elias, 1939: Vol. I, 201) — and the

relatively unbridled persistence of violence in relations *between* states. Yet there is always a close linkage between the two levels. Warfare, whether between the many small territories of Europe around the end of the first millennium AD or between states in the modern world, does not in Elias's view stem from any inherent and constant aggressive impulse in human beings as individuals. It stems rather from the structure of competitive figurations in which they are caught up. Thus, in the elimination contest of medieval Europe, even a peaceably-inclined individual magnate could be compelled to compete for territory because if a neighbour gained territory, even from a third party, that neighbour's resulting increased military potential would be a threat to the peaceably-inclined magnate. On the other hand, the same competitive figuration makes the process of internal pacification essential; internal dissensions are externally weakening, and internal order, organization and taxation strengthen military potential.

This two-way relationship is a continuing element in the growth of geographically more and more inclusive systems of inter-state tensions which have eventuated in the globalization of human society. Elias (1939: Vol. II, 96–104) shows how throughout the later Middle Ages, England and the various territories that were to constitute France formed a single system of tensions. The final expulsion of the English from the system permitted the further consolidation of the French kings' hold over the mainland part of the former more extensive system. The emergence of a more centralized French state in turn facilitated its further expansion east-wards, creating a new and wider system of tensions with the Valois (later, the Bourbons) and Habsburgs as the principal poles. Already by the time of the Thirty Years War in the seventeenth century, the system of tensions had spread to involve all the states of Europe. It then underwent further development through further wars. To the east, the Habsburgs and Hohenzollerns were creating empires of their own partly within and partly outside the old Imperial territory, but it was only after the Napoleonic Wars that Prussia and Austria achieved a duopoly in Germany; the war of 1866 then resulted in Austria's expulsion from the German Confederation and Prussia's hegemony over the remaining territory. The interplay of the internal and the external is seen especially clearly in the Franco–Prussian War which shortly followed and which led both to the consolidation of a single (though admittedly still federal) German state and set the scene for the two World Wars of the present century. Those are so called because, though both began in Europe, they unfolded within a system of inter-state tensions that was for the first time truly global in reach. And out of these struggles there emerged in turn the world-wide duopolistic hegemony of the two nuclear super-powers that has been a major preoccupation of Elias's old age.

The Pacification of Global Society?
Writing on the eve of the Second World War, Elias was highly conscious of the tensions propelling the states of the world towards a global conflict, but saw the possibility that in the long term the outcome might be something like a world government.

> [T]hat, in our day, just as earlier, the dynamics of increasing interdependence are impelling the figuration of state societies towards . . . conflicts, to the formation of monopolies of physical force over larger areas of the earth and thus, through all the terrors and struggles, towards their pacification, is clear enough. And . . . beyond . . . the tensions of the next stage are already emerging. One can see the first outlines of a worldwide system of tensions composed by alliances and supra-state units of various kinds, the prelude of struggles embracing the whole globe, which are the preconditions for a worldwide monopoly of physical force, *for a single central political institution and thus for the pacification of the earth.* (1939: Vol. II, 331–2, my italics)

In part, that passage still seems highly prescient, in view of the emergence after 1945 of inter-state groupings such as NATO, the European Community, the Warsaw Pact, Comecon, and some other inter-state groupings elsewhere on the globe. But in his writings since the 1960s, Elias has been far more pessimistic about his earlier vision of a single world monopoly apparatus with the capacity to punish states which breach the peace. In *Humana Conditio*, his reflections on the fortieth anniversary of the end of the war in Europe (1985: 112), he sees this as more remote than ever. He rates the chances of nuclear war between the superpowers as quite high. He surveys a great many instances of 'hegemonial struggles' between state-societies from antiquity onwards, and the 'hege-monial fevers' which members of competing survival units experienced in the course of their struggles with each other. There has been no case in history, he says (1985: 68–9), where competition between great powers did not sooner or later lead to war.

This competition has been a powerful force in the globalization of human society.

The most powerful state-societies are no less constrained than the smaller, less powerful state-societies which have been drawn into their orbit. Together they form a common figuration — a structural 'clinch'. The balance of power between interdependent states is such that each is so dependent on the others that it sees in every opposing state a threat to its own internal distribution of power, independence and even physical existence. The result of the 'clinch' is that each side constantly tries to improve its power potential and strategic chances in any future warlike encounter. Every increase in the power chances of one side, however slight, will be perceived by the other side as a weakening and a setback in its own position. Within the framework of this figuration it *will* constitute a setback. So counter moves will be set in motion as the weakened side attempts to improve its chances; and these in turn will provoke the first side to make its own countermoves. (Elias, 1970: 169–70)

The parallels between this figuration and that depicted by Elias much earlier in the elimination contest between small territories in Europe are evident, but now the scale is world-wide. Indeed the boundaries between opposing power groups are no longer simply geographical lines. Throughout the world, and especially in the poorer countries of the Third World, states' internal axes of tension fall into line, as if in a magnetic field, with the axes of tension between the great powers. It is particularly clear in the case of revolutionary and counter-revolutionary movements in the republics of South America (1970: 169). Every fluctuation in power chances — between Sandinistas and Contras, for example — disturbs the balance of tensions between the great power blocs, representing a potential gain to one side, a potential loss to the other. Moreover, these struggles have economic consequences:

In highly developed and relatively prosperous societies, the dialectical threat of force does not hinder, and may even positively promote, further development and increasing social wealth; yet in any poor country the polarisation of dedicated revolutionaries and counter-revolutionaries usually leads only to further impoverishment. On close examination, aid from the great powers proves to be a mere palliative. Basically it is meant not so much to assist the development of the countries concerned as to gain supporters for one side or the other. (1970: 171)

The rather bleak view found in Elias's later writings has not gone unquestioned. Using many of Elias's own ideas, Godfried van Benthem van den Bergh (1983, 1990) has arrived at a lower estimate of the chances that the rivalry between the superpowers will end in nuclear war. He argues that nuclear weapons have unintended benefits: they force the great powers to conduct themselves in a much more prudent and restrained manner than in prenuclear times,[3] and *may* possibly come to serve, in the absence of anything yet resembling a world government, as a functional equivalent at the international level of the central monopoly of violence held by states.

Both Benthem van den Bergh and Elias (1987b: 74–115) see the risk of a nuclear holocaust arising not because any group of people with the means to do so seriously wants to bring about such a war, but because the bi-polar struggle between the superpowers has assumed the form of a *double-bind figuration*. The compelling force of such an unplanned social process cannot be understood simply in voluntaristic terms — that is, in terms of the perceptions, plans and intentions of one side or the other considered alone. For the perceptions, plans and intentions of each side are in considerable part formed in response to the perceptions, plans and intentions of the other. The two sides are bound together in interdependence through the danger they pose each other. Moreover, a double-bind figuration tends to be self-escalating, not just because each accumulates more and better arms in response to the other's accumulation of arms, but also for a reason more characteristic of Elias's thinking: the reciprocal danger enhances the emotive fantasy and unrealistic ideology on both sides.

Elias's thinking about 'hegemonial fevers' in inter-state conflicts is linked in fact to two other elements in his work which at first glance may not seem relevant here: his theory of involvement and detachment in the development of knowledge and the sciences (1987b; see also Mennell, 1989: 159–99) and his theory of established-outsiders relationships (Elias and Scotson, 1965; Elias, 1976; Mennell, 1989: 115–39). The emotional fantasies and beliefs of the antagonists in relation to each other play as major a part in keeping the double-bind process going as does the competitive circularity in the development of weapons. Each side's they-image involves a distortion of the vices of the other side, just as its we-image is an exaggerated picture of virtue. (In *The Established and the Outsiders* [1965], Elias and Scotson depicted the process of distortion in the microcosm of a local community, where a dominant faction viewed itself in relation to an outsider group through the distorting lens of a 'minority of the best' and a 'minority of the worst' respectively.) Relaxation of the double-bind process may just be possible because fear of the bomb may outweigh the fear and hatred of the enemy; but it can only be very slowly achieved because it requires 'a change in the mentality of both sides, a higher level of detachment and self-control in their dealings with one another'. And this is extremely difficult because

> If the danger which one group of humans represents for the other is high, the emotivity of thinking, its fantasy-content, is also likely to remain high. If the fantasy-content of thinking and knowledge is high and thus its reality-orientation low, the ability of both sides to bring the situation under control will also remain low, the danger level and the level of fear will remain high, and so on *ad infinitum*. (Elias, 1987b: 99).

Nevertheless, the very existence of nuclear weapons since 1945 made the hegemonial fevers of the Cold War somewhat different from the many earlier ones. In contrast to all former weapons, which made the fighting and winning of wars possible, nuclear weapons have, as Bernard Brodie put it, only 'utility in non-use', for the prevention of war. The situation has been summed up as 'Mutually Assured Destruction', or MAD for short. But, says Benthem van den Bergh, the iron embrace of the nuclear powers is not so mad at all, and certainly the least mad of all the ways of thinking about nuclear weapons and strategic situations between great powers. *Nuclear weapons may thus have begun to function as an external constraint towards self-restraint* in international relations. Benthem van den Bergh sees an analogy with the civilizing process depicted by Elias within states. Peaceful conduct within states is not a gift from God: it requires the ever-present threat of the state's monopoly of violence, even if that threat, at least in Western Europe, has been pushed more and more into the background. In inter-state relations, nuclear weapons are the only conceivable alternative to a world monopoly of violence. The MAD balance may have acquired a civilizing function in international politics: it forces the political and military establishments of the great powers to restrain themselves and to act with great care and circumspection. Mutually Assured Destruction exerts pressures towards Mutually Expected Self-Restraint (in Goudsblom's phrase). Possibly the most graphic illustration of the 'civilizing' functions of MAD is the extra-ordinary lengths to which both sides have gone to eliminate the possibility of the accidental or unauthorized use of nuclear weapons. The common interests of the nuclear oligopolists, argues Benthem van den Bergh, may lead to their acting as an external constraint *forcing* other states to behave peacefully; but in the longer term, the existence of a functional equivalent for the central monopoly of the state could become a social constraint towards self-restraint, as it will change states' expectations of each other's conduct. He does not see this as *likely*, but as the only *possible* way in which a peaceful world can emerge.

Elias remains sceptical of this argument, even as far as it goes. His scepticism seems to stem in effect from the conclusion he drew at the end of *The Civilising Process*, that 'wars between smaller units have been, in the course of history up to now, inevitable stages and instruments in the pacification of larger ones' (1939: Vol. II, 331). He is inclined to dwell on the continuities between pre-nuclear and nuclear times; the dangers inherent in inter-state double-binds remain the same. Benthem van den Bergh in contrast emphasizes the differences. Before the nuclear age there were always pressures and incentives towards integration on a higher level through war, because there was always a potential threat from still other larger survival units outside. Now, with the factual integration of humanity as a whole in a world-wide system of tensions, there are no larger survival units outside the great powers regime to provide that incentive. And nuclear weapons make development to a higher level of integration through hegemonial war impossible: a nuclear war would result in a regression to a much lower level of integration.

Current developments in Eastern Europe may possibly lend support to Benthem van den Bergh, though the sheer speed of events may make both parties to the discussion seem unrealistically cautious in their estimate of the possibilities of the pacification of the global society. Time will tell: this, of all things, requires a longer term perspective than that of the instant commentator.

Conclusions: Micro/Macro Relationships

One of the *Leitmotive* of Norbert Elias's thinking is the long-term integration of humanity and the obstacles it encounters. He has tackled the subject from the earliest beginnings in the smallest survival units to the present tight mesh of inter-state and intra-state tensions worldwide, when humanity perhaps stands at a saddle point: the possibility of global pacification on the one side, and on the other the chances of destruction through nuclear holocaust or ecological disaster — both produced by the globalization of human interdependencies.

Elias's most historically detailed studies are of the middle phases of the process in one continent. He has not produced so detailed an account of the emergence of the modern world system as

Wallerstein, for example, though there are many points of contact between their approaches. Elias is sometimes accused of paying insufficient attention to the economic components of the process, but that is unjust. It was in reaction to a prevalent overemphasis on economics that he tried to show the equal centrality of violence and its control, intermeshing with economic development and with the development of knowledge, in the overall development of human society.

That such a comprehensive vision of the long-term structural integration of human society should be found in the work of someone popularly associated mainly with the study of changing manners and social habitus ought to be no surprise. Because interdependence is Elias's central category, he has always been able to bridge the gap between micro and macro-sociology with seeming ease. Note that he always speaks of *inter*dependence, not of dependency, for power relations are always bipolar or multipolar, and power ratios are an aspect of all human relationships from the most microscopic to the most macroscopic. Because Elias thinks of power in terms of flexible, labile, balances often changing in a discernible direction over time, he is able to bypass such debates as that concerning the definition of the periphery, semi-periphery and core in which world-systems theorists have tended to become bogged down. He seeks process theories in which 'the processes come into the foreground, with 'phases' or 'stages' no longer defined as stationary states but in terms of the very processes of which they are part and through which they are generated' (Goudsblom, 1989a: 18; cf. Mennell, 1989: 176–81). I would therefore argue that, if Elias's own writing about the globalization of human society has centred mainly on the chances of nuclear war, there is much in his underlying theoretical strategy of great value to others in investigating many other aspects of global society. To reach for just one example, a topic to which Elias himself has not returned since his earliest work, what about the prospects for the globalization of manners? After all, he began his study of the European civilizing process from the observation that the notion of civilization represented the self-satisfaction of Europeans in a colonialist age. What are the implications now for a world-wide civilizing process, considered as changes in ways of demanding and showing respect, when Europe and Europe-over-the-ocean no longer occupy the hegemonic position? Or do they?

Notes

1. Here and elsewhere Elias avoids using the word 'evolution' except in a strictly biological context; he prefers to speak of 'development' in a social context, to underline the very great differences between biological and social processes. Other writers, however, either do not make the distinction, or use the terminology in an opposite sense. For example, Stephen K. Sanderson in a recent paper (1989) and a forthcoming book (1990) argues for what he calls 'evolutionism without developmentalism'. Although I entirely agree with his argument — like Elias, he is pursuing a non-teleological, non-unilinear form of what I would call developmental theory — he employs the two words 'evolutionism' and 'developmentalism' in precisely the reverse sense to Elias's usage. That is, I think, because Robert Nisbet (1969) made 'developmentalism' a dirty word among American sociologists, whereas in the world of British anthropology and sociology the same connotations have remained attached to 'evolutionism'. The nomenclature is confusing, but in the underlying argument there is no disagreement.

2. It is pointless to list separately Elias's writings on the early origins of human-kind and on the present-day superpower balance, since he so often deals with both topics within the same book or article. Relevant sources are: *What is Sociology?* (1970: 138–9, 155, 168–72); *Humana Conditio* (1985); *Die Gesellschaft der Individuen* (1987a: 218–26); *Involvement and Detachment* (1987b), especially pp. vii–xv of the Introduction written for the English edition, and pp. 74–115 of the essay 'The Fishermen in the Maelstrom'; 'The retreat of sociologists into the present' (1987d). See also Haferkamp (1987), Mennell (1987) and Mennell (1989: 217–23).

3. At least in their direct dealings with each other; and their use of surrogates in countries throughout the world, to which Elias alluded in the passage just quoted, is itself in part a manifestation of the restraint enjoined on them in direct dealings.

References

Benthem van den Bergh, Godfried van (1983) 'Two Scorpions in a Bottle: The Unintended Benefits of Nuclear Weapons', pp. 191–9 in William Page (ed.), *The Future of Politics*. London: Frances Pinter.

Benthem van den Bergh, Godfried van (1990) *The Taming of the Great Powers*. Aldershot: Gower.

Elias, Norbert (1939) *The Civilising Process*. Vol. I, *The History of Manners*, Oxford: Basil Blackwell, 1978. Vol. II, *State Formation and Civilisation* [USA: *Power and Civility*], Oxford: Basil Blackwell, 1982 (orig. German edition 1939).

Elias, Norbert (1970) *What is Sociology?* London: Hutchinson, 1978 (orig. German edition 1970).

Elias, Norbert (1976) 'Een theoretisch essay over gevestingen en buitenstaanders', in N. Elias and John L. Scotson, *De Gevestingen en de Buitenstaanders*. Utrecht: het Spectrum (English orig. *The Established and the Outsiders*, London: Cass, 1965).

Elias, Norbert (1985) *Humana Conditio: Beobachtungen zur Entwicklung der Menschheit am 40. Jahrestag eines Kriegsendes (8 Mai 1985)*. Frankfurt: Suhrkamp.

Elias, Norbert (1987a) *Die Gesellschaft der Individuen*. Frankfurt: Suhrkamp.

Elias, Norbert (1987b) *Involvement and Detachment*. Oxford: Basil Blackwell.

Elias, Norbert (1987c) 'On Human Beings and Their Emotions: A Process-Sociological Essay', *Theory, Culture & Society* 4 (2–3): 339–61.

Elias, Norbert (1987d) 'The Retreat of Sociologists into the Present', *Theory Culture & Society* 4 (2–3): 223–47.

Elias, Norbert and Scotson, John L. (1965) *The Established and the Outsiders*. London: Frank Cass.

Festinger, Leon (1983) *The Human Legacy*. New York: Columbia University Press.

Gellner, Ernest (1988) *Plough, Sword and Book: The Structure of Human History*. London: Collins Harvill.

Goudsblom, Johan (1989a) 'Human History and Long-term Social Processes: Towards a Synthesis of Chronology and "Phaseology"', pp. 11–25 in J. Goudsblom, E.L. Jones and Stephen Mennell, *Human History and Social Process*. Exeter: University of Exeter Press.

Goudsblom, Johan (1989b) 'The Formation of Military-agrarian Regimes', pp. 79–92 in J. Goudsblom, E.L. Jones and Stephen Mennell, *Human History and Social Process*. Exeter: University of Exeter Press.

Haferkamp, Hans (1987) 'From the Intra-state to the Inter-state Civilising Process', *Theory, Culture & Society* 4 (2–3): 545–7.

McNeill, William A. (1982) *The Pursuit of Power: Technology, Armed Force and Society since AD 1000*. Chicago: University of Chicago Press.

Mann, Michael (1986) *The Sources of Social Power*, Vol. I. Cambridge: Cambridge University Press.

Mennell, Stephen (1987) 'Comment on Haferkamp', *Theory, Culture & Society* 4 (2–3): 559–61.

Mennell, Stephen (1989) *Norbert Elias, Civilisation and the Human Self-Image*. Oxford: Basil Blackwell.

Nisbet, Robert A. (1969) *Social Change and History*. New York: Oxford University Press.

Sanderson, Stephen K. (1989) 'Evolutionism without Developmentalism: Two Models of Explanation in Theories of Social Evolution', paper presented at American Sociological Association Annual Meeting, San Francisco, 12 August.

Sanderson, Stephen K. (1990) *Social Evolutionism: A Critical History*. Cambridge, MA: Basil Blackwell.

Taagepera, Rein (1978) 'Size and Duration of Empires: Systematics of Size', *Social Science Research* 7: 108–27.

Worsley, Peter (1984) *The Three Worlds: Culture and World Development*. London: Weidenfeld and Nicolson.

Stephen Mennell is Professor of Sociology at Monash University, Melbourne. His latest books are *Norbert Elias, Civilisation and the Human Self-Image* (Blackwell, 1989) and *Human History and Social Process* (with Johan Goudsblom and E.L. Jones, University of Exeter Press, 1989).

Privatization and the Public Influence of Religion in Global Society

Peter F. Beyer

Since at least the 1960s, many sociologists have put forward the notion that religion in the contemporary Western world has become increasingly privatized. Most prominently, Talcott Parsons (1966: 134), Peter Berger (1967: 133f.), Thomas Luckmann (1967: 103), and Robert Bellah (1970: 43) interpreted secularization in the modern world to mean that traditional religion was now primarily the concern of the individual and had therefore lost much of its 'public' relevance. People were voluntary adherents to a plurality of religions, none of which could claim practically to be binding on any but its own members.

While there are certainly important variations on this core idea, here cannot be the place to engage in a proper comparison (see Dobbelaere, 1984; 1985). Instead, in what follows, I concentrate on Niklas Luhmann's version, not only because I believe it addresses certain problems inherent in others, but principally because it allows a clear examination of the problems and potential of religion in contemporary global society.[1] The thesis that I explore posits that the *globalization of society, while structurally favouring privatization in religion, also provides fertile ground for the renewed public influence of religion*. By public influence, I mean that one or more religions can become the source of collective obligation, such that deviation from specific religious norms will bring in its wake negative consequences for adherents and non-adherents alike; and collective action in the name of these norms becomes legitimate.

This thesis depends on a specific analysis of privatization. Therefore, I begin by looking at Luhmann's analysis of privatization. The operative Luhmannian distinctions used in this analysis are those between professional and complementary social roles and between religious function and performance. I explain these terms below. I argue that, in so far as privatization refers to the rise of pluralistic

Theory, Culture & Society (SAGE, London, Newbury Park and New Delhi), Vol. 7 (1990), 373–395

religion among individuals, it reflects basic structures in modern society, structures which in themselves do not undermine the possibility of publicly influential religion. The problem of public influence is then broken up into three interconnected arguments. First, if religion is to be publicly influential, it is not enough that there be a high level of individual religiosity which adherents then translate into religiously inspired public action. It is also not enough that religious leaders and professionals form and concentrate that religiosity in organizations and movements which institutionalize religion. This is a prerequisite for religion as such, not just publicly influential religion. What is required for publicly influential religion is, at a minimum, that religious leaders have control over a service which is clearly indispensable in today's world as do, for instance, health professionals, political leaders, scientific or business experts. Second, the globalization of society significantly alters the ways that religion can attain such public influence. A global society has no outsiders who can serve as the social representatives of evil. Without these, the forces of good also become more difficult to identify, undermining, for instance, deontological moral codes and the salience of other-worldly salvation. Third, therefore, religion will have a comparatively difficult time in gaining public influence at the level of global society as a whole; but such influence will be easier to attain if religious leaders apply traditional religious modalities for the purpose of sub-societal, political mobilization *in response to the globalization of society*.

A Luhmannian View of Privatization

In key ways, Luhmann's social theory agrees with that of Parsons, Berger, and Luckmann. All four see institutional differentiation and pluralistic individual identities as basic features of modern society. The institutional spheres, which Luhmann calls functionally differentiated societal sub-systems, specialize around specific kinds of action, for instance, political or economic. Secularization is the consequence of the relative independence of these sub-systems from religious norms, values, and justifications. Luhmann, however, goes on to say that, in this socio-structural setting, religion not only retreats somewhat from many important aspects of social life, but also comes under persistent pressure to develop an institutionally specialized sub-system of its own. As with Berger, Luckmann, and Parsons, traditional religion suffers the fate of compartmentalization; but, with Luhmann, in principle not more so than other major functional areas of life, such as the political and economic ones.

The Luhmannian position begins to make a distinct contribution to the privatization debate when one looks at a central structural feature of these societal sub-systems: the differentiation of 'professional' and 'complementary' roles (see Luhmann, 1982a: 236; Dobbelaere, 1985: 381f). These roles are critical for structuring the relations of individuals to the major institutional domains. In the communally structured societies of the past, individuals belonged to specific status groups. Such membership largely predetermined access to societal functions: access to wealth, power, knowledge, religious status. To a great extent, it also determined the 'professions' a person could follow. In modern, functionally structured society, this way of determining the access of individuals to societal functions becomes problematic because it negates that dominance of functional differentiation. How, for instance, can economic rationality dominate in the economy if, not only the ability to pay, but also group membership determines who can be a customer? If functionally specialized institutional sub-systems are to be the prime structural features of a society instead of status groups, then status group membership cannot on its own determine access to societal functions. Something else has to do this. Accordingly, modern society has developed what Luhmann calls complementary social roles. As in past societies, an individual usually only occupies one of the specialized professional roles such as doctor, politician, entrepreneur, or priest; but now s/he also occupies an inclusive set of complementary roles such as patient, voter, consumer, or believer, one for each sub-system. These mediate access to the benefits of functions. Since, however, unlike with professional roles, the same given person can occupy all these complementary roles, the functional interference implicit in this concentration presents a problem similar to group membership: it threatens the relative independence of the major functional sub-systems. It is apparently too much to expect individuals to neutralize this implicit interference themselves in any consistent way. Individual persons do not necessarily divide their consciousness in the same way that society divides its communication, although some parallels exist (cf. Berger, 1979). A functional equivalent is therefore found in the statistical neutralization, as it were, of the consequences of this interference. We come to see many of the decisions involved in these complementary roles as a 'private' as opposed to a 'public' matter. Such privatization of decision-making accepts that we sometimes do consume according to religious conviction or cast our vote on the basis of aesthetic criteria; but such overlapping is in principle nobody's business but our own.[2] Hence, the individual pattern of interference becomes more difficult to communicate to the point of statistical or public significance.

From the Luhmannian point of view, then, privatization of decision-making is a consequence of central structural features of modern society. In principle, it does not refer more to religion than it does to politics or the economy. Especially in Western, First World portions of global society, individuals voluntarily choose their religious convictions and practices as well as their political ideas and action. These may include membership in a church or party, but need not. A person may vote regularly or s/he may not; s/he may pray or not. Given that few if any observers would claim that such privatization makes politics a minor player in global society, it is therefore insufficient to claim that religious communication must decline in societal (i.e., public) importance simply because of the privatization of much complementary role decision-making.

Religious Leadership and Publicly Influential Religion
In the Luhmannian scheme, a corresponding professionalization of public action is as important as the privatization of complementary role decision-making. The much discussed rise of the expert in modern society reflects a socio-structural situation in which professionals become the prime public representatives of societal subsystems. Typical features of professional roles, such as standards of competence and codes of professional ethics, illustrate this capacity. The normative rules of professional competence and professional ethics both stress functional, systemic priorities in professional action. They help to differentiate personal identities, including group identities, from what the institutional system does; and so reinforce the relative independence of both the social systems and the individuals involved in them.

To be sure, societal sub-systems do not consist of professional action alone. Privatized, complementary action is still an indispensable part of the system. Yet, because professionals more closely represent what each system is all about, the public importance of a system rises or falls with the public influence of its professionals.

The meaning of this hypothesis, of course, depends on the meaning of public influence. I have given a brief definition above and treat this topic in greater detail in the section on 'Globalization and Religion' below. Here it is enough to say that public influence refers to the level of importance professional action has outside the narrower audience of fellow professionals and voluntarily associated members of the public. Privatization of religion would then, in a Luhmannian view of the matter, translate into a combination of privatized decision-making in matters of religion *plus* a relative decline in the public influence of the public representatives of the religious system, the professionals or leaders.

An illustration at this point serves to concretize the argument somewhat. The issue of professional and, therefore, system influence manifests itself well in the recent controversy over the possibility of 'cold fusion'. From the narrower viewpoint of science, the work of Professors Stanley Pons and Martin Fleischmann may have been of great significance. It challenged some important prevailing assumptions in the fields of chemistry and physics. Yet what vaulted this issue onto the front pages of the world's newspapers was not the disputed scientific discovery as such, but its potential implications for everyone, including those uninvolved in science. The potential *applications* of this bit of pure scientific research are what give it its overriding public importance. And by extension, it is such far-reaching applications that lend the scientists and the entire science system their public influence. If their work had withstood the onslaught of scientific scrutiny, individuals, corporations, institutions, and countries that ignored or denied the new scientific norm would have faced possible negative sanctions ranging from loss of prestige to economic downturn. Even though Pons and Fleischmann were probably wrong, the episode demonstrates the power of the system that they represent as professionals.

The question for religion and religious leaders is under what circumstances will we all listen to the new revelation or the revival of the old? The answer cannot lie in religion doing what science does, what the economy does, or what any of the other specialized functional spheres do for us. The effectiveness of this specialization, what Parsons called adaptive upgrading, is, after all, one of the key benefits of the socio-structural shift to functional differentiation. The answer must therefore lie within the domain of religion itself. Like science, the economy, or the health system, religion must provide a service which not only supports and enhances the religious faith of its adherents, but also can impose itself by having far-reaching implications outside the strictly religious realm.

Part, but only part, of the answer lies in the strength of the religious institutions themselves: individual religiosity and organizational strength are essential if religion is to be a viable social force at all. Nevertheless, if the influence of religion is to go beyond the organizations and their immediate adherents, more has to happen. It is in this context that contemporary religio-political movements are of particular interest. They are explicit attempts to create the sort of public influence for religion that I am talking about. Whether in Latin America, North America, the Middle East, or elsewhere, these movements and their leaders assert that religious norms and values must to some degree be made collectively binding; that they go beyond the choices of individuals. These movements imply that religion offers a service that is necessary for everyone, and that is not the same or similar to what is offered, for instance, by the economic sphere or the scientific sphere.

The critical problem, of course, is to know what, sociologically, this essential religious service is. Answers such as 'ultimate meaning' (e.g., Bellah, 1970; Berger, 1967) or 'compensators for unavailable rewards' (Stark and Bainbridge, 1987) beg the question as to whether and under what social conditions these things are essential. Claiming that religion integrates societies, as does the Durkheimian tradition in sociology, makes the empirically unwarranted assumption that religion does or even can perform this task. I address this issue in some detail in the section on 'Globalization and Religion' below. Before proceeding to this, however, it is necessary to introduce a further Luhmannian distinction that plays an important role in subsequent arguments. It is already implicit in many of the preceding arguments about the possibility for public influence of religion in modern society.

Function and Performance

As noted, for Luhmann, the central structural feature of modern society is differentiation on the basis of function. Institutional spheres cluster around particular kinds of social action on the basis of relatively autonomous functional rationalities. These sub-systems include polity, economy, science, religion, law, education, art, health, and the family. The autonomy that each of them exhibits is real enough, but it is heavily conditioned by the fact that many other systems are also operating in the same social milieu. The above discussion of complementary and professional roles outlined a central structural feature of this 'both autonomous and conditioned'. One important theoretical consequence is that there is a difference between how a sub-system relates to the society as a whole and how it relates to other sub-systems. Luhmann analyses the former in terms of *function* and the latter in terms of *performance*. In the present context, function refers to 'pure' religious communication, variously called the aspect of devotion and worship (cf. Parsons, 1967: 393ff.), the cure of souls, the search for enlightenment, or salvation. Function is the pure, 'sacred' communication about the transcendent and the aspect that religious institutions claim for themselves, the basis of their autonomy in modern society. Religious performance, by contrast, occurs when religion is 'applied' to problems generated in other systems but not solved there (cf. Luhmann, 1977: 54ff; 1982a: 238–42). Examples of such problems are economic poverty, political oppression, or familial estrangement. Through performance, religion establishes its importance for the 'profane' aspects of life; but in so doing, non-religious concerns impinge upon pure religiousness, expressing the fact that other societal concerns condition the autonomy of religious action.

Function and performance are more than analytic categories dependent on Luhmannian theory for their importance. A real tension exists between the two. Historically, various religious institutions have sought to effect a clear separation between them. In Weber's terms, ascetic and mystic rejections of the world have sought to eliminate mundane demands from the purely sacred realm. The medieval church considered the ascetic monk on a surer road to salvation than those immersed in profane life; the elder Hindu, having completed his duty of raising his family, retired to the forest for the proper pursuit of religious goals. Nevertheless, function and performance are also inseparable and mutually reinforcing. Indeed, it is only in modern society and in the leisured upper classes of some traditional stratified societies that the two become clearly differentiated at all. Buddhism, for instance, did not become a world religion until it compromised its religious purity and made itself suitable for life in the everyday world. In modern times, the practical Catholic orders involved in education, public welfare, and health care were instrumental in allowing the Roman church to maintain its influence in predominantly Catholic areas such as Latin America, Quebec, and the Netherlands (see, for example, Mainwaring, 1985; Levine, 1981; Beyer, 1989b; Coleman, 1979).

This last example illustrates the critical importance of performance relations for religion in the modern world. As the example of

Pons and Fleischmann from the science system implies, the *functional* problem of religion in the modern world is actually a *performance* problem, but one exacerbated, if not caused, by the peculiarities of the religious function. Therefore, if 'pure' religion is at a disadvantage in modern global society, if it is becoming increasingly privatized, then a possible solution lies in finding effective religious 'applications'.

A further consideration concerns the role morality plays in the relation between religious function and performance. In the past as in the present, most religious traditions have linked religious communication and social problems through moral codes. The moralization of religion, or the development of a religious ethic, has allowed the interpretation of social problems as consequences of sin, ignorance, or similar contravention of religious norms. Conforming to these norms then becomes the solution to the social problems. Establishing religious performance through moral codes is, however, strictly dependent for its effectiveness on social structures that favour morality as a privileged form of social regulation. The frequently heard lament that our society is becoming increasingly immoral or amoral points to the fact that modern circumstances do not favor morality in this way. Business people put profit and market share ahead of moral considerations. Politicians lie, mislead, and otherwise compromise their principles in order to get and maintain power. Yet religious leaders continue to talk about sin, whether personal or social. The privatization and loss of public influence of religion are closely connected with the similar fate of morality. It is to a discussion of this proposition that I now turn.

Globalization and Religion
The notion that there is a religious system which is functionally differentiated within and out of modern society really only takes on its complete significance when one appreciates that this differentiation is intimately connected with the globalization of society. We cannot separate the secularization of modern society from its globalization. Here cannot be the place for a proper elaboration of this admittedly important statement (cf. Luhmann, 1982b; 1984). Suffice it to say that centering much communication around specific functions instead of specific groups of people (status groups) results in greater wealth, more effective political power, more sophisticated technology — in short, communication which breaks through geographic barriers until no unaffected population remains on

earth. The question of concern here is what does this imply for religion in general and for the task of religious leaders and their organizations in particular?

In Luhmannian theory, the characteristic communication of each modern functional sub-systems revolves around a central dichotomy which is also the focus of professionalization (cf. Luhmann, 1977: 193ff.). These dichotomies consist of a positive term and its negative opposite. Thus, for instance, the world of science operates with true/false, the economy with owning/not owning, art with beautiful/ugly (or, perhaps, inspiring/uninspiring). In religion, immanence/transcendence takes this place (see Luhmann, 1977: 46; 1987). Here, however, the situation is complicated by the holistic view of religion: just as religious commitment implies the whole person, so the religious dichotomy uses the whole world as its positive term, immanence. In other words, the world that, for instance, science approaches with the difference between true and false statements, religion identifies as the immanent. However, since the whole cannot as such be the topic of communication or the object of consciousness — i.e., it does not distinguish itself from anything that is not itself — the transcendent functions to give it definition. But, as every major religious tradition shows only too clearly, the transcendent is not anything which can be talked about except in immanent terms. Hence religion always deals with the simultaneity of immanence and transcendence, as in the Middle Eastern concept of divine creation or the Hindu concept of maya.

The only stable solution to this fundamental religious problem is to specify the transcendent in terms of immanent categories, especially those that structure social groups and social relationships (cf. Durkheim, 1965: 462ff.; Douglas, 1970; 1975). People see the rules that govern their everyday lives as reflective of the cosmic order. Bad things happen to them to the degree that they fail to live up to the ethical and ritualistic requirements of the cosmos through their social relationships (cf. Weber, 1978: 529ff.; Berger, 1967: 24f.). This close association of social and cosmic rules obtains in pre-literate societies, in traditional societies, and in modern global society. It also holds regardless of whether one is talking about conservative or transformative religion. The key point is that the cosmic order, however conceived, is ipso facto universally applicable. Since human beings have no choice but to express this universal order in terms of a particular social order, that social order becomes the battleground between ideal and real, expectation and disappointment, good and evil. Religion and its quest for 'salvation' (harmony, enlightenment, happiness) are then what life is all about. The problem of religious influence arises only when religion tries to encompass too many lives that are manifestly 'about' different things.

Historical and anthropological data show that there are many different ways to structure social existence, and hence many different constructions of cosmic order. This variety does not present great problems as long as communication between societies is restricted and internal variety is limited. When these have occurred, older societies have solved both these problems by emphasizing the boundaries between social groups. Differences in religious expression, including the behaviour that this implied, were one of the principal ways of drawing or maintaining these boundaries. Using terms more suited to the modern context, one can say that to be a member of a particular societal group was to be an adherent of that group's religion. In more complex older societies divided into stratified status groups, religious membership and social group membership were still more often than not identical; but the dominant status groups, in an effort to bolster and express their control over a greater social diversity, usually attempted to style their religion as definitive for the society as a whole, often in the form of an overarching cosmology that made the norms and values of the upper strata, that is, their moral code, the presumptive standard for all behaviour. Group membership and its defining norms were still intimately related to cosmic order; but now this association claimed to be relevant and binding for a far wider variety of actual life-worlds. The resulting pressure towards abstraction and generalization of the moral code produced more unified and hierarchical cosmologies, first in the form of hierarchical pantheons with the good gods at the top; then increasingly in the form of monotheistic or henotheistic views. These either identified the morally good with the transcendent as in the Abrahamic religions; and thereby more thoroughly moralized religion. Or they posited a 'transmoral' realm beyond good and evil as in the Tao, Brahman, or Nirvana. The esoteric, mystical, and socially elitist nature of these latter concepts indicates that too great an abstraction from specific group moral rules yields a religion with limited influence in the larger society (cf. Stark and Bainbridge, 1987: 113–15). Here, moreover, as in the ascetic and mystical movements of the West, religious function and performance were becoming clearly differentiated for the first time, foreshadowing the problem of religion in modern society.

The close association between moral codes, group membership, and religion in pre-modern societies did not solve the problem of inter-group or inter-societal conflict. Rather it merely structured it. Religion's role in this structuring was often critical. In situations where one societal group threatened another, or where there was simply competition, the enemy could be interpreted as the embodiment of evil, as the negation of the correct relationship between social order and the transcendent that one's own group represented. In justifying the conflict, religion promoted the survival or expansion of the group and its culture.

An example from traditional Christian theology can both illustrate what I have said thus far, and carry the argument further. Here, a personal, good God represents the unity of the immanent/transcendent distinction through his creation. The characteristics of this unity are relevant for human beings through moral behaviour that is conceived in terms of the affirmation or denial of the fundamental immanent/transcendent relation: i.e., God and his rule over creation. The possibility of affirmation or denial is represented in the first instance by the possibility of salvation or damnation, both dependent again on the quality of individual behaviour. The individual soul, the personalization of this overall quality (however determined), stands before judgement on the basis of its moral character. The possibility of denial or evil is personified in the devil, who embodies evil not simply as immoral behavior but as the denial of the dependence of the immanent on the transcendent and thus its unity and thus God. The key to the viability of the entire picture is the assumption that we can expect everyone to live more or less by the same moral code. S/he who does not, for whatever reason, acknowledge and live by this code denies God. Such a person is the morally and religiously other, the outcast, the one beyond the pale, concretized and made visible in the existence of true outsiders, whether Jews, barbarians, Saracens, or simply the enemy who personifies or carries the marks of the devil. To the extent that outsiders have the opportunity to become insiders, they can be 'saved' not simply by abstract morally good behaviour, but only by religious conversion (cf. Luhmann, 1987).

The consistent characterization of the transcendent as source and guarantor of the group's moral norms made it possible to give Satan this unequivocal, personal persence. And Satan was essential to show the importance of God and salvation. The religious leaders of traditional Christian society could represent threats to the group as outside threats, whether by actual outsiders or their imputed moral counterparts within the society. By tying the pure religious goal of salvation to a particular social order in this way, they also assured the relevance of religious norms and hence their own influence.

The societal shift to the primacy of functional differentiation undermined this symbiosis. The autonomy of functionally specific rationalities runs counter to a priority of communal group boundaries. For example, in societies where communal boundaries prevail, people eat according to the traditional norms of their group culture. What we do and what is good for us are the same thing. In modern society, whether one eats rice or potatoes with chopsticks or a fork are incidental or voluntary, privatized choices. On a public level, health considerations, universally applicable to all people, take priority. The resultant globalizing tendencies of society have radically altered the conditions under which the moralizing solution is still possible *on the level of society as a whole*, because the group now includes everyone. The situation of religion in global society alters correspondingly. S/he who used to be the unequivocal outsider is now often literally my neighbor, whether I approve or not. The outside/inside distinction readily at hand for reinforcing the internal moral codes of communal, and hence territorial, societies becomes at least difficult to maintain over the long run in a world of virtually instant global communication, itself a consequence of institutional specialization. Not only does the leader of the 'evil empire' reveal himself to be less than totally evil when met face to face; more importantly, it is increasingly difficult not to meet with him, not for moral reasons, but for primarily political and economic ones. In the process, morality has lost its central structural position. Translated into more theological language, the globalization of society does not lead to the death of God, as some theologians of the 1960s asserted. God is still in his heaven and his will still rules the world; but the visage of the devil is becoming increasingly indistinct. The result is that God can still be loved, but it is more difficult to fear him. He is still there, but does he make a difference? Is salvation still essential; or will it become the privatized proclivity of a minority, similar and not superior to other leisure pursuits? On the global level, the problem of specifying the transcendent and thus giving the central religious dichotomy meaningful definition must be addressed anew.

With this development, a prime historical solution to the problem of specifying the transcendent has been undermined, although only on the level of society as a whole. The conditions and implications of using the old solution have been altered. Religion and, in the current context, religious professionals are therefore faced with a dilemma: whether to address the contemporary problem of religious influence without the old solution or by reasserting it.

Each of these paths has its attendant problems. In what follows, I call them the conservative and liberal options. The first would correspond to the reassertion of the reality of the devil and the second to the acquiescence in his dissolution. Using the distinction as a point of departure, I want now to examine how contemporary developments in global religion reflect the structural tendencies outlined thus far. In the process, I again take up the various themes introduced above, but specifically the notion that, regardless of which option is taken, public influence for religion will be found in the direction of religious performance; while action concentrating on religious function will continue, with certain exceptions, to be the domain of privatized, highly pluralistic religiosity.

Private Function and Public Performance

The liberal option addresses the central problem of determining the transcendent only in a very weak fashion: there is evil in the world, but it cannot be consistently and clearly localized or personified. It is a limitation in all of us, in all our social structures. It is especiallly not to be found in the fact of pluralism, including religious pluralism. If anything, the opposite is true: intolerance and particularistic ascription are a prime source of evil. Religious professionals with this attitude tend to be ecumenical and tolerant. They see comparable possibilities for enlightenment and salvation in their tradition and in other religions. The central theological problem of this option, as critics (e.g., Kelley, 1972; Berger, 1979) point out, is that it makes few really *religious* demands: it conveys little specifically religious information that would make a difference in how people choose; or that people could not get from non-religious sources.

Professional responses to this problem under the liberal option reflect the difference between function and performance outlined above. In terms of function, the tendency is to orient the organization towards helping services, including the celebration of important life passages and, of course, the 'cure of souls' for those who feel the need (cf. Bibby, 1987 for excellent Canadian data). This response accommodates itself to what the private adherents evidently want.

Function concentrates on private choices. God is preached as benevolent and not wrathful: his only real request is that people imitate
his attitude in their relations with others. Evil exists but it is a
negative deficiency to be filled and not a positive presence to be
destroyed. Moreover, religious leaders with this ecumenical attitude
have picked up the universalistic orientations of elitist strains in the
major world religions: the possibility of enlightenment for all, the
possibility of wisdom for all, the possibility of salvation for all.
Now, however, as part of the globalization process, everyone is
included, and not just upper strata virtuosi with the leisure for such
functional specialization. The combination of pluralism and inclusion excludes very few from the virtually automatic benefits of the
religious function.

Religious leaders and organizations that follow the liberal option
therefore have difficulty in specifying both the benefits and the
requirements of religion in functional or 'pure' form. This indeterminacy has led them to a reliance on performance relations to re-
establish the importance of religion and hence the influence of the
religious system. Here, often globally oriented issues ranging from
gay liberation to political oppression are providing the opportunity
to show that religion leads to benefits and demands that are far from
insignificant.

To repeat, the Luhmannian view of performance sees it as the
attempt by one system to address problems that are generated in
other sub-systems but not solved there. As such, the problems
addressed by religious performance are not religious problems at all,
at least not directly. The solutions, therefore, while religiously
inspired, will tend to take on the characteristics of the target system:
economic solutions to economic problems, political solutions to
political problems, and so forth. The attempt to conform to this
structurally encouraged pattern is characteristic of the liberal option
inasmuch as it correlates with the basic structure of modern society.
There is the conviction that educational problems are not going to be
solved by adherence to the traditional faith; that health problems
are not going to be solved by meditation, political problems not by
the correct execution of rituals. Instead, the liberal option returns to
the communitarian past of religion to define its 'application' as that
which is concerned for the community as a whole. In this modern
case, however, humanity as a whole is the community and the
religious task is to work for the fuller inclusion of all people in the
benefits of this global community (cf. O'Brien and Shannon, 1977:

117-70, 307-46). Hence religious leaders of this direction style the problems of global society in corresponding terms: conflict among various sectors of the world community is attributable in large part to the marginalization of some (often the majority) from systemic benefits like 'adequate' income, political participation, health care, education and so forth. Yet, the notion of a global community is very general and very vague, including as it does a vast variety of group cultures and individual lifestyles. The styling of the applied religion in terms of a global community in fact reflects the benign functional message of the liberal option. Combined with the respect for the independence of other systems, notably the political, this may work against such activity being recognized as specifically *religious* communication, as something that religion does for us. While this is a problem, it does not mean that such religious activity cannot be effective.

An example may help to illustrate this point. Generally, liberation theologians (and their First World parallels) represent the liberal option. They are concerned with justice and peace, values that point to the egalitarian inclusion of those marginalized from the benefits of modern institutions. This 'preferential option for the poor' rejects traditional religious interpretations in favor of a contextual theology which uses present experience as the basis for finding the correct religious understanding. Liberation theologians do not present one particular group culture and its religion as being closer to the divine will than others. While the alleged opposition of the 'poor' and 'capitalism' sometimes comes close to being an opposition between good and evil, these religious leaders generally criticize the latter for its creation of vast, global inequalities and not for being an alien world view destructive of the true and good order that one's own group represents. Accordingly, they also do not discourage religious pluralism. The critics of liberation theology accuse them of having lost the specifically religious (e.g., Ratzinger) or of offering economic and political solutions that do not accord with economic and political realities (e.g., Novak) (cf. Berryman, 1987: 179-200). One attack is in terms of function, the other in terms of performance. In fact, liberation theology places primary emphasis on religious performance. While 'pure' religious belief and practice are important, they are so only to the extent that they contribute to the alleviation of social ills, leading to an emphasis on *praxis*. Essentially, liberation theologians respond to the privatization of religion by seeking a revitalization of the religious function in religious performances, particularly in the political realm. Sin becomes primarily social and the principal religious demand is for social justice (see Baum, 1975:193ff).

Seeking to establish religious influence by linking function and performance is, of course, not new or unusual. As discussed above, all religious traditions have historically done this. In modern circumstances, however, function and performance are more clearly distinguishable because we use function as a central way of dividing social action. Therefore, if working for social justice is going to be a recognized *religious* performance, then its necessary connection with religious *function* must be apparent, just as the necessary connection between Einstein's pure scientific endeavours and the building of the atomic bomb is apparent. The criticisms of liberation theology, that it is neither good religion nor good economics, indicate a problem here. And in fact, liberation theologians rely heavily on non-religious interpretations such as dependency theory and Marxist analysis to understand the problems; and prefer explicitly political courses of action. The connection with the theology is clearly visible in the writings of its proponents; but it is anything but necessary. In this light, it should not be surprising that liberation theologians are tempted to address the problem through an increasingly 'Manichaean' opposition of the poor and capitalism, with socialism, the group culture of the poor, as the vaguely defined, communitarian goal.

I do not want to suggest with this analysis, that liberation theology is not legitimate theology. If anything, the opposite is true. The issue here is rather the position of religion in global society and how the problem of privatization reflects this position. Liberation theologians are attempting to establish public influence for religion in the face of privatization. They are doing this through religious performances that concentrate on political involvement although they do not go so far as to advocate the legislation of religious norms. One can argue, as does Phillip Berryman (1984), that they have been somewhat successful in this endeavour (but see Mainwaring, 1989). Yet, whether this strategy will lead to a re-establishment of the public influence of religious communication in general in our society is still an open question.

While performance relations under the liberal option thus offer a possibility for religion to break out of its privatized functional ghetto and back onto the political stage especially, the possibilities are limited. In addition to problems touched upon in the example of liberation theology, the pluralism permitted on the level of function implies an equal pluralism on the level of performance. Therefore, to the extent that religious leaders, such as those in North American liberal Protestant churches, can control their organizational levers and take a unified public stand on issues, to that extent they risk losing an appreciable portion of their adherents, regardless of the particular stand taken (cf. Hadden, 1970; Bibby, 1987). Mobilization becomes a serious and constant problem in this respect. In the absence of additional, non-religious measures (especially direct political involvement), religious leaders are left with the kind of persuasion that in the Christian tradition is called evangelization: reliance on voluntaristic, private decision-making with its attendant fissiparous pluralism.

In spite of this difficulty on the part of the liberal option, its religious cosmos does correlate with the structural tendencies of a global society, as the above argument has outlined. To the degree that global society continues to become a more solid reality, the liberal option might be seen as the trend of the future. In the meantime and at least for the foreseeable future, however, it is not the only possible direction.

The conservative option (the reassertion of the tradition in spite of modernity), far from being merely a throwback correlating with bygone social structures, is in fact the one that is making religion most visible in today's world. It is a vital aspect of globalization and not a negation of it. Given the direction of the preceding analysis, this assertion requires a bit of explanation.

For private faith, the conservative option implies a reassertion of the traditional view of transcendence, often explicitly as a normative response to a society ('the world') that is seemingly heading in a different and evil direction. The present analysis would confirm this impression: the conservative option has fewer problems with transcendence but finds itself in conflict with dominant trends in global social structure. Nevertheless, religious leaders and professionals who orient their organizations to this kind of private committed religiosity are basically offering a variation on the liberal functional response: accommodation to private proclivities in matters of religion but with a holistic emphasis that can but need not result in sectarian organization. Conservative religion, from this point of view, only contradicts modern social structures to the extent that it emphasizes individual, personal holism in the face of differentiated (and hence impersonal) social structures. It concentrates on religious function and tends toward privatization, with the difference that the private religious selections more often include the element of holistic commitment and concentration on community solidarity. Conservative religion on the level of function responds to some of the possible disparities between the structure of personal systems and the societal system. It therefore reflects modern structures rather than negating them.

I want to make a similar argument with respect to the performance response under the conservative option: what seems to be running against globalization and modernity is actually better seen as reflective of it, albeit in a very different way when compared with the liberal option. To explain this requires a short digression.

Globalization, in the Luhmannian context used here, does not mean the inevitable, evolutionary progress toward a global spread of Western modernity. Such developmentalism is inadequate not only because the empirical facts negate such a proposition, but also because, from the theoretical point of view, globalization should have as profound effects on the formerly territorial societies of the West as it is having on other formerly territorial civilizations around the world. Up until the middle of the twentieth century, the West may well have believed that its successful imperial expansion of the previous four centuries was essentially a one-way street. Today this illusion is rapidly revealing itself for what it is.

The resistance to, or perhaps better, digestion of globalization in various parts of the contemporary world has given rise to movements informed by the conservative religious option: political mobilization as the service (performance) of the religious faith. Whether the complaint is 'Westoxication' in the Middle East or the difficulty of 'making America great again', the problem is similar. In the West, former 'outsiders' (the Soviets, the Japanese, the Arabs et al.) are undermining the long-standing political, economic, and general cultural dominance of the West. The West can rely less and less on its economic, political (especially military), and scientific might to assure the continued hegemony of its culture. On the home front, the functional differentiation which is such a key aspect of globalization continues to bring about rapid change in the old core structures: the family, morality and religion. In the non-West, in spite of increased political independence and/or economic power in many areas, Western cultural patterns still seem to be becoming increasingly dominant. What appears to some in the West as moral, economic and political decline of their own culture, appears to many in the non-West simply as continued Western cultural, economic and political imperialism. With its clear ties to communal group cultures, both in the past and still largely in the present, religion is an obvious candidate for structuring a response to both.

Many of the religio-political movements that have sprung up in recent decades all around the world reflect this development. In the West, for example, the New Religious Right in the United States battled to restore the old Western dominance. Traditional Christian moral values, combined with an emphasis on free enterprise and vigorous defence against Communism, would restore America as the great nation God intended it to be. In the non-West various Islamic movements from Indonesia to Northern Africa, for instance, are attempting to build concrete paths toward the long desired separation of modernization from Westernization. In many of these cases, and certainly in the ones just mentioned as examples, the religious leaders consciously adopt the conservative option. Whether it is the 'Evil Empire' or the 'Great American Satan', the reappearance of the devil as that which gives definition to the transcendent signals a return to the traditional way of making religion capable of communicating publicly essential information. Far from being a mere yearning for imagined bygone days, such reassertion is a logical outcome of a globalization which has generated and continues to generate fundamental conflicts among different regions of the world.

When political and economic responses to these conflicts fail, religious performance may be able to fill the breach. Since the adherents to the various religions around the world are still by and large localized, leaders can often express regional conflicts and disparities in religious terms. Here, the conservative option, grounded as it is in traditional, communally oriented societies, offers distinct advantages. Its solution to the problem of transcendence allows an approximate dichotomization of the world into the religiously pure and impure, into us and them. Such a clear religious message can, under the correct conditions, lead to successful mobilization of entire populations. Politicization on this religious basis then becomes a way for regions to assert themselves in the face of globalization and its consequences. Hitherto, the most visible examples of such conservative religious performance movements, in the Islamic Middle East and in the Sikh Punjab, have occurred after prolonged, unsuccessful political attempts to address problems attendant upon modernization and in the wake of significant increases in regional wealth (cf. Esposito, 1987; Arjomand, 1988; Leaf, 1985; Wallace, 1988). This combination of factors is probably not accidental. The modernization that correlates with globalization is not simply benevolent, let alone egalitarian. It destroys as well as creates. The attempt to gain some transcendent perspective on this historical process is understandable, especially when immanent techniques such as purely political nationalism, socialism, open-door capitalism, secularized education, and even economic progress all seem to fail. If the necessary definition of the transcendent means applying the religious correlates of bygone social structures to the very different divisions of today, then this only indicates that contemporary structures do not offer a self-evident alternative.

Religious movements grounded in the conservative option contrast with their liberal counterparts in a number of ways. Critical among these is the conservative notion that the public influence of religion should be supported by law. Important religious norms should be enshrined in legislation; they should not have to rely on a 'demonstration effect' for their influence. The conservative religious leaders of these movements lay great stress on a particular group-cultural moral code as the manifestation of divine will. In a global social environment which is generally corrosive of group cultural boundaries and which therefore encourages religio-moral pluralism, there is little hope that one cultural outlook will prevail on the basis of its own unique merits. The alternative is to gain control over a limited territory dominated by the particular culture and then control pluralism within it. This 'nationalism' has certainly been the goal of the New Religious Right in the United States, Sikh extremists in Punjab, the politicized ultra-orthodox camp in Israel, and Islamic 'fundamentalists' in the Middle East. The first and the last of these even envisage the global spread of their group culture after the initial national success. This difference between the liberal and conservative options emphasizes the degree to which the latter uses and reinforces the segmentary and territorial differentiation within the modern global political system of states. It is another example of how the conservative direction within global religion is reflective of the structures of global society and not just a reaction against these.

Indeed, what I have been calling the conservative performance option for religion in the modern world does not at first glance seem to accord well with a primacy of functional differentiation. One of the more explicit aims of many of the movements under scrutiny is to de-differentiate many functional areas, mainly religion and politics, but also religion and the family, religion and education, and others. However, de-differentiation in the absence of an alternative structural base, such as was provided by stratified status group differentiation in older societies, is still a response to problems of globalization in terms of a primacy of function. Religious movements like the Iranian revolution want to solve over-all societal problems by giving the religious system and its values first place among the various functional spheres. Like economic dominance in the nineteenth-century West or political dominance in the People's Republic of China, a strategy which attempts to combat the effects of functional dominance under the banner of the religious system can perhaps best be seen as a critical accom-modative response to a globalism in which function dominates.[3] It may stem the tide of modernization and some of the more disruptive consequences of globalization for quite some time in particular regions, perhaps even until the global system collapses under the weight of its own internally generated problems. But it does not negate the fundamental structure of global society.

Summary and Conclusion

In sum, regardless of whether the functional dilemma regarding the basic religious dichotomy is solved in a liberal or conservative direc-tion, religion in the modern world takes on a private or a public face depending on whether one is looking at religious function or religious performance. It is, therefore, not simply a matter of greater or lesser privatization. Privatized religion continues to develop in a myriad of pluralistic directions across the full range of religious possibilities from supererogatory asceticism to eudaemo-nistic liberality, from committed sectarianism to piecemeal bricol-age. For the leaders and their organizations, religion seems to be going in one of two directions: concentration on ministering to private religious choices or entering the political and public arena. The latter direction itself contains two possibilities: an ecumenical one that looks to the global problems generated by a global, func-tionally differentiated society; and a political-movement one that champions the cultural distinctiveness of one particular region through a reappropriation of traditional religious antagonistic categories. Both represent possibilities for publicly influential reli-gion that are direct consequences of the globalization of a society which encourages increasing privatization.

394   *Theory, Culture & Society*

Notes

1. Viewing the global reality as a society is not a dominant position, but it is a key aspect of the argument I present in this article. I have outlined my reasons for this stand elsewhere and therefore will not attempt to give a fuller justification here. See Beyer (1989a).

2. I should emphasize that the complementary roles themselves are very much public; it is only the way that an individual combines decisions within those roles that is privatized.

3. For the example of Quebec, see Beyer, 1989b.

References

Arjomand, Said Amir (1988) *The Turban for the Crown: The Islamic Revolution in Iran*. New York: Oxford.

Baum, Gregory (1975) *Religion and Alienation: A Theological Reading of Sociology.* New York: Paulist.

Bellah, Robert N. (1970) 'Religious Evolution', pp. 20–50 in *Beyond Belief: Essays on Religion in a Post-Traditional World*. New York: Harper & Row.

Berger, Peter L. (1967) *The Sacred Canopy: Elements of a Sociological Theory of Religion*. Garden City: Doubleday.

Berger, Peter L. (1979) *The Heretical Imperative: Contemporary Possibilities of Religious Affirmation*. Garden City: Doubleday.

Berryman, Phillip (1984) *The Religious Roots of Rebellion: Christians in Central American Revolutions*. Maryknoll: Orbis.

Berryman, Phillip (1987) *Liberation Theology: The Essential Facts about the Revolutionary Movement in Latin America and Beyond*. New York: Pantheon.

Beyer, Peter F. (1989a) 'Globalism and Inclusion', pp. 39–53 in William H. Swatos (ed.), *Religious Politics in Global and Comparative Perspective*. Westport, CT: Greenwood.

Beyer, Peter F. (1989b) 'The Evolution of Roman Catholicism in Quebec: A Luhmannian Neo-Functionalist Interpretation', pp. 1–26 in Roger O'Toole (ed.), *Sociological Studies in Roman Catholicism*. Lewiston, NY: Mellen.

Bibby, Reginald W. (1987) *Fragmented Gods: The Poverty and Potential of Religion in Canada*. Toronto: Irwin.

Coleman, John A. (1979) *The Evolution of Dutch Catholicism*. Berkeley: University of California.

Dobbelaere, Karel (1984) 'Secularization Theories and Sociological Paradigms: Convergences and Divergences', *Social Compass* 31: 199–219.

Dobbelaere, Karel (1985) 'Secularization Theories and Sociological Paradigms: A Reformulation of the Private-Public Dichotomy and the Problem of Societal Integration', *Sociological Analysis* 46: 377–87.

Douglas, Mary (1970) *Natural Symbols: Explorations in Cosmology*. New York: Vintage.

Douglas, Mary (1975) 'Self-Evidence', pp. 276–318 in *Implicit Meanings: Essays in Anthropology*. London: Routledge & Kegan Paul.

Durkheim, Emile (1965) *The Elementary Forms of the Religious Life* (translated by Joseph Ward Swain). New York: Free Press.

Esposito, John L. (1987) *Islam and Politics*, rev. 2nd edn. Syracuse: Syracuse University.

Hadden, Jeffrey K. (1970) *The Gathering Storm in the Churches*. New York: Doubleday.

Kelley, Dean (1972) *Why Conservative Churches Are Growing*. New York: Harper & Row.

Leaf, Murray J. (1985) 'The Punjab Crisis', *Asian Survey* 25:475–98.

Levine, Daniel H. (1981) *Religion and Politics in Latin America: The Catholic Church in Venezuela and Colombia*. Princeton, NJ: Princeton University.

Luckmann, Thomas (1967) *The Invisible Religion: The Problem of Religion in Modern Society*. New York: Macmillan.

Luhmann, Niklas (1977) *Funktion der Religion*. Frankfurt: Suhrkamp.

Luhmann, Niklas (1982a) *The Differentiation of Society* (translated by Stephen Holmes and Charles Larmore). New York: Columbia.

Luhmann, Niklas (1982b) 'The World Society as a Social System', *International Journal of General Systems* 8:131–8.

Luhmann, Niklas (1984) 'The Self-Description of Society: Crisis Fashion and Sociological Theory', *International Journal of Comparative Sociology* 25:59–72.

Luhmann, Niklas (1987) 'Die Unterscheidung Gottes', pp.236–53 in *Soziologische Aufklärung 4: Beiträge zur funktionalen Differenzierung der Gesellschaft*. Opladen: Westdeutscher Verlag.

Mainwaring, Scott (1985) *The Catholic Church and Politics in Brazil 1916–1985*. Stanford: Stanford University.

Mainwaring, Scott (1989) 'Grass-Roots Catholic Groups and Politics in Brazil', pp.151–92 in Scott Mainwaring and Alexander Wilde (eds). *The Progressive Church in Latin America*. Notre Dame, IN: University of Notre Dame.

O'Brien, David J. and Shannon, Thomas A. (eds) (1977) *Renewing the Earth: Catholic Documents on Peace, Justice and Liberation*. New York: Doubleday Image.

Parsons, Talcott (1966) 'Religion in a Modern Pluralistic Society', *Review of Religious Research* 7:125–46.

Parsons, Talcott (1967) 'Christianity and Modern Industrial Society', in *Sociological Theory and Modern Society*. New York: Free Press.

Stark, Rodney and Bainbridge, William Sims (1987) *A Theory of Religion*. New York: Peter Lang.

Wallace, Paul (1988) 'Sikh Minority Attitudes in India's Federal System', pp.256–73 in Joseph T. O'Connell, et al. (eds), *Sikh History and Religion in the Twentieth Century*, Toronto: South Asian Studies, University of Toronto.

Weber, Max (1978) *Economy and Society: An Outline of Interpretive Sociology*, 2 vols, Guenther Roth and Claus Wittich (eds). Berkeley: University of California.

Peter F. Beyer is Assistant Professor in the Department of Religious Studies at the University of Toronto, Canada. He has published a translation of Niklas Luhmann's work, *Religious Dogmatics and the Evolution of Societies* and is currently completing a book on religion and globalization.

Architecture, Capital and the Globalization of Culture

Anthony King

A topic as ambitious as that indicated in my title imposes both constraints as well as obligations: constraints in that if it addresses the concerns of practitioners in architecture and urban design as well as academics in sociology, geography and cultural theory[1], it cannot be theoretically over-ambitious; obligations, in that it must, however, find a conceptual vocabulary which is available to all. Moreover, the projects of these different audiences do not necessarily coincide: architects and urban designers have to design buildings and cities (or parts of them) in a way that sociologists do not have to design societies; or not, at least, in the short term (one might say that Marx left a large number of design briefs around which, had he lived long enough to pick up the fees, would have earned him a small fortune).

But the task of developing a common conceptual framework and vocabulary is clearly an urgent and important task. Architects, planners, urban designers, indeed all those professions which deal with the realities of the built environment, need (and in many cases, also want) to understand questions concerning, for example, the long-term economic, social or political outcomes of particular design policies or decisions, or the meaning of different building forms in various cultures, or issues relating to the social organization of space, whether at the level of the building or of the city. It is only quite recently, however, that social theorists have begun to take a serious interest in such questions (at a theoretical, not an applied level) and many of the debates are still confined to questions of 'space', 'social relations and spatial structures' and do not address, as I shall discuss below, a more differentiated notion of the built environment and its relation to a vast array of social processes.

The larger problem I want to address can be put, in over-simplified terms, in the form of three questions:

Theory, Culture & Society (SAGE, London, Newbury Park and New Delhi), Vol. 7 (1990), 397–411

1. What is the role of the multi-faceted forces of international capital (economic, political, technological, social), and the built environments which they help to produce, in contributing to the homogenization of culture on a global scale?

This hypothetical question can be broken down into two more specific issues:

2. What is the role of the physical and spatial built environment in contributing to a globalization of culture?

Here, I am suggesting that 'globalization' can mean either the creation of homogeneity (where everything becomes the same) or, following Robertson (1987), the creation of heterogeneity (or difference) as *a response to* globalization. I am subsuming under the word 'culture' both the material culture of the built environment itself as well as the systems of meaning, action and symbolic forms with which this is connected.

3. What is the more specific role of architecture, urban planning and design, understood as distinctive, professional cultural practices, in this process of globalization? Here, I am seeing architecture and urban design or planning as particular cultural industries which might be compared, for example, with other major spheres of cultural production such as the film, video, or music industries, the realms of television or advertising: the image-projecting and consciousness-transforming industries, all those industries which, in short, in the conditions of contemporary capitalism and along with a variety of other forms and processes, contribute to the constitution, confirmation or reconstitution of human subjectivity and cultural identity. I am suggesting, in brief, that architecture and planning, indeed, all the 'design professions', are potentially major influences in contributing to the transformation of culture on a global scale.

However, in talking about the production of the built environment, I also want to distinguish between the actions of individuals and organizations (maybe individual architects, firms of developers or municipalities, agencies of one kind or another) and the larger structures and conditions in which they operate: particular modes of production or forms of socio-economic organization and political control: free market capitalism, state capitalism, socialism, welfare capitalism; or distinctive regional or even national cultures. This is what we commonly accept as the structure-agency question.

It might be thought that to ask such questions is simultaneously irrelevant as well as intellectually misconceived, an example of a'totalizing discourse' which might be undermined from a variety of directions. I would suggest two very practical reasons why I believe such questions to be legitimate.

The immense acceleration in the processes of globalization and 'global compression' (to use Robertson's phrase) is most obviously seen in relation to the economy: the three major players in the internationalization of the economy since the 1970s have been the banks, the global corporations and the state (Thrift, 1986); it has been accompanied by the internationalization of production and of consumption, of twenty-four-hour global trading in securities, of revolutionary developments in transport and telecommunications technology and the massive growth in international labour migration. These, in turn, have brought the deterritorialization of cultures, the existence of cultures far from their places of origin.

Two particular aspects of the so-called new international division of labor which characterized these new developments in the capitalist world economy are of particular relevance to my theme. The first, drawing on the work of Friedmann and Wolff (1982, 1986), Sassen-Koob (1984, 1986, 1990), Soja et al. (1983), Soja (1988) and others, concerns the shift of manufacturing industries from once-industrial cities to lower labor-cost countries and regions (or to their automation) and their replacement by higher level, producer service functions (international banking, financial services, insurance, real estate, design services, etc.). Because such activities rely on advanced information technology and are labor-intensive in terms of 'think work', in which core post-industrial states have a major competitive advantage on a global scale, these knowledge-intensive (and also ideology-producing) services, fed by the major centers of education and research, are largely concentrated in the major 'world cities' of the USA, Europe and the Far East, along with the headquarters offices of global corporations and international banks. Here, they provide, in Sassen-Koob's (1986) terms the 'global control capability' in an increasingly global system of production. International contracts have become increasingly important for many architectural and engineering firms. In the mid 1970s already, one-third of US world-wide receipts on contracts for construction, consulting and design services were coming from OPEC countries (Sassen-Koob, 1984) and this has increasingly been the case for UK companies (King, 1990a). The

1980s has been the decade in which all companies, not least those in architecture and design services, have 'gone global'.

One of the best examples is that of Japanese construction contractors which have undergone a major process of internationalization in the last decade. The lack of public works in Japan and declining profits prompted large corporations to 'go global' in the 1980s, helped, of course, by the surfeit of Japanese capital looking for profitable sites for investment. Between 1981 and 1988, Kumagai Gumi, once a small-scale Japanese contractor, moved from 135th to 6th place in the world's top international construction contractors. In the process, they have had a massive effect on Australian urban and building development, leaving a string of luxury hotels, tourist resorts, condominiums and often unwanted developments around the Australian coast (Rimmer, 1988). The spectre of capital combing the world looking for profitable sites for investment and, if necessary, tearing down existing environments to achieve it, if not the major feature of the 1980s, has nevertheless been a striking characteristic of urban development in that decade. It is now well known that 70 percent of downtown Los Angeles is foreign owned (Wald, 1988: 8). Other world cities have equally been the recipient of foreign capital investment. In New Delhi, the capital of India, a massive building boom has been under way since the mid-1980s, a considerable part of it fueled by investment from 'NRIs' (Non-resident Indians), often from capital generated in the Gulf but also from other international sources. The developments have had a significant and major effect on Indians' traditional investment practices as, over the last decade, they have moved accumulated and inherited wealth out of investment in (especially gold) jewelry to investment in property and land. The result has been the growth of a new 'South City' in Delhi, a spate of luxury building on a scale not seen since the establishment of colonial New Delhi in the early twentieth century, and the creation of 'designer housing' which apparently combines features from Riyadh, South Kensington and Bombay (*Cityscan*, 1989).

London, which was one of a number of cities targeted by oil surplus funds in the 1970s, has been especially transformed in the 1980s, largely in the run-up to and aftermath of 'Big Bang'. Between 1985, when Japanese investment in British property was still rare, and 1987, Japanese banks' investment in UK property increased eightfold to around £250 million (King, 1990a: 108). Less well documented has been the laundering of drug profits and their investment in urban redevelopment round the world, including new developments in Dockland (King, 1990a: 148).

These are only some of the more obvious effects of the massive internationalization of capital in the last decade and their impacts both on architectural production and on the profession itself. The decade also saw the first case of an architects' firm being listed on the London 'unlisted securities' market. Because of the creation of the single European market in 1992, consultants are being employed to buy up small architectural firms in preparation for what some see will be a boom in design work following the establishment of the single market, and where firms in England, say, will do design work cheaper than those in France.

Thus, even at this relatively elementary level of world economic forces and their effects on urban and building development, we need a framework for understanding the mechanisms, the institutions, the meanings, and the economic, social and cultural consequences of these developments. How are we to understand this process of transnationalization in this process of the transformation of space and form? What difference, if any, will it make to people's social, political or cultural consciousness? What kind of symbolic invest-ment are they to make in these new environments, what meanings will they have and how will they mobilize these meanings for their own social or political purposes? More significantly, what are the prisms through which we should try and understand cultural resistance to these developments and the differences which are evident from one place to another? How relevant are the categories, for this purpose, of nation, locality, region, religion, class, gender, economy?

This, therefore, is what I would call the *external* justification for my theme: in a situation of 'global compression', I am concerned to find a framework for understanding transformations in space, building and urban form which extend well beyond the boundaries of the state. My *internal* justification comes from another, though related phenomenon: just as the new international division of labor is increasingly sending producer services in design outwards, to other countries in search of markets, so also is it bringing increasing numbers of protoprofessionals from so-called 'Third World' societies for professional education in countries at the core. As the quarternary sector of such countries expands, the educational component of that sector depends increasingly on this input of students from the global periphery. It is here where the totalizing theories are constructed. So the experience (for a few) of flying round the world and needing schemata to make sense of what they see is increasingly complemented in the classroom back home by looking round the graduate seminar table and seeing students from all over the world. It is these conditions which are giving rise to the construction of global theories. We can address our larger questions through a series of different stages in which parts of the problem have been formulated. The first of these we can call:

The Social Production of Knowledge

Much of academic work is concerned with filling in gaps, doing things which one thinks others have omitted; making visible what was previously invisible, creating discursive noise where there was previously silence. So, in the last twenty years, geographers have argued for the centrality of space and spatiality to the explanation of social process; in the urban field of sociology, transformed to urban political economy, capital became critically important in the 1970s and early 1980s, though later it emerged that politics had been neglected. My own experience, for what it is worth, of returning to Europe after living in India for five years, was to discover (in the early 1970s) that 'culture', in its old, 'anthropological' sense was being neglected in the study of architecture and urban form. After some years working under the paradigmatic shadows cast by Harvey and Castells it wasn't in any way a sure thing that 'culture', in any sense, existed.

Over the same period meanwhile, feminists had made more than apparent the invisibility of women in history, architecture, anthropology; at another conjuncture, the state was discovered: it had to be brought back in. Decades before, social historians had discovered there was a (generally male) working class. Since the 1970s, in architectural history, scholars have pointed out that insufficient notice was being taken of 'the vernacular' and 'ethnic architecture'; ethnicity, of course, and ethnic difference, has been a major area of neglect and subsequent discovery across the spectrum of intellectual enquiry. For Foucault, the discovery was even greater: it was the appearance of man (and maybe woman) in the sphere of knowledge, not to mention discursive formations. In cultural studies and elsewhere, what has been neglected is the question of subjectivity, and the constitution of the class or gendered subject. And culture, twenty years ago thought to be about values, beliefs, world views, or alternatively, about 'what you need to know to be accepted as one of them by any members of a cultural group' is now constituted through representation.

One could, of course, continue these examples, from discourses on language, religion, psychology, but what I want to ask is, what are the conditions under which these discourses are produced? Why does ethnicity, gender, class appear on the agenda? The answer, of course, is obvious enough but it raises questions not only in the sociology and geography of knowledge (who is producing it, who for and where is it being produced as well as sent to, and consumed) but also, in the history and political economy of knowledge (when is it being produced and who is paying for it; how is it being financed and for what purposes).

In one sense, knowledge is a very personal thing; it comes from personal experience, but personal experience which is situated and formed in particular social institutions and work contexts (like universities, departmental disciplines, professional organizations), in particular geographical locations (cities, regions, states, rich and poor parts of the world) and a product of particular temporal or historical periods, some of which are seen to be significantly formative (and in different states, according to different histories, acquire different labels, such as the 'Quit India' period, the 'Civil Rights' movement in the US or, in the UK, the apparently 'global 1980s'). So discourses, and the languages in which they're expressed, become fossilized, not only according to socially institutionalized disciplines (sociology, architectural history) and particular places (Chicago sociology, British architectural history) but also according to particular historical epochs (postwar Chicago sociology). And this brings me back to my own personal experience. For having discovered, after five years in India and returning to the UK, that it was 'culture' which was being left out, after a further few years working in London with students of building, planning, architecture and urban design from all over the world, it was obvious that two other massive realms were missing from the discourse about society and culture in the UK. One was the built environment, the other was the rest of the world.

The Built Environment
Until quite recently, with its appropriation in the debate on postmodernism, one of the main silences in social theory has concerned the built environment. This is not the place to discuss this at length nor to provide any theoretically coherent account except to

say that most of the work concerning, for example, the social production and organization of space, of the built environment, of questions of meaning, or representation and cultural identity produced in the last twenty years has (with a few exceptions) been undertaken in anthropology, archaeology, geography, social history, or various hybrid fields such as man(sic)-environment studies, though very little in social theory.

Yet just as the feminist critique has exposed the folly of constructing totalizing theoretical paradigms concerning class or employment without reference to gender, I would suggest it is equally fallacious to conceptualize society, culture, social organization or process without reference to the physical and spatial material reality of the built environment. For the most part, social theory deals with a world of social relations, of discourses about culture, in which the built environment, understood as the physical and spatial contexts, the built forms, the socially-constructed boundaries, material containers, the architectural representations, the socially-specialized building types, not only do not exist but play no role whatsoever in the production, and reproduction of society. It is as though it didn't matter whether all social life took place where it actually does or on a huge global beach, or if social subjects were somehow magically suspended in space. I am saying, in short, that the built environment, building and urban form in all their conceptualizations, do not just represent, or reflect social order, they actually constitute much of social and cultural existence. Society, as Prior (1988) has pointed out, is to a large extent, constituted as well as represented through the buildings and spaces that it creates.

Thus, if we are considering cultures in terms of the ways in which they are represented, either in a tangible, material sense such as in different kinds of texts and visual expression and in the production of different aspects of material culture, or in a non-material sense such as in music, oral culture and symbolic practices of different kinds, it can be argued that the demarcation, and subsequently, organization of space is, in virtually all cases, a necessary prerequisite for all forms of cultural performance and representation. Secondly, many of these activities equally presuppose some form of socially and physically constructed space.

Moreover (and still speaking with reference to social theory), if built environments, in all their various conceptualizations, are as important as socially-constituting mechanisms as I am arguing here, then they should (as indeed they do) provide us with some evidence, some data about the nature and organization of society and culture as well as its spatial expression or constitution. They should tell us (as indeed they do) about its social and spatial divisions of labor (on the basis of gender, age or region), about its economic, social and political organization as a whole.

The problem is, of course, that when you look at the built environment, at urban forms or hierarchies produced by a given economic and social formation, they do not fit into the politically or geographically-defined nation-state, such as the UK, or USA, which has traditionally been taken as the unit of analysis in social theory. This is most obviously demonstrated, and illustrated, by examples of colonial societies. In the early twentieth century, Britain, South Africa, India, Australia, Kenya, and many other places were, for the white British migrants who went there, in one sense, one single colonial society: not, in any way, a series of societal clones displaced round the world, but a single social and cultural system whose occupations, lifestyles, and sub-cultures, as well, of course, as built environments, were determined by their participation in a colonial mode of production which was in turn part of a larger international division of labor.

Sociology, as both Robertson (1988) and Wallerstein (1987) have reminded us, has not been very good at coping with social and cultural systems which spill over the boundaries of nation-states. And it is to the alternative theorizations of these two scholars which I would like to turn. It is in attempting to cope with the problem of understanding the production and social meaning of built environments, of buildings and architecture on a scale that is outside and beyond the boundaries of individual states that I believe both of these scholars have contributions to make.

The World as a Single Place

Though the phrase of my sub-title is Robertson's, it would be generally agreed that the most widely accepted paradigm within which this phenomenon is discussed is the world-systems perspective of Immanuel Wallerstein. Though the focus of Wallerstein's work has shifted in recent years, the main features of the perspective remain: that since the sixteenth century there has been one principal mode of production and that is the capitalist world economy, and this is a single division of labor within which are multiple cultures. Other essential elements of this capitalist world economy are:

production for profit in a world market; capital accumulation for expanded production as the key way of maximizing profit in the long run; the emergence of three zones of economic activity (core, periphery and semi-periphery); the development over time of two principal world class formations (the bourgeoisie and the proletariat) whose concrete manifestations are complemented by a host of ethnonational groups. This historically unique combination of elements first crystallized in Europe in the sixteenth century and the boundaries slowly expanded to cover the entire world (Wallerstein, 1979: 159).

Readers familiar with Wallerstein's work, and the critiques made of it will know that until recently, it has (as can be seen from these earlier sources) been principally concerned with the economic and political rather than the cultural (though see Wallerstein, 1990).

Yet there are at least two features of Wallerstein's notion of the world-system which make sense when discussing the production and meaning of built environments, both historically and today. The first is the notion of the international division of labor nested in ideas of 'core' and 'periphery'; the second is the notion that the world-system is indeed 'systemic' in that economic, social and cultural processes in one part of the world are systemically related (if not mechanically or in a determinate fashion) to processes in other parts. Let me illustrate this by reference to economic, social and spatial divisions of labor and their relationship to the built environment.

To understand any built environment we need to understand the economic, social and political formations on which it is based; we need to understand both a social and spatial division of labor. There is no adequate explanation of, for example, the growth in the nineteenth century in northern England of industrial 'cotton towns' (sic) without reference to the transformation of Egyptian agriculture, the huge rise of cotton exports (under colonialism) and the creation of colonial Cairo from the 1880s. They are both part of the same mode of production and the built environment and architecture is one of the major clues. Not because it is 'the same' but because it is complementary: the Classical Revival banks are in the City of London, loaning money (at prohibitive rates) to the Egyptians to import manufactured goods; the Classical Revivalized mansions are in Cairo and Alexandria belonging to the Egyptian comprador bourgeoisie or the families of European officials or merchants.

The same holds true in the last decades of the twentieth century.

No one can attempt to talk about New York and its buildings without reference to the world economy. The fact that New York has the largest number (56) of multinational headquarters buildings of any city in the world — only two of any of the huge Third World cities, many of which have larger populations than New York, have any multinational corporation headquarters at all (King, 1990a) — also explains back office functions located in the Caribbean and the low-rise factories which exist in Taiwan or the Philippines.

Yet whilst these notions, inherent in the world-systems perspective, do provide insights into especially economic processes and, by focusing on the level of the nation-state, on political processes as well, there are other dimensions which we need to take note of:

First, globalization processes are only partial; they affect some regions of the world-economy more than others, and within regions, some social groups or sectors more or less than others, and this is important if we are trying to understand the production of particular built environments. Second, by focusing on what might be seen as the dominant economic processes (the internationalization of capital), we may seriously underestimate the processes of economic, social and cultural resistance, both in terms of scale (i.e. how large are they) and intensity (how strong are they). Finally, if we are interested in identifying and documenting cultural difference, distinctive cultures and the way they are represented in architecture and urban form, world systems theory does not, as yet, have anything to say about this.

An alternative conceptualization is that of Robertson's (1987) theory of globalization, the term defined as 'the process by which the world becomes a single place'. What Robertson emphasizes is that it is crucial to recognize that the contemporary concern with civilizational and societal (as well as ethnic) uniqueness, as expressed in such motifs as identity, tradition and indigenization, largely rests on globally produced ideas. In an increasingly globalized world, 'characterized by historically exceptional degrees of societal and other modes of interdependence, as well as the widespread consciousness of these developments, there is an exacerbation of civilizational, societal and ethnic self-consciousness' (1987). Robertson has suggested that globalization theory turns world systems theory on its head by focusing first, on the cultural aspects of the 'world system' and second, by the systematic study of internal societal attributes which shape orientations to the world as a whole (Robertson, 1987).

Globalization, according to Robertson, involves the development of something like a global culture, not as normatively binding but in the sense of a general mode of discourse about the world as a whole and its variety (1987).

Both Robertson's and Wallerstein's theorizations, therefore, in different ways, argue against the homogenization of culture; that of Wallerstein, in a negative way, by implying the creation of processes which spark off cultural resistance and opposition: that of Robertson, by suggesting that the consciousness, or experience of globality will exacerbate, even provide new kinds of, cultural difference.

A third, and different argument put forward by Stuart Hall (1990) suggests that it is precisely in the nature of capital, in its constant state of expansion, penetration and internationalization, to work in and through difference, to celebrate, enhance and exaggerate cultural diversity.

To these propositions, other arguments might be added; firstly, that there is now no longer one core to the world system but rather, many cores exist, not least those located in Asia and Latin America, which are coming out with their own, alternative forms of cosmopolitanism (*Public Culture*, 1988). Cultural transformations are not just moving in one direction but many. If this is so, then my original hypothesis concerning a move towards a general, global cultural homogenity is, theoretically at least, not likely to hold water.

So far, however, I have been speaking of these theories as theories: let me say something about them as empirical data.

All theories are themselves cultural products, produced under particular conditions, by particular people and in particular places. If the criticisms of Stuart Hall are taken seriously, then all globalizing theories are 'the self-representation of the dominant particular'; they represent a 'certain configuration of local particularities which, in a hegemonic sweep, try to dominate the whole scene, to incorporate a variety of more localized identities into subordinate positions'.[2]

Other criticisms see these constructs — core/periphery, First World/Third World, center/margin — as just that, social constructs with no real referents in social reality. They are all 'defined in difference' in terms of 'the Self and the Other' (Wolff, 1990).

These criticisms I take less seriously; the fact that theories and conceptualizations are cultural products, social constructs, does not mean that they cannot take on their own reality. People do indeed take on identities and represent themselves as from the Third World, the periphery, as ethnic minorities or scheduled castes. The greater problem with these concepts is that they are generally binary constructs — black/white, male/female, self/other — as if there were no categories before, between, and after. As Arjun Appadurai once pointed out, some others are more other than other others.

Conclusion

What suggestions do these various innovations from social and cultural theory offer for the understanding of architecture, built environments, societies and cultures on a global scale? I shall conclude by reaffirming some basic propositions and suggesting some more for further analysis.

First, that cultures, sub-cultures and economic, social and political formations are not only represented but also constituted in and through spatial and built form practices and today (as well as in the historic past) these are constituted on a global scale. The relationship is not necessarily 'one-to-one' and there may well be some cultural lag over time but this does not alter the basic proposition.

Second, there is indeed a world or global culture which is largely the product of a world political economy of capitalism, as well as being the outcome of its technological and communicative effects. However, while there may well be a globalizing culture in relation to the built environment, it is not necessarily (and is as much likely to work against) a homogenizing one.

Third, that changes in the construction of space, its organization and physical containment and representation in building and urban form is a major factor in the transformation of (especially material), cultures on a global scale. However, form should not be confused with content nor should we fail to recognize that apparently similar forms can carry quite dissimilar meanings.

Fourth, and in regard to my propositions about the nature and organization of societies, people belong to many different cultures and the cultural differences are as likely to be *within* states (i.e. between regions, classes, ethnic groups, the urban and rural) as *between* states. Architects and designers move more easily between New York, London and Bombay than between Bombay and the villages of Maharashtra.

Fifth, nation-states constantly aim to construct, define and monitor national cultures within the politically-defined boundaries

of the state (Wallerstein, 1990). But these are constantly undermined, not only by cultural flows coming in from outside the state
but increasingly from autonomous and hegemonic professional sub-
cultures (such as architecture) which generally, though not
necessarily, have their values and roots in institutions derived from
capitalist social formations and practices which operate across
national boundaries.

Sixth, that history is at least if not more useful than theory in
charting the development of national, regional or international
cultures and the way they get represented in the built environment.
This can be more easily illustrated than explained; for example,
societies and built environments in particular parts of the world can
be understood better when conceptualized as 'post-colonial' or
'post-imperial' than as 'peripheral' or 'core'.

Finally, when it comes to the crunch, there's nothing like theoreti-
cally-informed empirical and archival research on the history of the
global production of building form (King, 1990b). We need careful
historical studies of the images, plans, ideas and symbols which are
increasingly making the world's cities simultaneously similar to, and
different from, each other.

Notes

1. This paper is a slightly revised version of a lecture given at the University of
Minnesota at Minneapolis in May 1989 and sponsored by the Program in
Comparative Studies in Discourse and Society of the Department of Humanities, and
Departments of Architecture, Urban Design, Sociology, Geography and Interna-
tional Studies. I am very grateful to John Archer for initiating the invitation.

The paper also draws on contributions to a symposium on 'Culture, Globalization
and the World-System' by Roland Robertson, Immanuel Wallerstein, Ulf Hannerz,
Janet Wolff and Stuart Hall held at the State University of New York at Binghamton
in April 1989.

2. Comments by Stuart Hall in a discussion following a lecture on 'Globalization
and Ethnicity', State University of New York at Binghamton, March 1989.

References

Cityscan (1989) 'Land South of Delhi. Moneyscape' (November): 21–8.
Friedmann, J. (1986) 'The World City Hypothesis', *Development and Change* 17
    (1): 69–83.
Friedmann, J. and Wolff, G. (1982) 'World City Formation: an Agenda for Research
    and Action', *International Journal of Urban and Regional Research* 6 (3): 309–44.
Hall, Stuart (1990) 'Globalization and Ethnicity', in A.D. King (ed.) *Culture,*

Globalization and the World-system. Binghamton: State University of New York at Binghamton and Macmillan (in preparation).

King, A.D. (1990a) *Global Cities. Post-Imperialism and the Internationalisation of London.* London and New York: Routledge.

King, A.D. (1990b) *Urbanism, Colonialism and the World-Economy.* London and New York: Routledge.

Prior, L. (1988) 'The Architecture of the Hospital: A Study of Social Organisation and Medical Knowledge', *British Journal of Sociology* 39 (1): 86–113.

Public Culture (1988) 'Editorial', 1 (1): 1–6.

Rimmer, P. (1988) 'Japanese Construction Companies and the Australian States', *International Journal of Urban and Regional Research* 12(3): 404–24.

Robertson, R. (1987) 'Globalization Theory and Civilizational Analysis', *Comparative Civilizations Review* 17: 20–30.

Robertson, R. (1988) 'The Sociological Significance of Culture: Some General Considerations', *Theory, Culture & Society* 5: 3–23.

Sassen-Koob, S. (1984) 'The New Labor Demand in Global Cities', pp. 139–72 in M.P. Smith (ed.), *Cities in Transformation.* Beverly Hills and London: Sage.

Sassen-Koob, S. (1986) 'New York City: Economic Restructuring and Immigration', *Development and Change* 17 (1): 85 85–119.

Sassen-Koob, S. (1990) *The Global City.* Princeton, NJ: Princeton University Press.

Soja, E., Morales, R. and Wolff, G. (1983) 'Urban Restructuring: An Analysis of Social and Spatial Change in Los Angeles', *Economic Geography* 59: 195–230.

Soja, E.W. (1988) *Postmodern Geographies. The Reassertion of Space in Critical Social Theory.* London: Verso.

Thrift, N. (1986) 'The Geography of International Economic Disorder', pp. 12–67 in R.J. Johnson and P.J. Taylor (eds), *A World in Crisis? Geographical Perspectives.* Oxford: Blackwell.

Wald, M.L. (1988) 'Foreign Investors Take More Active Roles', *New York Times. Real Estate Report on Commercial Property* (15 May) 5–12.

Wallerstein, I. (1979) *The Capitalist World-Economy.* Cambridge: Cambridge University Press.

Wallerstein, I. (1987) 'World-systems Analysis', pp. 309–24 in A. Giddens and J.H. Turner (eds), *Social Theory Today.* Cambridge: Binghamton.

Wallerstein, I. (1990) 'The National and the Universal: Can There Be Such a Thing as World Culture?', in A.D. King (ed.) *Culture, Globalization and The World-system.* Binghamton: State University of New York at Binghamton.

Wolff, J. (1990) 'The Global and the Specific: Reconciling Conflicting Theories of Culture', in A.D. King (ed.) *Culture, Globalization and The World-system.* Binghamton: State University of New York at Binghamton and Macmillan (in preparation).

Anthony King is Professor of Art History and Sociology at the State University of New York at Binghamton. He is author of *Colonial Urban Development, The Bungalow. The Production of a Global Culture, Global Cities* and editor of *Buildings and Society* (all published by Routledge).